A ...om
The Second ... ...he Istanbul

ANFIELD OF DREAMS

Neil Dunkin

KNOW!
THE SCORE

Know The Score Books Limited

118 Alcester Road Studley, Warwickshire, B80 7NT Tel: 01527 454482
Fax: 01527 452183 info@knowthescorebooks.com
www.knowthescorebooks.com

A CIP catalogue record is available for this book from the British Library
ISBN: 978-1-905449-80-4

Typeset by Andy Searle

Printed and bound in Great Britain by
Polska Print, Poland

Contents

About the Author

After his childhood and education in Liverpool and London, Neil Dunkin descended into the underworld of newspaper sub-editing, receiving indoctrination in the dark arts of this print jungle from a succession of wise scribes.

During a career that has taken him from the North-West of England to Fleet Street, he has explored arcane areas of several national titles and managed to come out unscathed, aided in no small measure by survival skills acquired in the Boys' Pen at Anfield.

A horizontal fixture to the bars of beer festivals throughout Hertfordshire, he has two children and, at the time of writing, was still married.

Winston Churchill quotation reproduced with permission of Curtis Brown Ltd, London, on behalf of the Estate of Winston Churchill.
© Winston S. Churchill.

Carl Gustav Jung quotation reprinted by permission of HarperCollins Publishers Ltd. © Carl Gustav Jung 1961.

Every effort has been made to trace other copyright owners and anyone claiming copyright should get in touch with the author at anfieldofdreams@hotmail.co.uk.

For Helen, Russ and Anne,
the best wife, mother and
soulmate in the world

Dedicated to the memory of
all those who did not come
home from Hillsborough

1
Depths Of Despair

You always pass failure on the way to success.

– Mickey Rooney

IT WAS the funeral at sea where everyone was laughing, even those who were grieving most.

As the coffin was carried by four pallbearers around the promenade deck of the mighty Queen Elizabeth, hundreds of mourners clapped and cheered in celebration of a fallen hero's committal to the mid-Atlantic depths.

Lancashire cotton brokers, Wall Street bankers, London lawyers, Boston professors, passengers from across the spectrum of British and American society joined the captain, officers and crew of the great liner to mark the demise of a friend whose name was inscribed on the coffin lid.

"Liverpool F.C. R.I.P.", the ship's painter had crafted in big black letters on the rough wooden casket, hastily nailed together by the carpenter.

For this was April 10, 1954, and news had come through on the Queen's ship-to-shore radio that Liverpool had lost 3-0 to Arsenal at Highbury.

Catastrophe of catastrophes, the Reds had been relegated, after 50 years in the First Division.

Within minutes, this calamity was bush-telegraphed from stem to stern and from top to bottom of the 83,000-ton vessel, the largest afloat.

Within seconds, the legion of Everton supporters in the crew, always partial to taking the mickey out of their Merseyside rivals, agreed this was an opportunity not to be missed. After all, as one team went down, they would pass the other coming up, because the Blues had sealed promotion from the Second Division. What a turnaround!

So Evertonians decided Anfield's ignominy deserved a funeral, out at sea. Yes, the last rites would be administered on the club from the opposite side of Stanley Park.

And when Liverpool fans learnt what was planned, they had to join in the fun. As one deckhand told his mates: "No use sulking, lads. Let's go down laughing."

He knew, like every crewmember knew, that football offered a healthy subject for banter during long hours of boredom in their oceanic community and the Reds were always ready to give as good as they got. At this time, though, they had to accept the forthcoming humiliation with the best possible grace, since a funeral did seem appropriate to mark their team's fall from grace.

All hands knew it would be a giggle, given that the chief mourner would be the ship's master. Commodore Sir Ivan Thompson had begun his seafaring life as a cadet on a tramp steamer sailing out of Leith and had risen to hold the most prestigious title in British shipping, Master of the Queens, Cunard's twin titans, Elizabeth and Mary. The whole world and his mother and great-aunts knew Sir Ivan was a Red 'un, holder of a season ticket in the Kemlyn Road stand. Now he too would have to grin and bear it during this maritime requiem.

Soon Liverpool loyalists and Evertonians-for-ever were congregating on deck. Some had made the long climb up greasy steel ladders from the sweltering hot engine room, others had slipped out of cool cocktail bars where they'd been serving Singapore Slings and Brandy Alexanders.

Down below, the Working Alleyway, the main street running practically the length of the vessel and containing services such as the bakers, confectioners, printers and hospital, had emptied of personnel because they wanted to watch, even those without the slightest idea how to lace up a caseball.

Before long the promenade deck was lined with onlookers, so many you could have sworn every one of the 2,300 passengers and 1,200 crew had turned up. At the front were chief mourners from every corner of Anfield – Kopites, Kemlyn Roaders, Main Standers, Paddockers, Anfield Roaders, dabbing eyes with hankies, shaking their heads and letting out sobs.

Americans, with no concept of what football was, never mind its importance to Merseysiders, looked on, amused, bemused and confused by these screwball Scousers.

"They're doing this? For a saaccer team? A funeral?" asked one Philadelphian who'd abandoned his stateroom after hearing a medley of applause and wailing.

"Yeah, dead funny, isn't it?" a deckhand from Bootle replied, with a broken-toothed grin.

Flanked by the throng, the coffin was paraded sedately along the deck by its bearers, wearing red scarves and bobble hats.

Since no one knew the words, some Evertonians had started humming the Funeral March, while others were getting their digs in.

"Couldn't kick the ball, now they've kicked the bucket," a Blues brother teased.

"Only cup they'll get will be on a saucer from Davy Jones's locker," another one quipped.

These jibes only served to turn up the mourners' volume and raise the intensity of their histrionics. One commis chef, eyes screwed shut in anguish, drummed his white-clad breast like Johnny Weissmuller's Tarzan, while an assistant purser noted for flamboyant theatricality after a couple of noggins of rum and peppermint threw himself at the ship's rail in a bid to hurl himself overboard.

Nevertheless, the corpse's dispatch could not be delayed. Its cortege moved to the stern and waited for Commodore Thompson to give the nod.

After a dignified pause, he could no longer preserve his mock-solemn face. Breaking into a broad smile, he raised his right hand and dropped it, signalling the act of committal to the deep.

Slowly the bearers slid the coffin over the rail, to the accompaniment of a brain-scrambling blast on the ship's hooter.

Liverpool's remains glided down the starboard side of the towering vessel until a strong upward gust of wind stalled their descent halfway and strove to blow them from whence they came. To no avail.

Before you could say Jacob Bronowski, gravity imposed its pull and, with a shrug, the casket resumed its progress.

At last it pierced the murky sea with a hollow splash, disappeared for a few seconds and surged back defiantly to the surface, before bobbing away in the Queen's foamy wake.

Now it was on a maritime roller-coaster, rising up and down to the ocean's rhythm and attracting the attention of a lone seagull which altered its flight path to hover briefly over the box in a fruitless quest for nourishment.

As this hungry migrant resumed its journey and the liner's engines thundered relentlessly on, the coffin shrank into a dot, glimpsed fleetingly on crests of waves.

By this time, most witnesses of the send-off had drifted away, leaving a handful of hardcore supporters of both persuasions at the rails.

They peered into the gloom until, finally, even the sharpest-eyed cabin boy who could spot the Statue of Liberty from 10 miles out was unable to espy the box any more.

The corpse of Liverpool FC had been laid to rest.

But as the laggards returned to their posts, one defiant Kopite, a steward from Crosby, delivered the parting shot.

"We'll be back next season – wait and see," he shouted with a toss of his Brylcreemed head at Toffees' fans.

He knew it and, to be fair, he was not alone in his certainty. All the Anfield faithful were convinced. No sweat, the lads would bounce up into the First Division, the place they'd graced for an eternity.

One season and that would be it; back where they belonged, in the top tier.

* * * * * * * * * *

As a boy growing up in Liverpool in the Fifties, one of the earliest, most critical decisions you faced, affecting the rest of your life and having an incalculable influence on your happiness, was which team to support.

Back then, my home town revelled in a raw passion for football matched by just a handful of places across the globe, such as Rome, Rio de Janeiro or Buenos Aires, where people's devotion to a club is magnified by rivalry with another local side.

On Merseyside, Everton were *the* club: more famous, more successful than their Liverpool neighbours, with a history and stature few teams could equal. Consequent upon this, the Blues had bigger crowds and a greater number of supporters, a statistic readily confirmed whenever the game was discussed in pubs and clubs, factories and offices, schools and colleges.

Nonetheless, as with most youngsters, my allegiance was not dictated by who was biggest or best. My club was decreed by contemporary interpretation of that law for 16th-Century kings, princes and potentates, "Cuius regio, eius religio", roughly translatable by this non-Latin speaker as "Whosoever rules the land dictates the religion of that land". In common parlance, the leader of the house – your father or mother – prescribed your football team.

Now this was never a subject, along with the extortionate price of nutty slack and the sexual transgressions of Tory ministers, that provoked feverish debate late Saturday night in the Standard boozer at the bottom of our street. No, Cuius regio, eius religio was not an issue for argument or deliberation, rather an unsaid, unwritten, unchallenged principle applying to families across Liverpool, and in its 20th-Century form for this lad without a dad, there could be only one ruler of my world: my mother, who had divorced my faithless father.

It was she who paid rent to the camel-coated landlord banging at our door; purchased our weekly groceries at the Co-op on Breck Road; watched her payment being inserted into a metal cylinder by the assistant, then catapulted by overhead pulley to the beady-eyed cashier in his roost at the back; checked the dividend total in her passbook as she walked out; cooked blind scouse for Monday's tea (blind because household finances meant it contained no meat); lit coal in the hearth with firewood chopped in our shed; whitewashed the walls of our backyard in spring with a bubbling lime mix; gave a cow bone from the butcher's to our dog Rick to chew; bought Geronimo the tortoise as my birthday present; treated me to barley sugars and dandelion and burdock from Pickett's corner shop; gave me sixpence for a lolly ice (not an ice lolly) from the street vendor on his tricycle with a cold box on the front; wet a hankie on her tongue to remove chocolate from around my mouth on our trips to town; and helped me with all those troublesome words in the Beano and Dandy.

It was she who tuned in to Billy Cotton, yelling "Wakey, wakey!" on our jukebox-sized radio, and rarely missed Family Favourites on Sundays; gave me one of her 15denier nylons to drape over the bottom of the bed for Father Christmas (that German-American impostor Santa Claus was unheard of) to fill with an apple, orange, chocolate coins, jigsaw, crayons, colouring-in book and Comet annual; got out her sheet music and played Lily of Laguna, Ain't She Sweet and other melodies on the upright Rushworth piano in our parlour every Boxing Day; accompanied you on the ferry, "over the water" to New Brighton for summer outings; dropped you off on Saturday at the children's matinee in Oakfield Road's Gaumont; joined in the chase when you scampered out, left arm grasping imaginary reins, right hand slapping your buttock in imitation of Roy Rogers galloping on Trigger; had a kickabout with you in Stanley Park's green acres; wiped away tears when you grazed your knees; washed you in a tin bath in the back kitchen on Friday nights; dried you all over with a fluffy white Terry towel; and at bedtime tucked you into cold sheets with warm, gentle hands.

Yes, it was Mum who did everything for me. And this all-powerful, all-loving lady of my life, this ruler of my heart also imbued me with my football faith, the club I was born to follow, and likewise she had adopted the Liverpool denomination because it was her parents'.

Like nearly every woman, she remained content to be an armchair supporter, keeping abreast of the club's fortunes through the *Liverpool Echo*, reports on the wireless and conversations with friends. As far as I could ascertain, she had never been to Anfield. Despite this, she was always true to her team and from the mists of infancy I accepted that, just as Liverpool was hers, so it was mine. By this quirk of birth, I was destined to be Red till dead.

Home for Mum, me and my sister and brother was the Lake District – rows of terraces forming a mini gridiron of streets whose names were taken from England's most beautiful region ... Coniston, Thirlmere, Windermere, Rydal. We lived in Ullswater, a street of English, Welsh, Irish and Scottish residents who rarely moved away, apart from when a wheezing lorry crept up to a house at dead of night and a desperate family undertook their moonlit flit, escaping the landlord's visit next day, spiteful lead pencil poised over his arrears book.

In estate agent speak, our house boasted three rooms downstairs, specifically a parlour (present-day reception room), kitchen (living room) and back-kitchen (kitchen), and three bedrooms upstairs. No bathroom, just a brick lavatory at the end of the backyard, containing a wooden bench with a circular hole over the pan and newspaper torn into squares – far more absorbent than the Co-op's glazed Izal toilet roll, which was as effective as a porcelain plate.

In the Fifties, Mum had no such contraption as a washing machine. Instead she used a dolly tub, a galvanised container filled with boiling water, and dolly legs, a wooden implement like a child's stool fitted with a long handle to mash clothes in the barrel.

If it was too wet to hang washing on the line in the backyard, she would put it on a clothes maiden, a cast-iron and wooden rack hanging on twin rope pulleys from the ceiling of our upstairs landing. In the back-kitchen, nothing so revolutionary as a fridge or freezer; anything from the butcher's was kept in a meat safe, a wooden box with a fine mesh door and four short legs to keep it off the ground.

For cooking, Mum juggled with a primitive electric oven and a single gas ring, on which she prepared her renowned treacle toffee, while for supper last thing at night we tucked into butties spread with sugar, brown sauce or dripping fat sprinkled with salt.

Ee, lad, must have been reet grim oop North. Well, no ... happen I had it reet cushy, apart from sporadic coal shortages when the house was a mite chilly, nothing an overcoat on the bed couldn't neutralise.

Most people had lived in Ullswater Street for years, so like villages in the West Lancashire countryside, it typified the kind of place where you felt at ease because you knew everyone and everyone knew you; familiarity breeds content. This sense of belonging applied particularly to Mum, who was manageress of Sayer's cake shop in Breck Road at the top of our street, dealing with shoppers appreciative of her cheerful smile, abiding courtesy and efficient service with strawberry tarts and hot steak pies.

Ours was a safe neighbourhood where to mug someone didn't mean to rob them, rather to offer a couple of bob as reward for some favour or helping hand, and almost every kid abided by the rule of "Respect people, respect property", because if they didn't, they got a good rattling from their Dah. So during summer holidays, front doors were never closed; they were left wide open all day, from 9 in the morning till 9 at night, children going out to play at will, returning for slurps of corporation pop from the back-kitchen tap.

According to residents of more affluent areas, your Aigburths, Childwalls or Crosbys, shops in Breck Road had burglar alarms fitted to their burglar alarms and local kids played tick with hatchets, when really the games in our car-free, carefree street were football, cricket, boxing bouts with mini-gloves and competitive sprints around the block. These activities sent exhausted boys to bo-boes, while the girls slipped into their beauty slumber after skipping, hopscotch, rounders, two-balls-against-a-wall and ring-a-ring-aroses.

Here the people might have been rough and ready, pugnacious and poor, but they were also kind and caring. Incidents of lawlessness were rare, although one fracas not far away did get in the paper, a sparring match between rival gangs of Teddy boys in Breckfield Road.

After the Teds, in their long velvet-collared jackets, tight trousers and brothel creepers, made themselves scarce because scuffers had rolled up, a hoard of abandoned weapons was recovered – knuckle-dusters, bicycle chains, wooden staves and lengths of lead piping.

This affray was a one-off. Nothing approaching its scale occurred again and peace resumed.

Our homes were built on rock-solid foundations: the family came first, but you also took pride in your neighbours and your street, evidenced in a small but no less significant way by the mothers who got down on their knees every week to scrub the front doorstep with a donkey stone, supplied by Arthur, a rag-and-bone man who rode into our street on his horse and cart. He gathered bundles of old clothes in exchange for knick-knacks such as packets of balloons and donkey stones, which women rubbed along the sandstone sills of their doors to make a neat, white strip.

Arthur's steed wasn't the only one seen around the Lake District. Our milkman filled customers' jugs from churns in the back of a horse-drawn trap and even dustbins were emptied into a garbage wagon pulled by a horse.

Along with the knife-sharpener on a cycle whose pedals turned a stone grinding wheel, another frequenter of our street was George, the vendor of bottles of Aunt Sally liquid soap for washing clothes, a lot cheaper than packets of Rinse detergent. He hauled his bottles around on a backbreaking handcart, roped up with a pair of black dogs as big as Shetland ponies, so any ne'er-do-well couldn't pilfer while their master attended to customers on doorsteps.

At time of misfortune, Ullswater's community feeling always came to the fore. When a newly married man was killed on a building site, within minutes of the news breaking, all the adjoining houses' curtains were drawn as a mark of mourning and women could be seen moving quietly from door to door, collecting for the family.

Whether they were skint or barely knew the bereaved, no one refused to contribute. Every home made a donation, even if it meant giving a few bob saved behind the clock on the mantelpiece for a piece of mutton on Sunday.

Using this collection, Ullswater folks would buy a wreath for the funeral, and an envelope with the balance would be presented to the widow, "From all your neighbours", a phrase that expressed a lot to those who had had black flowers of mourning cast into their homes.

In this way, the grief was shared. It was the done thing, the gesture that reassured: "We know what you're going through, we are with you."

Sorrow was seldom visited on our street, though. Instead, fun and games constituted the weekly norm for kids whose upbringing offered long periods of pleasure, at least once you escaped the benign discipline of Anfield Road primary school, a couple of corner kicks from Liverpool's ground. Despite the poverty afflicting some households who struggled to pay the rent, gas and Co-op bills, people enjoyed life, and mirth, music and dancing formed rudiments of your childhood.

Be it an engagement, wedding, Bank holiday, Christmas, Easter, the pretexts for a communal coming-together were numerous, not least when any wife became pregnant. Well before her confinement, knitting needles would click away into the evening in homes that often had no connection with the parents. In fullness of time, the mother would receive sets of woollens for her newborn and a hooley would be thrown for friends and neighbours, with beer, whisky and lemonade funded by the money-lender in Steer Street and supplied by Mackie & Gladstone's off-licence.

After Andrew's liver salts had suppressed hangovers, the street could draw quiet satisfaction from that stirring but vanishing phenomenon: snow-white nappies fluttering on a washing line in the backyard.

Our biggest thrash always came on New Year's Eve. At 6 o'clock that night, Mum would take me to Auntie Winnie's do in Margaret Street, where dozens of adults and children crammed into her terrace home, swigging Scotch and soft drinks, as suitable or not. Just before 7, the old people strode off to the pub, abandoning the house to kids who partied away, playing with their Christmas toys and games, eating mountains of nuts and boiled sweets, gulping buckets of cream soda and Vimto cordial.

At 11.45, the grown-ups would return in highest spirits, sweep up youngsters of all ages and meander off to the Breck Road-Landseer Road junction where hundreds congregated to see in the New Year. Everyone was merry – singing, laughing, carousing and dancing with friends, neighbours and strangers, and waiting for a ritual that occurred every year. A white-haired gent in his 60s, cockerel-proud in black tights, saluted the midnight chimes by shinning 20 feet up the ornate lamp standard in the middle of the junction, from where he waved regally to the throng below.

After that, to the accompaniment of ships' foghorns trumpeting from the Mersey, the gang of us went back to Aunt Winnie's for a shindig lasting till daybreak when we dragged ourselves home to the mewing of sleep-deprived gulls and the tang of sea-salt on the breeze.

There has never, before or since, been a happier way to embrace a New Year.

Vivacious, outgoing and intelligent, Mum kept to the Scouse precept of "Love life, love people, love Liverpool". Not to say her eyes were shut to any faults and failings, since she could be harsh on anyone who let the place down, castigating the slovenly litterati who dropped chip papers on our pavement. "No pride," she would murmur, picking up their rubbish.

And Lord protect the lowest forms of Pool life who violated anyone's home. If they'd caught a sneak thief, Mum and other women would willingly have chastised them with their fire pokers. Some possessed sufficient strength of will to be a handful for most blokes, exhibiting no fear and attesting to the truism that, pushed to their extreme, women are harder than men.

One neighbour who worked as the manageress of Church Street's Kardomah café was endowed with a pulverising grip in ham-shank arms that would have gladdened a brewery drayman. No lad could master her at arm-wrestling and whenever rowdy youths blighted her catering establishment, she did not hesitate to physically eject them if they failed to heed warnings. They did not come back.

But occasional instances of petty crime or boorish behaviour could never dilute Mum's loyalty to Liverpool, forged in the flames of the Second World War when her city got a bigger pasting than anywhere outside London, devastation that military histories have termed the Forgotten Blitz.

November 1940 offered a foretaste of what was to come. In a single night, the Luftwaffe dropped 350 tons of high explosive, 30,000 incendiary bombs and 30 blockbuster mines that claimed the lives of 300. When the Adelphi took a direct hit, plunging the hotel into darkness, the orchestra retaliated by playing There'll Always Be An England, sung lustily by diners and waitresses alike.

The following year, the Nazis returned with a vengeance, at the behest of Grand Admiral Erich Raeder, supreme commander of the German Navy and Hitler's ruthless henchman. He championed a plan to invade the United Kingdom, Operation Sealion, but advised the Führer that the Luftwaffe had to rule our airspace first, demonstrating its awesome might by teaching one city a lesson the country could not ignore. In a top-secret memo, he recommended that "an early, concerted attack on Britain is necessary – on Liverpool, for example, so that the whole nation will feel the effects".

His choice of city was a no-brainer because my home town presented an easy target for German aircrews; bounded by the Dee, Mersey and Liverpool Bay, the unmissable Wirral Peninsula stuck out in phosphorescent seas like a thumbs-up for enemy pilots navigating by moonlight.

Since Hitler had reportedly lived in Upper Stanhope Street with his half-brother Alois Hitler for six months before the First World War, he knew Liverpool and soon acted on Raeder's recommendation. Stung by his U-boats' failure to halt convoys sailing to the port from North America, the dictator resolved to devastate our city in one all-out campaign before reassigning his bombers to the Russian front.

In May 1941, his forces of evil descended on Merseyside in a week that would be seared on Mum's psyche.

From May 1 to 8, from 10pm till 6 next morning, squadrons of up to 500 bombers unloaded thousands of tons of high explosive and 112,000 fire bombs on the city, leaving 1,900 Liverpudlians dead and 1,450 gravely injured – so many victims that bodies were left rotting in the rubble and 554 had to be buried in a mass grave in Anfield cemetery on May 14.

The Blitz's biggest single death toll occurred when a parachute mine drifted onto a school used as an air-raid shelter in Durning Road in Edge Hill, killing 164 men, women and children, while one bomb landed 50 yards from our house, in Little Ullswater, a short extension of our street on the other side of Thirlmere Road. This claimed the lives of a family of four huddling in the tiny broom cupboard under the stairs, and Mum told me how vulnerable she felt as earth-shuddering explosions rocked the neighbourhood. Yet she also recalled the quiet courage of Scousers who might have retreated to their homes and shelters but would never surrender to Hitler's mass-murderers.

Defiant to the end, they refused to be cowed by the rain of death, like the woman amid exploding bombs in County Road, waving an axe at the funereal skies and screaming, "Come down here, you bastards, and fight like men". She'd have fought to the last, too.

As a way of reducing the hazard of flying glass, people glued white tape in X shapes on windows. They incited Lord Haw-Haw, the haughty British fascist who made propaganda radio broadcasts for the Nazis from Berlin, to sneer at Bootle's residents, telling them "the kisses on your windows won't help you". His taunting left Merseysiders unmoved and the Rev Leslie A Thomas from St Aidan's Church observed: "Our Liverpool people are and have been magnificent in their suffering."

Throughout the Luftwaffe's onslaught, Mersey dockers unloaded ships, a contribution to the war effort that cannot be underestimated, since the port became our country's saviour, receiving food, fuel and Allied troops.

Once peace dawned in 1945, my city, along with Bootle, Birkenhead and Wallasey, had played a momentous role in the Allied victory, especially the Battle of the Atlantic, the war's longest campaign. Escorted by naval commanders like Captain Johnny Walker, who sailed out of the Mersey to destroy U-boat packs, 1,285 convoys had succeeded in reaching our docks and 75 million tons of vital supplies had passed through the port.

The Luftwaffe might have murdered 4,000 Merseysiders, demolished 10,000 houses and made 70,000 homeless but Hitler had met his Nemesis, Nazism had been extinguished, and the Nuremberg War Crimes Tribunal would sentence Herr Raeder to life imprisonment.

Never again would Mum and her neighbours have to withstand aerial bombardment. She could face the future with hope, living in the place of her birth, where everybody was a character and a comedian, a singer and a storyteller.

My, how she loved her city and wanted it to do well. During the Fifties, however, one source of Mersey pride was to almost run dry: Liverpool Football Club.

* * * * * * * * * *

Fate decreed that Anfield football stadium lay a quarter of a mile from our home in Ullswater Street and the nearest part of the ground to our backyard was the Spion Kop, so close that, in the still of the living room, Mum could sometimes hear a distant, dull thud when a goal was scored.

Because of this proximity, most Lake District children supported the Reds but my pals were about to take on a distinctly blue hue. At the age of 10, I arrived at a pivotal juncture, the 11-plus exam that decreed whether you went with the clever Dicks to a grammar school or the Joe Soaps to a secondary modern.

For many boys, often bright lads, failing the exam was a priority, because they preferred to stick with mates who were heading to the secondary modern. They also had no desire to be a reluctant sprog, strong-armed every morning into grammar school uniform by their mother before being propelled through the front door into the street.

That uniform made you stand out. You were different, a know-all, too smart by half.

Once in a while, any homeward-bound boy in blazer and cap would offer entertainment for a ruffian shambling around the corner of Breck Road. If this lout fancied a bit of early-evening recreation and began a chase, you needed to be fleet of foot along the shortest route through back jiggers, the back entries, to your house.

Should your pursuer summon up a surprising turn of speed and grab you, he'd make you pay for having the effrontery to flee. Dragging your blazer inside out from its tail, over your head and shoulders, he'd truss you up like one of Bernard Matthews' oven-ready turkeys and haul you around in circles while administering roundhouse kicks to your backside.

After a few seconds' horseplay, the scruff would usually lose interest and let you go. If you were really unlucky, though, and had crossed a real nasty, he might rip your shoes off and lob them over a wall into someone's backyard. That meant you had to knock on the door to request their retrieval or slouch home in stocking feet, practising your explanation for an outraged mother.

As well as to dodge the bullies, would-be 11-plus failures had another justification for not wishing to make the grade: they argued O-levels in Latin or geography weren't essential to find a job.

They were right – once school was packed in at the tender age of 15, full employment awaited, with barely 500,000 on the dole throughout the land. If there were no vacancies locally in Prout's garage, Fusco's ice-cream factory or the Vulcan foundry, you'd always get sorted down at the port or in the Merch, the Merchant Navy.

Liverpool's Dock Road was heaving with lorries and along the quays every berth was hogged by ships from companies such as Ellerman Pappayani, Booth, Elder Dempster,

Blue Funnel, Bank Line, Harrison, Shaw-Savill, Pacific Steam, Fyffes and Ben. Want a job as a docker or a deckhand? You got it.

Regardless of this, Mum knew education was the key that could unlock the door to a far better future and with her encouragement, I contrived to pass the 11-plus at Anfield Road primary.

Now I had to choose a grammar school from three possibilities: the Institute and Collegiate in the city centre and Alsop in Walton.

Out of a dozen lads in Ullswater Street, just one was attending a grammar school, Alsop, so Mum consulted his mother and, swayed by her assessment, concluded it would be best for me.

An educational institution scoffed at by boys from rival schools as All Slops, No Tea, Alsop was situated closer to Everton's Goodison Park than Anfield, and when I entered the first form in 1955, I found myself among a minority of Red lads. Not that football rivalry created conflict. Alsopians might have had different allegiances but the Liverpool fraternity knew their place – in the Second Division, from which their team were toiling to escape.

No contest, Everton wore the rosette of Merseyside's top dogs and the Toffees' fame was so sweet that a club in Chile was even named after them. Or so I was informed by Gozzy Johnson, the school genius on all things football.

The Gozzy moniker had been conferred on Johnson because, in addition to wearing welder-friendly, thick-lensed glasses, he suffered from a severe squint that enabled him to stare at the blackboard and out the window at the same time. In Scouse slang, he was gozzy.

For those of us enamoured of American comic books, he resembled a loon from Mad magazine, with spiky hair that never did what it was told, teeth no two of which were at the same angle, and a pock-marked complexion redolent of the dark side of the moon, as depicted on the backcloth of a Flash Gordon film episode.

To add to Gozzy's dishevelled image, he always wore his Alsop tie with an oversized knot pulled halfway under one wing of his collar.

What also distinguished him from other boys was the fact that, regardless of the weather, hot, cold or tepid, he usually sported a splodge of snot on the tip of his nose. But he never carried a hankie, hence his alternative name of Greensleeves.

His futile attempts to delete this viscous appendage annoyed masters, so much so that one afternoon, our doggedly placid French teacher, Mr Cummins, got a cob on and resorted to a Gallic colloquialism, instructing Gozzy to "remonter ta grand'mère au grenier", or put your granny back in the attic.

This term for sniffing was a phrase few boys forgot. Later, with scant regard for context, some even incorporated it in the GCE French essay, to the bewilderment of examiners marking papers.

Normally Gozzy's nerdy demeanour would have made him easy meat for bullies but his encyclopaedic knowledge of football afforded some protection. Our school mastermind of the game didn't waste time reading Hotspur or Film Fun as he queued to buy a tube of Spangles from Mr Abrams in the tuck shop; he would be digesting Tommy Lawton's biography. Plonked down in one of Alsop's outside loos, this anorak in a blazer would be absorbing a Glasgow Rangers football programme and at the bus stop in Queen's Drive his face would be buried in the latest Football League annual.

His most trusted authority was Charles Buchan's Football Monthly, the soccer magazine he could commit to memory in an evening's voracious reading. While other boys were racing off to the corner newsagents, clutching 4 pence to catch the newest adventures of Dan Dare in The Eagle, Gozzy would already be sharing his armchair with Charlie, devouring all his facts, stats and stories.

If Liverpool recruited a new player from, say, Newcastle, Gozzy could give chapter and verse. Position, age, place of birth, previous clubs, Morris Minor or Austin A30, Capstan or Woodbine fags, Old Spice or Imperial Leather after shave, Brylcreem or Tru Gel, Rael Brook or Van Heusen shirts, width of trouser bottoms, whether he dressed to the right or left, Gozzy knew the lot.

He could even be credited with keeping up attendances at school. Boys were known to sag off in the morning but register with some spurious excuse in the afternoon because they had heard on the street about a Red or Blue signing and wanted this soccer compendium to regale them with all the details.

By any lad's teens, football had evolved into a focal feature of his life, more so even than girls, and at Anfield you earned your stripes in the Boys' Pen, an enclosure on one side of the Kop, with a wild and worrying reputation. My Everton pals enjoyed easier access to their games because Goodison had a gate at the Bullens Road end allocated to boys aged 14 to 16, allowing entry at cut price behind the goal with grown-ups who'd paid full admission.

This cheap admittance to a First Division game was a boon for youngsters, and not just Evertonians. As Liverpool and Everton home fixtures alternated on Saturdays, I sometimes went with Blue mates to watch the Toffees when our lads were playing away in the Second Division; this allowed me to see top-drawer football, invariably from the opposition.

The boys' gate at Goodison also tempted impecunious adults. Every so often a dad, miniscule school cap plonked on a mop of hair, would crouch down in the pack, bent on sneaking through the turnstile. Naturally, mounted police were alert to this scam and would bend down from their saddles to drag protesting middle-aged men out of the scrum of lads.

At Anfield, unless a boy was rich enough to pay full whack for the Kop of 3 shillings and 6 pence (today's 17.5p), he had to take his chance in the Pen, for the princely sum of 9 pence (4p).

This nest of vipers was notorious for scallies who wandered through, sniffing out money. "Gissus yer odds, lah" was their usual greeting for newcomers. "Pray, young fellow, be so charitable as to grant me any surplus change that you might poooooo."

If you pleaded poverty, the interlocutor would always dip into your pockets to validate the truth of that claim.

Now I wasn't a hard case who could tell these beggars to go jump in the Mersey; I was a medium-to-soft case, a nesh lad tarred with the customary taunt, "He couldn't punch a hole in a wet *Echo*". In truth I could … but only if I had to, which wasn't often.

Accordingly, the instant I began entering the Pen at the age of 12, I had to be canny, depositing any coppers in the Bank of Wolsey – down my sock.

Having walked up the steps into the enclosure and joined the raucous mob, I was careful about my accent, too. By comparison with other boys, I didn't talk broad Scouse, probably because Mum was mildly spoken, but out on the terrace, I exaggerated my Liverpudlian twang, since posh lads never ventured into the Pen.

I also adjusted my vocabulary to suit the language there. At home I addressed my mother as Mum and out in our street referred to her as such.

At Anfield, no one had a Mum – it was me Mam or me Ma, and that had to be remembered, otherwise you were singled out as a cissy. Anything that might differentiate you from other lads was not recommended.

This even applied to my first name. While Johnny, Joe, Jimmy and Billy were norms on the terrace, Neil sounded la-di-da, but I had an alter ego. On Merseyside, an anthology of alternative family names prevailed, taking precedence over the originals and becoming common currency at Alsop. In homage to Professor Stanley Unwin's garbled, Learesque speech on radio, lads added to this roll call of gibberish by creating a fresh nomenclature at school, a mix of traditional and modern that included Chimble (Campbell), Golly (Gallagher), Gibbo (Gibson), Groggy (Graham), Hairy (Harris), Yozzer (Hughes), Jonah (Jones), Macca (for any Mac or Mc), Muffin or Spud (Murphy), Thommo (Thomas or Thompson), Smigger or Smithy (Smith) and Wonkie (Wheeler). So my Dunkin was contorted into Dootch and it was he who first set foot in the Pen.

For my initial forays, I was chaperoned by Steve Jones, a Coniston Street lad who became a mate when we were both about nine and spotted each other lying on the pavement in Breck Road, the thoroughfare demarcating one side of the Lake District. The prostrate pair of us were practitioners of penny dip, a money-making venture for hunter-gatherer youngsters.

Here's how it worked. The majority of shops had an ancient cast-iron grid set in the pavement alongside the door, giving access and light to a cellar. Over the years, customers coming out of premises would accidentally drop coins as they pushed their change into purses or pockets, and a fair number would roll through the grille into a four-foot-deep cavity.

Fly boys knew such riches could be salvaged. A dessert spoon bent at right angle and bound onto the end of a long cane with string would be poked through the grid and manoeuvred to lift any copper or silver spied amid decades of dust, sweet papers, cigarette butts and chewing gum.

One Saturday morning, after unproductive exertion to dislodge a florin superglued in a crack, bending my spoon even more and nearly snapping my cane, Steve came to my aid. By nudging the recalcitrant coin alternately on each side, the pair of us extricated this booty and a childhood friendship was born. From then on, we spent many hours together, face down on the flags in Breck Road, Oakfield Road and Breckfield Road, searching for buried treasure, and loud was our elation if we salvaged anything as grand as a half-crown.

Before transferring to a secondary modern, Steve attended the same primary school as me, Anfield Road, and during my first days there I was informed of the pecking order of hardness, the league table of older boys who were the best playground brawlers.

At the base of this scrap heap were the cocks of each class, with cocks of each class year above them, rising up to cock of the school, a lad called Dawson who everyone obeyed. But over and above all the cocks in all the schools, one tough was acknowledged as the hardest case and I only ever saw him once.

I must have been about 13 and was in the Pen with Steve before a game with Leeds. Waiting for the teams to come out, the soprano hubbub suddenly stilled and the multitude parted as if by inaudible command.

A boy mooched through, eating chips out of their newspaper wrapping.

I say boy but an oblique glance, oblique because any direct regard would have been treated as a challenge eliciting a violent backlash, revealed he was 15 going on 25. He had lived and fought a lot, with a boxer's broad nose, sunken eyes and sour face that, despite its youth, bore the shadows of constant fatigue and brutality.

Even more striking, he gave off vibes that bellowed: "Out of my way!"

I got the message and averted my gaze.

The fact he was sucking on chips said everything. You scarcely ever saw that in the Pen. The appearance of any sustenance, be it a Wagon Wheel, Holland's meat pie or – delicacy of delicacies – a foot-long Curly Wurly toffee, occasioned plunder by a shoal of pimply piranhas, stripping you of your mouth candy in seconds, and even a glimpse of an apple core could unleash a feeding frenzy.

But this lad wasn't a super-tough brute extracting chips from a compact, handy-sized parcel clutched to his chest – he had the newspaper wrapping deliberately splayed out like albatross's wings, demanding space, room and attention. A challenge to everyone: Take a chip, if you dare. Proof this was one hell of a hard 'un.

Seconds after this boy-man/man-boy appeared, he was gone, subsuming himself lethargically in the crowd, which gradually resumed its chatter.

"Who was that?" I asked Steve, who knew everyone. "Cock o' the Pen," he replied quietly. "Just hope you never see him again, Dootch."

And I never did, in the Pen, the Kop or anywhere else in Liverpool.

What became of this lord of the fans? Did he get a job, marry, have kids, move into a council house in Winsford? I doubt it very much. That face left a feeling he was fated to die young. Probably, as punishment for gratuitous acts of violence, he went on to have several stays in Her Majesty's Hotel, Hornby Road, variously known to its lodgers as Joe Gerks, Walton Jail or Liverpool Prison.

There, during months of inactivity, he would have done as thousands of cons have done: stained his hands with roll-your-owns of cheap baccy, bit his nails down to the cuticle and used Cherry Blossom shoe polish and a needle to tattoo the statutory Love and Hate on the backs of his fingers. Perhaps, too, after he walked blinking into the bright light of freedom, he went straight to the tattooist in Hardman Street to put that emblem of the wanderer, a swallow, between thumb and first finger. With these tokens of incarceration for all to see as he lifted his pint in the Flat Iron down the road from the Kop, he would have planned his escape from the misery of existence.

Perhaps like lots of feral lads, he joined the army, got into the Parachute Regiment and was shot in the back during the communal conflict on Cyprus. Far more plausibly, because military discipline would not be tolerable to a loner like him, he went away to sea. I suspect that, late one night, after a bender in some dockside dive in Lisbon or Genoa, he quarrelled with a pimp or a pickpocket and bled to death from a stiletto wound to his heart.

Whatever did happen, I'd bet my last Liverpool programme he never saw middle age.

When Steve was barely out of nappies, his father took him for karate lessons, martial training that taught him how to handle himself, as I found to my cost one morning at the bus stop in Breck Road.

Approaching from behind while he waited, I clamped my hands over his eyes.

Woof! Steve's right elbow pistoned into my solar plexus, knocking the stuffing out of me. This reflex showed he was always on his mettle and he was the most street-wise mate I had, knowing all the tricks in the Scouse Lads' Survival Handbook.

For example, he would alter his walk to suit a potentially nasty situation. Striding through a neighbourhood where he didn't belong, if lads were on a corner ahead, he would clench both fists, swing his shoulders in a purposeful manner and stare straight ahead.

This assertive gait was meant to tell likely assailants, "I'm ready for action", and it could deter them. They would be more disposed to pick on some unassuming individual who kept his bonce down and slunk past or, most damning of all, crossed over the road.

In any disagreement demanding fisticuffs, Steve knew how to hit with venom, using a ploy he utilised one August Bank Holiday at Stanley Park's funfair.

Amid the dodgems, waltzers and toffee-apple stalls, half a dozen grown-up lads who'd all had a few jars were measuring the force of their haymakers on a punch ball, dangling from a chain in front of a big clock-face dial. Once this rubber sphere was slugged, it impacted on the glass dial and jerked a needle round to the number indicating the potency of your wallop, whether 50, 60 or whatever pounds.

After the tipsy tearaways had bashed the ball again and again to identify their champion, little Steve, all 14 wiry years of him, stepped up.

He pushed a penny in the slot, pulled the bag down to the right height and took aim.

Splat! His fist catapulted into the bag which crashed into the glass, jolting the needle to its mark.

70 pounds! The watching lads' eyes narrowed in disbelief. How come ...?

As we skipped away, Steve gave a big grin and pulled his hand out of his pocket. Opening the palm, he exposed a ball of copper coins. "The secret," he revealed. "Hold those dead tight – they make your fist a lot stronger. A belt with them, Dootch, could stop you getting splattered."

Pennies reinserted in pocket, he stuffed two fingers from each hand in his mouth and screeched the loudest whistle I'd ever heard, his way of crowing over his ingenuity.

Among other physical attributes, Steve was acclaimed for his expertise in one particular Lake District activity, bunking on the back of wagons, a motor sport played by lads when they reached their teens.

Before then, our most exhilarating pastime was careering down the nearest hill, Oakfield, an offshoot of Oakfield Road, in a steerie, a wooden orange box to which someone's dad had fitted two cross-members and four pram wheels. While this freewheeled or was pushed down the incline, best of all when wet or icy, the driver sat inside, steering with reins, a rope tied to each extremity of the articulated front axle.

As soon as you reached secondary school, though, the steerie became child's play and bunking was mandatory to establish your rank as a lad.

For this escapade, you sought out a lorry that parked in our street every week, driven by the original man in black.

Wearing black canvas kecks, a white-going-on-black shirt and black leather waistcoat to cushion his back from sharp pieces in the sacks, the coal merchant made his deliveries up and down the back jiggers.

Once completed, he would drive off slowly in his rattly ERF commercial, giving you a chance to bunk on the back: run and grab the tail of the flatback load area, where the pile of coal hid you from his cab.

As the wagon gathered speed in Thirlmere Road, dragging you along by your hands, you'd swing your legs forward and under the wooden boards and brace your feet against a lateral section of the sub-frame.

Horizontal position achieved, legs extended in direction of travel, head back from whence you'd been transported, this extreme sport would begin in earnest. While the lorry bounced along bumpy streets, you hung on for dear life, hoping the coalman wouldn't slam his anchors on, hurling you under the wheels or ramming the tail into your teeth.

Hands would quickly lose their grip and when the ERF slowed, you'd try to dismount. Lowering legs to ground, you'd hare along like international sprinter MacDonald Bailey, then leave go with your hands and trust to providence that residual velocity would not propel you nose first into the tarmac.

The longest distance I ever travelled was from Ullswater to the bottom of Thirlmere, about 100 yards. However, one afternoon when the coalman had made his last delivery, Steve became the undisputed champion bunker. By dint of resting whenever the wagon came to a standstill at junctions, he rode a quarter of a mile, from the Breck Road traffic lights to the coalyard in West Derby Road. So Steve was a hard-nosed lad and I regarded myself as fortunate to have him as a partner during my first tentative steps in the Pen.

Frankly, the longer anyone patronised this devils' nursery, the safer it became, although around Bonfire Night it was advisable to keep your hands resolutely in your trouser pockets, in case someone inserted a banger and blew your nuts off.

Once your mug became familiar and your eyes kept to themselves, you felt accepted and could join in the fun, outshouting the Kop where older brothers went. High-pitched like a cloud of cheeping sparrows, the Pen was always noisy in its support, deliberately sounding off when the rest of the ground had fallen silent. The boys mightn't have been louder but they went on much longer.

There were plenty of laughs, too. At every game, resident comics picked a quiet interlude to bawl some witticism about a player or to tell a joke they'd been saving all week. Immediately the Pen would crack off laughing, leaving the rest of Anfield mystified by what the kids found so hilarious.

So when a Swansea fullback was all over the show marking Billy Liddell, the South Walian panicked, miskicked and conceded a corner. As he lurched back to his position on the line, a Kopite gave him an employment reference. "You're shit," he cried.

"He's not that good" came the riposte from a Pen joker and all the boys chortled.

We'd scored against the Kop.

One Saturday, Steve introduced me to Fat Harold, a lad from Rydal Street who'd had run-ins with the police as he progressed from purloining bottles of milk on doorsteps to stealing from shops, misdemeanours that brought a term of residence in an approved school, a reformatory for delinquent boys.

Because of his dealings with Liverpool Constabulary, Harold wasn't keen on bizzies and contrived a way of exacting retribution.

In the Fifties, police officers patrolled Breck Road every night, checking premises were secure. As they plodded along the pavement, they would reach out and grip shops' doorknobs and latches to establish they were locked.

Harold scrutinised this with interest, deducing it offered scope to give an undesirable surprise to scuffers, an act of revenge in which his family's venerable mongrel would play a starring role.

One night Harold went in the backyard where Jess occupied his kennel and picked up a cob of dog dirt in a piece of newspaper. With this in hand, he sloped off to Breck Road, which was deserted at such a late hour, every shop long shut. Now he could execute his plan.

After establishing the coast was clear, he daubed some of Jess's turd on the doorknob of Sturla's. Then he moved on to the Co-op and repeated the process. After the baker's, the butcher's and the pet shop further along, he darted across the road, made sure once again that no one was watching, and gave the same treatment to Martin's bank, the men's outfitters, the Chinese laundry and, lastly, Buckley's the greengrocers.

By now Harold had used up the entire dollop but his trap had been set. He walked briskly over to Mackie & Gladstone's, shrank into the doorway, and waited.

It had turned chilly but on the corner of Richmond Terrace, a couple who'd just forsaken the pub were having a snog.

Harold watched, pondering what all the fuss was about.

He glanced away, peering down Breck Road. Yes! As reliable as the 1 o'clock gun at the docks, the night copper plodded into vision from Belmont Road, just before last knockings in the hostelries.

Harold peeped around the off-licence window, as the unsuspecting constable clumped along. He clumped and he clumped, without halting.

Flippin' heck! He wasn't checking doors.

A new boy who didn't know the form. Harold had gone to all that effort for nothing.

Past the bank, the men's outfitter, the Chinese laundry, the bobby walked, until he arrived at Buckley's and hesitated at the window, his attention arrested by a cardboard cut-out of a swimsuited nymphet nuzzling a juicy Cape orange.

For a few seconds, he was catatonic, fossilised in fantasy.

A motorbike roared past, sucking the scuffer out of his reverie. He turned to scowl at the noisy Norton clattering towards Everton Road.

He resumed his patrol. He was on the verge of passing Buckley's door when .... he hesitated.

Harold peeped round the corner of Mackie's, transfixed.

The constable had remembered something.

He studied Buckley's door, and elected to do the right thing. Extending his arm to the brass knob, he grasped it firmly – and recoiled in horror, face disfigured by disgust.

He gazed at his paralysed hand, edged it slowly to his nostrils and sniffed.

From across the road, Harold watched his victim mouth one word: "Shit."

Correct.

After the doo-dah, time for Del Shannon's da-doo-run-run-runaway. Harold didn't dawdle.

He nipped round the corner of Rydal Street and skedaddled home, leaving one cackhanded copper.

The following Saturday, news of this smear campaign spread through the Pen where everyone was agog. How could he do that? What balls!

Whenever we came out of the ground, Steve and I would tag on to groups of men heading along Oakfield Road, listening to their arguments about the match. In those days, cavalcades of supporters cycled to Anfield and parked their bikes in backyards of houses next to the stadium, for a penny a slot. As they pedalled away, these cyclists would decelerate alongside a discussion group, listen to conflicting statements and, if they heard something provocative, stick their oar in. Stalled in a slow bicycle race, they would give their input to the analysts on the pavement. Meanwhile, engrossed in the exchanges, we would bring up the rear, walking past the Lake District and onto Breck Road, in the hope of discovering whose motion was carried.

One location guaranteed to offer football polemics could be found in the lee of the Kop – Donaldson Street wash house, a council facility with two functions. Firstly, a laundry where mothers did their weekly washes using Reckitt's Blue starch; every day you'd see them pushing rickety old prams laden with steaming clothes back to their homes. Secondly, it was a bath house for locals. None of the homes in Ullswater had bathrooms, so if you'd outgrown the tin coffin carried from the coal shed into the back kitchen and filled with kettles of hot water, Donaldson Street was the place to do your ablutions. There you had the benefit of male and female sections, with women attendants to keep everything spick and span in cubicles where you soaked away the grime of docks, factory, office or school.

On reaching my teens, I would go twice a week: on a Tuesday, quiet apart from the occasional Johnnie Ray impersonator lamenting the fact somebody had stolen his gal, and a Friday, unfailingly boisterous as blokes got spruced up for the weekend. The pubs, the clubs and, inescapably, the footie were noisy topics for a soapy seminar as Reds and Blues cast judgement on teams while basking in their tubs.

Some clients had alternative plans for the weekend, not necessarily legal ones, and they would enter into private dialogues, using back slang to maintain confidentiality. In its most common form, this language of the underworld entailed pronouncing things back to front. For instance, police became slop, man was nam and pint was tenip. In another variant, the first letter or letters would be stuck on the end and the suffix "ay" added, distorting hello into ellohay or house into ousehay.

Elementary, but when spoken at speed very difficult to follow. Anyone could pick out the odd word but sentences were impossible, unless your ear was attuned to the speech pattern.

While I was growing up, my Anfield idol was Billy Liddell and my real-life hero was Mum's brother, Uncle Len. After his early education in that august academic institution, the university of Liverpool life, Uncle Len had joined the Royal Navy and spent many happy years sailing the Seven Seas and experiencing adventures in exotic ports of call, the stuff of fiction for a boy like me.

On leaving the Senior Service, he became an engineer with the Dunlop company in Aintree and travelled throughout Africa during the Fifties and Sixties, installing and servicing conveyor belts for the mining industry.

Every year, he'd return with his wife Kay for leave in Liverpool where he stayed with us in Ullswater and caught up with his many mates. In our back kitchen, before heading out, he would pay tribute to Gigli and Caruso by singing opera while shaving with a cutthroat razor brandished like a conductor's baton. Great to be back. Then he would don his immaculate blue blazer, embellished with its Royal Navy badge, and embark on a leisurely voyage around selected pubs using the overhead railway, the Dockers' Umbrella, that rattled along the waterfront.

For Uncle Len, nowhere could beat Old Mother Mersey, a haven that has bewitched seafarers for centuries. As the novelist Herman Melville wrote in Redburn in 1849: "Of all the sea-ports in the world, Liverpool, perhaps, most abounds in all the variety of land-sharks, land-rats, and other vermin, which makes the hapless mariner their prey ... And yet, sailors love this Liverpool; and upon long voyages to distant parts of the globe, will be continually dilating upon its charms and attractions, and extolling it above all other sea-ports."

In Melville's day, one attraction for crews who'd been becalmed in the doldrums or eviscerated by the Roaring Forties were the grog shops that promised to get you drunk for 1d and blind drunk for 2d. By the nature of their trade, mariners condense their rest and recuperation into a concise period of shore leave, so binge drinking was and is commonplace: arrive in port, hit the nearest bar, pile your dosh on the table and neck back liquor until not a farthing remains.

One Saturday night, after sojourns in ale houses on the Dock Road with a rumbustious finale in the Baltic Fleet, Uncle Len walked into our kitchen where I was reading the Eagle while listening to Radio Luxembourg on the transistor radio.

"Wait till you hear this," he said, and creased up in anticipation of the tale he was about to tell. "You know my mate Ronnie from the Throstle's Nest in Scottie Road?"

I nodded.

"Last night, about midnight, he was nicked. Outside the pub, outside the Throstle – a copper found him, paralytic, on his knees, trying to roll up a zebra crossing. He wanted it as a present ... for his missus. A zebra-skin carpet for the bedroom. Mad!"

Uncle Len was in bulk, and I couldn't help joining in.

We guffawed.

What a picture! Ronnie, kneeling at the side of Scotland Road, growing more and more frustrated as he wore his fingers to the bone, doing his damnedest to get a free black-and-white Axminster for his Judy.

Liverpool has been the scene of some weird goings-on in but someone trying to pinch the road surface ... an attempt at real highway robbery.

Evidently Ronnie's would-be larceny had been buzzing around city-centre boozers, inciting observations like "Must've had one for the road", "Fancies himself as a comic, the new Robb Wilton" and "Why'd he hang around and get arrested? Should've done a runner".

This story had set the seal on Uncle Len's night out, attesting to why he loved trips home: the craich, the yarns, the jokes, the well-oiled wallies banged up overnight in the cop shop.

In blissful mood, he went into the back kitchen, returning with a bottle of Ind Coope mild for himself and a glass of sarsparilla for me, and installed himself in the armchair next to the spluttering coal fire.

Now the serious conversation began. "How's school?" he asked.

"OK," I replied, overlooking the caning I'd just had for needless backchat to "Perry" Mason, the science master. "It's all right. I like French, Spanish ... not too keen on physics, chemistry. I've played for the under-15s, too." This impressed Uncle Len.

Now I disclosed something else of which I was quite proud: "I've started going to Anfield, in the Boys' Pen."

Uncle Len shook his head, slowly.

This was a man who had sunk many a jar for Liverpool in competition with San Francisco's thirstiest, who'd boxed for England in Sydney's roughest hostelries, who'd fought off footpads in Shanghai, who'd stared death in the face while serving on warships in the war.

Now, when I divulged I was entering the Pen, the fact he shook his head said everything.

Yet Uncle Len was fearless, a man's man, whose father – my grandfather – had a niche in naval annals.

During the First World War, Grandad had survived U-boat attacks while serving on the Titanic's sister ship, the RMS Olympic, the Germans' most coveted maritime target after it was commandeered and renamed His Majesty's Transport 2810 to bring thousands of Canadian and American troops to England. I knew little about Grandad's war service until, 75 years after it was posted, Mum gave me a letter from the White Star Line headquarters in Southampton addressed to him. It read:

> Mr R. G. Lee, 29th May, 1918
> Quartermaster at the Wheel,
> H.M.T. 2810
>
> *Dear Sir,*
> *We have pleasure in handing you herewith a cheque for £10 and take this opportunity of congratulating you on your very efficient handling of the wheel in prompt obeyance to Captain Hayes' orders, as a result of which the ship on which you were employed was able to ram and sink a German submarine.*
> *Wishing you the best of luck in your future career.*
>
> *Yours sincerely,*
> WHITE STAR LINE,
> P. E. Curry LOCAL MANAGER

So my Grandad, a humble Liverpool seafarer, had sunk a U-boat. Eager to find out more, I posted a photocopy of this letter to the Imperial War Museum and they replied with page after page of accounts of the sinking.

From these, it emerged that at daybreak on May 12, 1918, the Olympic, a 46,000-ton leviathan affectionately known as Old Reliable, had been cruising off the Lizard towards Southampton when the U103 surfaced directly ahead. Although the submarine was silhouetted against a low streak of dawn on the horizon, the Olympic was camouflaged by the sky's black background so the Germans were unaware of its presence. They soon woke up when Captain Hayes ordered "Full speed ahead!" and the Olympic's forward gun opened fire.

Despairingly, the U-boat commander, Claus Rücker, took evasive measures, trying to get into position to launch torpedoes at his attacker, but Grandad outmanoeuvred him. Steady at the helm of the Allies' biggest transport vessel, he bore down on the enemy, ripping apart the submarine with his Olympian tin-opener, a collision so violent that officers on the troopship's bridge were thrown off their feet and the bow was buckled eight feet to one side.

A total of 31 German sailors were rescued, including Rücker who three years previously had machine-gunned the crew of a British trawler, the Victoria, after torpedoing it.

Histories of the First World War record the Olympic's feat as the only known instance of a merchant vessel sinking a warship, so Grandad accomplished something unparalleled in naval warfare, with 5,000 American soldiers on board. Imagine if a torpedo had sunk that.

The White Star letter testified to Grandad's valour and now I was sitting in the kitchen in Ullswater Street with his brave son, Uncle Len, whose unspeakable verdict on the Pen tickled me. Why, it came nowhere near being as dreadful as most Scousers conceived but such was its notoriety.

My uncle shook his head and that was that. The subject was not referred to again.

The Pen was where I supported the Reds and I went in there until long after Uncle Len had returned to his expatriate life in Africa. Once I reached 15, though, the moment of realisation for every pubescent lad arrived: the child has mutated into a teenager. Time to migrate from the wild and wonderful Pen to the Kop, where big lads and men rubbed shoulders as equals, aired adult opinions and gabbed in deep voices about boozing, football and girls.

But those years in the Pen amounted to an initiation rite for any Liverpool boy, after which Elland Road, St James' Park, Stamford Bridge, Old Trafford, San Siro, Camp Nou, Maracana and Azteca would hold few misgivings.

Gosh! I'd even get out of Huyton's Eagle and Child in one piece. Need I say more?

2
The Messiah From Glenbuck

To be a champ, you have to believe in yourself when nobody else will.
– Sugar Ray Robinson

IN 1954-55, Liverpool's first season after relegation, the team performed as if they were in shock.

The club had spent 50 years in the First Division, so falling through the trapdoor devastated everyone, particularly our manager, Don Welsh. Despite a wealth of experience as a former Charlton and England inside-left, he found it difficult to motivate players and his lowest ebb came on December 11 when the Reds suffered their worst-ever defeat, 9-1 to Birmingham at St Andrews.

Attempts to blame this humiliation on a frozen pitch only added insult to the fans' depression. Didn't the Brummies have to cope with the slippery surface as well?

A few weeks later, consolation came with a 4-0 FA Cup success over Everton in front of 72,000 at Goodison. Hopes rose of a trip to Wembley but in the next round Huddersfield knocked the Reds out at Anfield, 2-0, and from thereon the campaign went downhill, with some supporters even fearing another slide, into the Third Division. By the season's close, however, Liddell had led a rally, rattling in 30 goals, so the lads finished 11th, doomed to another year with the second-raters. Kop fanatics were aghast.

The following season, 1955-56, the team pulled themselves together and made a determined challenge for promotion. For several months they were well placed to go up, as Kopites commended goalscorers with "For he's a jolly good fellow" and urged the Reds on with "Two, four, six, eight, who do we appreciate? Liverpool! Liverpool!" However, in the end, they missed out, finishing third. Since it was two up, two down, third was nowhere, a wounding blow to Welsh who resigned.

Boasting one of the Second Division's biggest squads, the lads had allowed their title push to fade away. Inside forward Jimmy Melia, who said the club had some 50 professionals, including six keepers and seven right-wingers, recalled Bob Paisley being told to play on the right by Welsh and muttering: "There'll be about eight of us up there."

Welsh's successor was Phil Taylor, who had come to Anfield as a player in 1936 and captained the side thwarted in the 1950 Cup Final by Arsenal. In all, he played 345 games for the Reds, so Kopites hailed the appointment of this club stalwart, praying it would mark a turning point.

Taylor did make Liverpool promotion contenders but at the campaign's close they were the Nearly Men again – and not just for one season. Three years in a row, they played well, often leading the table and seemingly bound for the top tier. Hold on. As the season reached its climax, just as night follows day, individual players would lose form and other results would go against them. So even though Liddell and Melia scored 20plus goals in each term, Taylor's teams finished third in 1956-57, fourth in 1957-58, and fourth again in 1958-59.

In those days, there was no hiding place for players who usually lived in the city. As Ronnie Moran said: "After the whistle, it was straight into the bath, then straight on the tram. Fans were still making their way home, so if I'd played a stinker, I'd slouch in the front seat with a cap pulled over my face."

Other clubs in the Second Division were more than grateful to see Liverpool staying down, because attendances in excess of 40,000 were the norm at Anfield, yielding much-valued income for visiting teams such as Cardiff and Coventry who split gate receipts 5050 with the Reds.

Towards the close of the 1958-59 season, I was playing keepy-uppy in the street by myself one Sunday afternoon when a neighbour, Taffy Griffith, doddered past on his way home from the Standard. A mate was heading in the opposite direction, so Taffy waylaid him to get something rather substantial off his chest.

The big issue was Liverpool's plight and he proceeded to rail against the Reds' inadequacies, Taylor's mistakes, the board's failures, the team's lack of skill and commitment, the players you wouldn't pay in brass washers. After this rant, he moved a bit closer to his pal, as if about to impart a secret, and said quietly: "You know, Jim. I can't help myself when it comes to that bloody team. I love it like you love a woman who's a bitch. You know, she treats you like a dog but you can't help loving her. Never change."

With that, Taffy pootled on, lapsing into the Welsh that some families spoke within their four walls in Ullswater. The sole word I could distinguish was Lerpwl, Liverpool.

Mumbling in his mother tongue, Taffy hauled himself up the steps into his house, one more tipsy victim of a passion that can inflict so much pain.

During this period of near-misses at Anfield, I and other lads in Ullswater were entering our teens, a phase that coincided with a growing appetite for football, not just for our club, be it Liverpool or Everton, but also for knockabouts in nearby Stanley Park, those acres of greenery dividing the Red from the Blue, Anfield from Goodison.

Our matches were held against other makeshift teams from rival streets in the Lake District, and since family finances couldn't meet the cost of proper football kit, we wore old white school shirts and black gym shorts that billowed down to your calves. Boots were leather gargoyles, misshapen lumps held together with sharp nails and usually passed down from an elder brother or even your father.

Some boys didn't possess such monstrosities – they wore rubber plimsolls used for PE at school and offering as much protection as ballet shoes when you wellied the case-ball. A rubber bladder inside a leather cover, this antiquated football was blown up like a balloon and sealed inside the case with a lace through eyelets. Hard and heavy when dry, it became a lead pumpkin in the wet, which explained why my big toe turned black overnight after taking a penalty and a gentle tug dislodged the nail. Worse still, head the casey and you'd teeter around with concussion. This was no joke for professional players, such as Jeff Astle. In 2002, a coroner decided the former England striker died at the age of 59 because of "an industrial disease" – brain injury caused by persistent heading of a leather case-ball. Lads in Liverpool were more than conscious of the harm inflicted on your skull, referring to anyone who was a nutter as a head-the-ball.

Still, the likelihood of cranial compression was far from our minds when we played footie one sultry September afternoon in Stanley Park in 1958.

The previous month I'd ventured away on my first trip without Mum. Normally during summer she would take us for a week to Squire's Gate holiday camp in Blackpool but instead I'd cycled with three schoolpals, Angus Bell, Jim Donohue and Eric Cole, around North and Mid Wales, staying in youth hostels. On my return, I fizzed with fitness and was burning off some excess energy in a game with other Ullswater lads against our rivals from the next street, Coniston.

Our side featured a guest player, Trevor, who'd moved away from the Lake District to live in a swish council house (with bathroom!) on a Kirkby overspill estate but still journeyed back to Ullswater to see his mates.

A fine footballer nicknamed Puskas, he had turned out for Liverpool Boys and was up for it when he heard we'd arranged a match with Coniston. Advantage, Ullswater.

Our temporary signing played a blinder up front, scoring four goals in a 7-5 victory, although he should have had a fifth when one shot bounced over the folded windcheater marking a goalpost. We said it was in, Coniston dissented, and after a barney we agreed to disagree. John Brodie, the Liverpool City Engineer who produced plans for the original Mersey tunnel, must have foreseen this type of dispute. In 1890, he hit upon an innovative way to end quarrels about whether the ball had passed between the posts – he attached the first nets to goals.

At full-time, Coniston's side drifted off home but our gang, having sated our thirst at the iron water fountain next to the Arkles Lane gates, lay sweating on the warm grass.

As we contemplated candy-floss clouds inching across the blue sky, bright spark Mick had a brainwave: "Wouldn't it be great to have our own kit? We've got no jerseys, no shorts, nothing. Some of us don't have boots. So ... why don't we ask Liverpool if they'll give us any old gear they've got? We're a local team, down the road from Anfield. When their kit's worn out, they probably just stick it in the bin. It'd do us."

Everyone guffawed. Crazy idea! No chance, we all agreed. Mick's gibbering because of sunstroke. Everybody dozed off again. But the sheer audacity of the proposition did have an appeal and like the occasional harebrained notion, the longer you mulled it over the less stupid it appeared. After further contemplation, unanimity was reached: an idea so outlandish it was at least worth a try. Nothing ventured, nothing gained.

So there and then, Rob, our captain, and me were delegated to pass on our proposition to Anfield's hierarchy.

The stadium was only a couple of hundred yards away, up the hill that gave our ground its name, a contraction of Hangfield or Hanging-field, the field at the top of a slope, and seconds after going in the main entrance from Anfield Road, Rob was explaining shyly to a receptionist what we proposed.

She didn't tell us to take a running jump. She listened, made a brief phone call and asked us to wait.

While we stood there, overawed by our surroundings, this regal home of League champions, and astonished at what we had been so bold as to try, a voice boomed out: "All right, lads! What can I do for you?" We turned and there, walking towards us, in shirtsleeves and red tie, was, wait for it, Phil Taylor. The Reds' boss! Meeting us! Someone we'd only seen previously from afar, on the touchline or in photos in the *Echo*. We were flabbergasted.

He shook our little hands and then listened as Rob told him awkwardly where we were from and why we'd come.

"Right," he said, with a reassuring smile. "Come with me."

We followed him through a door and down a corridor, past dressing rooms aromatic with embrocation and one room full of boots on wall pegs.

Strewth! These two ragamuffins from Ullswater were within Anfield's inner sanctum, being shown around by Mr Taylor. This was where the first team got ready for matches. Billy Liddell walked along these corridors.

We arrived at a door, which our esteemed guide opened, releasing the distinctive smell of Omo soap powder. Inside lay a large rectangular room with dozens and dozens of Liverpool jerseys, shorts and socks on hangers and racks.

"Look," Mr Taylor said. "This is where we keep all the kit. But I'm afraid, lads, we can't give you any. After it's used by the first team, it's passed on to the reserves, the A team, the B team, the youth team. By the time it's been used by everyone, it's not worth having."

Now we'd mislaid our tongues. At last, Rob blurted: "Erm, thank you … we understand", but my vocal chords were back on the grass in Stanley Park. I nodded.

Liverpool's manager closed the door to the kit room and walked us back along the corridor, asking about which schools we went to and what positions we played in our team. Back at the main entrance, he wished us well for the future and suggested that if we wanted to come for a trial, our parents should write to the club.

We walked into Walton Breck Road in a daze. We had met Phil Taylor and he was a super fella. Knackered or not, we sprinted the rest of the way to Ullswater to tell our mates what had happened. They were bowled over. They'd expected us to get the bum's rush the second we set foot in the ground. Instead we'd been invited inside the offices, walked the corridors, seen the dressing rooms and the kit room! We mightn't have come back with any football gear but everyone was emerald green with envy at what our bold initiative had accomplished.

For weeks, it was the talk of the Lake District. Embarrassingly, one Saturday night while I was queuing in our chippy, its owner, Mr Fox, pointed me out to the packed shop as the lad taken on a tour of Anfield by Phil Taylor. Everyone gawped and I blushed.

Upon my turn to be served with fishcake and chips, Mr Fox, Breck Road's respected cod father and a founding member of the Merseyside chapter of the Fish-Fryers' Hall of Fame, chose to mark my elevated status by giving me a bumper bag of scratchings, crunchy bits of cooked batter, topped off with a scollop, a fried slice of potato. For nowt! As I departed with my goodies bundled in a copy of the *Daily Post*, I felt like a Hollywood star.

A few months after our Anfield inspection, considerate, obliging Phil Taylor faced up to his blackest despair. In January 1959 in the FA Cup, the Reds lost 2-1 to the part-timers of Southern League Worcester City at their St George's Lane ground, the most dispiriting result in club history.

The players were gutted, a mood that rapidly darkened on the journey home when the coach carrying wives and families of the Liverpool squad broke down on Worcester's outskirts. The only option was to put everyone on the team bus, meaning more than 60 squeezed into a space for 40 on the long, uncomfortable return trip.

It was hardly any better for Scouse fans. As their charabancs trundled away through the frosty countryside, dejected Kopites were unanimous in their verdict: This wasn't good enough.

Once Liverpool resumed their League campaign, the fans' despondency deepened. Leading members of the first team failed to live up to reputations; injuries undermined team selection; promising replacements fell short; performances did not improve when crocked players returned; Lady Luck deserted the Reds as the bar or post intervened to block certain goals; refereeing decisions went against us.

Handicapped by these misfortunes, Liverpool slipped behind in the promotion battle, finishing fourth, and supporters quipped that the players didn't want to go up. But for the thousands who flocked to Anfield, backing the team through thin and thin, the indignity of being mired in the Second Division was acute, especially as Everton were entrenched in the top flight.

If only those staunch supporters could have foreseen their years of misery had a purpose.

When Bill Shankly, the man from Glenbuck, arrived and brought success, it was ohso-sweeter for the bitter failure that had gone before.

Phil Taylor's term of office was concluded just before Christmas 1959. The writing had been on the wall of Anfield's boardroom since the previous January when that Worcester City debacle had stunned everyone but directors agreed to give the manager more time. After the 1959-60 season kicked off, however, time made no difference, since the team were still treading water in the Second Division, offering little cheer to supporters. For months secret huddles had been taking place about a new boss and one candidate topped the list of possibilities: Bill Shankly of Huddersfield Town. Now the board got their wish.

The news came one afternoon when I was in my bedroom, grappling with my three-foot-long snake.

Let me explain.

After my tortoise Geronimo failed to come out of his shell and was laid to rest in our postage-stamp front garden beneath the irises, a school pal gave me an unconventional pet: a grass snake, which his father, a gardener on a country estate out at Croxteth, had caught.

I christened this creature Sybil, since it was a female, sexed, or so I was informed, by virtue of its short tail. No one else in Ullswater owned such an unusual reptile. Her grey-green body, golden eyes, yellow collar and black slashes along the flanks created a mobile kaleidoscope that shimmered and glimmered and glided over your arms when she was handled. Zig-zagging across the floor, she was all grace and suppleness and finesse, such a contrast with slow-motion, take-your-time, get-there-tomorrow Geronimo.

Sybil was my pride and joy and, the minute I arrived home from school, I'd race up to my room to see her in her wooden hutch, slumbering among bedding of damp straw, grass and leaves. One afternoon, though, I pulled the lid off to find the box – empty! Sybil had escaped!

The only possible explanation was she'd squeezed through a gap in the wood, barely big enough to poke two fingers in.

I searched everywhere for my little beauty, stripping the bed, pulling up the carpet and lino around skirting boards, removing books and toys from the cupboard. The space beneath my bedroom door wasn't big enough to allow her through – she'd have to be as flat as a pancake to wriggle under. It was a mystery where she had gone.

Settling down in the kitchen to do my homework, I couldn't concentrate. Without her feeds of minced meat, Sybil was bound to die. That night, I went to bed and, as I was dropping off, heard something slithering within the spring mattress.

Sybil! The little tinker must have sneaked inside through a tear in the fabric. How could I get her out? The only solution would have been to rip the mattress open. Mum, who wasn't keen on having a pet reptile in the house, wouldn't have been best pleased.

At least I knew where Sybil was hiding and hunger must drive her out. So it came to pass.

Two days later, I got home from school and hurtled upstairs, straight into my room.

Snake's alive! There she was, curled up on the eiderdown, oblivious to the world. My entrance shattered her snooze, and, with whiplash speed, she uncoiled and set off towards the headboard.

For a second, her sinuous motion hypnotised me.

Go! I woke up. No way was she going to scarper!

I dived headlong on the bed, grabbing her with both hands behind the head. Frantic for freedom, she flailed about but I held her firmly. Sybil was mine again. She coiled around my arm and ceased writhing. Now I could stroke her, scanning for any injury. She was fine and soon relaxed, the tip of her tail tickling my skin, flagging contentment.

Knock, knock! Someone at the front door interrupted my bout of serpent bonding. With Sybil secure in my hands, I went downstairs, to find a mate from up the street, Jimmy Shakespeare.

Jimmy's parents had recently made one of the most onerous judgements of their lives.

With a surname like that, they'd been dying for years to know if William the playwright might be a distant relative. After all, it was recorded that he spent the early years of his stage career in Prescot.

To put an end to this conundrum, they'd built up a nest-egg for "a gynaecologist" to investigate – but then their telly began playing up. Was it to be the Bard or a new blackand-white Pye set? Gynaecological, and even genealogical, examinations were shelved and TV won.

Now here was Jimmy Shakespeare at my door, just after I'd done my repo job on Sybil. He reached out to touch her bony head, twin black stripes running down from her eyes, like the tracks of tears. Then he remembered why he'd come.

"Have you heard? Taylor's gone. We've got a new manager. Bill Shankly, from Huddersfield. It's in the *Echo.*"

So on the day I recaptured Sybil, Liverpool bagged Shankly, introducing him to the press at Anfield (or in newspaper parlance, he was unveiled. What a vision – Shanks sitting motionless with a gossamer veil over his head, waiting for it to be whisked off by the chairman, like Paul Daniels uncovering a pigeon on the Wooky Hollow Club's stage.)

No, the Red Laird was introduced or presented to the media and he was to last a lot longer in L4 than Sybil at 48 Ullswater Street. Soon after apprehending her, I accepted that what my mother maintained was correct: keeping such a wild creature in a wooden cage was inhumane. I cycled out to Croxteth Park, with Sybil snug in my Campagnolo buttie bag, and liberated her in the thickest woodland I could locate. She was back from whence she came, where nature intended.

As she adjusted to her native environment, Bill Shankly was settling in to his job at Anfield. Now the board had found a man befitting the challenge. Shankly, a young tiger with young ideas, was obsessed with football and understood how diehard Reds' fans felt.

They were his kind of people. Working-class, honest, true, best friends and worst enemies. Most importantly of all, their ardour for the game was his ardour, since football dominated his being. As he professed when leaving Huddersfield: "I'm going to a place where they live, eat, sleep and drink football, and that's my place." If any man knew where he was coming from, where he was going and how he would get there, it was William Shankly.

Hewn and honed in the mining village of Glenbuck in Ayrshire, he was one of 10 children and became a footballer, like his four brothers. After joining Carlisle United in 1932, he made his mark as a tough-tackling wing-half and was transferred to Preston North End where he spent the rest of his playing days, totting up 313 games and 13 goals.

The high spot of his time at Deepdale was winning the FA Cup in 1938, although the lad who began with the Glenbuck Cherrypickers' team also took great pride in five international caps for Scotland. If the war had not intervened, he would have received many more.

In 1947, he hung up his boots for the last time in the Lilywhites' dressing room and switched to management, his football knowledge, motivational flair and coaching techniques bringing positions at Carlisle, Grimsby, Workington, Huddersfield and now Liverpool.

At Anfield, Shankly knew he'd taken on a real challenge, yet from the minute he joined he was hellbent on pursuing excellence. Nobody, but nobody, was going to block his plans.

Before the new boss arrived, every manager explained his team selection to the eight directors, who could overrule him. Now Shanks had accepted the job on condition the board handed over control of team and transfers and he even berated them for their lack of ambition. "My idea was to build Liverpool into a bastion of invincibility," he said. "Napoleon had that idea – he wanted to conquer the bloody world. My idea was to build Liverpool up and up until everyone had to submit and give in."

One of his first resolutions was to rejuvenate the training regime, specifying new standards of fitness and skill. In this period, the ball-starvation theory held sway: if you did not practise with a ball during the week, you'd be hungry to get it during the game. Bobby Robson tells how, in the Fifties, when players at Fulham and West Brom requested a ball for training, they were told: "What do you want it for? You'll get one on Saturday."

Technique was for Johnny Foreigner; the English forte was lap after lap of running. But, as Shanks pointed out, snooker stars didn't prepare for tournaments by loping round and round the table, so he shifted the emphasis onto ball skills and five-a-sides, with constant chipping, shooting, controlling, heading and movement. "This was where a great team would be built," he said.

At Melwood training ground, he erected shooting boards, two wooden walls set 15 yards apart. A player would stand in the middle, kick a ball against one board, collect the rebound, swivel, run a couple of yards and shoot against the facing board, over and over again. He also kept comprehensive logbooks of training and exercises carried out every day and, at the ground, put a notice, "This is Anfield", over steps leading to the pitch, "to remind the lads who they're playing for and the opposition to remember who they're playing against".

One key element that did not change was the coaching staff. Shanks underlined that if you aspired to a great team on the pitch, you required another one off it. He assessed the qualities and capabilities of Bob Paisley, Joe Fagan and Reuben Bennett before giving his judgement: they were staying, on one condition – "utter loyalty, to each other and to Liverpool FC". The new manager wanted the Boot Room Boys to share his destiny, telling them: "We'll make Liverpool great again."

All along, he emphasised this was a long-term project and did not feel disheartened when in his inaugural game the Reds lost 4-0 to Cardiff City at Anfield. "In a way, it's a good thing," he told the press. "You learn more from defeats than victories."

The learning process would take time and Shanks's team in transition ended their season in third place, missing out on promotion again. To Kopites' dismay, the next campaign, 1960-61, turned into a carbon copy of the previous one as the lads finished third again, despite going unbeaten in 14 matches.

Phil Taylor's "almost there" days were being duplicated and in some quarters there were whispers Shanks mightn't be the man for the job. Now, though, the boss who had refused to sign a contract because he wanted judging by results was going to banish the sceptics.

3
18 Steps To Heaven

Those who lose dreaming are lost.
– Aboriginal proverb

IN THE whole of Alsop school, "Stagger" Lee was easily the oldest boy. Because of an illness that kept him off for months in the upper sixth, he was doing an extra year before retaking A-levels and consequently had attained the advanced age of 18. I say he was a boy but he had become an adult, evident in the way teachers addressed him as an equal. So while younger lads who'd developed beyond the bum fluff stage nicked their cheek with a razor to proclaim they'd begun shaving, Stagger allowed spiky stubble to grow on his chin.

As a consequence of his maturity, he had travelled farther than anyone along those three seductive, post-pubescent paths leading to alcohol, music and girls. One July dinnertime, days before the break-up of 1961's summer term, we were chewing our mutton, boiled potatoes and cabbage in the school canteen when he told me about a club downtown in Mathew Street, with brill rock bands and oodles of talent.

I'd already heard mention of this joint, the Cavern, and it cropped up again when I nattered to other lads. Obviously it was a happening place, worthy of inspection.

My first fumbles with social interaction had come in Ellergreen Avenue's youth club but, now a 16-year-old, I was becoming more adventurous; the Cavern might satisfy my tender yearnings for pop music and female company.

In money terms, I was better off, too, ever since I'd wandered around St John's Market, asking if anyone was looking for a Saturday boy. Jan Zygadlo, a human ox, Polish war hero and owner of a stall selling Continental foods, had taken me on, enabling me to splash the cash after surviving on Mum's few bob of pocket money.

A couple of weeks after speaking to Stagger, I vacated the armchair from which I used to watch Val Parnell's Saturday Spectacular on TV and accompanied a schoolmate, Ian Brown, to the Cavern. Our intention was to have a few scoops in the Grapes in Mathew Street and, empowered by booze, move on to the club.

The Grapes was a dinky establishment, a Higson's house with a couple of small rooms. At 7.15 that evening it was so wall-to-wall with tipplers that soon after we arrived, a cockle-seller in off-white coat shouldered the door ajar, squinted at the throng and withdrew disconsolately with his wicker hamper of seafood to seek trade elsewhere.

Whereas I was 16, Ian was already 17, still not the legal age of 18 to buy alcohol. Despite this, he succeeded in purchasing two pints of mild without being challenged by the barman and we insinuated ourselves into a corner, to sip our bevvies while drinking in the atmosphere.

From snippets of dialogue I got the impression people gathered here before going to the Cavern.

Sure thing. At 8 o'clock, to a silent command, the pub began emptying.

Ian and I gulped down the remainder of our jars and strode out into the street.

Before we'd taken a few paces towards the small illuminated sign above the Cavern's door, a dull thump, thump pulsed into us, meeting us head-on. A few more paces and this bass beat was forcing its way between the cobbles.

Beneath our feet, a monster was panting and roaring and at the club's entrance we felt its hot breath. We could also distinguish drums, guitars, singing, rock music coming out of the hallway, along which lads in duffel coats and girls in gaberdine macs were queuing.

A dinner-jacketed figure who people addressed deferentially as Paddy was controlling the flow of clubbers, ushering them down stone stairs into a viscous underworld.

With each of our steps into this abyss, the music grew louder.

And the heat! I was easing myself into a tureen of warm soup.

At the bottom of the stairs I handed over my 1 shilling (5p) for membership and 3 shillings 6 pence (17.5p) for admission to a woman cashier behind a table and queued to leave my hound's-tooth overcoat in the cloakroom alongside.

While they dealt with clubbers, two girls were chattering away behind the counter. Suddenly they grabbed each other and did a high-speed, five-second jive to the music.

Laughing, they shuddered to a stop as quickly as they'd begun and resumed taking coats.

I slipped the cloakroom ticket in my pocket and pushed through the doorway to join Ian. Blinking, we found ourselves in a basement. We were inside the restless beast's stomach.

The only light came from a stage at one end and a snack bar at the other but soon my eyes adjusted to the murkiness. The room was bursting at the seams, boys and bints shoulder to shoulder along the sides while others sat in rows of chairs down the centre, watching a group of musicians generate this deafening noise.

Dressed in my only casual gear – grey Harris tweed jacket, black slacks, white shirt, blue Slim Jim tie – I wasn't prepared for the heat and humidity, with rivulets of condensation dribbling down the painted brick walls to form glistening pools on the concrete floor. But these tropical conditions were stoking up the excitement I'd first felt in The Grapes. This sweatbox was far removed from anything I'd come across before – not cold, conservative England but somewhere thousands of miles away, hot and humid, fervent and fiery, on the shores of the Mediterranean, in Latin America, in Africa.

What hit you most, though, in the chest, in the head, in every vital organ, was the beat. Wow!

On stage were four lads, three with guitars, one on drums, all in powder-blue suits, tight jackets and drainpipe trousers. They were singing Chuck Berry's Rock 'N' Roll Music and I'd never heard anything like it. The noise! How could four people create such a sound?

Look around. We were inside an amplifier. The Cavern's walls were trapping the music which pounded the bricks to escape.

Boy was I hooked, and when, with every chorus of "If you want to dance with me", the band stamped their Cuban heels in unison on the wooden boards, my heart was pumping in synchronicity. Sole music, indeed.

What a revelation. What a place.

Whoof! The group finished their number with a slam of their feet.

As the audience clapped, I asked a girl who they were. "The Four Jays," she informed me.

Never heard of them, but no argument, they were the bee's knees.

After a couple of thank-yous, the boys launched into Sweet Little Sixteen, a song my sister Doreen listened to on her Dansette gramophone, but Chuck Berry emasculated on vinyl sounded nothing like this. Nothing. The Jays' music was proving so infectious that girls in the seats were hand-jiving, flapping their hands to the rhythm.

Sweet Little Sixteen turned out to be the group's last number and the audience gave them a big hand. The Jays unplugged their instruments, carrying them away to the poky bandroom on the left from where the unseen "dee jay", Bob Wooler, began playing records.

During this break, Ian and myself took a closer gander at the club, three barrel-vaulted tunnels, side by side like a pack of cigars, divided by sturdy pillars. Its central area had the stage at one end, just wide enough to shoehorn a band in, with a proscenium brick arch above and its back wall covered in a gloss-paint patchwork of geometric mis-shapes. Bands had scrawled their names on these, "Zodiacs" and "Hurricanes" being noticeable.

Facing the performers was the audience, seated in rows, while through the vaults on each side, minute spaces among the standing crowd permitted limited body movement, vaguely discernible as dancing.

The Cavern was cramped, no bigger than our school gym, but its intimacy meant the band jumped in your face. Now I could appreciate why Mum loved live music. For years she'd been listening to singers and musicians at venues like the National Union of Railwaymen's social centre in Edge Hill or the Montrose Club in Richmond Terrace, and yonks ago she'd even mentioned this cellar in Mathew Street where they featured traditional jazz. Originally a fruit and veg business that went pear-shaped, its potential as a night spot was recognised by Alan Sytner, entrepreneur and future BMW magnate, who converted it into a copy of Le Caveau in Paris.

On its opening night in January 1957, such was jazz's draw that hundreds were locked out, while down below the Merseysippi Jazz Band blew the audience away. The Cavern was born.

Now, while I leant against a pillar waiting for the next act, those self-same Merseysippis clambered onto the stage again to maintain their tradition of musical syncopation and improvisation.

Chalk after the Jays' cheese. I'd noted the band's name in the *Echo* (how could it fail to register?) but I'd never heard them. They launched into Bad Penny Blues, casting a blanket of calm over the place. People broke off from dancing, sat down or gravitated to the snack bar. The atmosphere had changed. The beast was resting.

At school, someone had said that beatniks, those denizens of dingy abodes, lurked within this basement and I espied a cluster on the far side, farthest from the exit. Bods with unkempt beards and long-haired birds in ankle-length dresses were sitting along the wall, smoking Old Toxteth herbal tobacco in white clay pipes while musing on the music.

As the Merseysippis got stuck into their first number, some of the beatniks stirred from their lethargy and slouched onto the floor. Now they flaunted their quixotic dancing technique, which for some profoundly philosophical rationale buried deep within the subtext of a Jack Kerouac treatise was performed without a hint of happiness on their countenances.

To execute this Cavern shuffle, they faced their partner, crouched forward cheek to cheek and clutched each other's right hand, stretching down towards the ground. These conjoined arms now instituted a lateral swinging movement, which gradually spread to shoulders, upper trunk and hips. Once both bodies were entwined in this oscillation, they sashayed back and forth, flicking alternate sandaled feet out to the sides, in sequence with their hands.

Throughout this coordinated shamble, they remained oblivious to their partner and the few other dancers who'd taken to the floor.

After watching the beatniks getting into the swing of things, my mate and I squeezed through to the snack bar, which didn't serve alcohol, just fizzy drinks. We bought two bottles of dandelion and burdock and stood to one side, eyeing the talent along the counter.

Some selection. Apart from sporadic trips with Alsop sixth form to plays performed by girls at our sister school, Holly Lodge, we'd never been surrounded by so many Judies. This was where they got to at weekends. Plainly Stagger Lee's sexual antennae had been finely tuned when they detected the Cavern.

Once the Merseysippis had finished their set, another rock group stepped on stage, five of them and a frontman who was a big 'un, in a startling, stand up and fight check jacket.

Bob Wooler introduced them: "Kingsize Taylor and the Dominoes!"

Immediately the band blasted off with another Chuck Berry number, Memphis Tennessee, and the vocals delivered by Kingsize's huge frame were suitably forceful. He filled the tiny stage, strumming his guitar with bunches of bananas masquerading as fingers.

Now Ian and I were ready to break through the shyness barrier and get jigging. Edging through the ramjammed crowd, we joined a pair of lasses in some rhythmical writhing, since jiving as practised with Doreen in the parlour was impossible. All you could do was stand in one position, bend your knees, lift toes and heels, wriggle hips. Because of the headbanging beat, chatting-up was impossible, although that wasn't the object of the exercise. I simply wanted to share the gratification of movement to music.

After a couple of numbers, we were soaked in sweat – why was I wearing a string vest? – but the music drove us on, especially as Kingsize's repertoire got better and better: Blue Suede Shoes, Sherry Baby, Slippin' and Slidin', Maybellene, Great Balls Of Fire. All great numbers.

Before we knew it, the evening had swept past and my watch was showing 11.30. Time to catch the bus.

We thanked our partners, offering the customary farewell that we hoped to see them again in the Cavern. Truthfully, we weren't too fussed.

Coats repossessed from the cloakroom girls, by this point in non-jiving mode, we dashed to Rigby's pub in Dale Street, from where the last Corporation carriage of the evening transported us home, dead-beat but tingling. Why does live music make you feel so alive?

Next day the Cavern's sounds swirled around my head. I couldn't wait to get back but restrained myself until the following Wednesday, when I returned with Ian specifically to hear one band.

Of all the favourites cropping up in teen tattle – Gerry and the Pacemakers, Rory Storm and the Hurricanes, Faron's Flamingos, Derry and the Seniors, Swinging Blue Genes – one group stood out, not just because their name was so unusual but also because their shows were so raved-about. This night they were first on the bill, so the pair of us got downtown sharpish.

At the bottom of the cellar steps, the air was crackling with electricity as we wormed into a gap to one side of a pillar.

The place was crammed. There must have been 800 down there. On a Wednesday!

On stage, four lads were readying themselves.

The Beatles.

To the left, George Harrison was standing alongside Paul McCartney, who adjusted the Reslo microphone's height by another inch. On the right, John Lennon was planted at a second mic, staring into the distance. You could see he had attitude. Little wonder Cynthia Lennon was to say: "He was always danger, he was always trouble."

At the rear, behind his drums, Pete Best applied a final twist to a butterfly screw on a cymbal and gave a "boom! boom!" with the foot pedal of his bass.

Paul glanced around, establishing everyone was set up, then gave a nod to Wooler in his bandroom hideaway.

Time to liberate the tigers from their cage.

"Hi, there, cave-dwellers," Wooler began. "Welcome to the best of cellars. We've got the hi-fi high and the lights down low, so here we go with the Beatles' show!"

Bang!

"Gonna tell Aunt Mary 'bout Uncle John ..."

Paul tore into Long Tall Sally with the ferocity of a fist to the face.

The audience, particularly the girls, went mental.

Clearly the Beatles had a big following and their screaming fans wanted them to know it.

As they thrashed their guitars, John and George gave full throat to the vocal backing while, head cocked to one side, Pete caned his drums, crashing out a sledgehammer beat.

The foursome looked the part, too. Whereas other groups wore suits, the Beatles' black leather jackets and trousers with black T-shirts gave them a menacing air.

Yes, they were different, and not only in their get-ups. Until now, the bands had had one or two singers but John, Paul and George all did solos.

Pete weighed in once with Matchbox, leaving the others to perform a mix of hard and soft numbers – Good Golly Miss Molly, All I Have To Do Is Dream, Shake Rattle and Roll, Red Sails In The Sunset, Tutti Frutti, If You've Got To Make a Fool of Somebody, Some Other Guy.

They even did Ain't She Sweet, which Mum played on her piano, and she'd have been intrigued by their rocking interpretation of this oldie.

They couldn't go wrong. If they'd sung Land Of Hope And Glory or She's A Lassie From Lancashire, they'd still have been sensational.

One rip-roaring moment came with John's recasting of Money, which Barrett Strong had made a hit in the States. I'd heard the original single, brought back from New York by a seafaring mate, but Lennon gave it real bite, snarling the lyrics.

As their show drew to a close, Ian and I had to concede the Beatles were special, very special, handling their instruments as effortlessly as combing their hair. Never a bum note, you'd have thought they'd been touring years to achieve that polished, powerhouse sound, yet they had a freshness, a raw vitality you didn't get from old-timers churning out the same material night after night.

No argument, the Beatles were a class apart. And what a catchy name, too. Buddy Holly's Crickets had been eclipsed and it would be a long wait for the next most memorable ones, the Epileptic Tits, to do their manic jitterbug all over a Merseyside stage.

To wind up, Paul put his guitar to one side, grabbed a mic and began belting out What'd I Say. As he bawled away, he jumped around the stage, so that the other mic stand wobbled back and forth, provoking a nodding donkeys' routine by backing singers John and George.

This stonking finale brought the house down. At the end, no encores – the Beatles unplugged their kit and minutes later were carrying it through the audience, stopping briefly to exchange words with some girls.

Then they were gone, off to their next booking that night – the Tower Ballroom in New Brighton, Knotty Ash village hall, Aintree Institute, wherever.

For me, an epiphany had occurred in Mathew Street. I had become a Beatles fan because they were the best. Other groups such as the Four Jays and the Dominos were good, very good, but the leather-backed creepy-crawlies took the biscuit.

From there on I was in their thrall – and the Cavern's. *The* place to be, its stone stairway became my 18 steps down to Heaven during the rest of that summer of '61. Even though I explored other venues for my teenage kicks – the Mardi Gras, Orrell Park Ballroom, Iron Door, Jacaranda, Rialto – the Cavern outdid them all for music and atmosphere. Nowhere bettered a smelly cellar bursting with adrenaline and bodily warmth.

Nonetheless, my weekly visits would have to end. Before completing my A-levels in June, I determined to ignore the advice of Mr Warren, Alsop's headmaster who had urged me to go to university.

My decision stemmed from a turn of events in Ullswater Street: we had a new ruler of the household, a stepfather hogging the sofa in our living room.

His arrival triggered friction over what I regarded as bullying and on his return from the pub one Saturday night, a quarrel deteriorated into a scrap, during which I managed to grab his head in an arm lock, cracking it against a glass panel in the kitchen door.

Only Mum's intervention averted what could have been a messy conclusion.

After that, fearing someone might get hurt, I reasoned my future lay away from the Lake District. University represented one bolt hole but Mum would likely have to offer financial assistance and she wasn't flush with cash. For an independent life, employment appeared more viable. Since the Civil Service had been advertising posts in London, I applied, the interview went well and they offered me a job at the Board of Trade's headquarters in Whitehall, conditional on three A-levels, in French, Spanish and history.

While awaiting my results, I busied myself doing casual clerical work for the Inland Revenue in India Buildings in the city centre, which offered one irresistible perk; during the week, the Cavern was open from noon to 2pm. So I became a patron of these midday gigs where, for a shilling – a solitary shilling! – youngsters from nearby insurance and government offices could eat their sandwiches while listening to bands.

Most were content to sit and nibble away but some did exploit the space for an activity that was impossible at night, jiving.

If you were on your tod and on the prowl for unattached lasses, you could always split up a couple of dancing girls by asking any other single bloke if he'd make a duo with you. Nobody ever refused. All very laid-back.

That summer, the Beatles were in permanent residency and one sunny August day, I descended into their lair. In the cloakroom, a girl with bobbed hair and somewhat prominent nose took my coat and handed over a ticket. My first glimpse of Priscilla White, aka Cilla Black.

Inside the Big Beat Basement, as it was nicknamed, about 100 teenagers, mainly girls, were sitting around, watching the lads perform on the stage, so I commandeered a chair and settled back to listen.

They were singing quieter numbers than in their evening shows, such as Over The Rainbow, Falling In Love Again and Besame Mucho, a pleasant diversion from the normal stomping play-list and testimony to their versatility, although they wound up with Reelin' And Rockin', which did wonders for the digestive system.

Session over, they had no need to race away to another booking and hung around the snack bar, passing the time of day with anyone and everyone. Having eaten my corned beef sarnies, I was listening to the next group when George Harrison, bottle of pop in hand, sat down beside me.

Once the music ended for a break, I said, "All right, George. How're you doing?" and we began chinwagging like mates, the way Scouse strangers do on a bus or in a bar.

He told me the Beatles were chuffed with their audiences and bookings were coming thick and fast.

"We've been in Hamburg, the Top Ten Club," he said. "Hard work, playing for hours, but we had a great time."

The music resumed, halting our brief conversation and leaving me to think George was an ordinary, down to earth guy, no big-head. He could have his pick of 100 Judies but still came over as one of the lads, like the other Beatles nattering to whoever in the club. What I did not appreciate then was how all their hard graft in the Top Ten, 92 nights of marathon shows, starting that April, had helped perfect their inimitable musical style. For £3 each a session, the Beatles put their heart and soul into their craft, doing hundreds of cover versions and exploring every facet of their instruments.

Back in Liverpool that summer, their technique and finesse had moved on to a higher plane.

Now they were ready to dazzle Merseyside and the world.

* * * * * * * * * *

In August, news arrived that I'd got three A-levels, my entry pass for the Board of Trade. The following month, after Mum's tearful goodbye in Ullswater, I caught a coach from Skelhorne Street for my eight-hour journey to London, a city at the other end of England where the Civil Service had arranged accommodation in a hostel.

It was situated in a road called Craven Hill in Bayswater, so after arriving at Victoria coach station I negotiated the tube system to Queensway and then trekked with my wizened leather suitcase through the streets.

The traffic, the congestion, the noise – Liverpool this wasn't.

As I turned into Leinster Terrace, a woman, 40 going on 60, neck transplanted from a turkey, face heavily plastered by Max Factor, strongly scented by Woolworths and gaudily dressed in a blue PVC coat from C & A, positioned her pair of ponderous boobs to block my progress.

"Fancy a bounce, dearie?" she inquired

A bounce? What's that? Perhaps trampolining is big down here.

Too weary for any form of energetic exercise, this 17-year-old mumbled his apologies, did a neat sidestep and hurried away to the security of the hostel. There the warden showed me to a room containing beds for myself and five other lads whose career paths had all led them to the metropolis. This was to be my dormitory home while I worked as a filing clerk in the Commercial Relations and Exports Department of the monolithic BoT building, on the opposite side of Whitehall from Downing Street.

Thanks largely to a boss, Joe Buckingham, who took me under his wing, I settled into my duties, which transported me every day to exotic countries such as Brazil and Japan via the classified diplomatic reports in my in-tray. My horizons were expanding.

As there had been an intake of school-leavers, I soon made friends with other teenagers, bending their ears with descriptions of Liverpool's vibrant music scene. They must have reckoned this boy from the North Country was unhinged, the way I droned on about it. Surely nothing ever happened in faraway Liverpool?

I was missing the Cavern, until I had an idea: Why not re-create its lunchtime bops in our office?

I plucked up courage; Mr Buckingham, could we bring a record player in to listen to music during our midday break?

Certainly.

My boss fixed us up with a lecture room where, after eating in the canteen, we would play our singles, EPs and LPs on a portable Dansette and gossip with colleagues from other departments.

As the opening bars of the Sixties wafted down Whitehall's corridors of power, our numbers swelled to about 20 youngsters, listening to Elvis, Cliff, Duane Eddy, the Ventures, whoever's discs were available for spinning on the turntable, although no one brought along a compilation of romantic ballads advertised in the *New Musical Express*: "Nights of Passion, in 7-inch and 12-inch versions". That advert didn't soothe my juvenile sense of inferiority

Away from Whitehall, hostel life was reasonably agreeable, and I got a real kick out of our football games in nearby Hyde Park at weekends. As the only fact you knew about some team-mates from other dorms was their place of origin, the action would be punctuated with cries of "Shoot, Sheffield", "Man on, Manchester" or "Get rid, Billinge Stump", which puzzled onlookers.

My free time in the capital lacked one important feature, though: live music. When it came to going out on the town, London wasn't bubbling like Liverpool. Back home, groups were practising and playing in pubs, clubs, church halls, school halls, dining halls, garages, gardens, garden sheds, coal sheds, front rooms, side rooms, bedrooms, back rooms, backyards. Everybody seemed to be learning songs, strumming a guitar, bashing a snare drum, blowing a mouth organ, and not an evening went by without dances in one district or another as teenagers constantly discovered new venues and bands. Down in London, music didn't matter so much. Something you paid occasionally to listen to, it wasn't on your mind, in your ears, on a daily basis and you certainly didn't go to the trouble of performing it, like so many lads in the Pool.

After three months in the hostel, I and four other inmates teamed up to rent a flat in Streatham, moving into our new address in Mount Ephraim Road just before Christmas 1961. Now, as well as a career down south, I had a room, rather than a dormitory bed.

Since leaving the sixth form, my circumstances had altered drastically, and the same could be said about the situation at Anfield. With the Reds missing out on promotion twice, in 1960 and 1961, Shanks made a hard-headed review of his bloated playing staff and resolved to have a clear-out. In all, a whopping 24 were shown the exit gate. He also concluded the team were crying out for a strong spine – goalkeeper, centre-half and centre-forward – and in the close season of 1961 grafted on two thirds of this backbone, recruiting Ron Yeats and Ian St John, who arrived from Motherwell for £37,500, a Liverpool record. Since the board had balked at an earlier bid for another striker, Brian Clough, it was widely believed Shanks threatened to resign if cash wasn't found for the Saint. The directors heeded his warning and the manager got his striker, just as he nabbed Yeats, a man-mountain of a stopper, for £30,000.

The strapping centre-half had been put on the transfer list by Dundee United who told him to go to the Station Hotel in Edinburgh where someone was waiting for him to put pen to paper. Yeats had no inkling who the potential buyer might be but, striding into the hotel's lobby, he spotted a group of Dundee officials with people he didn't recognise; Shanks and the Liverpool party.

As Yeats walked towards them, Bill came to meet him, growling: "Bloody hell, you're a big lad. You must be seven foot."

"No, I'm six foot two," replied Yeats.

"That's near enough seven foot for me, son," retorted Shanks.

After the manager introduced Yeats to his directors, the defender floored them all. Since his geography wasn't too hot, he inquired: "Where's Liverpool?" Shanks was miffed. "What do you mean, where's Liverpool? We're in the First Division, in England."

Yeats was confused. "I thought you were in the Second Division."

"Second Division?" Shanks barked. "We are at the moment, but when we sign you, we'll be in the First Division next year."

This declaration of faith in the future won Yeats over; he had no qualms about heading south. Back at Anfield alongside his new signing, Shanks told journalists: "With him in defence, we could play Arthur Askey in goal" and "Walk around him – he's a colossus."

Abso-bloomin'-lutely! Yeats was to have a colossal influence on the team's chase for honours.

My lust for Anfield – and the Merseybeat – had turned into a long-distance affair, involving a hitch-hike from Streatham about once a month for home games. An ideal Saturday double: Kop in the afternoon, Cavern at night. My life in London coincided with a storming start to the 61-62 season by the Reds, who won 10 and drew one of 11 matches. Shanks was taking us up, up and away.

Throughout most of the campaign, Liverpool led the table but, as bells rang out for the dawn of 1962, they had one unexpected rival for promotion, Leyton Orient, making the New Year fixture at their place into a six-pointer.

That Saturday, Euston station was awash with Scousers when I rendezvoused with Steve Jones at the left luggage office. How refreshing to hear so many happy voices. I'd really missed the accent that Fritz Spiegl, musician and expert on our dialect, defined as one-third Irish, one-third Welsh and one-third catarrh, caused by the perpetual draught from the Mersey Tunnel.

I accompanied Steve down the escalator into the tube, where hundreds of Red men were waiting to trek out east. My Boys' Pen mentor, who'd never been south of Talacre before, was wide-eyed at the way trains flowed in, each one shaving off a row of passengers along the platform edge – "like a wood-plane", as this apprentice joiner put it.

By the time we got into Brisbane Road stadium, the majority of Scousers were already occupying one of the goal terraces, although hundreds more were scattered along the other sides for a game that had all the intensity of a Cup tie. Orient were no pushovers, matching the Reds for commitment, and our lads relied on Alan A'Court to score twice in a 2-2 draw that Steve and I considered a fair reflection of play.

After the match, we squirmed into another tubular tin of human sardines (surely underground tickets should carry a government health warning) and, regurgitated at Euston, said our goodbyes. While my mate headed off on the football special, I was going in the opposite direction, taking the Northern Line to Streatham.

I felt empty inside. I wanted to be travelling home to my mother's city and my mother city, enjoying the comradeship of the shirt, the analysis, jokes and songs that bind supporters.

Cheer up, I told myself. Be positive. The Reds are doing great and you *will* be there when they clinch promotion.

As mentioned, hitching was my mode of transport for trips north. Assisted by obliging lorry drivers and sales reps, some of whom detoured to drop me nearer my destination, I never had serious difficulties getting back to the Lake District, although the slog south on Sunday nights could be problematic because of the quiet roads.

My only disrupted trip was in February 1962; heavy snow stopped all traffic and I spent an hour curled up in a phone box in rural Staffordshire. Still, just after 1am, I was toasting myself in front of Mum's hearth.

My most pressing journey took place a couple of months later. The afternoon of Friday, April 20, I stood by the side of the A5 where it dissects London's North Circular Road, and raised my thumb to passing traffic. Mr Buckingham had allowed me to finish work at 3.30 so I could take the tube to the starting line of my 200-mile hitch for the game of the season.

Next day the Reds were playing Southampton in L4 and both points would guarantee promotion. As I'd vowed, I would be there.

The trip up the new M1 went well, despite a detour around Brownhills in the Midlands because of motorway construction work, and by 9pm I'd reached Haydock on the East Lancs Road, that artery pulsing between Liverpool and the rest of England.

The continental divide between North and South had been traversed; I was back in familiar territory, evident when opening any evening journal, be it in Liverpool, Preston, Bolton or Blackburn, and spotting the perennial one-paragraph North Country kitchen drama, "Chip Pan Fire" – just as you could tell you were in London by reading its local papers, the *Evening News* or *Evening Standard*, and seeing their splash, "Snowflake Falls On Capital". Or if two flakes fall, "Blizzard Conditions Cripple Capital".

Still, mates in the Merch swore they could only be in New York when their eyes alighted on headlines like "Buggery Rap Rumpus Probe". Trust the *Daily News* to get to the bottom of any sex and violence story.

Minutes before 10pm, I pushed through the front door in Ullswater to let Mum know I was home. "Want some supper?" she asked.

"No, thanks. Back soon," I replied, dumping my holdall and haring off to the street's most hospitable haunt.

Every Lake District road possessed an institution that under one roof combined a social centre, music hall, Comedy Store, snack bar, debating chamber, dating agency, conference centre, citizen's advice bureau, property exchange, rehearsal room, rehab unit, doctor's surgery, DIY clinic, lodging house – it was the pub; in our case, the Standard, an Ind Coope hostelry.

I knew it would be under siege and, inside the public bar, regulars were well conditioned, the atmosphere similar to the eve of a Bank holiday weekend. Everyone was going to the Saints game, everyone was bouncy.

After a couple of milds had oiled my tongue, Danny, the Standard's manager, invoked his quirky method to announce the cessation of licensing hours at 10.30pm and make strangers scarce: he called on everyone to drop their pants for a rectal inspection.

As he collected glasses, he yelled "Arseholes, please." At least that's what his smoke-cured larynx came out with but in reality he was shouting "Last orders, please."

Invariably this induced one response: outsiders bolted for the exits.

My pot drained, I strolled home to Mum's teasing welcome of "You dirty stop-out" and a plate of her scrumptious corned beef and piccalilli butties. Hunger has always been the best sauce.

Next morning, after some staccato slumber, I lay in bed ruminating on the Reds as a gale rattled the ill-fitting sash window. Would the footie fairy answer my prayers?

Steve had arranged to meet in the Standard at midday for a few liveners and, with those down our gullets, we headed along Thirlmere Road through rain that wasn't so much stair rods as railway sleepers.

At the ground, thousands were queuing in Kemlyn Road but by 2 o'clock, thoroughly soaked, I had heaved myself into the turnstile's jaw, paid my money and hurdled up the steps into the back of the Kop. Now for the right result.

Kevin Lewis didn't let us down, wrapping up promotion with a brace in a 2-0 win.

After the whistle, overjoyed fans poured onto the boggy turf, compelling the team to run for the dressing room. Shanks ordered them out again, into a mob of celebrants, with one Kopite in a white cork motorcycle helmet prominent among the dark, sodden horde as he bear-hugged Yeats.

Miracle of miracles, after eight years and seven months in the Second Division, the Reds had recovered their first-class status. Since being relegated, they had finished 11th, 3rd, 3rd, 4th, 4th, 3rd and 3rd. By the close of 61-62's campaign, having led throughout, they were champions, eight points ahead of Orient and unbeaten at home, where the average gate was 39,000.

Along with Roger Hunt, who amassed 41 goals, including five hat-tricks, one player merited more credit than most for the team's accomplishment – Yeats. Week in, week out, the colossus confirmed what an admirable recruit he was and in return Shanks had kept his vow when they met, gaining promotion in the defender's first season.

At the end of his trophy-laden career, Yeats was to say that getting out of the Second Division remained his supreme feat.

The evening of our triumph, Steve and I joined a euphoric knees-up in the Standard, where even that most vital member of bar staff, the landlord's highly-strung Alsatian, seemed good-tempered. Since Kopites were buying, Evertonians toasted Liverpool's resurgence, too, with an added incentive to party; derby games were back on the calendar again.

So when my woozy head hit the feather pillow, the lads were back in the First Division and I nodded off to one of life's comforting truths: dreams do come true.

4
Heartbeat Of A City

Whatever you do, or dream you can, begin it. Boldness has genius and power and magic in it.

– Johann Wolfgang von Goethe

D URING the Sixties, it is no exaggeration to say you were blessed to be a Scouser. Since the Merseybeat had turned Liverpool into the capital of popular music, teenagers from Toronto to Tokyo and Stockholm to Sydney yearned to be in my home town.

Why did a city of half-a-million, tucked away on England's north-west coast, have such an impact on global culture? First, we need to acknowledge that its musical biography did not begin with the Beatles. In the Fifties, it had already produced Michael Holliday, Lita Roza, Frankie Vaughan and Britain's original rock 'n' roll idol, Billy Fury, while local singers Jackie and Bridie, the Spinners, Glyn Hughes and Tony Murphy had spread the folk gospel for decades, introducing young Scouse ears to standards such as Maggie May and The Leaving Of Liverpool.

Historically, however, the city's cultural lineage can be traced back centuries, to include unheralded contributors such as John Newton, a captain of Mersey slave ships, who renounced his trade to become a church minister and composed that much loved hymn, Amazing Grace, in 1779.

Looking back over the years, you soon identify one fundamental factor in the region's musical flowering: its role as a crucible for elements from all the home countries, be they English ballads and Welsh choral singing or Scottish folk songs and Irish jigs and reels. Yet, despite soaking up these home-grown influences, Merseyside's face has always been turned to the sea, rather than the Lancashire hinterland. So, into this melting pot you can also toss rhythms and people that travelled along maritime routes from North and South America, Africa, the Caribbean and Asia, connections going back centuries and encompassing Europe's oldest Chinatown whose residents put down roots because of the silk trade.

Stir all those ingredients together and you have a multi-ethnic blend with one final catalyst: Scousers enjoy performing in public. As Shakespeare phrased it in As You Like It: "All the world's a stage – and yon Scousers are always seeking to steal the limelight."

Well, at least he did in the play's first draft in the long-lost Upper Parliament Street folio.

Mum typified this desire to perform and whenever she held parties during the Fifties and Sixties, her nimble fingering of our piano topped the bill, to the accompaniment of friends on guitars or accordions.

Not everyone could afford an accordion or violin from Hessy's, Frank Hesselbaum's old-established emporium in Whitechapel. For the cash-strapped, music was created with a mouth organ, tin whistle, tambourine, jew's-harp, kazoo, triangle, a pair of bones from the butcher played like castanets, a comb covered in paper which you blew to make a buzzing backtrack or, a rare skill, knocked against your teeth with finger tips to create rhythms.

Tap-dancing was also a popular pastime and out in the street one mate, Alan Rogers, would demonstrate the steps taught at classes in Richmond Baptist church hall. With taps screwed loosely onto his shoes to make that distinctive jangling noise, he enjoyed making sparks fly from the flagstones.

Our road also acted as an open-air theatre through which singers and minstrels processed with antwacky, loosely-strung guitars. Fallen on hard times, they were seeking to raise a few pennies, although sometimes an amateur vocalist would feel too shy or ashamed to perform, cap in hand, in the middle of the street. Instead he would stand in the back jigger and give forth with his interpretation of Frankie Laine's Rawhide, backed by wailing jigger rabbits, stray cats.

Among the nomadic entertainers was Jake, an escapologist, half man, half whisky, who would do his show on the debris, a piece of empty ground where the house had been razed by a Luftwaffe bomb.

An assistant, usually as bladdered as his boss, would bind this part-time Houdini in heavy chains and locks, then stow him inside a sack on the ground, which itself would be bound with a rope.

After much writhing, grunting and groaning, the sack would stand up – and fall to the floor, uncovering the sweaty star in all his unfettered grandeur.

Cue for applause and for his assistant, the bottler, to produce the hat for a whip-round that the Standard's till would soon swallow up.

Sunday mornings brought another type of performance as the Boys' Brigade band from St John's church marched down our street, drums thudding and trumpets blaring. In the assembly hall at Alsop, we also attended concerts by the Royal Liverpool Philharmonic Orchestra, who opened unsophisticated ears to the fresh, lush tones of orchestral works.

Sitting in front of me on the balcony for one of their visits were two sixth-formers who'd launched their own rock group. As the Phil's violin section attacked the opening bars of Beethoven's Fifth Symphony, the lads turned to each other and pursed their lips in mutual appreciation of its thematic textures, a couple of members of the Beat Generation harking to classical music's splendour.

Alsop's Christmas carol concert was another musical event most lads embraced, although on one occasion an angry outburst by the headmaster brought it to a dramatic halt. As the school launched into a carol, Mr Warren, standing on stage with the teachers, threw a quite uncharacteristic fit, stamping his foot and bellowing: "I will not have you singing 'While shepherds washed their socks by night'. Boys, you WILL sing the correct words!"

Our next attempt proved acceptable but the whole school was dumbfounded by the head's intervention. No matter how the carol is sung, you can detect this mutilation of the verse, or even naughtier adaptations, if you listen out for them.

It was as well my childhood was favoured with live entertainment because in the Fifties BBC radio's Light, Home and Third programmes gave minimal coverage to pop music. One show I did listen to on Saturday mornings during my early teens was Children's Favourites, presented by Uncle Mac, who selected youngsters' requests, often folksy songs such as Burl Ives's The Man Who Swallowed A Fly, Pete Seeger's Little Boxes or Lita Roza's How Much Is That Doggie In The Window.

Then, in 1957, an earthquake convulsed England. Bill Haley and the Comets came over from the States to perform Rock Around The Clock and popular music changed irrevocably. Mind you, may the Almighty preserve any Children's Favourites listener who had the audacity to ask for Haley's hit.

When Uncle Mac deigned to read out a request for a rock number, his tone would harden; you could detect that he did not deem it proper for kiddies to be corrupted by amplified guitars and heavy drumbeats. Verily, the devil's own music.

If you wanted the hottest releases, you tuned into Radio Luxembourg, "Your station of the stars", transmitting from the Continent on 208 metres medium wave. Most sixth-formers at Alsop listened to Luxie between 11 and midnight on Sundays when it broadcast the Top 20, sponsored by Horace Batchelor who could sell you a fool-proof system for landing the football pools. In point of fact, the station offered snippets of the hit parade, because the primitive relay equipment and adverse atmospheric conditions caused transmissions to fade in and out.

Although Mum was a skilled pianist, the gratification she drew from entertaining was not passed on to me. I never had any inclination to take up an instrument or to perform in public, although I did pass one musical milestone at Christmas 1956 when I walked hesitantly into Toyland, a toy shop in Townsend Lane that stocked a small selection of vinyl, and bought my first 45rpm, Tommy Steele's Singing The Blues, a British cover of Guy Mitchell's American hit.

One Fifties sound that teenagers adopted was skiffle, a fusion of American blues and Country and Western whose leading exponent, Lonnie Donnegan, achieved stardom with Rock Island Line and Bring A Little Water Sylvie. Inspired by him, hundreds of bands sprang up around Liverpool. Down at the Standard, a group used to practise in the parlour at weekends and during our kickabouts in the road you'd hear them rattling away. Another early enthusiast was John Lennon, founder in 1956 of the Quarry Men, named after Quarry Bank High School, with a line-up that would incorporate Paul McCartney, George Harrison and Stuart Sutcliffe.

Skiffle was do-it-yourself music, not requiring a teacher for demanding instruments such as the piano and trumpet. A bass comprising a broom handle stuck on top of a tea chest, with a piece of string tensioned between the two and strummed for a "dum, dum, dum" tempo; a washboard scratched with metal thimbles on your fingertips; a couple of hand-me-down guitars; an ancient snare-drum, and, hey presto! your group was born. Now you could express yourself through words and music, conveying thoughts and sentiments like people have been doing since the advent of time. As Louis Armstrong put it: "All music is folk music. I ain't never heard no horse singing a song."

Skiffle thrived for a couple of years, until rock blew it away. Bill Haley set the ball rolling but the craze gathered momentum through being featured on television, radio's new rival. One evening in 1958, our minuscule black-and-white telly brought my lyrics of illumination, the Oh Boy! pop programme, when Cliff Richard curled his lips over Move It. The song was brill, the singer the height of cool in fitted jacket with narrow lapels and tight kecks … and the hair! His quiff was bigger than the kids' slide in Stanley Park.

After that, every teenage lad in the Lake District couldn't wait to get down to Burtons or Brass & Jackson to search pattern books and cloth samples for a suit like his.

Overnight, Move It proved a sensation and in Cliff and the Shadows, Britain had unearthed its first rock band, greeted at the Liverpool Empire in 1958 by a rapturous audience that included Lennon and McCartney.

Since their skiffle days, the Scouse mates had been pushing the musical envelope, tapping in to the rich heritage of a city whose seafaring routes had become conduits of American music. Most families had a member who went away to sea, perpetually returning from New York, Miami and New Orleans with discs to entertain pals and girlfriends. Accordingly, Liverpool teenagers were listening to and lending out the records of Elvis, Fats Domino, Little

Richard, Chuck Berry, Jerry Lee Lewis and Buddy Holly long before most of the British public had heard them.

A new city-centre venue was also about to leave its imprint on the scene. During the late Fifties, the Cavern jazz club had begun experimenting with skiffle spots and mine host Bob Wooler encouraged Ray McFall, who bought the club from Alan Sytner in 1959, to try local line-ups, considerably cheaper than jazz ensembles. As groups swopped skiffle for rhythm and blues and rock 'n' roll, McFall started booking beat bands in 1960, the very first being Rory Storm and the Hurricanes. From thereon, rock music took over and took off.

While Cavern audiences were warming to the latest sounds, the Quarry Men skiffle group had morphed into the Silver Beatles: guitarists Lennon, McCartney, Sutcliffe and Harrison and drummer Pete Best, who performed on both banks of the Mersey until they hit the jackpot in 1960, a booking from mid-August to the end of November in Hamburg. There they were contracted to mach schau, make a show, almost every night for 15 weeks at the Indra and Kaiserkeller clubs in the red-light area.

On return to Liverpool, the slimmed-down Beatles (in name and configuration, since Sutcliffe was pursuing an art career) resumed their appearances at popular night spots – Wallasey's Grosvenor Ballroom, the Casbah club in West Derby, Neston Institute, Aintree Institute – and debuted in the Cavern at lunchtime on February 9, 1961.

Across Merseyside, fans clamoured to see them, with so many bookings piling up that on occasions the lads did three engagements in a day, one at lunchtime and two in the evening. A prior commitment brought an intermission in April; they returned to Hamburg for a three-month stint at the Top Ten Club that entailed seven-hour sessions on weekdays and eight hours at weekends. Once they got home again in early July, I heard them live for the first time in the Cavern and went on to watch them up to four times a week, at noon and night.

Inexorably, audiences were elevating the boys to No 1 in the First Division of Mersey bands and just as Shanks had crafted promotion for Liverpool FC and was aiming for greater glory, so another manager, Brian Epstein, was formulating his masterplan for the Beatles.

Epstein's father owned NEMS, North End Music Stores, in Walton and in 1959 he opened a city-centre branch in Whitechapel. Stocked mainly with furniture, the new offshoot also accommodated a basement department for jazz, pop and classical records which would-be buyers could ask sales assistants to play on turntables behind the counter, linked to speakers in numbered booths.

This subterranean listening post quickly became hectic on Saturdays when lads would riffle through rows of discs that also acted as magnets for teenage girls with headscarves over their hair-curlers and love bites on their necks. One ritual for youths was to call at a tailor's such as Burton's, weighing up the catalogues of cloths and styles on a table outside, without any intention of buying, then continue to NEMS to pass judgement on the latest releases from Decca or Capitol. Down the flight of stairs lay free entertainment for penniless teenagers crushed into booths to hear their fave artists. If you did have a fistful of ackers, though, and returned home with a suit or an LP, a sizeable measure of credibility could be gained as you swaggered along the street with your booty.

While Brian Epstein was running the downtown NEMS and attending to customers, youngsters started asking for My Bonnie, a German release by Tony Sheridan and a Liverpool band, the Beatles. Epstein had never heard of this group but, curious about why they were so popular, he checked them out in a nearby club.

One lunchtime in November 1961, he descended into the Cavern, the dingy cellar coming as a culture shock to a young businessman who attended recitals in the genteel Philharmonic Hall. On a stage barely 12 foot wide, the Beatles were singing Kansas City and Epstein recognised them as youngsters who hung around his music department.

"This was quite a new world for me," he said. "I was amazed by this sort of dark, smokey, dank atmosphere, of this music playing away. The Beatles were just four lads on that dimly-lit stage, somewhat ill-clad and their presentation leaving a little to be desired. But, among all that, something tremendous came over and I was struck by their music, their beat and their humour. And afterwards I was struck by their personal charm."

In the ensuing days, Epstein grew increasingly certain the band had potential. On Advent Sunday, December 3, he invited them to his office in Whitechapel at 4.30pm to discuss being handled by him and three days later, the deal was done. Now their new manager faced his biggest hurdle: getting them signed up by a record company. He acted speedily, using what contacts he had, and on New Year's Day, 1962, "Merseyside's fabulous combination", as they were advertised in some Lancashire papers, auditioned for Decca at their studios in North London.

Even though Epstein and the lads had been quietly confident, Dick Rowe, one of the company's executives, informed them they would not be getting a contract because "groups with guitars are on their way out".

An exasperated Epstein told Decca bosses: "You must be out of your minds. These boys are going to explode. I am completely confident that one day they'll be bigger than Elvis Presley."

Go tell that to the birds, because the capital's showbiz moguls regarded Liverpool artists as acts from the back of beyond. As Marianne Faithful put it later: "I know we looked on them as very provincial, very straight, sort of a little bit behind London people, which is very patronising, not really true."

While Epstein was trying to arrange the Beatles' big break down south, Merseyside was rocking to hundreds of groups, an estimated 250 in 1962 alone, lumbering from date to date in ancient Commer vans with their primitive instruments. "I think there were more people in bands than there were audiences," said Brian Jones of the Undertakers.

Not quite. With growing numbers of teenagers switching on to live acts, more and more church halls, coffee bars and clubs started booking groups, so many that Gerry Marsden stated it was possible to go to a different place and listen to a different line-up every night for six months. The Liverpool sound was also benefiting from a ripple effect as its popularity spread and bookings arrived from Wales, Yorkshire, the North East and Scotland.

Now, like Kopites supporting the Reds, Merseyside teenagers followed their fave bands, tracking their movements through the *Echo* or *Merseybeat* newspaper, whose first edition in July 1961 carried an article by John Lennon with the title Being A Short Diversion on the Dubious Origins of Beatles.

To Epstein's annoyance, the record industry's movers and shakers were still expressing dubious opinions about his group's prospects during the winter of 1962, so he decided a makeover was in order. On their previous return from Hamburg, the lads had been wearing black leather gear. He jettisoned this, dressing them in made-to-measure Beno Dorn suits, and also toned down their Scouse accents, to help outsiders understand them more readily.

National exposure came soon afterwards in March 1962 when they were booked for their radio premiere on Teenager's Turn, a BBC music show from Manchester.

Overnight the Cavern's bush telegraph spread the word and no one could afford to miss their slot. The lads, our lads, on the wireless! Can't believe it.

The programme was scheduled for broadcast at 5pm on a Thursday afternoon, so that day I took a tiny Bush transistor radio into the office at the Board of Trade and at 4.55, just before clocking-off time, hurried out to Embankment Gardens alongside the Thames.

The weather was the answer to a taxi driver's prayer, intermittent heavy rain, and I lowered myself gingerly onto a sopping bench under dripping trees. There I twiddled with the tranny's knobs, tuning in to the Light programme.

As, heads bowed, commuters scurried past to their semis in Hatfield and Dartford, I held the radio to my lug-hole and listened.

The moment arrived.

"A new group from Liverpool. The Beatles."

The opening line of Memphis, Tennessee set me a-quiver.

"Long-distance information, give me Memphis, Tennessee, …"

I closed my eyes. The Embankment had vanished, the office workers had evaporated, the rain had dried up, and I was 200 miles north, in a hot, humid Cavern, smelling the sweet aroma of teen spirit.

The lads wound up Memphis Tennessee and, without pause, whipped into Please Mister Postman. Another pick of the pops … and they didn't even consult me.

After pleading with the postman to deliver a letter, the sooner the better, the lads finished their mini-session – to be replaced by the Northern Dance Orchestra. After the Lord Mayor's Show…

For a few precious minutes, my tranny had let me escape from London, this itsy-bitsy box of tricks had transported me home.

I switched it off. The spell was broken.

I was alone on a bench on the Embankment, rain trickling down my neck, apprehension inside me. The rest of the country had heard our band and the genie was out its bottle.

Through one radio performance, Liverpool had divulged a bit of its secret and the Beatles had lost some of their innocence.

What next? Might the curtain fall on their Cavern days?

Well did I wonder. Within months, the foursome auditioned at Abbey Road studios in London for George Martin, the artist and repertoire manager of EMI's Parlophone label, who signed them up. Pop music would never be the same again.

Before they recorded their first disc, Epstein called Pete Best into NEMS and dropped his bombshell: the drummer was out, replaced by Ringo Starr from Rory Storm and the Hurricanes. How cruel on Pete. You graft away for two years and, stardom beckoning, you're sacked.

Cavern regulars were dismayed, particularly as Pete had a legion of female admirers. Whenever the Beatles played, you soon twigged he was the teen heart-throb, the strong, silent type smouldering at the back – "mean, moody and magnificent", in Bob Wooler's terminology.

One reason tendered for his dismissal was the others wanted a musician with superior technique. Yet, to the question, "Is Ringo the best drummer in Liverpool?" John answered: "He isn't even the best drummer in the Beatles." That might explain why Ringo wasn't allowed to perform on the group's debut disc, corroborating for some Cavernites that Best was shown the door because of jealousy. For John, Paul and George, he was possibly too handsome, too attractive to members of both sexes.

So Pete was dealt one of the lousiest hands in showbiz's poker game. As Love Me Do was about to bring the Beatles' first chart entry, he was doing the Mersey rounds again as new drummer with Lee Curtis and the All-Stars.

5
The Scouse Sixties

Hope sees the invisible, feels the intangible and achieves the impossible.
– Anonymous

WHEN the first whistle shrilled for the 1962-63 season, Kopites believed the Reds would prosper in the First Division. To everyone's consternation, their form proved patchy. During the first few games, the most encouraging result was 2-2 with Everton at Goodison in front of 73,000 – with another 150,000 wishing they were inside – and although this stalemate pleased Merseyside's Red half, our lads were soon treading water in the table's lower reaches.

Shanks prescribed his remedy. Since resolving to give the team a steel spine, he had transplanted two thirds of its backbone, the centre-half and centre-forward, Yeats and St John. Now he completed his blueprint by grafting on the last vertebra, a keeper.

Under Phil Taylor, Tommy Lawrence had been a member of the A team but Shanks spotted the makings of something better and moved him up to the reserves. Despite a bulky physique that Kopites seized on with the name of Flying Pig, Lawrence's athleticism and command of the area soon got him upgraded to the first team in October 1962.

Another welcome addition was Willie Stevenson, a £27,000 buy from Glasgow Rangers who helped push the lads into the top half of the League until they were challenging for the title.

However, Lawrence was Shanks's master stroke and he took part in one of the finest games ever at Anfield.

The Easter of 1963, I had enough cash to get the train from London for the Good Friday shoot-out with Spurs, kings of English football and front-runners for the Championship. Since it was a Bank holiday, like most of the Kop I was wearing my best gear – charcoal-grey, three-piece Burton ensemble, white Rael Brook shirt and maroon Tootal tie. Our lads out on the pitch weren't smart enough, though, as the White Hart Lane maestros indulged in all their silky skills to take a 2-0 lead during the first half.

At the break, which lasted 10 minutes, an ancient Anfield ritual took place when two brawny, besuited blokes carried a weighty advertising hoarding around the running track. This solid wooden placard, hanging down from a hefty crossbar and borne on aching shoulders, was pasted with a poster detailing the following week's boxing and wrestling programmes at Liverpool Stadium, a capacious hall behind Exchange Station in the city centre.

As their billboard weighed a ton, the pair of bearers would rest it on the ground at the halfway line on the Kemlyn side. While they paused for their breather, the half-timescores man was putting cards with large numbers into slots in the perimeter wall alongside letters for each of that day's fixtures, as printed in your programme – A, B, C, D, etc.

In the Fifties and Sixties, there were no technological marvels such as announcements on the public address system or, wondrous contrivance, a dot-matrix screen. You relied on this system of cards with numbers to display the state of play in each game.

As the scores man was consulting his list, the front bearer of the Stadium's billboard nattered to him about the action on the pitch and gave a thumbs-down, indicating the Reds were on a loser.

Fair comment. But wait a while. During the second half, the match was turned on its head, endorsing the maxim that half-time is when the manager earns his corn. The Mersey upstarts scored not one, not two, not three, not four but FIVE goals in a coruscating comeback. Within 10 minutes of the restart, Stevenson and Melia put us level, then St John nudged us ahead and Lewis and Melia gift-wrapped a princely 5-2 victory.

St John had said, "There's no noise like the Anfield noise and I love it!" and the 54,000 in the ground went doolally, rejoicing with a chorus of "London Bridge is falling down, falling down, falling down, / London Bridge is falling down, poor old Tottenham. / Build it up in red and white, red and white, red and white, / Build it up in red and white, poor old Tottenham."

An early example of the Kop's flair for adapting songs to situations.

That afternoon our team had stubbornly refused to give up, abiding by Shanks's gospel that there is never a lost cause, and at full-time I tottered into Walton Breck Road, my mangled clothes fit for the rag-and-bone man. Back inside the Standard, everyone was as bedraggled as me and we all needed a good gargle.

Your health! Bottoms up! Barrels away! Chin, chin!

The Reds had put down a marker, although one Evertonian did deride our fightback: "Five breakaways! I ask you!"

This result made waves throughout football, since Super Spurs were a formidable team, the double-winners in 1961. Yet that 5-2 scoreline was to mark the pinnacle of a season in which the Reds finished eighth in the League and were defeated in the FA Cup by bogey team Leicester. Despite dominating the Hillsborough semi-final, we lost by the only goal to a team who had already seen us off twice in the League.

So 1962-63 served as a period of consolidation for Shanks and his team. Little did Kopites know that the lads' recovery against Spurs was an early pointer to their desire and determination. With these qualities, trophies would only be a matter of time.

* * * * * * * * * *

In the summer of '63, after two years working for the Civil Service, I conceded I'd made a mistake; I should have gone to university. Even though I'd entered a Civil Service competition, as they termed it, for promotion and been moved up to the executive grade, I felt I could do better for myself. Bolstering this conviction was a realisation that school pals now well into their university courses were living it up, more so than those who'd plumped for full-time employment.

Take Angus Bell, my best mate at Alsop. While reading medicine in Edinburgh, he was enjoying a frenetic social life and sleeping with a skeleton at his digs in the New Town. OK, it wasn't in his bed – it was under it.

Angus had bought this dumb flatmate because he was required to know all about the bones of the body and, as well as poring over the 1,458 pages of Gray's Anatomy, he was taking a close interest in the anatomies of his female classmates, entering realms of wonder that made me feel a tad disadvantaged in London.

The downside of going to university would be my forfeited salary, but I judged I could cope on a student grant and seasonal casual work, while having some fun, too.

The die was cast. In September I quit the Civil Service to do a Bachelor of Arts degree in French in London, where my Board of Trade boss, Joe Buckingham, offered accommodation in his Streatham home, not far from my former digs in Mount Ephraim Road.

Joe's wife, Jackie, was not only French – a bonus for my studies – but also a cook marinaded in God's kitchen. A lad raised on blind scouse and Sunday mince was about to be introduced to a gourmet lifestyle à la Buckingham. Consequently, as the 1963-64 football season got into its swing, I was settled in London, receiving my initiation into the exotic flavours of boeuf Bourguignon, melon, roast duck, Armagnac, saucisson, Champagne, fresh pineapple, garlic and pets de nonne, those melt-in-your-mouth miniature doughnuts that emit a dainty puff of air as they fry in hot oil, hence their French title of nun's farts.

In tandem with my culinary studies, I was evaluating the virtues of Romance philology and Rabelais and running my eyes over Erich Auerbach's Mimesis (not a pretty sight first thing in the morning). This research extended to a couple of girls at college, although my main romantic focus fell on a Liverpool lass I'd begun courting in the summer. She enticed me into coming home as often as practicable, enabling me to partake of Merseyside nightlife, Huyton love life and Anfield sporting life.

The Reds' League campaign did not open auspiciously. In the first three matches in L4, they went down 2-1 each time to Nottingham Forest, Blackpool and West Ham, prompting Shanks to tell directors: "I assure you, gentlemen, that we will win a home game this season." He duly delivered with a 6-0 clobbering of Wolves in the next Anfield fixture.

Our 3-1 victory at Stamford Bridge brought a foretaste of troubles that would plague football. Minutes before kick-off, a column of Chelsea fans rampaged over the back of the away terrace, driving me and the rest of the Scousers from behind the goal to a spot near the corner flag. Police intervened quickly but this was the first instance I'd encountered of an organised mass charge. Sporadic scuffles, yes, but systematic assault, no.

The season had brought two far-reaching developments at Anfield. In August, Shanks clinched the signing of elusive winger Peter Thompson from Preston for a record £40,000. Then, October saw an event that would resonate through generation after generation of Red supporters – You'll Never Walk Alone was first played at the ground.

Even though Brian Epstein had opposed its release as a single, Gerry and the Pacemakers had taken their interpretation of this evergreen to No 1 in the hit parade and when it was broadcast on the Tannoy system as the Reds came onto the pitch, Kopites joined in. The following home game, they gave full voice once more to it, repeating the process at match after match until YNWA turned into the crowd's curtain-raiser.

This uplifting lyric, written by Rodgers & Hammerstein in 1945 for the film musical, Carousel, became indelibly linked with the Kop, accompanying triumph and tragedy, reverberating wherever football is played, and evolving into an anthem for fans of most persuasions. So, in 1963-64 Liverpool gained their inimitable theme tune – and they also won Shanks's first Championship.

The early Sixties had brought radical changes to football: the maximum wage – £20 a week in the season, £17 in the summer – was abolished and players won freedom of contract, allowing them to change clubs. Now, too, psychology was playing an increasingly influential role in the game. To motivate his team, Shanks used exaggeration, offering ludicrous assessments of opposing players and teams. Melia said: "We'd be up against Manchester

United and he'd say, 'Bobby Charlton looks terribly tired, Denis Law is pale and George Best has been on the town all night – he looks awful'. We knew he was making it up but it relaxed you."

With the aid of such mental techniques, Shanks piloted the Reds through a purple patch in 1963-64, during which they hoarded 47 points out of a possible 60, including seven consecutive victories in March and April. After beating their main title rivals Manchester United at Old Trafford through a Yeats goal, the pair faced each other in April in L4 where the Mancunians went down again, losing to one strike from Ian Callaghan and a brace from Alf "Arrers" Arrowsmith.

During the game, Law cut a forlorn figure and the next day a match report said "the greatest inside forward in Britain found his fangs drawn by Gordon Milne, with surely one of the most magnificent displays in the half-back's career". All in all, it was a tremendous performance by the Reds, who were concentrating on the League, since Second Division Swansea had knocked them out of the FA Cup. The Swans won 2-1 at Anfield in round 6, with Shanks blasting: "It's the biggest travesty of justice in football history. The real score should've been 14-2."

A fortnight after we'd taken United's scalp, I was back in the Lake District for our fixture with Arsenal that could decide the title. I'd just polished off Mum's heart-attack breakfast of egg, bacon, fried bread and black pudding when the door knocker banged. It was a Sikh, a bulky, bearded chap, dressed in a purple turban and black serge overcoat.

"Good morning," he said, opening a senile suitcase that contained an assortment of brushes, for shoes, hair, clothes, home. "Would you like buy?"

"Sorry," I replied. "I'm a student. Got no money."

True. We also didn't require any brushes, large or small.

The Sikh fixed me with his brown eyes. "If I do magic, you buy?" he asked.

My curiosity stirred.

"What kind of magic?"

"I show."

The Sikh reached into his pocket, fishing out the stub of a thick lead pencil and a slip of crumpled paper, size of a Rizla.

He scanned my face again and asked: "You have wife?"

What's he on about?

"Wife?"

"Yes. Wife, woman."

"You mean girlfriend?"

"Yes."

"I've got a girlfriend. Yes."

At this, he cupped the paper in his palm to conceal what he was doing, and painstakingly wrote something. Then he screwed it up and placed it in my right hand, which he clasped like a ball.

"What is name of woman?"

"Frances," I replied. The Sikh stared into my subconscious for a few seconds and let go of my hand.

He jabbed a finger.

"See."

I opened the paper and, in crude capital letters, as if written by an Anfield Primary six-year-old, was "FRANCES". My Huyton lass!

"How'd you do that?"

"I am Jesus, I am holy man," the Sikh responded, apparently disclosing something commonplace.

I had no alternative but to select a small shoe brush and pay 2s 6d to this eastern magus.

He closed his case and went on his way, leaving me stumped.

How had he done it? I'd never met him before, never clapped eyes on him. How could he have known who I was going out with? Might a neighbour have told him? Impossible. Hardly anyone in the street could name my girlfriend, I'd had so many. Anyway, even if they could, why would they impart that knowledge to a door-to-door salesman?

It didn't add up and the more I tried to explain it, the more illogical it became. It was magic, no more nor less, but then some people – a tiny handful – do have faculties that logic or science cannot explain. Still, if this Sikh had such rare abilities, what was he doing selling door-to-door? He should have been a millionaire, feet up alongside the pool in his Formby mansion, sipping a brandy.

At 11 in the morning, still perplexed by my brush with the brush man, and musing that our players needed to conjure up some magic on the pitch, I clogged it to Anfield.

Outside, the streets were seething but by 2pm I'd squeezed my frame into the back of the Kop. From there, I watched the Reds nail down the championship with a 5-0 demolition of the Gunners, an exquisite exhibition of free-flowing football in which Thompson shone with two superb goals.

Kopites were on cloud nine, roaring and chanting without drawing breath and London reporters who'd trekked north had never experienced such vocal support. They had discovered our *Singing* Sixties. The following day, the *Daily Express* revealed: "The Kop chant and its perfect timing were a puzzle, but the secret was a brawny docker in a red and white suit who the Kop chorus christened Sir Malcolm (after the conductor, Sir Malcolm Sargeant), who conducts their more ambitious choral arrangements from a position directly behind the goal. 'What happens,' he said, 'is that anyone with an Ee-aye-addio on his mind shouts it out, and if we like the idea, we give it four beats and then let go. We've got some pretty sharp boys here'.

"The climax of Sir Malcolm's performance came a few minutes from the end of the game when he raised his arms in the air and the Kop thundered out: 'Oh when the Reds go marching in'."

Remarkably, Anfield was not full, holding only 48,000, 6,000 less than capacity, all because of Shanks. In the morning he'd arrived at the stadium to find thousands standing around outside. Concerned about people travelling long distances, he went on radio at midday to warn that if they weren't already at the ground, they wouldn't get in. So thousands who abandoned their journeys missed the Reds' drubbing of Arsenal but the Championship was ours. We could not be caught by United, even though we had three away fixtures to play.

At the final whistle, the team, a couple of small boys in tow, jogged around with a replica of the League trophy made from plastic and cardboard because the real thing had not been sent to Anfield. As the crowd roared their approval, I felt numbed by the game and what Shanks had achieved in his second season in the top division. Not only had he won promotion but now our lads were the best in the land. A fate accompli for a manager fulfilling his destiny with the Reds.

His team of Lawrence, Byrne, Moran, Milne, Yeats, Stevenson, Callaghan, Hunt, St John, Melia or Arrowsmith, and Thompson had brought Liverpool's sixth title and first since 1947. To chalk up their 92 League goals, including six each against Ipswich, Wolves, Stoke and Sheffield United, they had adhered to Shanks's simple instruction, "Pass and move", a reworking of the Continental credo that players without the ball were as influential on the field as those with it. During training, Ronnie Moran, the coach, would constantly urge: "Pass, move, pass, move." This uncomplicated formula had brought the League pennant to Anfield.

After Liverpool mauled Arsenal, I got wasted in the Standard. It must have been a rare old evening because Black Maggie dumbfounded everyone by coming in twice with her earthenware jug for best bitter.

This lady, in her 80s and perpetually dressed in widow's weeds apart from a starched white apron, lived at the bottom of Ullswater and entered the pub every night to have her pitcher filled with frothy ale as a takeaway.

Nobody could ever remember her getting seconds so she must have been toasting the Reds' brave new world, too.

* * * * * * * * * *

When the 1964-65 season opened with a home game against Arsenal, Anfield had a completely different side – of the ground. Fans occupying the

6,700 seats in the rebuilt Kemlyn stand were now protected from the weather by a cantilever canopy, rather than the ancient barrel roof.

The fixture was also a TV milestone: at 6.30 that Saturday evening, a new programme, Match of the Day, aired highlights on the latest channel, BBC2.

Introduced by Kenneth Wolstenholme from what he referred to as Beatleville, the broadcast could only be viewed in the London area, so a piddling 22,000 watched Hunt hook the ball over Gunners keeper Furnell for the show's first ever goal.

The technology used for the programme relied on razor blades to splice film together. With seconds to spare before transmission, the editing was a bit too sharp – it showed Yeats taking a throw-in ... to Yeats, who came within inches of scoring. In spite of this, two other goals from Gordon Wallace made it 3-2 for the Reds and Match of the Day had spun its strand of TV history.

That same month of August, Liverpool were making their debut in the European Cup against Reykjavik. As there were no flights to the Icelandic capital from Speke Airport, the squad flew to Prestwick in Ayrshire where they had a five-hour wait for a connection to Iceland, a delay that Shanks, ever a man of simple tastes, decreed should be filled with a charabanc trip to Butlin's holiday camp in Ayr.

As their coach pulled up at the entrance, the gatekeeper was unimpressed.

"Who are you lot?" he asked.

"Bill Shankly and Liverpool football club. We're on our way to Reykjavik, in Iceland."

"I think you've taken the wrong road" came the gateman's reply.

Shanks's reaction is unrepeatable in a family publication.

Once the team did arrive in Iceland, they won 5-0, Wallace grabbing Liverpool's first European goal, while the tie was wrapped up with a 6-1 Anfield romp, noteworthy for support given to the visitors by Kopites who cheered their rare attacks and booed the Reds'. Shanks even went to the touchline to yell at Yeats: "Let them score!" Subsequently, an Icelandic player received the ball on the centre spot and was shepherded through our defence to slot home.

The Kop roared with glee. The visitors could have their consolation goal because we were through.

The next round pitted Liverpool against daunting Continental opposition, Anderlecht, who had provided seven members of the Belgian national side, the Red Devils, that had just outplayed England at Wembley.

For the Anfield leg, Shanks decreed a revolutionary change. Abandoning the club's white shorts, white socks and white piping on red jerseys, he introduced an all-red strip. The original colour combination now seems dated, a relic of Victorian days when gentlemen players wore canvas knickerbockers on Eton's playing fields, but Shanks's idea to go red, signifying passion and blood, was radical in the Sixties, making Liverpool the only British team to play in that one colour.

The day before the tie, Yeats was asked to try the kit on, blowing the boss away. "Christ, son, you look seven foot tall," he raved. "We'll play in all-red from now on. Real Madrid play in all-white, Liverpool in all-red."

The new strip certainly paid off on the pitch as we spanked Anderlecht 3-0, and Shanks had no doubt about its crimson impact. "There was a glow, like a fire was burning inside Anfield," he said.

Once more, the Scot's brand of psychology was called upon for this tricky pairing. Beforehand, he told his side: "You're playing a load of rubbish tonight." Afterwards: "Congratulations, lads. You've beaten one of the best teams in Europe."

In the away leg, the Reds came out on top again, Hunt nicking a late winner. Now the Continent was taking notice of these Scouse novices.

In the FA Cup in January, Liverpool faced Fourth Division Stockport County at Anfield, a tie that Shanks missed because he had gone to West Germany to run the rule over the Reds' next European opponents, Cologne. On his return, he landed at Manchester where he noticed an airport worker with the Saturday evening football paper.

Eager to know how his lads had fared, the boss asked if there'd been any shocks in the FA Cup. "Yes," the man answered. "Peterborough beat Arsenal." Shanks hadn't the faintest interest in this upset. Glancing over the worker's shoulder, he ran his eyes down the page and spotted the Liverpool result, 1-1. He hit the roof. "What! What do you call that if it's not a shock?"

The Reds won the replay 2-0 at Edgeley Park.

In the next round, they overcame Bolton at Burnden Park and then were paired with their bogey team, Leicester, who had not only knocked them out in the semi two years before but had prevailed in six of seven previous meetings. I returned home for our cup showdown and travelled with three mates by Lawrenson's coach to Filbert Street on the Saturday morning. As we entered the outskirts of Leicester, news came on the charabanc's radio that intruders had painted the goals and touchlines red during the night. This put everybody in good humour.

Once the tie kicked off, Gordon Banks turned into Leicester's saviour, thwarting our attempts on his goal. The Foxes did make a couple of breakaways but after 90 minutes, the score remained 0-0, a moral victory for us. The travelling support rejoiced; the replay at Anfield would be a golden opportunity to bury our Leicester hoodoo.

My pals and I were on such a high that we set out in search of an off-licence for some celebratory bottles of brown. Nowhere was open, though, and we returned empty-handed to the street where all the coaches had been parked. It was deserted. Every chara had gone.

My muckers scampered off to the station for a train but, strapped for cash, I had to resort to hitch-hiking. Having walked to a main road leading west out of the city, I planted myself on the pavement, red scarf around my neck, thumb in the air.

Seconds later, a Morris Minor pulled up, bearing three Red men who'd been toasting our draw in a pub. "In you get, lah," was their reassuring injunction.

I eased myself into the rear, alongside an old stager who'd supported Liverpool since way back when, and the whole of our return journey to Lancashire was enlivened by the discussion that flows whenever fans of the same creed are pitched together.

Jimmy, my companion in the back, had a wealth of knowledge, with tales of Mersey immortals such as Albert Stubbins, Dixie Dean, Cyril Done, Jack Balmer and Billy Liddell.

Billy. What a player! A placid giant possessing a cannonball shot, he was with the Reds from 1938 to 1960, netted 229 goals (as a winger!) in 536 appearances and was never booked.

Yet he wasn't even a full-time pro, fitting football into the profession of an accountant and training only twice a week. Despite this, when the Reds were in the Second Division, his tireless raids down the flanks led Kopologists to rechristen the team Liddellpool.

I listened enthralled to Jimmy's reminiscences about the greats and we soon got home, passing the Liverpool sign on the East Lancs Road at about 10 o'clock. Now silence reigned inside the motor.

Rain was slanting down on row after row of sullen terraced houses, the only bright spots being the street lights. We slid past Sparrow Hall flats, gazing out at the desolate surroundings. Then Jimmy, an ashes-to-Anfield fan if ever there was one, whispered a few words, not to us but himself: "Dirty, scruffy old Liverpool. God bless it."

Yes, yes, yes. God bless it.

The lads could certainly count their blessings in the replay in L4. In a hard-fought tussle, Hunt broke the deadlock with pile-driver past Banks. Our Leicester jinx had been banjoed and Liverpool were through to a semi with fashionable Chelsea at Villa Park.

First, though, the lads had unfinished business.

The Wednesday before the FA Cup decider, they faced Cologne in a European Cup quarter-final play-off, the culmination of one of the longest-running ties ever. In Germany, the Reds ground out a 0-0 draw but minutes before kick-off in the return leg at Anfield a snap blizzard covered the grass with a thick layer of snow on which neither team could keep their feet. With the pitch markings also invisible, the referee had no option but to call the game off.

An announcement followed that supporters should hang around, so vouchers for the rearranged tie could be distributed at the exit gates. During the wait, as minutes dragged and the Arctic cold began to bite, a band of Kopites resolved to warm themselves up: they legged down the field to hurl a barrage of snowballs into the Annie Road fans.

Glad to pick up the gauntlet, Annie Roaders unleashed a retaliatory fusillade at their assailants, who slammed into reverse. Then a ball was tossed onto the ice rink of a pitch and an impromptu kickaround ensued – no sides, no rules, just a horde of Jimmy Piss-Quicks booting the ball anywhere, pursuing it up and down the field, a swarm of bees after a child's sticky lollipop.

When the ball stalled abruptly in the snow, lads overran it and skidded to a halt in a heap of bodies. As they got to their feet on the treacherous surface, latecomers came sliding in and knocked them over again, like skittles in a bowling alley. Meanwhile, the ball had been hacked up the other end, chased by the rest of the ruffians in this game of kick and rush, push and pull.

Dozens of Keystone Kopites were floundering on their knees and the more bevvied they were, the more madcap the fun. One bloke was so unsteady that, after being decked, he tried to stand up – and immediately slipped over. After a couple of attempts to attain the vertical, he gave up, crawling off to the paddock. Spectators were in stitches.

Having congregated in the centre circle, the rabble launched a mass charge on the Kop goal, the ball zinging here, there and everywhere. One attacker took a swing at it, missed, fell on his backside and brought down two other participants who went headlong over his prone body.

The ball broke to a burly bod who, shouldering a rival to the turf, toe-ended it into the net. It was booted out, and belted back in by supporters who wrestled each other for the privilege of fulfilling their fantasy of scoring at the Kop end.

In possibly, probably, categorically a unique occurrence, mediaeval mob fute-ball had been re-enacted in a modern-day British stadium and by the time the vouchers were ready for collection, this rib-achingly funny night had erased any disappointment at the postponement.

The match was rescheduled for a fortnight later but ended goalless again, leading to a decider in neutral Rotterdam where 51,000 watched a nailbiting

2-2 clash on a pitch of porridge. St John and Hunt bulged the net for us but the Germans clawed themselves back level.

Extra time failed to produce a winner, so the rules decreed that the toss of a coloured disc would decide, one side red for Liverpool, the other white for Cologne.

The referee threw the disc into the air and it landed – on edge in the mud! This tie was never going to end.

The ref tried again.

At the second toss, Yeats peered down and then leapt for the moon while the rest of the team joined in a mass pogo. The disc was showing red, Liverpool had won and thousands of travelling Scousers went demented. It had required five hours' play for the Reds to reach the European semi-final.

Three days after that strength-sapping set-to, Liverpool faced Chelsea at Villa Park to decide who would go to Wembley for the FA Cup showpiece. Since I had my head buried in textbooks in London, Mum queued six hours at Anfield for two tickets and I presented the spare to Rick Davies, a student pal.

Beforehand, papers in the metropolis were adamant the Blues would win and on the morning of the tie, when Rick and I travelled by train to the Midlands, the *Express's* back page was dominated by its star football reporter, Desmond Hackett, chortling "It's Chelsea". After Liverpool's draining battle with Cologne, the Blues' manager, Tommy Docherty, was also sure his men would get to Wembley, a confidence Shanks used against the Londoners once he learnt they'd already prepared a Cup Final brochure.

With his customary sense of theatre, he picked his moment. Minutes before the Reds stepped out onto the pitch, he marched into their dressing room and, eyes ablaze with indignation, told them what Chelsea had done.

"They think you're not worth turning up for," he boomed. "They're already at Wembley. Now go out and show them!"

Nothing could have been more guaranteed to motivate the team and Tommy Smith said: "After that, there was no way we were going to lose."

The semi had a cultural context, pitting the Mersey sound against the swinging King's Road, and Liverpudlians struck the appropriate chord when Thompson dribbled to the edge of Chelsea's box and rocketed the ball into the rigging. A quarter of an hour later, St John was fouled by "Chopper" Harris and Stevenson lashed the spot kick home to send the Pool through.

In the other semi, Leeds overcame Manchester United, meaning a new name would be engraved on the cup as neither the Tykes nor the Scousers had ever won it.

The Monday night before the final, I headed from Streatham to the West End with one objective in mind: a ticket for Wembley, no easy touch since out of a 100,000 capacity, the FA had granted a miserly allocation of 15,000 to Liverpool, which could have been sold 10 times over. In a pub off Leicester Square, I soon bumped into my first couple of Reds, scarves knotted around their necks, pint pots in their hands, laughter on their lips.

The advance guard had arrived in town for the big day but when I inquired about spares, they only had their own tickets.

Over the next three nights, that response was repeated in assorted inns and taverns as London's bright lights lured more and more Reds. Wherever I wandered, I didn't get a sniff. Nowhere, in Soho, Tottenham Court Road, Charing Cross Road, Leicester Square, Haymarket or Oxford Street, was there a ticket to be had.

Last throw of the dice: I would go to Euston on the Saturday morning, wait for trains from Lime Street and ask around. Among the hundreds of supporters passing through the station, there had to be one spare. So at 9am on May Day, 1965, I caught the tube from Balham to Euston. No sooner had I surveyed the arrivals board and installed myself at the platform exit for the next Lime Street service than a challenger turned up.

A short, thick-set chap with flat nose and eyes hidden by dark glasses asked if I had a ticket to sell. I recognised him – Alan Rudkin, Liverpool's European bantamweight champion, who had just chinned Belfast's Johnny Caldwell for the Commonwealth title. I explained that I was in the same boat, desperate to get to Wembley.

Alan had queered my pitch, though. If anyone came along with a spare, it would be a walkover for a Scouse hero, one of the world's best pound-for-pound boxers who needn't break sweat for a first-round knockout in Euston's ticket tournament.

Move to the opposite side of the station, I thought.

This I did and, minutes after the next Lime Street train arrived, Eureka! I struck gold. A lad from Netherton had a spare, which he was willing to sell at face value. All of 7 shillings and 6 pence. That afternoon I'd be attending my first Cup Final.

Shanks had said: "If our fans at Wembley can make as much noise as at home, I don't think there's a team in the world that can live with Liverpool." He wasn't to be disappointed. Once I got inside the stadium, there seemed two Scousers for every Leeds fan and at kick-off the noise was ear-splitting.

Wembley was showing its age, though. Where I was standing next to the pitch, the terracing was so shallow that after a few minutes a neck brace would have come in handy to watch the action, which brought an early setback for us. In the sixth minute, Byrne broke his collarbone in a nasty collision with Bobby Collins and, since substitutes were not allowed, our fullback had to play on. Leeds were unaware of his fracture, otherwise they would have attacked incessantly down the right wing, but the injury compelled Liverpool to revise their tactics and the match deteriorated into a stalemate, with only a handful of scoring opportunities.

Goalless after 90 minutes, extra time loomed, which Gerry must have dreaded, even though he hadn't put a foot wrong, chasing and tackling like the fittest man on the pitch. Now, on the restart, he excelled himself; a charge forward and he centred for Hunt to break the impasse with a header.

Our Red noses were in front.

Leeds refused to lie down; Bremner equalised. Would fate deny us the silver once again?

Not when the Saint performed his miracle, leaping like a salmon to convert a Callaghan cross. 2-1.

Shanks had told St John: "If you're not sure what to do with the ball, just pop it in the net and we'll discuss your options afterwards." The centre-forward had digested this advice and, once the ref blew for the end, the FA Cup was ours.

Yeats and Milne, who hadn't played because of injury, carried the venerable trophy to the Scouse end, while Thompson hugged a bulky teddy bear wearing Liverpool colours, its gobstopper eyes dilated with amazement at the jubilant terraces. "Ee-aye-addio, we've won the cup," the Red hordes sang to their heroes.

Our lifetime's dream had turned into reality and Willy Stevenson reflected: "Leeds bottled it. They didn't want to lose, whereas we wanted to win."

Once the lads dragged their weary legs off Wembley's lush turf, I joined the columns of dehydrated drinkers heading into the West End where tills soon bulged with the Red pound and we partied big-style in Soho's Coach and Horses.

Some day and some way to heal 73 years of hurt.

Never one to rest on his laurels, Shanks was already eyeing the future. "I want to build an invincible team," he growled, "so they'll have to send a team from Mars to beat us."

The Sunday after the final, 500,000 people, equalling Liverpool's entire population, flocked to the city centre to watch the team's victory parade. They had unfinished business, though. After a break in invigorating Blackpool, they were back at Anfield on Tuesday for the European Cup first leg with Inter Milan, holders of the European and World Club titles and indisputably the best side on earth.

Even though the semi was scheduled for 7.30, streets around Anfield were chocker by midday and I got in at 4pm, an hour before the gates were forced shut, leaving thousands outside.

With kick-off drawing near and Kopites pleading, "Ee-aye-addio, we want to see the cup", Shanks was about to pull the ace out of his shirt sleeve.

Inter, encouraged to run out first for the kick-in, ignored tradition by trotting down to the Kop, where a wall of noise forced them into a hasty U-turn for Annie Road. Only when the Italians had been unnerved by their intimidating reception did Shanks show his card: out onto the pitch he sent the FA cup, borne aloft by our injured duo, Milne and Byrne, one arm in a sling because of his broken collarbone.

The din was pitiless from every corner of the stadium, rammed to its gunnels with Scousers, and Inter's players were visibly shaken. With global stars such as Jair, Mazzola, Suarez and Facchetti, they oozed class but once the whistle blew, a tidal wave of Red attacks rocked them back on their heels.

Despite that two-hour slog at Wembley, Liverpool were unstoppable. Within four minutes, they went ahead, through a precise Hunt volley. Mazzola equalised to briefly stem the onslaught until a free-kick routine straight out of Melwood's coaching manual wrongfooted Inter's defence, Callaghan sliding home. After that, the Milanesi held out until the 75th minute when St John made it 3-1, although a perfectly good goal by Chris Lawler was also disallowed by the referee for an offside that his linesman did not signal.

Throughout this pulsating encounter, Kopites hardly drew breath for their roars, chants and Beatles songs, compelling reporters to pick them as Man of the Match.

For Shanks, it was the greatest game he'd ever witnessed while St John described it as "the night Liverpool came of age". Reflecting on Hunt's opener, Helenio Herrera, Inter's eminent manager, declared: "That wasn't a British goal, it was a Continental goal", before conceding: "We have been beaten before but tonight we were defeated."

Later that evening, in every pub in every street, strong ale was taken and I got nicely sozzled in the Standard. Then, after towels were thrown over the pumps, I did the unprecedented: I went back to Anfield.

During the Thirties, unemployed men who couldn't afford entrance money would hang around outside, listening to the noise of the match. Now, with 11pm chiming, I stood on the pavement opposite the Kop, shut my eyes, heard the chanting and singing and even sensed the electrical charge the ground gives off.

Our third goal had just gone in when "We love you, yeah, yeah, yeah!" snapped me out of my trance. Voicing their adoration, three tiddly laddies were heading home and I did too.

Next day brought a ghastly sequel to a marvellous game: the body of Jimmy McInnes, Liverpool's secretary since 1955, was found in the turnstile area at the back of the Kop. Overcome by life's pressures, a vulnerable soul had been seduced by the terrible beauty of suicide and hanged himself.

This tragedy cast a pall over Anfield and put into perspective the mockery of a game in Milan.

After the first leg, every Kopite believed we could and would win the European Cup. Nothing could hold us back. How naive. How little we knew about the Machiavellian manoeuvres of Italian clubs, the swampy undergrowth in which unworldly Liverpudlians had never set foot.

Albert Camus, the existentialist goalkeeper and French novelist, wrote: "Everything I know most certainly about morality and the obligations of man, I owe to football." He attributed some of his fundamental beliefs to the game, saying: "I learnt that the ball never comes when you expect it. That helped me a lot in life, especially in large cities where people don't tend to be what they say they are."

Well, Shanks and his players would now receive a lesson in immorality.

After the Nerazzurris' humiliation at Anfield, Milan's press demonised Liverpool, depicting Scousers as drunken barbarians and their players as drug-takers, pages of poison that were administered daily until the return in the San Siro.

Beforehand, rumours circulated that the Reds would not go through and Shanks himself was told they would lose. The rumour-mongers must have had their ears glued to the doors of Inter's offices because the second leg was a farce, riddled with bizarre refereeing decisions that began with six Liverpool fouls in the first eight minutes.

However, St John stunned the 90,000 tifosi inside L'Opera del Calcio, football's opera house, when he bundled the ball into the home side's goal. For no obvious reason, Spanish referee Ortiz de Mendibil disallowed it and then Inter's Corso fired home straight from a free kick that Mendibil had signalled was indirect.

There was worse to come. As Lawrence bounced the ball in the 18-yard box, preparing to lump it upfield, Peiro nipped around his blind side and toed it out of his hands. A simple tap and the ball lay in our net. Even though the forward was offside, the referee did not blow.

Liverpool's bench were apoplectic because on the Continent every keeper was protected from opposing forwards. If an attacker so much as brushed against a goalie, he risked being booked.

After that, ruling after ruling penalised the Reds, who went down 3-0 on goals and 20-3 on fouls. As the teams pushed into the tunnel, Smith was unable to curb his anger, swinging his foot at the ref, but team-mates restrained him.

Shanks blasted Inter for taking performance-enhancing pills: "They were drugged to their eyeballs! No one could beat us 3-0 without drugs!" Years after, he cursed the match: "They had Mussolini reffing for them and his nephews running the lines. Of all the people I've seen and met, that referee is the one man who haunts me." And in 2001 Smith didn't mince his words: "The referee was bent and, if he's still alive, he can sue me."

Eventually the truth did come out. In an exhaustive *Sunday Times* investigation, The Years of the Golden Fix, Brian Glanville and Keith Botsford concluded that Inter's success in the Sixties had been "the fruit of bribery and corruption". Three years in a row, they tried to buy off referees in the second legs of European Cup semis at the San Siro and twice their palm-greasing paid off with victories in the final.

In 1964, Tesanic, the Yugoslav officiating at the Italians' tie with Borussia Dortmund, was said to have been handed a brown envelope. Coincidentally, he failed to notice that Inter's Suarez brutally curtailed one German player's participation in the Milan leg. However, Tesanic was incapable of keeping his mouth shut, revealing all to a fellow Yugoslav while holidaying on the Adriatic at Inter's expense. Cat out of the bag, Dortmund protested to UEFA who gave them short shrift.

As regards the Liverpool semi, Glanville uncovered evidence that a bribe was paid to de Mendibil, who had a sick child requiring expensive hospital treatment, while some reports alleged he received so much cash he bought a villa. However, testimony that the Spaniard exchanged shirts with Inter's president in the boardroom afterwards may be unfounded.

The following year, the Black and Blues' hat-trick of plots to influence officials came to nought because Hungary's Gyorgy Vadas spurned their blandishments – enough money for a fleet of Mercedes – and Real Madrid knocked them out.

Vadas's integrity did not earn him any merit marks. He was notified by the Hungarian Football Federation secretary, who was privy to the bribery conspiracy, that he would never officiate at another international match. He never did.

Glanville and Botsford also documented cases of Juventus and AC Milan "looking after" officials. But the long-term fallout for Liverpool from Inter's match-fixing was a 12-year wait to reach another European Cup final and the Italian authorities required another 40 years to amass irrefutable proof of the corruption rooted in calcio.

Although the Reds' first season of Continental endeavour might ultimately have been heartbreaking, our management and players had embarked on a learning curve about overseas trips: the hotels, airports, delays, food, tricks and traps. On the pitch, they also hit upon two watchwords, patience and possession, which would help bring trophies.

After the Inter fiasco, Liverpool finished seventh in the League and would compete in the Cup Winners' Cup next season, while I was hundreds of miles away in France. As 1965-66's fixtures opened in August, I was beginning a year of my degree course in Poitiers, working as an assistant who presided over English conversation classes for groups of trainee teachers. I was also receiving personal tuition in international relations at the university and soon learnt the French have sex lives where we have hot-water bottles and Witney woollen blankets.

My accommodation in a boarding school's dormitory wing was a room furnished with a bed, wardrobe, desk, chair, washbasin – and my trusty tranny, which relayed BBC football programmes once its aerial was connected to the iron radiator by a length of wire. This alliance of radio and radiator kept me posted about the Reds' dismissal of Juventus, Standard Liege and Honved on their European travels.

Anecdotes would divulge that the Honved tie caused ripples in Ron Yeats's home, all because of a Granada TV crew that travelled to Budapest to film a documentary, The Kop Goes East.

After Liverpool earned a commendable 0-0 draw, Shanks permitted the players to unwind at a nightclub, where Rowdy hauled himself up on aching limbs to do the twist with a go-go dancer, an event captured on celluloid by the camera crew. Next evening, our captain arrived home on Merseyside and told his wife about the quiet night he'd spent in the hotel after the game.

Hardly had he spoken than the telly showed pictures of him jig-jigging with this curvaceous dancer. Boing!

In the Cup Winners' semi, Liverpool crossed swords with a Celtic side intent on reaching the final because it was to be held at Hampden Park. A coachload travelled from the Standard to the away leg at Parkhead where, in front of 80,000 fans, the Pool went down, 1-0.

While the pub lads walked back to their coach, one of them was the victim of a snide attack. As a Bhoys supporter, green scarf muffling his face, strode past, he tossed his head so that the peak of his flat cap gave a glancing blow to Phil's cheek.

Odd, Phil thought, like a phantom butt. What was all that about? Then he got his explanation.

Warm blood was oozing down his cheek.

The Celt, who had melted away into the gloom, had a razor blade secreted in the edge of his tam's peak, and that had inflicted the wound. The cut was only a nick, but what if Phil's eye had been slit by the blade?

Once the lads returned home, this incident led the agenda in the Standard, firing everyone up. Liverpool had an extra reason to knock the Bhoys out.

The return, in front of a rain-soaked capacity crowd, took on a surreal air because steam from drenched clothes rose like smoke from the terraces. On the pitch, there were fireworks when Smith's thunderflash of a free kick levelled the tie on aggregate, then Geoff Strong put us ahead with a looping header.

Over in Poitiers, a Scouser banged his radiator in elation.

Wait! Not over yet.

With seconds to go, a Celtic goal was disallowed for offside. Out of sheer pique, Hoops fans in the Annie Road end resorted to brawling among themselves and bombarded the turf with empty bottles of heavy. At the whistle, so much glass littered Anfield that Shanks asked Jock Stein, Celtic's boss, whether he wanted a share of the gate receipts or the deposits on empties.

So Liverpool reached the Cup Winners' Cup final where they met Borussia Dortmund, conquerors home and away of West Ham. At Hampden, the Germans proved crafty opposition, with Hans Tilkowski in tiptop form between the sticks. Sigi Held put them ahead, Hunt equalised to send the match into extra time, and Reinhard Libuda snatched the silver with a 30-yard effort that hit the post, thumped down onto Yeats's hip and squirted into the goal as the skipper made a despairing effort to keep it out.

The Reds' first European final had ended in failure.

Over in Poitiers, a Scouser banged his radiator in exasperation.

As Chelsea had won 2-1 at Anfield in the FA Cup, Liverpool were now giving their all in the League and Hunt led the way, grabbing 29 goals that included a hat-trick in nine minutes against West Ham at Upton Park. Fittingly, our goal machine sealed the title with the clincher in a 2-1 disposal of Chelsea.

During our campaign, we used just 14 players and five turned out in every game: Lawrence, Byrne, Yeats, Smith and Callaghan. Nine squad members appeared in 40 or more of the 42 matches and Rowdy remained the unyielding hub of our defence.

"He frightened half the country out of playing by his sheer presence," said Everton's Joe Royle. "He was the hardest centre-half I played against."

So, in three seasons, our defensive rock, and Shanks, had won a scintillating haul of two League titles and the FA Cup.

6
Sound That Rocked The World

To accomplish great things, we must dream as well as act
– Anatole France

IN ONE of history's mystifying coincidences, Liverpool's domination of English football overlapped with Merseybeat's supremacy in music across the world and, inevitably, the Beatles laid the foundations of its chart breakthrough.

Before they did, one member of the band had to recover from a painful upset.

In August 1962, a fortnight after Pete Best's sacking, George was sporting a black eye when he travelled to Abbey Road with John, Paul and Ringo to lay down their first songs for Parlophone. An irate fan of their former drummer had inflicted the shiner during a scuffle in Mathew Street, obliging the studio photographer to capture only George's right profile.

Conceivably, this put a damper on the recordings, which were deemed unsatisfactory by George Martin. He got the Beatles to repeat them a week later, adding new material and using a session drummer; Ringo played the tambourine and maraca.

Martin was happier and on Friday, October 5, 1962, the debut single was released – Love Me Do, with PS I Love You on the flip side.

At this time I was working in the Civil Service in London, so I hotfooted it to HMV's shop in Oxford Street to buy a copy. The following Monday, the disc went straight onto the turntable at our midday gig in the Board of Trade, enabling guys and gals to listen to a group I'd been raving about. Whitehall was being introduced to the Cavern quartet.

On the back of my purchase and saturation sales in Liverpool, Love Me Do entered the chart at a lofty No 17. I was over the moon. A moderate start, but the momentum soon built up. At the turn of the year, Please Please Me reached second and then From Me To You went one better in April 1963, hitting top spot. Now office mates who hadn't been too fussed about Love Me Do were buying Beatles records.

John, Paul, George and Ringo weren't the only Scouse stars making waves. Other Cavern favourites had been given recording contracts as Epstein extended his empire, adding Billy J Kramer and the Dakotas, the Fourmost and Cilla Black to his roster of acts. In fact, another of his signings, Gerry and the Pacemakers, trumped the Beatles in March, becoming the first Merseybeat band to reach No 1 with How Do You Do It and notching up two more chart-toppers, I Like It and You'll Never Walk Alone.

During 1963, Liverpool groups could do no wrong and, down in Streatham, I was heartened to see bands turning into household names, like Billy J and the Dakotas, who took pole position in the hit parade in May with Do You Want To Know A Secret, and the Searchers, who succeeded them in June with Sweets For My Sweet.

Every week I kept abreast of the Merseybeat mania sweeping Britain by reading the *New Musical Express* and *Melody Maker*, which vied with each other for stories about the phenomenon. As often as practicable, I also went home to catch up with the music scene, although the Beatles' Cavern appearances got rarer and rarer.

The lads were moving on since their Please Please Me success, selling out bigger and bigger venues across the country. In February they fulfilled their last lunchtime date in the Cavern and on Saturday, August 3, they played their final evening booking there. In all, they had performed on that teeny stage on 274 occasions, including 150 midday gigs.

Farewell, Mathew Street, hello, world. Building on appearances across the country and extensive TV and radio exposure, the lads logged their second No 1, She Loves You, in August.

In London's Tin Pan Alley, the big noises were bewildered by the Mersey sound's takeover but as they sucked on their cucumber-sized cigars, they soon spotted a business opportunity. These country bumpkins from Liverpool were lording it in the charts when everyone knew the metropolis was the centre of the showbiz world. Why not launch a battle of the bands, a musical duplicate of Liverpool v Arsenal? A pop duel, Merseyside v London, North v South, could be a real money-maker.

And that's what Denmark Street engineered, a war of the airwaves, turntables and clubs. They backed various southern bands – the Dave Clarke Five, Brian Poole and the Tremeloes, The Who – until credible challengers were unearthed in the form of the Rolling Stones who in July released their first disc, Come On. Years later, a similar rivalry was contrived on TV after Coronation Street drew bumper audiences; the BBC's high command ordained that a London soap was essential to challenge Granada's working-class saga and EastEnders was born.

Since the Beatles were regarded as Scouse charmers and Mum's blue-eyed boys, the Stones were promoted by their management as the band with attitude, the rebels, seldom smiling, vaguely threatening, as they gazed impassively at camera or audience. Many kids liked them expressly because their parents didn't, a plus for record sales.

Not a big enough plus. In December 1963, at the end of my first term of university studies, the Beatles set an extraordinary benchmark for pretenders to their throne: seven songs in the Top 20, including I Want To Hold Your Hand at No 1. They were evolving into the universe's most celebrated rock band, due in no small measure to their rhythms and lyrics, transcending the "I remember, last September" norm prevalent in the charts. In all conscience, one *Sunday Times* writer, Richard Buckle, went so far as to extol Lennon and McCartney as "the greatest composers since Beethoven".

By now, the foursome had decamped from their Liverpool homes and relocated to London; Epstein was planning to crack the States through his Operation USA, although initial transatlantic soundings weren't favourable. To test the water, George Martin sent a copy of Please Please Me to a Capitol Records executive in New York, who responded: "We don't think the Beatles will do anything in this market."

A newspaper report backed this up, detailing American teenagers' indifference to our lads. "We don't want the Beatles over here," a girl declared. "We've got Elvis and don't want English groups." Yet when the band arrived in New York in February 1964, I Want To Hold Your Hand was already No 1 and their performance on the Ed Sullivan Show was watched by an audience of 73 million, nearly half the population. That same night, the crime rate slumped to its lowest in 50 years.

The most famous people on the planet, Merseyside's dearest sons were sending out a sonic boom that rattled radios and record players everywhere and two months after their Sullivan appearance, they occupied the top five places in the US charts, a feat never equalled.

Through these Scouse invaders, Americans were also rediscovering their long links with Liverpool, going back to the millions of emigrants who sailed from the port and the armies of soldiers who disembarked there during two world wars.

Now any Scouser travelling abroad had turned into a celebrity, too. From Alaska to Zanzibar, strangers wanted to talk to you about the place whose music was rocking the cosmos and Heswall's John Peel became an early beneficiary of this attention, passing on his Liverpool knowledge to radio listeners in Dallas.

Back in the UK, the Beatles led the charge as Merseybeat songs held top spot in the hit parade for 51 of the 60 weeks between April 1963 and May

1964, bolstered by the debut of BBC TV's Top of the Pops. Indeed, so many groups were flooding out of Liverpool that one German magazine advertised in the *Echo* for musicians to pose in a mass photo shoot on St George's Hall steps. Some 300 turned up, with guitars, trumpets, saxophones and drum kits, creating an iconic image that symbolised the Scouse Sixties.

While the Beatles were taking America's hit parade by storm, they were also making a feature film, A Hard Day's Night, which received its Merseyside premiere at the Odeon in London Road in July 1964. The lads flew home for the event, to be welcomed by 200,000 in the city centre.

Seemingly their influence knew no bounds; political commentators contended they tilted the balance in October's General Election when populist Huyton MP Harold Wilson hijacked the Liverpool sound to give Labour a youthful makeover and sweep into government, ending 13 years of Conservative rule.

Muhammad Ali was another luminary who fell for the lads' charisma. After meeting them in Miami, he wrote a tribute, rhyming: "When Liston picks up the papers / And sees the Beatles came to me / He will be angry / And I'll knock him out in three." Actually Sonny lasted till round 6.

As happens so often, high profiles can bring unwanted baggage. During one of my trips north, a school pal working part-time at NEMS passed on a snippet of gossip: Epstein was homosexual. Stories were circulating about liaisons with two Beatles and an altercation at Paul's 21st birthday party in Liverpool when Bob Wooler teased John about his closeness to the Beatles' mentor. Lennon reacted by snotting the Cavern DJ.

Brian's sexuality was none of my business, or anyone else's, but during the Sixties homophobia was a badge of honour flaunted by males unsure which way they themselves swung. As the English essayist William Hazlitt pointed out: "Violent antipathies are always suspicious and betray a secret affinity." In more extreme examples, these distressed individuals would seek salvation by working over "queers" or "arse bandits", a fact of which Epstein was only too aware, having suffered at least one queer-bashing in his youth.

Brought up with an open mind, I felt no qualms about associating with homos or heteros and would sometimes drink in the Magic Clock, a pub off Queens Square noted for three singularities: its walls and ceiling were festooned with cuckoo clocks; its clientele was a sociable blend of straights and gays, including actors from the Royal Court Theatre across the road and certain masters from Alsop; and its playlist of background music always showcased the latest hits.

Disparaged by the afflicted as the Shirt-Lifters' Arms, this tavern was far-famed among mariners, notably Cunard's cabin staff whose homosexuality helped them gain employment because habitually they were favoured with two attributes: they maintained superior standards of cleanliness and hygiene, and they never harassed female passengers.

One evening I was having a jar in the Clock with Rob, my teen companion on Phil Taylor's guided tour of Anfield. Having enlisted in the Merchant Navy, he introduced me to Dave, a Welsh seafaring pal who within minutes felt compelled to unburden himself, speaking despondently about his homosexuality. Consumed with self-hate, he'd allowed himself to be physically abused during voyages and rolled up a shirt sleeve to expose half-a-dozen cigarette burns on his arm.

"Stub a fag out," he urged. "I don't care. I'm going to kill myself, after my mother's died."

"Why?" I asked. "Your sexuality isn't your fault. It's the way you've been born."

I mentioned Jean Genet, the French playwright who during his youth despised himself because of his gay inclinations. Once he'd surrendered to what came naturally – "I'm homosexual ... how and why are idle questions. It's a little like wanting to know why my eyes are green" – he defined the love that dare not speak its name as "un don de Dieu", a gift of God.

Dave listened, unmoved, and although we chatted amiably for the remainder of the night, he was clearly in a different hemisphere.

As we left the Clock, Dusty Springfield was on the jukebox, lamenting the fact that she just did not know what to do with herself. My parting words to Dave: "Just accept it."

Never make a Samaritan volunteer, would I?

I didn't see or hear of him again, so I've no idea if he did harm himself. Perhaps he found inner peace, settled down with a partner and is now reading this.

I hope so. But Brian Epstein would have understood his torment.

* * * * * * * * * *

Although the Liverpool sound ruled the world in 1964, London's pop moguls were already looking ahead to "the next big thing". While Epstein artistes such as the Beatles, Searchers, Gerry and the Pacemakers, Cilla Black and Billy J Kramer were still hip in the UK charts, Tin Pan Alley was seeking fresh blood and Sandie Shaw, Millie Small, the Four Pennies, Herman's Hermits, Nashville Teens and Peter and Gordon all reached No 1.

At Christmas, the Beatles notched up their sixth chart-topper, I Feel Fine, but in the New Year Mersey groups didn't enjoy such rude health. Although the Beatles hit the heights with Help! and Day Tripper, no other Liverpool band reached No 1, a feat that was accomplished by new acts like Tom

Jones, the Hollies and Moody Blues, as well as America's Roger Miller, Righteous Brothers, Byrds and Sonny and Cher.

Irresistibly, Liverpool's musical star was on the wane and by 1965's close, the city's long night out was winding down as the Clayton Squares became one of the last Scouse groups to get a studio deal; their single, Come And Get It, failed to register.

Into 1966, and the Beatles continued to reap the benefits of their worldwide popularity, undertaking tours of Germany, Japan and the Philippines, where President Marcos's wife, Imelda, invited them to a palace lunch. Epstein had long enforced a policy that the lads should not attend official functions and conveyed his thanks but no thanks to Mrs Marcos.

She was not amused, treating the rejection as a snub to her, her family and her people. Filipino anger boiled over at Manila airport where a mob manhandled Epstein and the Beatles as they dashed for their plane.

More turmoil awaited them. In an interview with the *London Evening Standard*, John made the observation, based on their universal host of fans, that the band were "more popular than Jesus now". Unnoticed in Britain, this throwaway line was seized upon five months later by US newspapers who splashed it over their front pages. Within days, Bible Belt radio stations blacklisted Beatles songs, bonfires of their LPs and memorabilia were organised and the Ku Klux Klan damned the band as brainwashed communists.

In response to this "holy war", John retracted his statement, apologising for any offence caused, and the lads ignored death threats to complete a slew of stadium concerts in America. It was to be their farewell tour. Performing in front of audiences had lost its sparkle for the foursome. As John admitted later: "We always talk about Hamburg, the Cavern and the dance halls in Liverpool because that was when we were pretty hot musically. We never talk about after that because to us that was when live music stopped existing."

But by February 1966, live shows had been silenced in the Beatles' former home. With Merseyside's music scene losing its impetus, the Cavern had closed in February because of financial problems. Although reopened in July, its halcyon days would never return.

7
1966 And All That

Dreams aren't a matter of chance but a matter of choice. When I dream, I believe I am rehearsing my future.

– David Copperfield

THE radiant summer of '66. Back home in Liverpool after my Poitiers year, I revelled in my break from university, earning a few bob as a labourer on a council housing site in Great Homer Street, where Unit Camus was building 16-storey blocks of flats.

First day in the mess hut, a plumber queried: "Haven't worked for nine months? Been inside?"

Why disabuse him? I laughed his question off, but word about this ex-con must have spread, because my on-site respect rating rocketed.

"Neil, could you …?"

This from the hard-nosed general foreman!

Clocking up all the overtime on offer and saving every penny, I amassed enough cash for my holiday: a cut-price student flight to Barcelona, followed by a month's hitching around Spain.

Through treeless landscapes and blistering heat, I thumbed my way into deepest Castille where a lorry dropped me off at remote crossroads, miles from my destination of Avila, fields of yellow straw extending to the horizon, not a sliver of shade, not a vehicle or soul to be seen.

Standing there in khaki shorts, canvas Army-surplus shirt and desert wellies, I removed my sticky rucksack and contemplated the mirage shimmering down the road, pools of sweat from the baking earth. Out of this watery haze, figures emerged, a dozen men on tiny donkeys who trotted in my direction, laughing as they looked forward to their siesta.

Drawing closer, they fell silent and stared at me, an alien abandoned in the midday sun, until one broke the ice, inquiring where I came from.

"England," I replied.

Second question, without hesitating: "Leeberrpole?"

Not London, Birmingham, Glasgow. Liverpool. The first place in England coming to his mind.

When I answered "Sí", he eyed me as if I'd landed from Outer Space, before click-clicking his donkey on its homeward path.

In the UK, my city's brilliance might have faded but, for this peasant, the Beatles' birthplace still shone bright. Perhaps he was an avid reader of Allen Ginsberg's poetry, recalling his pronouncement on a visit to Merseyside the previous year: "Liverpool is at the present moment the centre of the consciousness of the human universe."

That moment might have lasted in a Sierra Guadarrama backwater but, one week later in Sevilla, a gipsy was more conscious of my pecuniary potential than my Beatles associations. Near the Giralda cathedral, he rushed up, agitated, sweating profusely, begging for help.

His grandmother was terminally ill. In hospital. In Granada.

Intake of breath. Had to get there before she died. No money for a train.

Further intake of breath. Kind señor, would you buy my gold ring with three diamonds? Only 20,000 pesetas.

I smelt a rat. But after showing me the hallmark, a lion stamped inside the shank, he proved they were real diamonds by coaxing me into a doorway and using them to etch a line in a glass panel.

This Andalusian rodent smelt markedly more fragrant.

The distraught grandson sweated and sweated, begged and begged, until I haggled him down to 2,000 pesetas, about a tenner. A whacking reduction for him, a lot of dosh for me, but I was convinced the band of gold was worth it. Rather me than some other tourist.

Transaction done, it was mine.

Some 2,000 miles later, after my swing through Spain and a side-trip to Morocco to sample the flawed allure of hitching in that country (discard all preconceptions about East Lancs Road civility – drivers picked you up and, once you were settled inside, demanded, aggressively, substantial sums of dirhams), I flew home for that summer's big football jamboree, the World Cup.

One of my first destinations in the Pool was O'Hare's pawnbrokers on Breck Road to seek an expert valuation of my Spanish ring.

£50? £100? £1,000? I was on tenterhooks. Those diamonds were whoppers!

The manager put his eyeglass in, gave a millisecond's scrutiny to the gipsy gold and tossed it back on the counter. "Not worth tuppence – paste jewellery," he said.

That little rascal in Sevilla had seen me coming! While he was receiving his Oscar at the Latin American movie awards in Madrid, I was reflecting on the theatrical tour de force he'd given to hoodwink me. What a lesson in life, too: honesty is the best policy – but never trust anyone who feels the need to say so.

At least I'd only been conned out of a few quid and it was brill being home. With the World Cup about to kick off, Merseyside was in festive mood, partying in streets and pubs to celebrate an event that had lured fans from across the globe, including many Brazilians. I would be seeing all the matches at Goodison, too, having forked out for a book of tickets.

The Saturday night before Brazil's first fixture, against Bulgaria, I met up with an Alsop pal, Stan Hayton, who had also returned home, after a year in Coimbra and Sevilla as part of his Latin American studies at Liverpool University.

Soon to be married, Stan was winding down his last few weeks of bachelor life, so we went for a couple of jars at the Crown in Lime Street. After that, we ambled to Wood Street, with vague intentions of going in the Beachcomber, a club which the previous Christmas had been the setting for a prank by me.

Recently home from Poitiers, my eye was caught by a pretty girl collecting glasses. When she came close, I went for it, mentioning how tickled I was to be back among gorgeous Liverpool women after my monastic months in France.

The glass-collector informed me she hailed from Chester, that city aglow with good-looking lasses, and was reading chemistry at Liverpool.

Ice broken, sap rising. I plunged in, straight to the chase: "Dance with me."

"Can't – I'm working." She paused. "Anyway he's there."

She nodded towards the far side of the room. There, perusing the dancers, was one of Clubland's best-known bouncers, black as a Nubian slave, bulging with more muscle than Charles Atlas and crowned with Floyd Patterson's handsome countenance.

I thought for an instant. The glass-collector was not about to become the lass of my life but I fancied the challenge.

"If he goes, will you dance?"

She half-nodded.

Before she could change her mind, I ducked into the crowd surrounding the dance floor and squeezed through in a wide arc until I arrived directly behind Mr Nubia.

Now!

Thrusting my head into his left ear, I blurted: "Quick! Fight downstairs!"

Without a sideways glance, the bouncer tore out the room.

Pleased with myself, I pushed smartly back to the Chester cutie who'd observed everything.

"What did you say to him?" she asked.

"Nothing. Let's dance."

Speed was of the essence now.

She placed her tray against the wall and we bopped away to the Supremes' You Can't Hurry Love. O-o-o-o-o-oh yes you can, if one of Merseyside's most fearsome doormen might be hunting you down.

Once our rapid twirl was terminated, my playmate disengaged to collect more glasses. My three-minute fling was over.

Soon after, the bouncer showed up again, face simmering, as if some pissed prat had just spewed all over his immaculate dinner jacket. Any amateur animal behaviourist could discern that his dander was so far up that it was gouging holes in the star-spangled ceiling.

He glared at male faces, straining to finger the prankster.

He hadn't seen me, though, had he? At least I hoped so. Just to be sure, for the rest of the evening I strutted my stuff in unlit corners, in case someone did point me out to the client security operative. But I'd met the challenge; I'd thrown some shapes with the Venus from Deva.

Six months on, here I was with Stan, back outside the Beachcomber after my thumbing expedition around Spain, about to watch the World Cup. The pair of us hesitated, peering into the entrance, pondering what to do. Then our decision was made for us.

"Couple of Brazilians here," the doorman muttered to the cashier.

Freshly tanned after our fry days and sun days in the Iberian Peninsula, the pair of us must have looked Latin.

The doorman – not so much Mr Nubia, more Mr Knotty Ash – gestured. "Come on in, lads," he urged. "No charge." For a pair of impoverished students, an offer we couldn't refuse. We entered.

At the bottom of the stairs leading to the dance floor, we conferred. "Let's carry on with this Brazilian caper," Stan suggested.

"We can talk in Spanish," I agreed. "No one'll know it's not Portuguese. Should be a hoot."

Too true. Every time we asked girls for a dance, we adopted this sham Brazilian accent, explaining we were football fans, Marcos and Luis, come all the way from Rio to Merseyside for the World Cup.

We couldn't go wrong. Not a single knockback. Seemingly every Judy in the place wanted to be with us; some, incredibly, even offered to buy beverages. Never in the memory of man ...

We were spoilt for choice, but what dictates your choice? For any horny lad, the biggest factor in your selection of a lass is her boobs, those succulent orbs of desire which Harrison Marks had been bold enough to bare in pin-up magazines published in Soho Square.

After playing the field for an hour, we copped off with a couple of girls, both big-busted, overflowing handfuls, all of 34BB – on both sides.

We'd found our dancing partners and they figured they'd scooped Vernons pools. Jane and Barbara, both from Gateacre, were soon eating out of our hands, captivated by tales of life in Copacabana with our wealthy families – the beaches, music, carnival, jungle, football.

Seeing as we'd never been within a million miles of South America, we wove some vivid tales. How did we keep our faces straight?

A couple of toe-twinkling jigs and one dance-floor smooch later, the girls implemented a choreographed movement, piloting us deftly to a banquette in a recess. There, before we could gird our loins, they instituted intimate tonsil examinations.

As Barbara's head buried itself deep within Stan's trachea and Jane was on her toes, clambering inside my oesophagus (such innocence!), my sole visible eye locked onto one of Stan's.

I winked. Twice.

This was unreal. Our amorous adventure had become a breeze, all because of superficial tans and fake Latino accents.

By the last bars of the DJ's closing number, Nat King Cole's When I Fall In Love, I'd engaged in some Playtex-fumbling and picked up on a hint of feminine arousal.

Jane was eager to extend our friendship into the wee hours for round 2, perhaps with a night cap in our hotel, the Adelphi?

During a trip to the gents, Stan and I had already prepared for this proposition. Sorry, Jane. Early tomorrow we're going on a coach trip to Chester and we feel very tired. We need to sleep. Undaunted, the girls proffered a phone number and we promised to ring.

Outside in the street, the four of us did our concluding stint of tongue-twizzling before the boys from Brazil hared off to their hotel. More truthfully, our bus stops, Stan for West Derby and me for Breck Road.

What fun we'd had – and oh to be a Brazilian in England every day!

The fact Brazil were playing in Liverpool had Scouse mouths watering; the best football team ever in the home of the world's most successful pop group ever. Before the tournament kicked off, people speculated whether these unrivalled talents might meet. That's what the Beatles desired, going so far as to offer to put on a show for the samba kings. Brazilian officials cold-shouldered their proposal; for a conservative management, the band's long hair and unruly sense of humour represented decadence, nonconformity, a threat to player discipline.

Edson Arantes do Nascimento, alias Pelé, was disconsolate. A Beatles fan, he'd missed out on a private performance that even presidents and prime ministers had never been offered.

Graver disappointment lay in wait for the Black Pearl, whose two goals as a 17-year-old helped bring victory in the 1958 World Cup final. Once Brazil embarked on group games, their opponents' prime objective was to prevent him playing, by fair means or foul. Bulgaria's Zhechev put the boot in first, inflicting so much damage that Pelé missed the next tie, with Hungary.

Although still not fit, he returned for the match with Portugal and was kicked from pillar to goalpost by his man-marker, Morais. In one assault, the fullback, who'd blundered upon the new sport of footbody, tripped the Brazilian cynically, then jumped onto him with both feet as he fell headlong.

Along with every non-Portuguese in the Goodison crowd, I howled my disgust at this despicable double foul. Indisputably, Morais should have been sent off, yet the English referee, George McCabe, turned a blind eye.

Despite the ministrations of Brazil's witch doctor, an Amazonian medicine man who sprinted onto the pitch with pouches of potions and pick-me-ups dangling from his belt, Pelé had to go off, a supernova extinguished by an alehouse team.

As he trudged away, a grey blanket draped over his shoulders to ward off the cold and damp, he was the personification of misery. Could you blame him? His World Cup was over, as it was for Brazil's 10 men, who lost 3-1.

Their supporters' drums and chants of "So mais una! Just one more goal!" had been left unanswered.

On return to South America, Pelé admitted he felt betrayed by referees who failed to protect him from violence, leaving one of his legs so badly maimed it required months of treatment. After three World Cups, he had no enthusiasm for being kicked to smithereens and swore never to play in the tournament again. Nevertheless, time was the ultimate healer. Eventually he would regain his love of international football and achieve more glory with Brazil.

Even though the samba rhythms had been silenced, the World Cup served up an unforgettable quarter-final at Goodison where Portugal trailed North Korea's Diddy Men by 3-0 within 24 minutes. Then Eusébio grabbed the game by its throat, getting four goals in a 5-3 comeback. A match and a star to grace any competition.

England were also progressing. After a Hunt brace disposed of France, they advanced from the group stages to a quarter-final at Wembley, where they overcame Argentina 1-0 once the South Americans' captain Rattin had been sent off for arguing. That set up a semi with Portugal at Goodison.

As Scouse fans were salivating over the prospect, FIFA upset the applecart. Motivated ever so marginally by the extra income that might be generated, the body's organising committee moved the goalposts 200 miles south: they shunted the tie down to Wembley, blithely ignoring fixtures drafted months before.

This ruling affronted Merseysiders waiting patiently to see Alf Ramsey's men. Eager to show how the national side could be backed in one of those rare eventualities when they escaped Wembley's silent, strangling tentacles, Scousers also wished to voice support for the squad's local players – as well as Hunt, there was Callaghan and Byrne alongside Everton's Alan Ball and Ray Wilson.

The sudden switch of venue caused consternation for Portuguese officials whose carefully laid plans revolved around playing at Goodison. Now, on the eve of their country's biggest ever match, the squad was ordered to London.

Eusébio was distraught. "Liverpool had become like my home," he said, convinced that Portugal could get past England there. In his hotel room, he wept.

Worthless tears. For the game's guardians, gate receipts were the bottom line. From a selfish standpoint, too, why should they stomach a horrid journey by ramshackle British Rail to some godforsaken northern outpost of football when they could be chauffeured in Humber Snipes across town to their stadium of choice?

With FIFA pooh-poohing their objections, Portugal caught a train south, while Liverpudlians got West Germany v Soviet Union at Goodison, where a banner in the main stand described the change of venue as an insult to Merseyside. FIFA felt ashamed, I'm quite sure.

During the Sixties, the Soviet Union was very much a closed country, with harsh restrictions on citizens travelling abroad. At a subdued Goodison, I stood near the first Russians I'd seen, a handful of fans waving a large red flag with hammer and sickle in one corner. These few Russkis were outnumbered by thousands of West Germans, who whooped it up as their team won a drab game, 2-1, assisted by death throes on the grass after every tackle to gain free kicks.

Simultaneously at Wembley, England bagged their place in the final by the same scoreline, Bobby Charlton notching a couple and Eusébio converting a late penalty. So we would face West Germany for the world crown.

Every Englishman's match of a lifetime came on Saturday, July 30, 1966, a day my mate Stan could not forget because he got married at midday in St James's, West Derby.

Dressed in my brand-new suit from Alexandre's in Church Street, I was rather gratified that Stan and his to-be had decided against top hats and tails, since formal gear had marred another mate's wedding a few weeks before.

At the reception in Litherland Town Hall, the groom's father was blotto, as he'd every right to be when his only son and heir was fleeing the nest. Suddenly, though, dad was afflicted with an overwhelming compulsion to spend a pound, so he teetered off to the Gents, plonking himself on the carsey in the nick of time.

Joyous relief!

However, being a docker who'd never previously worn a monkey suit from Young's Dress Hire, he'd committed a cardinal error: sitting with his coat tails inside the bowl.

Unaware of this, the hapless chappie got a load off his mind, did himself up beautifully and, fully re-energised, resolved to give his much trailed Fred Astaire demonstration.

An exuberant shriek announced his return to the crowded floor as he whirligigged into the dancers – with the back of his trousers looking like a diarrhoeic dog's dinner.

Some show-stopper. Niftily, the groom hastened to his dad and steered him out of the ballroom. One extra-quick quickstep later, father and lad were back in their nearby Bootle terraced home for a high-speed hose-down.

In all honesty, the bride's parents might have been marginally peeved but the celebrations did resume at full throttle. Everybody knows shit can happen, even in sleepy Litherland.

This misadventure entered local folklore and now, on World Cup day, Stan and his besuited guests were about to enjoy a more auspicious function. Service and photographs completed at the church, a Monte Carlo rally of guests' cars tore downtown for the shindig at the Strand on the Dock Road. Everything had to be wrapped up by 3pm, kickoff time at Wembley.

Stan's uncle gave me a lift and, amidst the grinding of his Morris Minor's gears, he joked that if the West Germans did win, at least we knew that twice this century we'd stuffed them at their national sport.

Inside the hotel, wedding breakfast and speeches were expedited as the TV deadline neared, until with five minutes to go, the best man squeezed the trigger on his starting pistol: "Ladies and gentlemen, you may now go into the lounge."

Immediately he led the sprint – bride, groom, bridesmaids, page boys, guests in hot pursuit – and soon the TV room was jammed as we sat down with the 32 million tuning in all over the UK.

Every newspaper had forecast an England triumph but Haller gave us an early jolt; he slotted home for the Germans in the 13th minute. Soon afterwards, Bobby Moore won a free kick on the left, swivelled his hips and centred for Geoff Hurst to head the equaliser. Next, Hurst shot, the ball rebounded off a defender, Martin Peters pumped it in.

As 90 minutes were almost up, and the cup was within touching distance, a grievous blow. Free kick to West Germany and Weber scrambled it in. 2-2, extra time and another surge in the Strand bar's takings.

During the break before play resumed, Ramsey walked around, instructing his men not to sit on the grass. "Look at the Germans, lying there," he was saying. "They're all knackered. You've beaten them once, now you've got to go and beat them again."

The match recommenced. Alan Ball crossed, Hurst controlled and let fly with a shot against the underside of the bar. The ball squirted straight down …. Had it gone behind the line?

Kenneth Wolstenholme, the BBC's commentator, blurted: "The linesman says No."

The Strand was in turmoil.

On the black and white screen, Gottfried Dienst, the Swiss referee, jogged to Tofik Bakhramov, his Russian linesman, and after a curt consultation pointed to the centre spot.

Goal!

It must have been a good 'un because when Hurst's shot ricocheted down, Hunt was our nearest player to the ball and turned away at once, right arm aloft saluting the goal. If it hadn't been in, Roger would certainly have lammed it home.

This controversy was to have no bearing on the outcome. In the closing seconds, Hurst ran through and toed the ball into the roof of the net, eliciting Wostenholme's epochal words: "Some people are on the pitch. They think it's all over. It is now. It's four."

At the whistle, wedding guests and Wembley crowd combined for "Ee-aye-addio, we've won the cup", the Kop chorus adapted from a Liverpool skipping song, "Ee-ayeaddio, the farmer's in his den". As this echoed across the airwaves, Jules Rimet's trophy was presented to Moore who led his red-shirted team-mates around the pitch.

Barely 18 months before, Bobby had been diagnosed with cancer; now he had captained his side to the World Cup.

From there on, the do in the Strand became memorable, if you could remember it, since everyone got plastered, including the bar staff. At about 10pm, I lurched out, commandeering a cab to take me to the Lake District. Michael Jackson, the Beer Hunter, has written that "no other city can match Liverpool by the square mile in the architecture of alcohol" and every hostelry along my route home bulged with architectural connoisseurs. The length and breadth of the town, from Commutation Row to Kremlin Drive, from Larch Lea to Zig Zag Road, whole streets were going on benders, while someone had already painted "World Cup 66" in white on the front wall of their house in Islington. An early reminder for anyone who might have forgotten what came to pass five hours previously…

Inside the Standard, it was like derby day, Reds and Blues contorted in every nook and cranny, and it took so long to get served you were compelled to remain there until way past closing. But if ever Englishmen had justification for a stay-behind, it was Saturday, July 30, 1966.

A couple of weeks later, in a glittering preamble to the Charity Shield game at Goodison, Ron Yeats carried the League Championship trophy around the ground, flanked by Everton's Brian Labone with the FA Cup and Hunt, Ball and Ray Wilson with the Jules Rimet statuette, the only instance of these three trophies being paraded at the same time.

No one could have foreseen that England's primacy in football symbolised the decade's zenith.

After the Roaring Twenties, Thrifty Thirties, Fighting Forties and Freezing Fifties, the Scouse Sixties had established themselves as the 20th Century's seminal epoch and the city of Liverpool provided their launch pad and backing track.

Terence Stamp believed "England was a good place for a young boy to be in 1966", yet the best spot to be during that decade was my town, the world capital of music. Thanks to the Beatles, Gerry and the Pacemakers and an army of bands, Liverpool plugged into the international grid, powered up as the galaxy's hottest, coolest spot, and electrified millions on every continent.

Wherever they hung out, every teenage devotee of pop craved to be there. Just as North American runaways still head for Seattle or Vancouver, the perceived end of their rainbow, so youngsters across Europe seeking escape from drudgery and despondency dreamt of my city in the Sixties. Some even absconded from their homes in Germany, Greece and elsewhere, reappearing hungry, worn-out but happy on the streets of Merseyside for police to take them into safekeeping.

By a chance of birth, I lived those teenagers' dreams. And if you were raised in Liverpool and came of age during that best of eras, you couldn't help feeling optimistic about your life and your future.

When the lad riding an Eddie Soens bike swopped it for an E-type Jaguar, purely because of a few guitar chords, then anything was possible.

* * * * * * * * * *

Two months after England's World Cup exploit, my girlfriend and I had been to the Bear's Paw for cocktails with Stan and his new bride. Arm in arm with our partners, we were walking along Church Street on our way home when, Crikey! who should be standing at a bus stop but the tonsil twins, Jane and Barbara.

They clocked us and, in unison, their jaws dropped.

Not a word. The pair gawped, baffled by what they were beholding.

Had the Brazilian lads met these Liverpool girls in some club, fallen madly in love and decided to forgo the glamour of Rio for the earthy chemistry of life on the Mersey? Or had a couple of likely lads hoaxed them in the Beachcomber?

Eyes straight ahead, Stan and I walked by, leaving the lasses to wrestle with their mystery.

* * * * * * * * * *

The autumn of 1966, I began my final year at university, just as Liverpool were embarking on their second European Cup campaign. Drawn against Petrolul Ploesti, they won 2-0 at home but went down 3-1 in Romania, a 3-3 aggregate that brought a replay, since the away goals rule had not yet been introduced. In neutral Brussels, the lads prevailed, 2-0.

Next they met Ajax in an Amsterdam fog that cloaked the Olympic Stadium's opposite ends, a pea-souper so thick that at one stage Shanks sauntered onto the pitch to give directions. His intervention failed to stem attacks by the Dutchmen who triumphed 5-1.

Undaunted, our manager quipped: "5-1. That should help make a game of it when they come to Anfield" and "We just can't play these defensive Continental sides", before turning serious to promise: "We're going to batter them in the second leg."

Alas, the Reds didn't batter them enough because young Johan Cruyff notched both the visitors' goals in a 2-2 deadlock in L4. Afterwards, Shanks praised his opponents: "They're some team. They'll win the European Cup, without any doubt."

A prophetic statement. Ajax moved on to conquer Europe in 1971, 1972 and 1973, endorsing the merits of manager Rinus Michels' philosophy of total football, whereby any team member could play in any position; everyone could attack, everyone could defend. His PITS coaching programme, developing personality, intelligence, technique and speed, became the Continent's norm.

After losing to the Amsterdamers, Liverpool finished fifth in the League and gained no compensation from the FA Cup, reaching the fifth round where more than 100,000 fans watched Everton pip them 1-0 in the first British match shown on closed-circuit television. The actual tie at Goodison drew a 64,851 attendance while 40,149 viewed it on four cinema screens at Anfield.

Typically, it was a 100mph collision, bearing out Joe Royle's assessment of these tribal conflicts: "A derby was like 90 minutes of lunacy. It took me about three years to get a kick."

One player who loved these confrontations, though, was Emlyn Hughes, who joined the Reds from Blackpool in February 1967. Later he said: "The greatest day of my life was when Shanks signed me for Liverpool Football Club. I went from being Emlyn Hughes, footballer, to Emlyn Hughes, Liverpool footballer.

"It was a world record transfer fee for a teenager but in the dressing room, there was Roger Hunt, World Cup winner, Gerry Byrne, World Cup winner, Peter Thompson, World Cup winner, Ian Callaghan, World Cup winner, Tommy Lawrence, Scotland's goalkeeper, Ronnie Yeats, Scotland's captain, Ian St John, Scotland's centre-forward. What had I done in the game? Nothing."

Once Emlyn had turned out a couple of times as left-back, Shanks reckoned he was too fit for the position. "I had too much energy as a kid," the new boy said. "I was mad, bonkers. If there was a wall there and the door was there, I'd have made another door there. I'd have gone through that wall because it was quicker."

Shanks pushed Hughes into midfield where his high-energy game earned the nickname Crazy Horse from Kopites, who also adapted Manfred Mann's tune Mighty Quinn into "You'll not see nothing like the mighty Emlyn".

The Reds mightn't have won any trophies in 1966-67 but I did snatch some honours, passing my final exams in June 1967, the summer of flower power when beatniks turned into hippies. Days after I'd made the transition to scion of the University of London, the biggest TV audience in history joined me to watch the Beatles sing All You Need Is Love in the first global satellite programme, Our World. Featuring contributions from several countries, this was devised to unite peoples of the five continents in a goulash of music and documentaries which the BBC dished up in black and white. The Beatles, our Beatles, my Beatles had degenerated from an adoring audience of 800 in the Cavern to 400 million viewers all over the universe.

Meantime, I had been reclassified from student to graduate. Blessed be the Bachelors of Arts for theirs is the kingdom of employment. The realities of working for a living beckoned.

The Board of Trade had offered refuge from a volatile home and they were willing to take me back but I could not see myself spending the rest of my days as a civil servant. I knew what pressed all the right buttons, though. Ever since my first glimpse of the Curly Wee cartoon strip in the paper, I had fancied being a journalist, so I applied to several media organisations, including Granada TV who wrote back that no suitable vacancy existed in their "Currant Affairs Department".

After I'd been raisin my expectations, too…

Despite this brush-off, I knew I had a face that was perfect for newspapers and things did work out because the *Daily Post* and *Echo* group accepted me for their trainee scheme, to my unfailing gratitude. Since my stepfather had passed away during my stay in France, I could reinstal myself in Mum's house in Ullswater Street; regular trips to Anfield and Merseyside's night spots were back on the agenda.

My stint as a cub reporter on the *Echo* introduced me to the extremes of emotion. One of my first jobs was a fatal accident, a schoolboy run over by a bus in Park Road. At the scene, sickly red sand verifying the point of impact, I got the facts from police and then set off on the task I was dreading: the death knock. Our news desk had told me to go to the lad's home, speak to his parents and ask for a photo.

As I pressed the door bell of their terraced house, I felt apprehensive. Here was I, an outsider, intruding on a family who minutes before had lost a loved one. How would they react? How would anyone react? You'd probably go berserk, chase me, and understandably so.

But no. Once the parents heard I was from the *Echo*, they invited me in like an old friend and opened their hearts about their beautiful little lad. If anything, they were glad to unburden themselves to a reporter from the paper they trusted and when I sought the favour of a photo, they found one.

I returned to the office with my story and picture, thinking it was an exercise I did not wish to repeat too often.

As luck would have it, the news editor did not delegate me such alarming tales as "Man battered to death with iron bar during game of poker" or "One-legged man was mentally unbalanced" or "Headless woman in topless bar" but I did get numerous stories with happy endings, like going to tell a reader he'd won Place The Ball, a competition to mark with an X the spot where a football had been airbrushed out of a Liverpool or Everton match photo. Bearing news of this £3,000 bonanza, I felt like a real-life Father Christmas, although when the winner lived in a detached house on Queens Drive, with a Jaguar and Austin 1100 outside – two motors! – he didn't get overexcited. A few thousand quid was no big deal; buckshee Caribbean cruise, that's all.

Daddy Chrimbo got a lot more gratification calling at two-up, two-downs in Garston or Kensington, for whose residents the prize was a windfall that could revolutionise their lives.

Kinnell! That exclamation of Scouse surprise would rend the air, a bottle of Bell's would be rescued from the back-kitchen cupboard and a few oversize measures would glug down this scribbler's craw. And I was getting paid to do this.

As part of my *Echo* induction, I was granted a short-term residency in our Fleet Street office, Mersey House, which brought one fringe benefit: a dalliance with a Soho stripper. Here's how it came about.

On my first Saturday night in London, I went pub-crawling in the West End with a university pal, Bob Adams, and we finished up in a strip club on the corner of Berwick Street. Since it was crowded, we had to sit at the back but were soon down on our marks for the stampede of high-hurdlers, clambering over the theatre stalls to get nearer the stage as other punters vacated their seats. Finally we landed in that gynaeological examiners' delectation, the front row. From there we appraised the innermost charms of the "exotic dancers" until, after several eyefuls, our retinas were taking a jaundiced turn. Should we swop bosoms for burgers in a Wimpy bar?

Before we could come to a decision, the MC announced the next act: "Vivi!"

The curtain opened to reveal a stunner, an Asian lass, about 20, with an hourglass figure. Beautiful. But the second thing to strike me was her girlish smile.

In those days, strippers performed on a circuit of Soho venues, sprinting through the streets in relays to their next curtain call and arriving so bushed that they behaved like robots on stage. Listlessly they would peel off their clothes, minds far away on some sunny Costa Brava beach.

Vivi was different. It was like her opening night. Glowing with a cute innocence, she performed as though she was keen to impress and to entertain.

I was certainly impressed and entertained.

At the end of her act, Bob and I heaved ourselves into the street where I hovered around the club's door.

"I'm going to ask her out," I said.

"Come on," my mate scoffed, striding away.

Hardly had I spoken than my Asian princess hurried out of the club with her holdall.

"Excuse me, Vivi," I began. "Just seen your show ... Must say, you were the best of all the girls."

Vivi flashed a smile and murmured: "Thank you."

Before she could flee, I got down to the nitty-gritty: "May I see you some time?"

Looking vaguely, very vaguely, curious, she smiled again.

At last! That rough-edged charm I'd cultivated with girls in Breck Road bus queues wasn't ending in a slap.

"It's difficult," she replied. "I'm only off one day a week ... Monday ..." She hesitated ... until my job description of ace reporter with the *Liverpool Echo* swayed her. "OK, give me a ring."

There and then, Vivi the stripper told me her phone number, before trotting off to her next show while this stagedoor Johnny sprinted to Bob, monitoring us from up the street.

I needed to write those phone digits down before they got garbled in my effervescent brain.

Bob didn't have a pen but a French tourist did. I scrawled the precious number on my hand.

The following Monday, unable to restrain myself any longer, I rang Vivi and she was home. Surprisingly, she remembered me and, without any coaxing, agreed to meet outside the Berwick Street club on the Sunday at 11pm, when she knocked off work.

Pinching a line from posters for burlesque pageants at the Pivvy, Liverpool's Pavilion Theatre, "Strip, strip, hooray!"

To my amazement, Vivi didn't stand me up. Ten minutes after the appointed hour, she came out, looking ravishing, and greeted me with another heart-melting smile.

Since she was feeling peckish, she suggested going for a curry in Chinatown where her life story came out as we grazed on our suppers: childhood in Sri Lanka, qualification as a nurse, move to a hospital in London, struggle to survive on her salary. Offered more money to be a Bunny Girl in Park Lane's Playboy Club, she took it, sharing the company of the rich and famous.

Offered even more money to be a Soho striptease artiste, she took that and was now sharing the company of an Old Alsopian in the Won Tong restaurant.

We were really hitting it off, too. At the end of our meal, I offered to drive her home in my precious, first-ever motor, a Ford Anglia van.

"I'll get a taxi," she said. "It's a long way."

I insisted, and it was a long way ... to Croydon.

There she invited me inside her flat, poured me a Grouse whisky and put on some relaxing music.

Johnny Bach's Air on the G String? Not quite. A soothing sitar lulled me while she disappeared for a shower, returning in a purple and gold sari that set off her olive skin perfectly.

I won't make your toes curl with an in-depth account of the rest of our night. For that, you'll have to get on the waiting list for the digitally remastered classic DVD from Blockbuster's adult section. Let's just say Vivi knew all the Tantric moves, techniques never envisaged in a million years in the Lake District's back jiggers or Standard's public bar.

With her tender guidance, for hour after hour I swam ... and swam ... and swam into the open arms of an Indian Ocean of love and next morning I exited her flat like a zombie, utterly drained.

Twice more we met for Scotch, sitars and zombification and the final time she revealed she'd been offered a job in Pigalle's Crazy Horse Saloon for shedloads of dosh.

As an afterthought, she also mentioned she'd been summonsed to appear at Lewes Crown Court on a charge of appearing in a lewd display.

A lewd display!

Holy Buddha! This butter-wouldn't-melt-in-her-mouth innocent had turned into the woman of my fantasies.

Next time I phoned Croydon, no reply; after several more calls, the line had gone dead.

While my Tantric therapist was bewitching France's bourgeoisie with her cherubic smile and bouncing boobs, my night classes in the rudiments of her Eastern art were over. But everyone should draw inspiration from this short-lived fling: never underestimate yourself.

If a lad from Ullswater Street, driving an Anglia van (£130, good heater and roof rack, no radio), can pull a stripper, then anyone can. Just ask the character in the Ferrari Dino parked down Berwick Street, studying Vivi as she clambered into my Ford 105E. Must've wondered what the hell she was doing with a plonker like me. A Kopite, mate. What more'd you want?

Not long after the conclusion of my initiation into Sri Lankan hanky-panky, I returned to the *Echo*'s Liverpool office as a major story with Merseyside ramifications broke: Brian Epstein was found dead in bed at his Belgravia home, leaving the Beatles inconsolable. "If anyone was the fifth Beatle, it was Brian," said a grieving Paul.

Unknown to nearly everyone, Eppy had been seeking to disengage from pop, approaching Robert Stigwood, the impresario of Grease and Hair renown, to see if he would buy 51 per cent of his NEMS company.

At the age of 32, Brian wanted out of management. As the Beatles cautioned, money can't buy you love, and a solitary existence had been sapping Epstein's spirit. In a revealing interview with *Melody Maker,* he was asked: "What is the thing you fear most in life?" His answer: "Loneliness. I hope I'll never be lonely. Although one inflicts loneliness on oneself, to a certain extent."

A few months later, he was dead.

At the subsequent inquest, the coroner delivered a verdict of accidental drugs overdose after hearing testimony that Brian had taken pharmacological substances, including LSD, Lucy in the Sky with Diamonds, the hallucinogenic that swept you into heaven or hell, as I knew so well.

One Saturday afternoon, in a student experiment, I tried "acid" at the home of Jim, a mate who had got hold of a small phial of the chemical.

He poured it into a glass of water, I sipped it all away.

Sitting on a settee, I waited for the hit.

For 10 minutes, nothing ... until suddenly the living room carpet came alive, the commas of its Paisley pattern leaping out like lunatic pistons. I looked through the window, at a tree. Leaves expanded into dozens of balloons which burst through the glass.

A noise from the kitchen. Jim's wife had arrived home with her shopping.

A stupefying perfume made my head swim; she was taking potatoes out of her bag.

She came into the room and demanded to know what was going on.

You've taken LSD? Bloody fool!

She sat down in an armchair, staring. She was angry, very angry.

But her dress ... look at her dress!

It had dissolved into an SS officer's black uniform, with FIVE jackbooted legs!

I stared at this diabolical vision, real but unreal, trying to make sense of it.

I screwed my eyes shut. "You've had LSD," I told myself. "This isn't happening. You can fight it and stop it, fight it and stop it, fight it and stop it ...."

But my psychedelic nightmare was only just beginning. There were hours and hours to come.

Why didn't Timothy Leary tell it like this? The apostle of acid called on America's youth to turn on, tune in and drop out, but where would it all end for me? Would I dive off the top of a tower block, like others had done, believing they could fly?

Not yet. A fresh terror awaited. All four walls of the room began moving ... inwards. They were sliding together. I was being crushed.

"Get me out!"

Jim bundled me into the hall, where he buttoned me up in my overcoat, and the pair of us stepped through the front door into a downpour. Clasping my arm, he shepherded me down the street, into another, and another, and another, and another, an endless walk through teeming rain, a search for sanity as we trod miles of pavement while I fought the lysergic acid diethylamide eating into my brain.

A thousand times I must have repeated, "You've had LSD. This isn't happening", until by evening, after five hours' walking, the chemical began wearing off.

Jim guided me, soaked and exhausted, onto a bus and somehow I contrived to navigate to Ullswater Street.

When I walked into our place, Mum was on the settee, watching telly. I slumped down beside her, my head in ferment. If I went to bed and fell asleep, would I find myself back in the heart of darkness?

I had to confess.

"Mum, I took LSD at Jim's."

"Why?"

Silence.

Mum reached across and took my hand.

I peered at our hands, hers holding mine. I glanced at her face.

Tears were glistening on her cheeks.

How could you? As if she hadn't been through enough …

You selfish, thoughtless bastard.

Racked by guilt, I hauled myself off to bed where, thank God, I wasn't plagued by any more demons.

Next morning, having survived my blackest nightmare, I made a vow: I would not allow anything – or anybody – to torment me again.

So this bad trip terminated my dabble with dark, satanic thrills; from then on, I never went near LSD, or any other mind-blowing narcotic.

* * * * * * * * * *

For 1967-68's campaign, Shanks strengthened his squad with Tony Hateley and Ray Clemence, and our season opened well, five wins in eight games. Then the unthinkable happened to me.

After an hour's shuffle up and down Kemlyn Road before the derby, the Kop gates were closed, leaving myself and hundreds more outside and 54,000 inside.

I tramped back to Ullswater where I listened to radio reports and constantly went out in our backyard to join a column of carefree flies dancing the polka in the warm air. Perhaps they were getting in the mood for a Liverpool triumph.

By listening to Anfield, the roars, groans and silences in the distance, I could gauge how the action was panning out and it sounded an even encounter. What I didn't hear was an outpouring of noise for a goal.

Twenty minutes from the end, I legged it back to Walton Breck Road; the threequarter-time gate was open at the Kop end, enabling fans to leave early and myself to gain entry for free. Minutes after I'd wriggled into the back of the terrace, Kopites chanted "Part-time supporters" at the first Kemlyn Roaders opting to leave for an early bus.

They should have stayed in their seats. As I stood on tiptoes to see over heads, Hunt whipped the ball into the net. We'd won.

Our master marksman grabbed more goals in the Inter-Cities Fairs Cup, where the Reds romped past Malmo and Munich 1860 (an 8-0 pasting on our turf) but then came a cropper 1-0 home and away to Ferencvaros, who had the distinction of being the first Continental side to win at Anfield.

After knocking out Bournemouth and Walsall in the FA Cup, Tottenham were our next opponents, a tie that brought my first chance as a trainee journalist to write a story relating to football.

In March 1968, the Reds drew at White Hart Lane and were scheduled to replay the following week. Having queued hours for a pair of tickets, one fan from Princes Park placed them in a cupboard for safekeeping, only for his five-year-old daughter to fish them out and slice them up with scissors. So he rang the *Echo*, for advice and our newsdesk arranged for him to go to Anfield with his kiddie to receive replacements. I was given the story.

At the ground, Peter Robinson, Liverpool's secretary, exchanged the shredded paper for new tickets while I compiled quotes and notes and an *Echo* snapper took photos. That evening the paper published my report – the oik from Ullswater had arrived and, boy, was Mum made up. Me writing about our club.

The tickets were worth replacing because the lads did get past Spurs, only to lose to West Brom in the quarter-finals, while on the League front, a dearth of goals consigned us to third place. Greater glories were on hold.

The following season, our newsdesk allocated me another football job when the South American champions visited Anfield. Before Estudiantes de la Plata went to Old Trafford for the first leg of the Intercontinental cup final, they watched us playing Manchester United and, since I had a smattering of Spanish, the sports editor enlisted me to translate for *Daily Post* reporter Jack Rowe.

With St John and Alun Evans, England's first £100,000 teenage signing, on their marks, the Reds strolled to a 2-0 win, and the Buenos Aires team were in awe of the Kop. In the Main Stand, Jack got me to put questions to Estudiantes' coach, Osvaldo Zubeldia, who enthused: "Our fans aren't so passionate as yours – they don't sing like here." His opinion of Kopites: "Maravilloso, marvellous."

Then I accompanied Jack to the boardroom where Shanks came in to answer the media's questions.

My hero! I'd never been this close to him. And that voice, although sometimes I had to listen intently to twig what he was saying. You couldn't ignore him, though; his Ayrshire accent gripped your scrotum with talons of steel. No wonder my legs felt like jelly.

The muscularity of his speech and force of personality dominated the hack pack, just as they ruled players like Alec Lindsay. After switching from Bury, the fullback described his initial impression of his new boss: "He frightened me to death. It wasn't what he said, it was the way he looked at you. He'd growl."

Now, as Shanks growled his shafts of enlightenment in the boardroom, Peter Robinson intervened to say a representative of Anderlecht was on hand and would like a word. In his deeply guttural voice, Shanks rasped: "Aaaaay, aaaaay. Dizzy spake Aynglish?"

Our manager was ushered away, leaving me to pity the Belgian, who probably spoke textbook Oxford English, scratching his head to translate Merseyside's modern-day Rabbie Burns.

This assignment in 68-69's season constituted my first and last residency in Anfield's press box. I didn't fit in there. Watching us score goals brought the constraints of a lone away supporter in the home end – embedded in a cohort of journos, shouting their copy down the phone above the noise, you couldn't let yourself go.

The Kop was my rightful place. Forget the comforts of an eyrie in the Main Stand, give me the mateyness of Walton Breck's terrace.

From my spec there, I saw the Reds losing on the toss of a coin in the Fairs Cup after an aggregate 3-3 with Athletic Bilbao, while Leicester proved our bogey team again in the FA Cup. Despite these exits from the knockout competitions, Liverpool could not capitalise on their lack of fixture congestion in the League, finishing runners-up to Leeds.

The Tykes sewed up their title with a 0-0 stalemate at Anfield, Kopites lauding them with chants of "Champions! Champions!" In gratitude, Don Revie sent a telegram to the club, stating: "We nominate you as sportsmen of the century."

The 1969-70 campaign brought early reverses; Second Division Watford notched up a 1-0 victory in the FA Cup at Vicarage Road, while Manchester City knocked us out of the League Cup, 3-2 at their place. Despite stuffing Dundalk 14-0 on aggregate in the Fairs competition, the lads also came to grief on the newly-introduced away goal rule, after a 3-3 deadlock with Vitória Setúbal from Portugal.

Although Liverpool entered broadcasting annals in November when they saw off West Ham 2-0 at Anfield in the League, Match of the Day's first game in colour, their fifth-place finish signalled lack of consistency. Shanks now had enough proof that his great Sixties side required overhauling; he had to create his second squad of champions, since the old icons could not go on for ever.

While St John and Yeats's careers in L4 were winding down, our knight in shining armour, Sir Roger Hunt, had already ridden off into Lancashire's hinterland to join Bolton.

After Alf Ramsey was made a Sir, the Kop conferred the same accolade on Roger, not just because of his World Cup deeds but also in tribute to his flawless disciplinary record and expertise as a striker; he totalled 286 goals between 1959 and 1969, a club record, and his 41 in Division Two in 1961-62 remains Liverpool's best for a season. On his return from Bolton for a testimonial, a 55,000 crowd roared its appreciation for one of Anfield's most loyal servants.

As a wind of change blew through L4's corridors, the closing sentences of the Beatles' lengthy chapter in cultural history were being written. Beneath overcast skies, they performed their last gig together, on the roof of Apple's offices in Savile Row. The Four Lads Who Shook The World were on the verge of splitting up. Once John married Yoko Ono and Paul got hitched with Linda Eastman, countless teenagers felt forsaken and the band's terminal dissolution came in 1970 when they went off to pursue individual interests. As the four followed their separate paths, Swinging London was laid to rest.

The Sixties, the century's sweetest decade, had run its course, leaving its legacy for this lad: I would be able to tell my grandchildren that, once upon a time, the Beatles performed for me in the Cavern while I nibbled my butties.

* * * * * * * * * *

Having bid farewell to Hunt, St John and Yeats, Shanks set about reinvigorating his squad for 1970-71 with recruits who showed guts and determination, spurning one player who had "a heart the size of a caraway seed". John Toshack, Larry Lloyd and Ray Clemence, left-footed but right-handed, were signed up, along with Steve Heighway and Brian Hall. Both graduates, one tall, the other short, Kopologists dubbed them Big Bamber and Little Bamber after Bamber Gascoigne, question-master on TV's University Challenge.

While a student at Liverpool University, Hall spent his summer vacation working as a bus conductor and training between shifts at Melwood where he turned up one day in uniform, ready for work. Spotting this diminutive figure in his Corporation Transport outfit, Yeats quipped: "Looks like we've signed Jimmy Clitheroe." But the lad collecting fares was also going to amass trophies.

Shanks was building a team to garner more silverware, with the Fairs Cup tipped to be first of many as the lads marched through to its quarter-finals.

There they met Bayern Munich, backbone of the German national side. Even though Bavaria's Reds boasted maestros like Gerd Muller and Franz Beckenbauer, who wore leather ski boots during boyhood to refine his ball skills, they were no match for the Mersey Reds at Anfield. An Evans hat-trick sank them and the Munich return ended 1-1.

In the semi, Liverpool were drawn against Leeds and after Revie's men grabbed a 1-0 win in the first leg, they shut up shop at Elland Road to thwart our European ambitions.

Now the FA Cup offered some solace for L4's men, who were drawn against League champions Everton in the semi. Second-half goals from

Evans and Hall cancelled out an early Blues effort, putting Liverpool in the final.

"Sickness wouldn't have kept me away from this one," Shanks said. "If I'd been dead, I'd have had them bring the casket to the ground, prop it up in the stands and cut a hole in the lid."

Our opponents at Wembley were Arsenal in an encounter forgettable for 90 minutes but thrilling in extra time. On a stifling hot day, Heighway ran himself into the ground, taking on defenders with his arms held out like a matador flourishing a cape at a bull.

After normal time, he opened the scoring and the Gooners' keeper, Bob Wilson, made a point-blank block of a Hall shot to keep his side in the game. However, once Eddie Kelly equalised, Charlie George was given space to fire home the winner from outside the box. Already crowned League champions, Arsenal had done the double.

One factor in their victory was their shirts. With the pitchside temperature a stamina-sapping 100 degrees, they wore short sleeves, whereas the Reds chose long ones, unsuited to the muggy conditions. So bare arms helped the Londoners get their hands on the cup.

Yet Hughes believed our lads had come of age. "We were all babies," he said, "but we grew up as men that day."

8
That Scarf Is Somebody's Life

It may be those who do most, dream most.
– Stephen Leacock

WATCHING Liverpool's Wembley defeat in May 1971 was the club's newest recruit, Joseph Kevin Keegan, who had joined from Scunthorpe United a few days before the final in a £35,000 transfer deal Shanks termed "robbery with violence".

Although Keegan had quit school at 15 and taken a job at a brassworks in Doncaster for £4 a week, he was determined to become a footballer. A trial at Coventry brought an early setback – he was "too small" – but a scout spotted him in a pub team and Fourth Division Scunny placed the 17-year-old on their books.

Three years later, after Liverpool received encouraging reports on the Iron's budding star, Shanks made his move. A meeting was arranged at which the Reds' manager told Keegan they wanted him. Then he threw down his trump card: "We're going to offer you £45 a week. We think that's very fair."

Keegan was underwhelmed. "I was hoping for more," he said. "I'm on £35 at Scunthorpe, when I play." In truth, it was £25, but Shanks upped his figure to £50 and the deal was done.

Initially the Anfield hierarchy regarded Keegan as one for the future but during five weeks of training before 1971-72's campaign, it became obvious he was good enough for the first team and on his Anfield debut against Nottingham Forest he scored at the Kop end after 12 minutes.

Shanks had decided that although KK wasn't the most gifted youngster, his determination and enthusiasm could be honed into an exceptional talent, with one priority to reinforce his physique through weight-training and dinners of steak and milk. After a few months, the lad had turned into a solid muscleman. In his sturdy 5ft 8in frame, he became the team's pocket dynamo, giving his all for the cause and epitomising that Scouse adage, Little man, big heart.

Keegan soon learnt the manager wasn't interested in the opposition, their strengths, weaknesses, tactics and strategy; his sole concerns were *his* team and what *they* could do. KK recalled: "Shanks used to say football was a simple game complicated by coaches."

The boss also employed an unorthodox technique to encourage anyone who had a tear or pull that prevented him turning out.

"He wouldn't speak to you," said Clemence. "It was like putting a bell round your neck and walking round Melwood. His philosophy was that if he made injured players feel like lepers, then they'd be back quicker."

This indifference to the ailing must have struck a chord with John Lambie north of the border. After being informed a striker had concussion and didn't know who he was, the Partick Thistle boss looked on the bright side.

"Great," he said. "Tell him he's Pelé and get him back on."

Shanks would have warmed to that. For him, good players always kept fit and, if they were indisposed, they had let the club down. Scorn rather than sympathy was what they merited, summed up in one remark: "That bastard Callaghan's injured."

* * * * * * * * * *

Even though Keegan established himself in the team, the first half of 1971-72 brought knockouts in the Cup Winners' and FA cups and a mid-table position in the League. The New Year heralded a revival; the Reds went on a roll, 15 games without defeat, and vied for the Championship with Derby County and Leeds.

On the season's closing day, Derby led by one point, having completed all their fixtures, whereas postponements meant Liverpool had one match left, away to Arsenal on a Wednesday night, while Leeds were visiting Wolves. If Leeds lost and we won, we would be champions. Highbury would be no walkover but our relentless charge up the table left Kopites feeling the dominoes could fall in our favour.

By this stage, I'd quit the *Echo* to join the *Daily Express* in Manchester as a sub-editor ("You're the sub-editor?" Mum asked proudly. "No, there are dozens," I enlightened her about these roomfuls of journalists hired to edit reporters' copy.)

Another change of scene: recently married, I'd migrated from Ullswater Street to a new home in Standish, 20 miles from Liverpool, so for our title-decider with Arsenal I took the train to Euston from my nearest station, Wigan.

Despite being given wrong directions to the ground by a couple of wide boys in Holloway Road (Ha, funny ha), I did arrive at Highbury minutes before kick-off, joining the Scouse army who'd journeyed south from Merseyside.

The game developed into a cagey, goalless stalemate but during the second half trannies crackled into life with news that Leeds were trailing 2-1. The silver was within our grasp. Liverpool besieged the Gooners' goal and in the very last minute, the Reds got their reward; Toshack toed the ball into the onion bag.

The travelling support went through the roof. The title was ours.

No! The linesman had raised his flag. The goal was disallowed.

Offside. Gutted.

When the whistle pierced the air seconds later, Brian Clough's Derby County, sunning themselves on a beach in Mallorca, were champions.

My journey back to Wigan was sombre, in a carriage devoid of Liverpudlians. No one to discuss the game with, no one to share your despair. If only that goal had stood ...

Shanks's squad needed more time to gel, as well as recruits to spice up competition for places. His next signing was Peter Cormack, who joined from Forest, although another target rebuffed his advances. Shanks wasn't bothered. "I only wanted him for the reserves," he said of Celtic's Lou Macari.

He had great expectations of his Keegan-Toshack spearhead and, the following season, 1972-73, those hopes were realised as Liverpool entered uncharted territory in Europe. After overcoming Eintracht Frankfurt, AEK Athens and Dynamo Berlin in the UEFA Cup, they saw off Dynamo Dresden 2-0 at Anfield and then faced a daunting trip behind the Iron Curtain for the second leg.

Once the team got off the coach at their hotel in East Germany, they were greeted by hundreds of Dynamo fans, chanting "Dresden, Dresden" and hurling abuse. Shanks could not disregard this hostile reception.

Without regard for his own safety, he marched straight into the crowd and launched a charm offensive, chatting, pressing the flesh, doling out LFC badges, smiling and laughing. Soon the Germans were won over and once he rejoined watching British reporters, he confided: "They're good people."

The game had a good ending, too: 1-0 for the Reds.

In the semi-final, a Heighway away goal eliminated holders Tottenham Hotspur, 2-2, putting Liverpool into the two-leg final with Borussia Mönchengladbach, who could call on 11 internationals, including Bertie Vogts, Gunter Netzer and Jupp Heynckes.

The first match took place at Anfield in rain so torrential that the referee abandoned play after 30 minutes, rescheduling it for the next day. This delay allowed Shanks to make a decisive change. During the half-hour of action, he noted the Germans' defence was vulnerable in the air, so he substituted Toshack for Hall in the replay. The big fella's flick-ons enabled Keegan to score twice in the first half while Lloyd headed home from a corner after the break.

The match drawing to a close, BMG were offered the lifeline of an away goal when they were awarded a penalty. Now Clemence showed the importance of doing your homework. A couple of weeks before, he had studied Heynckes's spot kicks and observed that he repeatedly shot to the right. When the German ran up, Clem dived to the right, and saved.

That handiwork was to prove vital because in the second leg the Reds were engulfed in wave after wave of Gladbach attacks, orchestrated by their coach, Hennes Weisweiler, who had formulated the ground-breaking concept of "pressing", utilising players' technical pace to possess not just the ball but also space on the pitch. Capitalising on this tactic in Dusseldorf's Rheinstadion, Heynckes netted twice in the first half to set up a frantic second 45 minutes, Liverpool's backs to the wall as they protected their 3-2 aggregate lead.

The lads stood firm. While the Reds' first European trophy was being presented, Kopites sang, "Come and behold them, they're the Kings of Europe", and Shanks said afterwards: "People on the Continent are beginning to get frightened of Liverpool. Gunter Netzer told me so tonight."

League sides also had good cause to fear the Reds. During their campaign, they set a record for consecutive home wins in the First Division, 21: the last nine fixtures of 7172 and the first 12 of 72-73.

Anfield had become a fortress where Shanks could nurture his new team of legends. At its defensive core, Yeats had been replaced by the commanding Lloyd, the first player to use TV film to contest a sending-off. On the opening day of 72-73, he got a red card but an FA disciplinary committee quashed it after viewing the evidence.

From then on, the Reds virtually monopolised the League's top spot and a few weeks after a new Main Stand opened in March 1973, they clinched their eighth championship, outplaying title rivals Leeds, 2-0. The only English club to have won a European and domestic trophy in one season, they finished three points clear of Arsenal, with Leeds third.

At full-time of the last game, against Leicester, Shanks walked to the Kop to receive their adulation. As he approached the ecstatic terrace, a Liverpool scarf was thrown towards him, landing behind the goal and for some reason a policeman kicked it away.

Shanks gave him a filthy look. "What're you doing?" he demanded. "That scarf is somebody's life." Picking it up, he wrapped it around his neck. That scarf was his life, too.

For Match of the Day audiences, the season's most riveting encounter had been at Anfield where Birmingham led by two goals twice. A Lindsay brace and Cormack peach made it 3-3 until Keegan flicked on to Toshack to score the winner.

For Kopites, however, the tastiest fare was our 2-0 defeat of Everton at Goodison. In the last 10 minutes, Hughes clouted in both goals at the Bullens Road end where the Red men were massed, and tore around like a headless chicken, arms waving in the air.

"We were ready to explode," said Emlyn. "We had great players, great team spirit, a great stadium and a manager who was the best ever. Liverpool were the fittest team of their generation. Nobody outplayed us, outran us, outbattled us."

Shanks's great team, mark II, owed a lot to the partnership of Keegan and Toshack, whose synergy on the pitch was judged so unnatural that an experiment was carried out on TV to check if they did have extra-sensory perception. The two sat back to back and KK held up cards with different symbols and colours, which Toshack had to guess. He got nearly all of them right. Uncanny.

Not really. As Tosh disclosed later, what viewers did not know was he could see the cards reflected in the camera lens directed at his face.

Keegan might not have had a telepathic influence on his sidekick but he did have an effect on me. Since moving to Standish, I'd indulged myself by buying an MGB sports car, Madge, which I loved driving cross-country after a match, accelerating past slower vehicles, decelerating, then surging in front of the next motor. Subconsciously, I was mimicking KK's playing style – slow dribble towards a defender, sudden injection of pace, followed by another slowdown.

So Kevin turned into my driving instructor, demonstrating how to get the maximum satisfaction from Madge, although Standish's bobby did not consider her up to the Road Traffic Act standard. One morning I came out to find a Greater Manchester Police notice of intended prosecution under the wiper, requiring me to attend the station in High Street and listing five offences, from contravention of waiting regulations to unnecessary obstruction.

All these had been crossed out but the issuing constable had written in a supplementary misdemeanour: "Criminal neglect – badly needs washing."

You're a card, Jim.

My solitary trips from Standish in Madge had been favoured with an ideal journey's end: the Reds were champions again, and I had a killer weapon for the good-natured banter battle with compositors and printers in the *Express* office. Always primed for a concerted ambush if Liverpool lost, United fans among them could steel themselves for an ear-bashing from this Scouser, a settling of the record that would animate our postproduction wind-downs in Slack Alice's or the Portland Lodge.

The 1973-74 season had an emotional opening when Stoke came to Anfield. After being blinded in one eye in a car crash, Gordon Banks, the Potters' goalie, had been forced to retire from active service and assume a coaching role. On the pitch before the game, Shanks made a presentation to the tearful England great as Kopites regaled him with You'll Never Walk Alone. Then a Heighway corker grabbed the points.

All League fixtures had to be rescheduled, though, when a three-day week was imposed on industry by the Conservative Prime Minister, Ted Heath, because of a miners' strike. To save electricity, floodlit matches were cancelled, extra games taking place on Sunday afternoons. During this disrupted campaign, Liverpool could not overhaul the pacesetters, Leeds, who deservedly took the title; the Reds were runners-up.

In the European Cup, we were knocked out by stylish Red Star Belgrade, 2-1 winners home and away. After that, the lads' only prospect of a trophy lay in the FA Cup where they vanquished Bobby Robson's Ipswich 2-0 at Anfield, Hall grabbing the first from a slide-rule Callaghan pass, and Keegan wrapping it up with a simple tap-in.

In the semi, after nullifying Leicester 0-0 at Old Trafford, the replay took place at Villa Park, where the ball hit Hall during a goalmouth mêlée, rebounding into the Foxes' net.

Our second was no fluke. Toshack lobbed the ball to the edge of the box and Keegan zinged in a delicious dipping volley. Socks around ankles to avoid cramp, Tosh netted a third, to make the score 3-1. Liverpool were back at Headquarters. Their opponents: Newcastle United.

The Magpies had reached Wembley with Malcolm Macdonald in the career-best form. Two years before, on his St James' Park debut, he'd got a hat-trick in a 4-3 win over the Reds and during the weeks leading up to the final, he blustered about what he was going to do, even casting aspersions on the abilities of Hughes and Smith. That fired up the pair. Emlyn recalled: "We didn't have pace, we couldn't jump, he was too quick, he was too strong, and that was just meat and drink for us."

What a banquet awaited Kopites. Before kick-off, the BBC interviewed both teams as they lined up on the pitch, beginning with Newcastle and their manager, Joe Harvey, who was plainly nervous. As the camera swivelled onto Shanks, he blurted out: "Jesus Christ! Joe Harvey is beaten already and the bloody game hasn't started."

Emlyn reckoned this was a deliberate ploy to rattle the Mags and the remark might have preyed on their minds because Liverpool dominated every phase of play. First, Hall ducked under a cross to allow it to reach Keegan who half-volleyed home. Shanks used to tell KK: "Just go out, son, and drop a few hand grenades all over the place." Now the hitman had set off the first Red bomb.

Next, Heighway went on a diagonal run in the penalty area and larruped a reverse ball beyond Newcastle keeper McFaul into the net. Shanks turned to ecstatic Scousers with his right hand in the air, index finger extended. The lads, and their manager, were No 1.

Once the game resumed, he stood with arms out, conducting the team on the field, his hands wafting from side to side to signal mobility for players who he wanted to sweep from defence into attack and vice versa. Pass and move was the directive.

The lads obliged with a sumptuous display of skill that ended with the ball in the bag.

Lindsay to Keegan, just outside Newcastle's 18 yard box. Cross-field ball from Keegan to right wing, where Smith lazily laid it off with the outside of his right foot to Hall. Hall passed back to Smith who had hared into space by the corner flag. Smith hit the ball to Heighway, who provided a wall pass back to Smith. Smith crossed low and hard into the goalmouth to Keegan who stretched a foot out and pinged the ball home from two yards out.

The move went: Lindsay-Keegan-Smith-Hall-Smith-Heighway-Smith-Keegan-goal!

As the Red Army gave full voice to YNWA, the BBC's David Coleman observed: "Newcastle were undressed, they were stripped naked."

The score stuck at 3-0 in a one-sided game that signified Supermac's uppance had come. Emlyn said later: "I did feel sorry for Malcolm Macdonald because he never had a kick of the ball, but Newcastle never touched the ball in the 90 minutes."

"Liverpool, Pride of England", as one banner styled them, had been ruthless; they knew what they had to do and had fixated on doing it. "A hell of a lot of football is about psychology," Keegan explained. "The six inches between a player's ears can be the most important part of his body."

Back home with the cup, Shanks told thousands packed outside St George's Hall: "Since I've come here to Liverpool, I've drummed into my players they're privileged to play for you. If they didn't believe me then, they do now. I've drummed into them they must be loyal, they must never cheat the public."

They hadn't cheated at Wembley and now their boss had been installed in Anfield's pantheon. Not only had Shanks rescued the club from its Second Division morass but he had also borne out his statement that "Liverpool Football Club exists to win trophies", leading them to three League titles, two FA Cups and one UEFA Cup.

After the victory over United, two fans prostrated themselves before him on Wembley's grass, kissing his shoes. In jest, he asked if they could polish them while they were down there.

This instinctive act of homage showed the adulation lavished on Shanks.

To Kopites, he had become the God-King you could touch.

9
28,000 Heads

Hope is a waking dream.

– Aristotle

A BLOOD-SOAKED hill in Africa and the most famous terrace in any stadium in the world.

The site of a British military defeat and the football stand that has witnessed a unique series of triumphs.

Natal's "acre of massacre" and the end of a ground acclaimed for its fervour, humour, singing and never-say-die spirit.

These two spots on the face of the globe might be 100 years and 6,000 miles apart, by train, troopship and hard marching for soldiers who sacrificed their lives under a scorching southern sun, but they are linked by a name that galvanises every Liverpool fan and arouses awe everywhere.

Spion Kop.

Two words that speak volumes about Scouse courage and Liverpool Football Club's glorious history.

Spion Kop.

Say it with pride, say it with humility.

For a battleground gave its name to part of a football ground, perpetuating the heroism displayed by Liverpudlians and Lancastrians during the Boer War in South Africa.

This conflict over land and rights broke out in 1899 when British settlers were attacked by descendants of Dutch colonists who invaded Natal and the Cape Colony and besieged Ladysmith, Mafeking and Kimberley. With urgent appeals being made for reinforcements, thousands of Scousers joined the Imperial Volunteers, departing from Lime Street station on the long journey south to take up arms for Queen and country in the Dark Continent.

On arrival at the battlefront in Natal, they learnt their commander, General Sir Redvers Buller VC, was not having a good war. While Napoleon chose generals he thought would be lucky, fortune had chosen to turn its back on Buller, his attempt to relieve Ladysmith's 12,000 British troops failing disastrously when he could not get his army across the Tugela river at

Colenso. One detachment which marched out of Buller's base at Frere was led into a loop of the river where Boer sharpshooters lay in wait, virtually surrounding Tommies who not only lacked good maps but also dependable intelligence. The upshot was heavy losses among the British ranks as they were ordered into an abattoir to die.

Sir Redvers persisted in trying to make a bridgehead north of the river but suffered so many setbacks that troops mocked "Sir Reverse". But his most ignominious fiasco, in the war's bloodiest battle, was to occur at Spion Kop, a bare, 1,450-foot-high plateau of rock called Spioenkop by the Boers, Spy or Lookout Hill in English. The enemy were well dug into this, as well as neighbouring Goenkop, Twin Peaks and Conical Hill, which blocked the way to the beleaguered enclave of Ladysmith.

Army scouting parties had reconnoitred the area, mapping out a route around Spion Kop to avoid a full frontal assault up its steep slopes but Buller, big cheese of the Zulu Wars, knew better. Blinded by those twin tyrants of arrogance and complacency, he determined this table of land should be taken because of the vantage ground it provided.

From the comfy canvas chair in his capacious tent, sipping Lapsong Souchong out of an Aynsley china cup, he conceived a pleasing strategy: go straight up and over the Kop.

For overall mission command, Buller turned to General Sir Charles Warren, a Royal Engineer with scant experience of battle who had recently arrived in Africa. Worryingly, Buller, who was infamous for his short temper and hasty antagonisms, did not rate the chap and this inept choice of commander hinted at a disaster in the making.

On January 23, 1900, at dead of night, 1,700 men, many of them Liverpudlians from the 2nd Lancashire Fusiliers, 2nd Royal Lancasters and 1st South Lancashires, crept up the plateau's flank and charged its summit. Taken off guard, the Boers fled under cover of a blanket of cloud, leaving the victors to dig trenches to defend their exposed positions, a task far more difficult than they could have imagined. The ground, which sloped away, was rocky, so they struggled to dig hollows deep enough to protect a man lying full length. In reality, they were digging their own graves.

As day broke and the sun banished the gloom, Liverpudlians and Lancastrians were horrified to see that not only did Boers occupy hills overlooking the plateau but they were also holding a ridge at Spion Kop's far end.

"At last the mist lifted," a war correspondent wrote. "The curtain rose upon the performance of a tragedy." Once visibility became crystal-clear, the Boers opened up, turning the Kop into a hill of horror.

Private Matthew Kelly recorded the battle's onset: "About 7am the sun breaks through the clouds and we see a long grassy ridge about 1,000 yards in front but commanding our ridge. About 8am the Boers open a terrific fire from every place except our extreme rear. We take the best cover we can get. Captain Birch gets shot in the head just above the eye. The fire is terrible, ever so much heavier than what I had seen before or since."

Prone in their shallow trenches, the British were caught on the horns of a deadly dilemma: they had to return fire or face being overrun. But when they raised their heads over the low parapets to take aim, the Boers opened up with Mauser rifles.

There was worse, though. Along one part of the summit rim, the enemy line was barely 30 yards from ours, enabling a signaller to direct salvoes from Boer artillery hidden behind the hills, to devastating effect. With shells slamming into the Kop at the rate of 10 a minute, screams from soldiers with horrific injuries rent the air, while others gave up their lives with a muted groan.

Acts of heroism were legion. As a company officer, Captain Muriel, was giving a cigarette to a injured comrade, he was shot through the cheek. He continued directing his men and, minutes later, a bullet passed through his temple. One Scouser, wounded three times, carried on firing and when the British lines were under pressure, a cry went up from the trenches, "No retreat, no retreat".

A Boer commander urged an isolated group of South Lancashires to lay down their arms. "When I surrender, it will be my dead body!" Colour-Sergeant Nolan shouted back.

Now the African sun was burning into the Brits, "rooineks", or rednecks, in Boer slang because of the savage blisters on their white skin. With temperatures rising and enemy bombardment taking its toll, Major General Sir Edward Woodgate used a heliograph to signal to Buller that the position was indefensible and his men were thirsting for water.

His last plea was: "Help us."

Soon after, while he was giving orders, a bullet hit him in the forehead and he died instantly, whereupon another officer, Earl De La Warre, asked: "Why are we here? Why have we come up this murderous mountain to be shot down?"

By this juncture, Warren, safely observing the battle from camp two miles away, should have climbed the hill to assess operations. He declined to do so.

Now no one on the Kop knew who was in charge. As the situation deteriorated by the minute, a soldier viewed the battle theatre: "The most awful scene of carnage. Men blown to atoms, joints torn asunder, headless bodies, trunks of bodies. Awful, awful."

At 2.30pm, Colonel Alexander Thorneycroft assumed command and sent a message to Warren: "We are badly in need of water. There are many killed and wounded. If you really want to make a certainty of the hill for the night, you must send more infantry and attack enemy's guns."

At long last, Buller saw sense and ordered reinforcements onto the Kop. One of them, Private Packer of the Middlesex Regiment, recollected: "It was a very high mountain. It must have took us nearly an hour to get up there. Some places were sheer rock – we had to pull one another up. We came under fire and one officer wanted us to charge the Boers. We all got up to charge and he went down with five or six bullets in him. So that stopped the charge."

Crouched on the summit rim, the Boers were also sustaining losses and feared they were losing. As some fled, running down the back of the Kop, the battle could have gone either way, but at nightfall an order was given for British forces to retreat. Thorneycroft sent a final message to Warren: "Regret to report that I have been obliged to abandon Spion Kop as the position has become untenable. I have withdrawn the troops in regular order and will come to report as soon as possible."

Demoralised and dead on their feet, Liverpudlians and Lancastrians hobbled down the hill by moonlight, leaving their casualties because of a lack of able-bodied men to carry them. On their descent, they met Winston Churchill, a 26-year-old war correspondent with the *Morning Post* who had chosen to see the combat at first hand. He remembered: "I found Colonel Thorneycroft surrounded by remnants of the regiment who had fought for him like lions and followed him like dogs."

The young reporter was bearing an order from Warren for the commander to hold his ground but Thorneycroft was drained. "I have done all I can and I am not going back," he vowed. Churchill went on: "I will describe the scene as I saw it from below. I shall always have it in my memory – that acre of massacre, that complete shambles, at the top of a rich green gully, with cool granite walls (a way fit to lead to Heaven), which reached up the western flank of the mountain.

"To me, it seemed our men were all in a small square patch. The Boers had three guns playing like hoses upon our men. It was a triangular fire and our men on the Kop had no gun. Men must have felt they had lived a long life under that fire by the end of the day."

Churchill's account wasn't tabloid sensationalism, given that in such a small area the British death toll numbered 332 and the wounded 563, with 163 taken prisoner. A further 642, many shellshocked, stumbled down to safety. Since the Boers had the sense to concentrate on fighting an artillery battle, their casualties were light, only 68 dead and 150 wounded.

The morning after our troops pulled out, the enemy retook possession of the hill and found a red carpet of mangled corpses straddling the summit, some of which they looted for belts, boots and socks. One witness of this plundering was Mahatma Gandhi, a young lawyer working as a volunteer stretcher-bearer for an Indian medical unit that treated British wounded.

Even Boers were moved by the slaughter. Surveying the dead, one conceded: "We wouldn't have stayed and fought like the British did in such hopeless conditions", and a surgeon attending to the maimed and mutilated agreed: "We Boers would not, could not, suffer like that."

The Spion Kop disaster was an object lesson in three consistent failings of the British campaign in South Africa: wretched leadership, bad communications and limited reconnaissance. Churchill had no hesitation in allotting blame, denouncing the officers' "astounding inefficiency". Now the penny dropped. Buller bowed to the inevitable and changed his obtuse tactics of full frontal assault, launching an onslaught on the Boers' eastern flank that compelled them to give ground until Ladysmith was relieved.

Back on Merseyside, the eventual success of this "excellent major, mediocre colonel, abysmal general" provided scant amends for families who, day after day, had been reading lists of the dead in newspapers. They would not forget the shambolic events and in 1906, Ernest Edwards, the *Echo's* sports editor, suggested a fitting way to remember their lost ones.

That summer, Scottish architect Archibald Leitch redesigned Anfield, with a grandstand beneath a barrel roof, paddocks on all sides and a lofty terrace behind the Walton Breck goal. Compounded of soil from the footings and cinders from a gas works, this uncovered slope would hold 20,000 spectators on steps made from wooden railway sleepers.

Once Walton Breck's embankment was finished, Ernest Edwards put forward his suggestion for its name. In the daily column he wrote using the nom-de-plume Bee, he proposed it should be called Spion Kop, the idea coming at a game in which the swaying crowd behind the goal recalled an account of the battle: "They ran forward, bending their bodies into a curve, as men do when they run under heavy fire; they looked like a cornfield with a heavy wind sweeping over it."

Since Liverpool had just become League champions for the second time, chairman John Houlding and his directors agreed to mark their feat by sending players on holiday to Paris and adopting Edwards's proposal. So an *Echo* journalist helped commemorate the battle at Anfield, bequeathing a place of remembrance for fallen heroes. Although other stadia adopted the Kop for their principal standing area behind one goal, Merseyside's blood ties with South Africa ensured Anfield became the site of football's most renowned terrace.

In 1928, two decades after the ground's wholesale redevelopment, Kopites were given a sturdy umbrella to keep them dry, a roof over their embankment which was the biggest single-span structure at any English stadium – 80ft high, 425ft wide and 135ft deep. Beneath this, 28,000 could stand on 100 concrete steps, most of them protected from the elements. The record attendance was set in 1952 when 61,905 sweated gallons during an FA Cup tie with Wolverhampton Wanderers, a total never exceeded, not just because of alterations such as seating but also because supporters in the Fifties were smaller and leaner. With people's frames getting statistically bigger over the decades, it became physically impossible to squeeze that number in again.

Toddling into the Boys' Pen for the first time during the late Fifties, I never foresaw what happiness I would find at Anfield and throughout the Scouse Sixties, the Spion Kop, that hellish hill for Scouse volunteers in South Africa, became paradise for me and thousands more.

To get into this Elysian field, I used various entrances, depending on the length of queues. Alongside the Albert pub in Walton Breck Road, turnstiles at the Kop's base opened onto a broad staircase, rising into the sky like a Mayan pyramid. Running up these was a test of your calf muscles but the exertion brought reward at the top where a balcony afforded a citywide panorama, ranks of terraced houses dwarfed by the Anglican cathedral and its Catholic counterpart, Paddy's Wigwam, sometimes referred to as the Metropolitan Cathedral of St Patrick, with the Welsh Hills on the horizon.

Other gates could be found at the corner of Walton Breck and Kemlyn roads. Through these, three routes fanned out: turn left to the bottom of the Mayan staircase; straight ahead up steps to a walkway that extended across the whole width of the Kop, splitting it into upper and lower sections; or go right into a corridor that led past a tea bar into the lower terrace.

Since it afforded a definitive vista of the Kop, this tea-bar corridor route was my preference.

Beyond char-garglers and crisp-crunchers, you arrived at a sloping platform that jutted into the embankment from its right-hand corner, with steps down to the pitchside walkway.

From this concrete ramp, first-timers were stopped in their tracks by a side-on view of the vast terrace, so intimidating you couldn't take your eyes away.

Tilting upwards, far, far into the distance, lay a hill of 28,000 heads, 28,000 heads that behaved like sand, sliding and eddying and forming rivulets that flowed down the slope like a wind-brushed dune on Formby beach. But these grains of sand were roaring, singing and clapping. A vision of man at his most mesmeric.

Apart from being a vantage point for the whole Kop, this ramp also permitted latecomers to spot pals. Blokes would rush in and stand, scanning the heads until waving arms and shrill whistles indicated where mates stood.

A thumbs-up and the dilatory would dive into the sea of bodies and swim unseen up the incline, always resurfacing alongside their muckers, even though the Kop was as solid as the pawnbroker's on Christmas Eve.

Newcomers conjectured how Kopites could navigate through this molten multitude and when I chanced upon a French coffee-table book about the days of sail, it offered a revealing insight into the Scouse sense of direction. Its author recorded that during the 19th Century crews from the imperial city of Liverpool became the most sought-after in Europe because of their prowess rounding Cape Horn. For these acknowledged champions of the Southern Ocean, the Continent's nobility and wealthy would gladly pay a high premium to ensure safe passage as far as America's Pacific coast.

So if your forebears could plot a course through those treacherous waters, bringing a three-master into Valparaiso or San Francisco with all hands on board, then it was no great shakes for modern-day Liverpudlians to heave themselves through 80 yards of terracing to their mates, even after a skinful of Bent's bitter.

Appropriately, our seafaring heritage was commemorated at the side of the Kop, on the Walton Breck-Kemlyn corner, by the club's flagpole, a towering tree trunk which was the top mast of one of the earliest iron ships, the Great Eastern. Designed by Brunel in 1860, the vessel ended its days in a Mersey breaker's yard in 1888, gifting its splendid mast to Anfield.

The irony of linking up with pals on a chock-full Kop was that once the action started, you could soon be separated, dragged in different directions by the ebb and flow of humanity. Fight as you might, it was impossible to thwart the crowd's grip, so you could even lift up your feet and be carried around the steps, without touching the ground.

Just as a tiring swimmer should never resist a strong current but go with the flow whilst seeking to move to its edge, similarly you bowed to the Kop's turbulence, allowing it to take you wherever. This meant that when we played Inter Milan, I began with five mates but never saw them again until I landed back in the Standard afterwards.

Above all, the trap to avoid was getting stuck behind a barrier, your stomach cleaved by the bar. At every goal, Kopites would avalanche and the tonnage threatened to split your body in two, even bending pennies in your pockets. The only escape was to wait until the rib-crushing compression slackened, creating a breathing space that allowed you to squirm under the barrier and out the other side where conditions might be bearable.

In worst-case scenarios, Kopites would lift winded fans out of the squash and manhandle them over their heads, letting them tumble like discarded rag dolls down the slope to St John Ambulance volunteers on the touchline. Generally, they would recover within minutes and could enjoy the goalmouth action from the front of the Kop. Some even feigned illness to get this good spec.

At one match, the scrunch was so disagreeable that a supporter, brave or foolhardy, escaped by climbing up onto the framework of steel supporting the roof and stepped gingerly along the girders to a spot above the goal. There he sat on a beam, legs dangling 70 feet over the crowd. From his roosting place, he watched the whole 90 minutes, while he smoked fags and applauded Liverpool attacks. As I shuffled out at the end, the spiderman was edging back warily to safety, empty concrete steps waiting to break his fall. The roof was being abandoned to its resident pigeons once again.

In the terrace's centre, the most pressing threat of interruption to any match was a distended bladder, because the gents was a 10-minute round trip away. Needs must; sometimes you had to relieve yourself amid the throng, a desperate measure that explained why my first sight of Niagara evoked Anfield. "When I saw this, I felt at home," my postcards of the falls disclosed. "Reminded me of the Kop steps at halftime."

Fortunately, fans about to burst could avail themselves of one unlikely accessory, "using their Echie", an *Echo* newspaper rolled into a tube through which the spate might be funnelled straight down to reduce splashing.

Another Kop peculiarity was its microclimate. When packed, a human hot-plate switched on, giving off several degrees of extra warmth that goalies, defenders and touchline photographers could feel on their backs.

Rainy days brought another climatic abnormality, fog. After queuing hours for big matches like our Cup Winners' tie with Celtic, spectators would be soaked but, once compacted on the terrace, they would dry out. As wet clothes gave off steam, a low-level cloud drifted onto the pitch, compelling you to watch through mist.

The Kop's most noticeable feature, however, was the sheer volume of its noise. Standing in the middle, it was impossible to gauge how loud the support was but you knew the tidal wave of intimidation unsettled opposing players and their supporters in the Annie Road end, like a university mate who came to watch Blackburn Rovers. After his maiden visit to Anfield, he told me he had to avert his eyes on kick-off, peering down at his feet because the Kopites' roar felt so menacing.

Such ferocious encouragement was said to be worth a goal lead and Shanks believed the crowd served as a 12th man for his team. "When we're attacking the Kop, the fans suck the ball into the net," he said. "And when the opposition attack, an invisible force heads the ball out of the Kop net."

Down at Wembley in the cup final with Newcastle, our vocal support and invisible force had helped drive Liverpool on to glory. Now, though, Shanks was to leave Kopites speechless.

10
Paisley, The Champion Manager

Don't be pushed by your problems, be led by your dreams.

– Anonymous

BEFORE the 74-75 season kicked off, Shanks addressed his troops on the first day of training. "Thanks for last year," he said. "Championship medals are in a box there. Now forget it. We start at the bottom again."

But he was preparing to pull a bombshell out of another box.

On Friday, July 12, a press conference was called to introduce Ray Kennedy, signed from Arsenal for a whopping £180,000. Then Shanks casually announced he was retiring at the age of 60.

"It's a family decision," he said, leaving reporters stunned and the club's president, Tom Williams, in tears. "It was the most difficult thing when I went to tell the chairman. It was like walking to the electric chair. That's the way it felt."

Several times previously Shanks had threatened to pack the job in but Bob Paisley and Joe Fagan had dissuaded him. Now, after 15 years at Anfield, his conclusion was irreversible. He was feeling tired, ready for a rest, keen to spend more time with his wife Nessie.

For Kopites, his resignation represented a bolt from the blue and some went into denial, refusing to believe it. This genius who was also your best mate had transformed our club into one of Europe's top sides. How could he be replaced?

Shanks's last fixture in charge was the Charity Shield with League champions Leeds United, led out by new boss Brian Clough, since Don Revie had got the England job. The game was notable on three counts: the first Charity Shield clash at Wembley; the first on TV; and the first in which red cards were flourished, a useful innovation as this usually staid preamble to the season produced fireworks.

With the score 1-1, Bremner gave Keegan a sly dig in the face; KK retaliated, delivering a straight right to the Scot's jaw that John Conteh would have admired. More fisticuffs ensued and the pair were sent off.

Days before, in a case of mistaken identity, Kevin had been given his marching orders in a friendly in Germany. Now red-carded again, he was incensed, removing his shirt and hurling it away as he marched off to the dressing room. Succumbing to the urge to imitate, Bremner ripped his jersey off as well.

The score remained 1-1 until the 90 minutes were up, after which the Reds won 6-5 on penalties. The Shield belonged to Liverpool and Shanks, who basked in the result all the more, having poked fun at opinionated Clough: "He's worse than the rain in Manchester. At least God stops that occasionally."

Once the victory parade around the pitch had been completed to chants of "Shanks, Shanks", this simple man walked off into retirement.

His many qualities always shone through – passion, generosity, compassion, decency, tenacity, humour – but in his autobiography, he stated that he wished to be remembered as "a man who was selfless, who strove and worried so others could share the glory, and who built up a family of people who could hold their heads up high and say, 'We are Liverpool'."

In truth, if Bill had never been manager, you'd have found him standing on the Kop, among "the most knowledgeable crowd in the world, and also the fairest". When his side lost, he ached like any Kopite did and purged his anguish by devoting Saturday night to a deep clean of Nessie's cooker in their three-bedroom semi at 30 Bellefield Avenue, West Derby. Children from the street used to knock on his door, asking him out for a kickabout on the nearby playing field, an invitation that this winner of titles and trophies could not refuse. Many are the tales of how he invited strangers into his home after they got nattering outside and habitually he would leave our Main Stand to hand complimentaries to ticketless fans in the car park. At away games, he even gave money to those who were down to their last penny.

As the team coach neared opposition grounds, he would ask the driver to pull up and order his squad off to meet our supporters. "Never forget these people put money in your pockets and food in your mouths," he used to say.

Most of his acts of kindness went unpublicised. The Kop fanzine, which came out in the Sixties, threw light on one example, brought to its pages by the mother of a girl who was marrying a Kopite. She wrote to the club, asking if Shanks could send greetings to the couple. Next thing, the manager and half his team – St John, Callaghan, Yeats, Byrne, Lawrence, Hateley – arrived at the mum's house in Anfield to convey their best wishes to the incredulous groom and bride. That was the calibre of Shanks.

Because of this genuine affinity, the mutual fondness of manager and fan has never been matched anywhere, never mind surpassed. Shanks and Liverpool were made for each other. "If I had a business and needed a workforce to be successful," he remarked, "I'd take them from Merseyside and we'd wipe the floor with everybody. They've got hearts of gold and they can work.

"All they need is to be handled like human beings, not bullied and pushed around. Merseyside is a distressed area with a lot of unemployment, but they've got a big spirit."

And the player who came closest to his heart for courage? Gerry Byrne for the agony he endured with that broken collarbone during 1965's Cup Final.

A man of the people, for the people, Shanks's dry wit and over-the-top utterances were incomparable, offering an insight into football's most loved folk hero. Here are some examples, just to give you a flavour:

● When he was Carlisle manager, the team traipsed into the dressing room at the break, 2-0 in arrears. The instant Geoff Twentyman came through the door, Shanks tore into him. "What did you pick when they tossed the coin at kick-off?" he demanded to know.

"I called heads," replied the captain.

Bill blew his top.

"God! You NEVER call heads!"

● En route to a fixture at Tranmere, Shanks had to get off Carlisle's coach to seek directions to Prenton Park but a passer-by couldn't help. The manager climbed back on board, shaking his head.

"Can you believe it?" he complained. "Imagine not knowing where the football ground is."

● Tommy Lawton, the England legend of the Thirties and Forties, visited Anfield, giving Shanks an opportunity to introduce him to teenagers on the ground staff.

"This is the greatest centre-forward who ever lived," he told them, listing his skills and scoring feats.

Lengthy eulogy over, Bill turned to his guest and commanded: "Now, Tommy, tell these lads who was the best wing-half you ever saw and why I was."

● Shanks's advice to St John when he signed for Liverpool: "Son, you'll do well here as long as you remember two things, don't over-eat and don't lose your accent."

● Tom Daley, Grimsby's keeper, played in the same reserve team as Shanks during the Fifties and recalled: "We were at home to Scunthorpe Reserves and the ball went into the stands. Shanks went to take the throw-in and started talking to the crowd. He was having a great time taking questions and the referee had to go over and give him a telling-off.

"At the turnaround, Shanks was fuming. 'I was just telling them about the first-team game away last week, trying to get a bit of atmosphere'."

- After Liverpool's squad landed at an airport in Italy, the boss was surrounded by a babble of local hacks, all jabbering away, crying out for answers to convoluted questions. Having listened patiently, Shanks instructed his translator: "Tell them I disagree with everything they're saying."
- About St John: "He's not just the best centre-forward in the British Isles but the only one."
- When one scribbler had the temerity to state the Reds weren't playing as well as they had been, Shanks was ready with his put-down: "You're right. We're struggling at the top of the League."
- To a journalist who criticised Hunt for failing to score enough goals, the manager retorted: "Aye, he might miss a few but he gets in the right place to miss them."
- Disappointed that a youngster who'd had a trial was not being kept on at Melwood, a scout protested: "But he's got football in his blood."

"You may be right," Shanks conceded, "but it hasn't reached his legs yet."

- Bob Paisley, answering a phone call from Germany, passed on this message: "It's Adidas, Bill. They want to know if you'll accept a golden boot for your services to football." The boss agreed: "Aye, tell them I take a size 13."
- In 1970, Liverpool had flown to Hungary to meet Ferencvaros in the Fairs Cup. In the foyer of the team's Budapest hotel, Shanks spotted football writer Horace Yates from the *Liverpool Daily Post* and confronted him.

"Your paper is crap, you write crap," the manager stormed. "Crap, crap, crap. I won't talk to you or your paper ever again. It's total crap."

He continued in this vein for several minutes, refusing to allow Yates to get a word in edgeways, until his torrent of invective was interrupted by a local reporter. Impatient for some quotes as his deadline loomed, he patted Shanks on the shoulder. The boss swivelled round and jumped down the Hungarian's throat: "Bugger off. I'm talking to a friend."

- On learning the hotel in Budapest did not stock the team's preferred refreshment, Coca-Cola, Shanks's temper did not improve. "It's a conspiracy, a war of nerves," he raged.
- Journalist John Keith recounts how one of Liverpool's official party walked into Shanks's hotel room before a game in Eastern Europe to find Shanks on a chair, eyeballing the light fitting.

"I know you're in there, spying on us," he shouted at the light. "Come out, you cowards."

- One teenager, a wisp of a boy, earned plaudits in Anfield's youth squad but the manager thought he should bulk up, arranging a diet of steak and milk à la Keegan for him during the summer. Before the next season began, the youngster came to see Shanks who commended his physical development and stressed the great future he could have.

Once the boss concluded his words of praise, the lad spluttered what he had been dreading to confess: "Mr Shankly, I'd like a week off. I've got a girl in the family way."

Shanks leapt up from his desk and strode out into the corridor. "Bob, Joe, come quick," he bawled. "We've created a bleeding monster!"

● On being told he had never experienced playing in a derby, the boss responded: "Nonsense! I've kicked every ball, headed out every cross. Once I scored a hat-trick – one goal was lucky but the others were great goals."

● After Alan Ball signed for Everton, Shanks rang him to say: "Congratulations, son, on your move. You'll be playing near a great team."

● On hearing a manager was ill: "I know what's wrong – he's got a bad side."

● When asked to choose what he disliked most about football: "The end of the season."

● About a hard-fought 1-1: "The best side drew."

● After thrashing opponents: "We beat them 5-nothing and they were lucky to score nothing."

● To a supporter at Anfield: "Where're you from?" "I'm a Liverpool fan from London." "Well, laddie, what's it like to be in Heaven?"

● Shanks and Tommy Docherty were at a game, watching a player tipped for great things. "100,000 wouldn't buy him," said the Doc. "Aye," said Bill. "And I'm one of the 100,000."

● To the Brussels hotel receptionist who queried his reply of "Anfield" for his home address: "But that's where I live."

● In a South Wales hotel the night before a game, the boss led his squad, coaching staff and directors into the lounge where Coronation Street was engrossing two old ladies. As another channel was showing boxing, Shanks asked politely if the TV could be switched over.

The old dears dug their slipper heels in: Sorry, they wanted to watch Corrie. Unperturbed, Bill's voice of reason settled the disagreement: "I'm a democrat. Hands up all those in this room who want to watch boxing."

● In 1973, the *Daily Express* enlisted computer boffins at Liverpool Polytechnic to program a match between the England team and a side comprising internationals from the Forties and Fifties. Once players' career details had been keyed in, the computer printed out an account of the action, which included the fact that Tom Finney was stretchered off after a Hughes tackle.

The Express carried a report of the game and that morning Shanks stormed into Melwood's dressing room.

Flinging down a copy of the paper, he monstered Emlyn: "If you touch Finney again, son, I'll kick you up the arse."

● In 1968, the boss's reply to a barber who asked "Anything off the top?": "Yes, Everton."

• When Tommy Smith injured his knee, he got Joe Fagan to bandage it and begged him not to breathe a word to anyone. While the Anfield Iron was on the treatment table, however, Shanks walked in and saw there was a problem. Immediately he instructed Smithy to remove the bandage. Tommy refused, saying: "Get lost, it's my knee."

Bill flashed back: "It's not your knee, son. It's Liverpool Football Club's knee."

• During a Monday night fixture at Wolverhampton, Tommy Lawrence suffered a serious muscle tear in his leg, which was no better by the following Friday. Even so, Bob Paisley advised the goalie to tell Shanks he was all right.

To confirm this, Shanks put him through his paces on the pitch. At the end of their session together, Lawrence was called over and asked how he felt. "I'm fit," he replied. The manager went ballistic. "Fit? You're a cripple, a bleeding cripple!"

• Having completed 241 successive League games, Chris Lawler was being treated by medical staff for a bad injury. "There's no way he can play on Saturday," Paisley counselled Shanks. "What!" the boss screamed. "He's a bloody malingerer."

• Peter Thompson recalled: "It was quarter to 3 on match day at Anfield and there was no sign of Shanks. Suddenly he came in. His shirt's torn, tie undone, jacket hanging off, hair all over the place. 'What's happened, boss?' 'I've just been on the Kop with the boys.'

"He'd gone in with 25,000 of them and they'd been lifting him shoulder high, passing him around, and he loved that."

Shanks was back on his beloved terrace in November 1975, after he'd quit as manager. He thrilled thousands of Kopites by walking unannounced into the middle to watch the whole of the game with Coventry. At the end he was lauded with "Shankly is a Kopite" and garlanded with so many scarves you could barely see his head.

• Ray Wilson, who Shanks coached at Huddersfield, said: "When I signed for Everton, I hadn't realised how intense the Liverpool-Everton rivalry was. I'd be talking to Bill as I remembered him at Huddersfield and he'd be telling me it was a disgrace I'd got picked for England. I was the worst fullback ever."

• Ronnie Moran told how Shanks wasn't interested in seminars about tactics; he preferred five-a-sides in which he could take part, and if his lot were losing, play would carry on until they managed at least a draw. The goals were simply poles pushed into the turf, without any crossbar, an omission that led to numerous disputes.

On one occasion, a team-mate of Shanks scored what he regarded as a legitimate goal to make it 2-2 but their opponents maintained the shot was too high to count. The boss turned to the silent knight, Chris Lawler, for his verdict.

"You're honest," he flattered. "Wasn't that a goal?"

"It wasn't," answered Lawler.

"Jesus Christ," Bill fumed. "You don't open your mouth for five years and then when you do, it's a lie!"

● On the subject of tactics, Moran said: "Bill used to lay out two teams on a Subbuteo pitch and growl, 'Now then, this is them and this is us'. Then he'd give a huge grin and sweep the other team on the floor. 'Ach, who the hell cares what they can do? Let's talk about us'."

● About one team talk before a match, Anfield youth coach Tom Saunders said: "Bill began to speak and continued for 15 minutes. Not about football or the opposition. No, boxing was the sole subject for a quarter of an hour." Then, with a brusque "Don't let's waste time – that bloody lot can't play", he sent his team out.

● When Anfield got new dressing rooms, the boss showed a journalist around, pulling a chain to demonstrate how the toilets flushed. "It fills again in 15 seconds," he informed the hack proudly. "A world record."

● After Shanks signed the teenage Emlyn Hughes, they hurried in the manager's car to Lytham St Annes to register his transfer at the FA offices. However, their journey was delayed when the vehicle was involved in a collision that led to a police officer's attendance. As the constable took down Bill's details, Shanks lost his rag. "Don't you know who's in this car?" he demanded. "No, not me."

He pointed at Emlyn: "The future captain of England."

● The boss loved to tell a joke about ageing. "When you're young, you play football," he said. "After that, you move on to cricket. When you're too old for that, you play golf. Now all I can play is marbles. Which proves that as you get older, your balls get smaller."

● A new reporter introduced himself. "Hello, Bill," he said. "I'm Erlend Clouston, of the *Daily Post*." "Aye," said Shanks. "Erlend Clouston? Is that a name or a disease?"

● After Clemence allowed himself to be nutmegged for a goal, he apologised, saying: "Sorry, Boss, I should have kept my legs together."

"Your mother should've kept her legs together," Bill retorted.

● About skinny Phil Thompson: "He's tossed up for legs with a sparrow, and lost."

● To an apprentice: "The trouble with you, lad, is that your brains are all in your head."

● Before a game with the Gooners at Anfield, Shanks timed his dig at Bob Wilson perfectly. As the keeper came within earshot, the Reds' agent provocateur asked a commissionaire: "Are Arsenal at full strength tonight or is Wilson playing?"

● After a goalless draw, the manager pleaded: "What can you do when you're playing against 11 goalposts?"

● About Matt Busby: "He says he's got a bad back. I tell you he's got two bad backs and not much of a midfield either."

● Ever alert to Italian deviousness: "I'm not giving away any secrets like that to Milan. If I had my way, I wouldn't even tell them the kick-off time."

● Asked by a reporter if he'd enjoyed his Christmas, Shanks responded: "Aye, not bad. Four points out of six."

● Don Revie said: "Bill would call me every Sunday morning, eulogising his players. Every one, including the substitute, even if he had not played. To him, every player in that red strip had everything: a right foot, a left foot, tackling, heading and stamina. No player had a weakness. They were each the best player, position for position, in the world. "When I managed to get in a mention of one of my players, he'd just say, 'A fair player, nae bad', leaving me wondering how Leeds ever managed to win a match with no great players, not even good ones, for all that Bill would admit to."

● Arriving to present trophies at a Merseyside amateur boxing club's fight night, Shanks was told by an official: "You're on first, Bill. Three three-minute rounds."

Splat! Shanks landed his KO: "My bouts never last three rounds, son."

● To the mass media flashgunning pictures of him at his retirement announcement: "Hold on a minute, John Wayne hasn't arrived yet."

● After finishing, Shanks hosted a Radio City chat show on which he asked one of his guests, Harold Wilson: "Who do you think was the first Socialist?" Unprepared for such a tricky question, the former Prime Minister hesitated before suggesting Ramsey MacDonald.

Bill disagreed. "No. Jesus Christ, son, Jesus Christ," he corrected.

● At Dixie Dean's funeral, Shanks said: "I know this is a sad occasion but I think Dixie would be amazed to know that even in death he could draw a bigger crowd than Everton on a Saturday afternoon."

Only Shanks could get away with a tribute like that. A master archer who stuffed his quiver with one-liners for the media, his wisecracks answered many a reporter's prayers. Tongue firmly in cheek, he uttered these outrageous gems, as well as some flawless pearls of wisdom:

● "Some people think football is a matter of life and death. I'm very disappointed with that attitude. I can assure you it's much, much more serious than that."

● "There are two great teams on Merseyside, Liverpool and Liverpool Reserves."

- "Me having no education, I had to use my brains."
- "I was the best manager in Britain because I was never devious or cheated anyone. I'd break my wife's legs if I played against her but I'd never cheat her."
- "Tommy Smith could start a riot in a graveyard."
- "If Everton were playing at the bottom of my garden, I'd draw the curtains."
- "Of course I didn't take my wife to see Rochdale as an anniversary present. No, it was her birthday. Would I have got married in the football season? Anyway, it was Rochdale reserves."
- "If a player isn't interfering with play or seeking to gain an advantage, then he should be."
- "Listen, son, you haven't broken your leg. It's all in the mind."
- "We murdered them 0-0."
- "There's Man United and Man City at the bottom of the First Division and they'll take some shifting."
- "Football is a simple game made complicated by people who ought to know better."
- "Football matches are played on football pitches and not in exercise books."
- "Football is a simple game based on the giving and taking of passes, of controlling the ball and of making yourself available to receive a pass. It's terribly simple."
- "If you can't make decisions in life, you're a bloody menace. You'd be better becoming an MP."
- "My life is my work, my work is my life."
- "Paddy Crerand's deceptive – he's slower than you think."
- "I don't drop players, I make changes."
- "It's great grass at Liverpool, professional grass."
- "If brains were gunpowder, he wouldn't have enough to blow his cap off."
- "The difference between Everton and the Queen Mary is Everton carry more passengers."
- "Liverpool was made for me and I was made for Liverpool."
- "George Best is probably a better player than Tom Finney, but then Tom Finney is 50odd now."
- "If it had been a boxing match, it would've been stopped at half-time."
- "The trouble with referees is they know the rules but they don't know the game."
- "A lot of football success is in the mind. You must believe you are the best and then make sure you are."

- "If you're first, you're first. If you're second, you're nothing."
- "Ain't life great, lads? All you need is the green grass and a ball."
- "The only thing in football that surprises me is that people are surprised."
- "At a football club, there is a holy trinity – the players, the manager and the supporters. Directors don't come into it. They are there only to sign the cheque, not to make them out. We'll do that. They just sign them."
- "No one was asked to do more than anyone else ... we were a team. We shared the ball, we shared the game, we shared the worries."
- "The fans here are the greatest in the land. They know the game and they know what they want to see. The people on the Kop make you feel great, yet humble."
- "The Kop's exclusive, an institution, and if you're a member of the Kop, you feel you're a member of a society. You've got thousands of friends around you and they're united and loyal."
- "I came to Liverpool because of the people. They have a fighting spirit with fighting blood in their veins, but mixed with tremendous kindness. They will threaten your life one minute and give you their last penny the next."
- And finally, in his autobiography, Shanks explained his personal philosophy: "I believe the only way to live and be truly successful is by collective effort, with everyone working for each other, everyone helping each other, and everyone having a share of the rewards.

"It's the way I see football and the way I see life."

☀ ☀ ☀ ☀ ☀ ☀ ☀ ☀ ☀

Once Shanks made clear he was set on retiring, the board knew who would replace him – Bob Paisley. Although he had always shunned any limelight, Shanks's right-hand man agreed to step up for one overriding reason: it was best for the club and staff, guaranteeing continuity and avoiding the disruption any outsider might cause.

A more unlikely figure than Paisley to run one of England's premier clubs would be hard to find. In cloth cap, cardigan and slippers, he could have been your favourite uncle, yet he knew how to keep the Anfield machine on track, saying: "I'm only a modest Geordie but get me cornered and I'm a mean bastard."

One early difficulty was Shanks, unable to leave go of the club he adored. Weeks after the Charity Shield, he reportedly put out feelers about getting his job back but the response was negative. Even so, he carried on turning up in his tracksuit at Melwood every morning as though nothing had changed and some players addressed him as boss in front of Paisley.

Shanks's long goodbye needed to be curtailed: something had to be said and one day it was. After that, he ended his visits to the training ground and popped up at Everton's Bellefield and over the water at Tranmere. Having made his decision to quit Anfield, he watched from afar as the new manager built his own dynasty.

The son of a North-East miner, Bob Paisley came to Liverpool in May 1939 from the Bishop Auckland amateur side, only to have his career interrupted by the outbreak of the Second World War that September. Answering the nation's call to arms, he joined the Royal Artillery and spent his war years in Egypt, Sicily and Italy with a unit full of Scousers. That led him to say: "Ninety per cent of the regiment were from Merseyside, so I got to know the Liverpool character. From a psychological point, that was a big asset. I've had a fair time to judge Liverpool people and I think they're tremendous."

Peace proclaimed, he returned to Anfield, winning the League in 1947 and transferring to the coaching staff in 1954. Through hard work and purposeful study, he made steady ascent of the managerial ladder, becoming a member of the Boot Room inner circle, until Shanks's departure gave him the ultimate job.

For the first five weeks of his inaugural 1974-75 season as manager, Paisley coped without Keegan, who was suspended after his Charity Shield spat with Bremner. Despite his absence, Liverpool notched up a record in the Cup Winners' Cup, trouncing Norway's Stromsgodset 11-0 at home as nine players scored; only Hall and Clemence did not get on the sheet. In the next round, however, Ferencvaros knocked us out and our FA and League cup campaigns ended, too.

The League turned into a keenly contested affair, with Liverpool, Everton, Stoke and Derby all on 47 points at the top in April 1975, but County nabbed the Championship pennant. Paisley's first camapign was not without pointers to the future, though, as he made two inspired additions, Northampton's Phil Neal and Terry McDermott from Newcastle.

By virtue of being League runners-up, Liverpool competed in the 1975-76 UEFA Cup, progressing to the semi-final where they became one of a handful of teams to eclipse Barcelona – and Cruyff – in a European tie at the Camp Nou. Toshack grabbed the glory with a goal that silenced 70,000 Catalans and stirred a whirlwind of cushions at the end.

In the Anfield return, Phil Thompson made it 1-1, securing a two-leg final with Bruges and Paisley's chance of a trophy.

By this time, I was making my pilgrimages to Anfield with some Wigan mates, Bill Crawford, Bill McMath and Dave Wakefield, and the four of us travelled there for the home tie.

Technically polished and highly rated on the Continent, Bruges rocked everyone by racing into a 2-0 lead within 12 minutes and then resorted to strongarm tactics to foil the Reds as they strove to rescue the tie. The referee ignored the Belgians' persistent fouling, so a section of the crowd launched into that lament of desperation, "The referee's a wanker".

Next to us on the Kop with her dad was a girl, about 13, who listened to this and then asked him: "What's a wanker?" His answer was curt, silencing any more dialogue: "Tell you later." The felicities of fatherhood.

In the 59th minute, the Reds finally smashed through Bruges's wall. Kennedy hit the bull's-eye and a couple more were added by Case and Keegan, leaving the second leg nicely poised at 3-2.

Driving back to Wigan along the East Lancs, the four of us were ebullient about our prospects over in Belgium but by the M6, our conversation had moved on to other topics. Dave, a traffic cop, mentioned he was driving a new police car on the motorway, a supertuned, three-litre Ford Capri S. "It'll take anything on the road," he said.

"Not necessarily …," I disagreed. "If the other driver knows the road well … He'd have a fighting chance," Dave conceded grudgingly.

Discussion over.

Two days later, 11 in the morning, I drove away from my Standish home in Madge on the commute to Manchester and was leaving the village's 30mph zone in Rectory Lane when I glanced in my rear-view mirror.

Cop that! On my back bumper, in his supertuned Capri, was Dave, grin as wide as Liverpool Bay. He knew what time I went to work and had waited to throw down the gauntlet.

You're on, mate. Tape down your toupee.

The lanes between Standish and Bolton, where the M61 swings down to Manchester, are a driver's delight of serpentine bends, right angles around square fields, a narrow bridge over the Leed-Liverpool canal.

Overtaking calls for a clinical assessment of what lies ahead. In 10 miles, there is one reasonably long straight, but I felt that if I gave it the bifters, Dave would be hard pressed to pass.

I wound up Madge and her rubber legs tore into the tarmac. Through the bends, at 50, 60, 70 miles an hour, we belted, with Dave poking my tail pipe, his face the incarnation of single-mindedness in my mirror.

Thou shalt not pass, I kept saying. Thou shalt not pass!

He didn't. He couldn't.

Until we entered a hedge-lined, left-handed bend leading into the straight.

As I slammed into third gear, Dave seized his moment; he accelerated past – on the wrong side of the road. From his high chair in the Capri, he could see around the curve and check for oncoming traffic.

Swine!

Now he'd nosed ahead, it was nigh impossible to overhaul him but he wasn't going to lose me. Foot to the boards, I overtook cars, lorries, a scooter, to hang onto his bumper until we reached the M61 roundabout, one behind the other.

With a regal wave, Dave sailed off in the direction of Bolton nick while a chastened MG owner swept down the slip road onto the motorway for Manchester.

Smart Alec had won the day, although the good folk of Worthington, Haigh and Aspull must have surmised they'd been chomping on magic mushrooms when they had visions of a sports car chasing a police car.

Our rural chase was a teen romp and, next time we met, Dave didn't breathe a word about it; his thoughts and mine were on the League title. On May 4, the four of us travelled to Molineux to see Liverpool play Wolves in a must-win match if we were to snatch the Championship from Queens Park Rangers, who had completed their fixtures and lay one point ahead, with a better goal average.

Wolves also had to beat us to avoid relegation to the Second Division and their programme summed up the showdown on its cover: "Wolverhampton Wanderers FC proudly present the Final Act of the great First Division drama against Liverpool, the Pride of the Kop. Curtain rises 7.30pm".

Molineux's 48,000 capacity could have been filled twice over as 20,000 Scousers squeezed into the ground for Wolves' "Match of the Century" and the atmosphere was electric. What's that, though? In the mass of Reds behind our end, a banner bore three black letters, one above the other, "QPR".

Rangers fans in the middle of our lot! Gerraway! Take a closer look.

The initial capitals spelt out "Quality from Paisley's Reds".

As BBC cameras were filming this decider, QPR's team had been invited into TV studios near their Loftus Road ground to watch the live coverage and have their elation captured on film – if they won the Championship.

The game began well for the BBC's guests, who whooped as Steve Kindon gave an early lead to Wolves. The Londoners' big star, Stan Bowles, was unable to take any more; he had to leave the building because of the unbearable tension.

At the break, it remained 1-0 and an insipid Liverpool could see their ambitions being dashed, until a climactic turnaround in the second half; Keegan, Toshack and Ray Kennedy all struck gold in the last 14 minutes to make it 3-1.

The Reds were Champions again and Paisley had won his first League title, on "the greatest night of my football life".

History was repeating itself, because in 1947 our manager had earned a Championship medal as a player when Liverpool got the better of Wolves in their last fixture of the season at Molineux. Nearly 30 years on, Scousers were rejoicing once again inside that very ground and no one wanted to leave. Once we did, we'd lost our bearings and couldn't remember where the car was parked. We covered every compass direction until, an hour after full-time, we blundered upon our motor and crawled north up a congested M6. So many Liverpool fans were on the motorway that traffic ground to a halt and lads got out of their vehicles, waving flags and dancing in the fast lane.

Having won his first trophy, Paisley could now get a second, in the away leg of the UEFA final. For this, thousands of Scousers descended on Bruges, Venice of the North and a beer buff's righteous abode where Leffe and Chimay ensure life is irredeemably intoxicating.

The game itself demonstrated Liverpool's growing maturity and confidence on the Continent as Keegan blasted in a free kick from the edge of the box to make it 1-1, clinching the silverware.

In his second season in charge, Paisley had duplicated Shanks's League and UEFA Cup double and had also revealed a way with words befitting the Ayrshire wit.

At the end of a campaign in which a solitary goal at Turf Moor gave victory to the Clarets in an early round of the League Cup, Bob produced this reminder for their manager.

"I remember Jimmy Adamson crowing after Burnley had beaten us that they were in a different league," he said. "At the end of the season, they were."

* * * * * * * * * *

After serving their international apprenticeship in the UEFA competition, Liverpool were bidding for the biggest prize of all in 1976-77, the European Cup, and they made steady progress into the quarter-final. There they were pulled out of the bag with St Etienne, widely regarded as Europe's finest team since outplaying Franz Beckenbauer's Bayern Munich in the final at Hampden the year before. Despite this, the French had lost 1-0 and, spurred by a sense of injustice, were fixated on winning the trophy in the next summit venue, Rome.

For their home leg against the Reds, they produced a secret weapon, a lumbering Argentinian centre-half, Piazza, selected with the express purpose of marking Toshack. "This thing", as Hughes dubbed him, did manage to stifle Tosh by being all over him like a rash and at full-time classy striker Bathenay had given a 1-0 lead to les Verts. Losing by a solitary goal was an excellent result for Liverpool who raised their arms in jubilation as they trudged off the pitch at the Geoffroy Guichard stadium.

The second leg on March 16, 1977 turned into one of Anfield's most memorable European games. When Dave, Bill, Crawfie and myself reached the ground three hours before kick-off, thousands had already mustered outside, regimented lines coiling back and forth, up and down the length of Kemlyn Road. Thousands were shuffling away from the gates in a long loop that curled back again towards the ground before turning away once more from the turnstiles where mounted police blocked latecomers trying to sidle into the head of the queue.

The mood was good-humoured but the closer the turnstile, the deeper your apprehension that a copper would force himself into the entrance and the door would shut because the Kop was full.

My fingers were crossed this wouldn't befall me tonight of all nights. It didn't. Minutes before the gates closed at 6 o'clock, Wigan's flab four clicked through, to join a full house of 55,000 inside.

Arriving on the team coach, David Fairclough said: "There were so many people and such an atmosphere I got this feeling something special was going to happen. When we went out on the pitch before the game, that feeling was reinforced."

The vibes were extraordinary, due in no small measure to 5,000 noisy Stephanois, St Etienne fans, whose iridescent green colours glowed through the Annie Road gloom, and once both teams ran out, Liverpool got their wish; they won the toss, so could attack the Kop in the second half.

A perfect start, too. Within two minutes, the Reds earned a corner which Heighway tapped short to Keegan on the left wing. He dribbled a few yards before lofting what could have been a centre into the goalmouth. Curkovic, the French keeper, flapped his hand – and the ball sailed over his head into the angle of the net.

Annie Road's Red sector underwent a convulsion that would not have disgraced the Kop. Sanity restored, Kopologists proclaimed their linguistic aptitude by adapting St Etienne's chant, "Allez les Verts, Come on you Greens", into "Allez les Rouges, Come on you Reds".

Although the aggregate score remained 1-1 at the interval, I felt the lads would score another at our end to guarantee progress but Bathenay had a different script tucked in his boots.

Six minutes of the second half gone, he surged forward and let fly with a swerving shot from all of 30 yards, beyond Clem's despairing reach. The Stephanois went barmy as Bathenay milked their plaudits.

The Greens were nearly there; because of the away goals rule, the Reds would have to score twice.

Believe! On the hour, Callaghan hoisted the ball into their 18-yard box. With Piazza welded to his back, Tosh turned and laid it off his thigh to Kennedy, who drilled home. 2-2, game on and the Kop cauldron was bubbling. A quarter of an hour to go, Toshack was crocked and replaced by Fairclough. As the clock ticked down, the tie could have gone either way until, with six minutes remaining, the instant came that every Liverpool supporter would cherish.

Using his immaculate left peg, Kennedy flighted a long pass over St Etienne's defence to Fairclough on the halfway line. In one flowing move, the Bionic Carrot let the ball bounce, nudged it with his chest, surged past defender Lopez, and slotted under Curkovic. 3-2!

The Kop was the epicentre of an earthquake that shook distant Shotton.

Arms aloft, Fairclough ran to the terrace. "Ray's pass was so good it invited me to attack," Supersub recalled. "It seemed so quiet as I homed in but the noise after it hit the net was the loudest I've ever heard."

After that, the whole ground gave full throttle to You'll Never Walk Alone. St Etienne were crushed and, once the referee blew, nobody wanted to leave, not even the magnifique Stephanois who applauded both teams off.

Kopites were already warming up for their mass migration to Rome and, to the tune of Que Sera Sera, implored: "Tell me Ma, me Ma, / I don't want no tea, no tea, / I'm going to Italy, / Tell me Ma, me Ma."

As they sang away, the PA announcer revealed Bayern had been knocked out, news we passed on to French lads walking through Stanley Park. They didn't feel quite so bad about losing. When they reached their coach in Priory Road, their adieu was "Win the cup".

In France, that cradle of enlightened thinking, fans upheld a tradition of backing any club that turfed their team out of a competition. Then, if their vanquishers won the silver, they could console themselves with the knowledge they'd lost to the best side, not some minnows who vanished without trace. After our pulsating encounter, the Stephanois took this doctrine a stage farther: they launched a branch of our supporters' club in their elegant city and also renamed the goal terraces in their Geoffroy Guichard ground as les Kops. How gracious can you be in defeat?

The day after the game, I left home in Madge on the drive to Manchester. It was raining steadily but the sun was shining inside my motor.

What a night, last night. Every Kopite knows how it is. When the lads are playing badly, you can't sleep. Then, when they're playing beautifully, you can't drop off, either. Last night, the noise, the tension, the goals, Ginger's winner ... they'd kept me awake hours.

With the action still ricocheting around my head, the journey to the motorway soon passed and I found myself at the crossroads in Aspull village centre.

On the junction's other side, parked on the common at right angles to the road, was a police Range Rover and through rain sluicing down my windscreen, I made out Dave Wakefield at its wheel.

The Capri must be having a decoke.

Dave's head was buried in a book, since he was reading for a law degree.

How could he apply himself to the intricacies of jurisprudence after what we'd been through just hours before?

I drove across the junction and slowed as I passed his parking spot, wiping condensation off the side window with my hand to verify it was Dave.

Yes.

I pulled up, peering back over my left shoulder to catch his eye. He was transfixed, though, by some convoluted case law and refused to look up. Possibly, though, he was nodding off.

I gave a couple of beeps on my horn. Dave raised his head, assessing this unwanted interruption.

I gave a wave. Now, identifying the car, my mate realised who it was.

Putting his book to one side, he switched on his engine and slid sedately out into the road, turning left to glide alongside for a yap.

I wound down my window.

As the bonnet of his motor crawled into view, I screwed my nose up in feigned disgust for the most pathetic pillock in Christendom and began wafting ridiculously lethargic V-signs at him.

The Range Rover stopped next to me.

Dave stared.

Except it wasn't Dave.

It was a bobby I'd never set eyes on.

Aaaargh! Horror of horrors for me, gross disbelief for him.

His face furrowed with incredulity. This just didn't happen on a wet Thursday morning in Aspull.

The driver of a sports car stops, waves to a traffic cop, honks to attract his attention, then gives a load of Harvey Smiths. What on earth …?

But, more relevantly, what on earth was I going to say? Your call, Neil.

Now the copper's expression had altered, ominously. He appeared irritated, verging on cross. In truth, he had a face like thunder.

He moved forward to park directly in front of Madge, where I suspected he was minded to discuss my digital dexterity.

Ages ago, Dave had advised me that, if pulled over by police in the rain, it was always good practice, a gesture of subservience that could earn Brownie points, to get out your vehicle and go to them, rather than the other way around. Now I was going to put this advice into practice – as speedily as I could.

I jumped out into the deluge and, pulling my collar up, dashed to the Range Rover.

"Awfully sorry, officer," I gasped. "Mistook you for Dave Wakefield, my mate."

The officer blew a gasket.

"Bollocks!" he spat. "Do I look like Dave Wakefield?"

I hold my hands up; he didn't. Undeniably that grey hair and lined face made him quite a bit older.

"No, not really, not from nine inches away," I explained. "My window was misted up – couldn't see properly. Sorry!"

Before he could take the questioning any farther, I legged it back to Madge, slipped slickly behind the wheel and took off down the sodden street. Through the wind and rain, I wellied it to Manchester. Phew!

Next day Dave rang to say a senior sergeant had approached him in the canteen at Wigan nick, wanting to know if he had a pal with a white MGB GT, registration number XKB 612J. Dave confirmed this, and the sergeant walked away, without explanation. So the moral is: Get your hand signals right when you're being observed by a traffic cop.

After our epic with ASSE, the Association Sportive St Etienne, the crowd before our next League match against Leeds was like I'd never heard, buzzing, as if Anfield had been converted into a stupendous beehive. Everyone was droning on about our prospects in Europe.

Minutes before kick-off, the bees were stilled when Kopites struck up again with "Allez les Rouges". The Stephanois had left their mark on our collection of chants, voiced again in the semi-final with Zurich which could be placed in the stroll-in-the-park category; we won 3-1 in Switzerland and 3-0 on our patch.

As the Kop had predicted, we would be migrating to our first European Cup final, in Rome, where the skilful Borussia Mönchengladbach awaited.

Meanwhile, Liverpool moved inexorably towards the Twin Towers in the FA Cup, their toughest challenge seemingly a Maine Road semi with Everton. The lads romped home 3-0, to set up a Wembley decider against Manchester United. By our big day out, we'd already won the League title and we performed like true champions against the Old Trafforders, bossing them around in the first half without any reward. After Alan Kennedy hit a post, Stuart Pearson put them ahead briefly, until Jimmy Case equalised through a sublime strike: back to goal, he received the ball on his knee and pivoted to volley in.

A freakish incident handed victory to the opposition; Macari hit a speculative shot that deflected off Jimmy Greenhoff's chest into the onion bag. A soggy goal any Scouser would have welcomed.

United manager Tommy Docherty had said: "I loved going to Anfield even though all you ever got was a cup of tea and a good hiding. You came away a bit wiser." This time he came away from Wembley with the silver.

Liverpool's treble chance of trophies had gone, although now they had bigger fish to fry: the European Cup.

Ever since the lads reached the Rome final, the *Echo*'s classified pages had been bloated with For Sale adverts: TVs, hi-fi systems, guitars, lounge suites, cars, bikes, scooters, anything to raise cash for the trip. Moneylenders also coped with a rush of business, while pawnbrokers were chocker with people hocking a watch or jewellery for journeys by road, rail and plane. Really skint fans set off hitch-hiking a fortnight before the match but my mates and I could afford to travel by train and were thrilled to receive our cardboard tickets, emblazoned with the words "Liverpool Lime Street to Rome and back".

At midday on the Monday before the game, we took one of 11 departures from the station on the first leg of a 1,000-mile journey to Italy, through England, Belgium, Germany and Switzerland.

Our train transported us to Folkestone where we embarked on a Belgian ferry for Ostend. Once up the gangway, we made for the saloon bar, settling down on a bench seat along the bulkhead.

Just as well we'd got there sharpish – the place was soon brimful with fans. Now our Channel crossing had begun, the air of expectancy was tangible. We were well and truly on our way to Rome and everybody appeared in good spirits, mainly shots of duty-free Scotch and vodka.

Our buoyancy was rudely punctured when we realised we were in the presence of thieves.

Eyeing the Red men squashed against the bar, we saw a crime being committed. Three barmen were working up a sweat to satisfy the thirsty mob and while they were haring back and forth, a sneak thief reached over the counter to snatch a carton of 200 cigarettes, which was spirited away to an accomplice lurking behind.

Very smart. You require brains bigger than a bus to do that, don't you?

Here was our team about to play their biggest game ever and this no-mark, in his 30s, face like a smacked arse, was doing his light-fingered bit to help the cause.

What a godsend for tabloid hacks, possibly on hoolie-watch on that very ship, their poisoned pens ready to pour out the vitriol for next day's lead story. "KOP YOBS ROB FERRY" – you could picture the headline splashed over front pages. A fillip for our team when they woke up in Rome next morning and manna for those who thrive on spreading a negative image of Scousers.

"Honda? Toyota? Nissan? Want to build a factory in the North? Take my advice – forget Merseyside. Always nicking stuff. Remember that ferry? What'll they do to your factory?"

And because of such a destructive stereotype, another dagger is thrust into Liverpool's bleeding heart, its unemployment rate is ratcheted up again and generations have to abandon the place of their birth to find work in Manchester and London, Toronto and Sydney.

Yes, Scousers have paid a heavy price for stolen property. Every scally's knock-off T-shirt, can of lager, bottle of whisky and diamond ring has cost us all.

Sadly for this cross-Channel pilferer, two police officers were monitoring his misdemeanour – Dave and Bill, who was also a copper.

After witnessing the theft, they engaged in a brief discourse about powers of arrest in international waters and as they did so, another pack of fags was filched by the thief.

How can you describe such an individual? A man of straw?

No, that's insulting to straw.

One of life's perpetual losers? Definitely.

As Mrs Beeton might have said: "If it was raining soup, he'd have a fork in his hand."

His petty crime showed what a miserable existence he'd led and it was not going to get any better.

My mates were about to flex the long arm of the law. Alpha males in any bunch of blokes, Bill and Dave pushed through to the ciggy snaffler and stood over him, blocking out the light.

Rattled, you could see him thinking: Two – two! – heavies. What's going on?

Then Bill spoke softly: "Police. If you want to see the game, you'd better pay for those fags."

The low-life's face was a comedy picture; he'd suddenly been afflicted with a severe case of strangulated bowel.

"Can't be real," you could imagine him thinking. "Middle of f****** Channel, miles from f****** Merseyside, looking forward to farting, puking and plundering my way across f****** Europe and my first act of f****** larceny has been rumbled by f****** Scouse scuffers. Would you f****** credit it? Evidently f****** not."

In seconds, the chip on this downtrodden laddie's shoulder must have grown into a sack of spuds.

"Right, right ... no grief," he spluttered. There was a brief, over-the-shoulder confab between Dole Model No 1 and Dole Model No 2, who flicked a glance at the force-issue stone faces bearing down on him.

Get a move on!

No 2 fumbled three Benson & Hedges cartons into the arms of No 1, who delved in his pockets for notes and thrust them at a barman.

So you do have some dosh, mate!

No hanging around. He snatched his change and flushed himself into the press of tipplers, as fast as a rat up a drainpipe.

Never again did we see him on the ferry, or during the rest of our journey.

I'd wager this incident was not his last, since he was one of those incorrigible derelicts doomed to be no-hopers because they assume crime is clever.

It's not, and the world's jails, not least Joe Gerks, are bursting at the seams with common thieves, too thick to learn. And having been inside Joe's joint – as a visitor – I can confirm it's a place to be avoided like the plague, fouling you with its all-pervasive odour of sweat, urine, excrement, dysfunctional bodies, decaying flesh and hopelessness.

After this spot of low-key, high-seas drama, our voyage was uneventful until Belgium's coast hove into view. Everyone thronged the rails, watching the port of Ostend come closer, admiring the white hotels along its seafront, and squinting over the roofs towards our far-off destination of Italy.

Soon after disembarking, we entered the dockside station where Belgian Railways had laid on a corridor train. We piled into a compartment with a couple of other Scousers, the guard's whistle lanced through the warm evening and our locomotive was quickly making tracks.

Rome here we come.

While we sped across the Belgian flatlands, night fell and the six of us agreed a sleeping rota in the empty luggage rack, a narrow hammock of trawler netting that allowed us to indulge in snoozes for two hours at a time. Years before hot-desking and hot-bedding, we'd invented hot luggage-racking.

With these periods of rest punctuating the journey, we clanked across the Continent towards our destination, gazing, dozing, eating, chewing the cud. Surprisingly, the final popped up only once in conversation. "I think we're going to win in style," one of our fellow travellers stated as we rolled through the Swiss Alps.

At 8am on Wednesday, Liverpool's day of destiny, our 40-hour trip terminated when our train nudged the buffers in Rome's Tiburtina station. Now we could see the sights.

First though, I had to store my customised Union Jack in a safe place.

Since Dave and Bill were coppers and Crawfie was a solicitor specialising in criminal law and, as a lad, I'd been waved down by a bizzy one evening in Arkles Lane for not having lights on my push bike, I'd decorated the flag's red cross bar with white lettering, "Walton Jail D Block".

A joiner pal had also given me eight bamboo poles that slotted together with Yorkshire copper couplers, like a chimney sweep's brush, to form 12-foot-long rods for insertion in flaps on each side of this banner. For carrying over my shoulder, the whole caboodle of flag and sticks was wrapped in a sling fashioned out of leather straps.

Being the standard-bearer, I'd put quite some effort into this little enterprise, with a self-publicising motive. Inside the Olympic Stadium, that Union Jack would mark the spot where we were standing and families and friends had been primed to watch out for it on TV that evening.

My package deposited securely in Tiburtina's left luggage office, we struck out for the centre of Rome, arriving by chance at a public baths after five minutes' walk. Donaldson Street by the Tiber – molto bene. Two days in a hot, sticky rail compartment were erased by a good scrub in the shower cubicles where we luxuriated in the sudsy removal of 1,000 miles of grime.

We had the place virtually to ourselves. Not for long. By the time we walked out after our ablutions, the bath house was loud with Liverpool voices. Every cubicle was occupied while more Reds queued to gain entry.

Crisply refreshed, we hit the town – our first destination the Colosseum, followed by the Spanish Steps, Trevi Fountain and Pantheon. Next stop the Vatican, to which we caught a bus, full of Liverpudlians singing, "Italy, Italy, we're the finest team in Europe and we're going to Italy".

Sitting opposite me was a comely lass who stood up to get off. She leant over and, with a coquettish smile, whispered: "Tutta Roma per Liverpool, The whole of Rome is for Liverpool".

Very nice. Her remark, too.

At the Holy See, the swarms of coach roaches scuttling into St Peter's on their guided tours could never have anticipated the tableau set before them, a piazza awash with Scousers being snapped with bemused cardinals, priests, nuns and monks. Presumably photos even exist of lads being greeted by the Pope in his private suite because, time and again, Reds have shown they can get where castor oil can't.

Having admired the basilica's beauties, the four of us were growing peckish. Down a side street, we came across a trattoria and wandered in.

It was 5pm – we were the first diners. As we stood in the dim interior, waiting to be seated, there was a simmering atmosphere, distinctly strained. You could sense we'd walked in after a row between the morose maitre d' and the stir-crazy cook glowering through the service hatch, face like Dolomitic thunder.

The saying goes that God sends meat and the Devil sends chefs. Well, for anyone making eye contact, this fiendish cook was itching to dish up his special of the day, a thick knuckle sandwich.

He was not a happy Roman bunny. No, signor.

We were hungry, though, and bided our time. Once the maitre d' had seen fit to show us to our table, calculating that tips from four customers were better than none, we told him a few jokes about psychotic Sicilians and the tension abated palpably.

After making our selections from a menu that featured "delirious meat sauce", preparation of which must have explained the chef's mood swings, he buried his skull in pots and pans and soon we were tucking into pasta perfection.

The flavoursome food, crisp Chianti, companionship of great mates, lingering hint of menace in the kitchen area – these stimulating ingredients tempted us to settle back for a binge but my flag was waiting to be retrieved. After a ta-ra to the trattoria's terrible twins, Dave accompanied me to Tiburtina while Bill and Crawfie went off to the ground, where we agreed to hook up at the Liverpool end.

A bus conveyed us to the station's left luggage office and I speedily regained possession of my flag and poles. Brace yourself, Olympic Stadium.

Not yet. As the evening rush hour got into gear, commuters crowded around Tiburtina's bus stops and the district was gridlocked. We could have waited ages so piled into a taxi, stressing to our driver that he'd get a lorra lira if he reached the ground pronto.

A juicy carrot. Plainly Enzo had graduated with laurels from the Bullitt school of motoring in Turin. Every road might have been solid with traffic but our demon driver got through, overtaking on the wrong side, bouncing along pavements, cutting up bus queues. Italy's legions of motoring chauvinists have a catchphrase, "Signorina al volante, pericolo permanente – when a woman's at the wheel, there's always danger", but with Enzo's pedal to the metal, we were the ones scrabbling to examine our travel insurance for exclusion clauses for rally driving.

As we careered along one road, the windows of blocks of flats blazed with reflections of the setting sun. A hot night was in prospect but Enzo's road-craft was giving us a cold sweat. Yet, despite defying the laws of physics, he did get us to the stadium unharmed and the instant he screeched to a halt, we spotted Bill and Crawfie amid the milling crowds.

Kick-off was minutes away and I had my flag to hoist high. Family, friends and neighbours would be able to see Walton Jail's branch of the supporters' club, all present and correct.

Hold your water, though.

As we filed towards our turnstile, a policeman gestured at my poles in the sling. For security reasons, he wanted them handed over.

I protested, he insisted, the assurance of Bill's warrant card was rebuffed with the flick of a tanned hand, and there could be only one upshot. As I gave him some stick, the carabineri tossed my poles onto a pile by the gate. I didn't know whether to laugh, cry or burst out in pimples.

After its 1,000-mile journey, my Union Jack would not be waving above the masses on its long bamboo rods and folks back home in front of the telly wouldn't be yelling, "There they are!"

At least after our frenzied dash from Tiburtina, we were inside the ground and when both teams walked out, it was like a home game for us, Scousers everywhere. The barbarians weren't hammering at the gates of Rome, they'd overrun its citadel.

In the middle of our end, surrounded by red-and-white-check flags, was a 40-ft-long banner that would go down in Anfield folklore, "Joey ate the frog's legs, made the Swiss roll, now he's munching Gladbach" – and it was on poles! How'd they managed that?

Once play commenced, Scousers paid homage again to St Etienne with "Allez les Rouges" and the Reds got our show up and running. Heighway slipped the ball through to McDermott who, from the edge of the penalty box, zeroed it past the German keeper, Kneib. For the rest of the first half, we controlled the game but after the break, Mönchengladbach's Simonsen nailed an explosive 20-yarder into the net.

Liverpool were under the cosh and Clemence pulled off a crucial save from Heynckes. If that had gone in, making it 2-1, we might have struggled.

Cometh the hour, cometh the man. On the eve of the final, Smithy had said he was going to retire afterwards and now he chose his moment to make history. Klinkhammer gave away an unnecessary corner, Heighway lofted the ball towards the near post and Tommy rose like a muscular Masai amid puny pygmies, spearing it diagonally into the top left corner with his head of iron. In his 600th appearance, he'd whipped in his most important goal ever, turning the Stadio Olimpico into a Mersey madhouse.

Keegan was playing out of his skin and proved to viewers across Europe what a star he was. Ever since shackling Cruyff in the 1974 World Cup decider between West Germany and Holland, Gladbach's captain, Berti Vogts, had been lauded as one of the game's most unyielding defenders. Now KK gave him the runaround.

He surged into BMG's box and floundering Vogts scythed him down. With the coolest of heads, Neal fired the spot-kick home. 3-1 and Gladbach were munched.

The Mighty Reds had beaten the gallant Whites.

At the last whistle, we Kopoholics did a synchronised jig, elated beyond belief, but Crawfie broke away. He was weeping. Rubbing his eyes, he mumbled: "Sorry, mates."

No call for an apology. We're champions of Europe and you're a Kopite, someone who loves emotion and needn't be ashamed of showing it. Flood the stadium, Crawfie.

When Emlyn hoisted the cup aloft, it beamed out shafts of light from hundreds of flash bulbs – a sight etched on your soul, a vision Pindar could have been portraying in his verse about victors in the Greek games being bathed in "a god-given splendour and rays of light".

Watching our splendid team process around the running track with that cup, our cup, I knew my lifelong dream had come true. Nothing could better this.

Once they had trooped down the tunnel, we dragged ourselves outside to catch a bus to the city centre. Creamcrackered, all we craved were some shots of anaesthetic in a quiet bar, and that's what we had until closing time when we walked to Tiburtina, ready for our return journey.

At daybreak, our train pulled out and I stood in the corridor, watching Rome slide by until I was joined by a lad from Penzance, zipped up in a white boiler-suit covered with players' names in red letters.

"That was some night," I said.

"Yeah," the Cornishman agreed. "And what a way to finish off. We went to the Holiday Inn, got into the room where the team was having its do. They let us in. The cup was there, on a table, and we had scoff and booze. It was jammed with our lads."

In the following days, it emerged that hundreds of fans shared the food and ale at the post-final buffet in the city-centre hotel.

Bob himself refused to touch a drop of alcohol, saying: "The Pope and I are two of the few sober people in Rome tonight." A beatific smile on his face, he was content to sup in the atmosphere on his "perfect day". He had resolved to remember every second, sticking to the example of American socialite Nancy Astor who confessed: "One reason I don't drink is that I want to know when I'm having a good time."

Our manager stayed dry despite having a compelling motive for hitting the bottle. "This is the second time I've beaten the Germans here," he said. "The first was in 1944 – I drove into Rome on a tank when the city was liberated."

As well as hungry supporters, another gratifying arrival at the Holiday Inn hooley was Vogts, der Terrier, who came to offer his congratulations and join in the Scouse fun. How many losing captains would have the good grace to do that? His gesture added lustre to an occasion characterised by honoured guest Shanks as "the greatest night in Liverpool's history".

Say that again: "The greatest night in Liverpool's history". And again: "The greatest night in Liverpool's history". And again … [That's enough. – Editor]

How great was illustrated when our train screeched to a standstill in Milan. On the platform, a lecture theatre of students chanted "Mee-lan!" and exchanged banter with Scousers but, once we set off, they clapped us on our way.

The Red express halted again that night, in Germany, alongside a freight train whose guard passed on news hot off the presses: Keegan, scorer of 100 goals for us, was joining Hamburg in a bank-busting £500,000 transfer. The Two Million Marks Man, as German radio labelled him, had accepted a £100,000-a-year contract, more than quadrupling his salary.

Money talks and talent walks.

The rest of our trip slumbered by until midday on Friday when, back on British rails, a red signal delayed us in South London. What is it they say? Travel broadens the mind, commuting kills it? To any observer, this was no commuter train, populated by grey people in grey suits. Red and white flashed through every window and, now we were motionless, flags hung out of carriages.

From within a factory adjoining the track came a dribble of workers, all black – "Must be the night shift," one wag quipped in these politically incorrect days. The onlookers knew who we were, giving us a clap.

A few miles farther on, we halted on an embankment above the gardens of terraced houses. Through the door of one property, a white-haired gent stumbled, carrying a cane with a tiny Union flag on the end. He walked down the lawn towards our train, waving his flag, and yelled a single word: "Fantastic!" We cheered.

After four days in trains and one day in Rome, we arrived back in Wigan at 6pm on Friday, the night of Smithy's sell-out testimonial at Anfield. A fairytale ending to his years with the Reds. While no truth could be attributed to the rumour Germolene would be applied to his studs if he was in a good mood, Tommy knew how to greet fancy-Dan wingers.

This arch exponent of the dark arts of defending admitted: "I would say, 'Come near me, son, and I'll break your back'. I played against Best and after a few shouts in his ear he used to go for a cup of tea."

When Smithy was born in Scottie Road, they broke the mould and he deserved every penny from his Anfield send-off after shedding blood to bring success to our club. And what success.

In May 1977, Liverpool became football's most garlanded team. On the 14th, they took the League championship for a record 10th time. On the 21st, they lost the FA Cup to a deflected goal. On the 25th, they won the European Cup in Rome.

For every Kopite, 12 unforgettable days.

* * * * * * * * * *

During a sultry summer, Merseyside's Red half was in seventh heaven and even Blues acknowledged their rivals had turned our city into the capital of club football, home of the European champions who were now aiming for more silverware.

When the new term opened with the Super Cup, Liverpool met Keegan's Hamburg, holders of the Cup Winners' Cup, and hammered them 6-0 at Anfield, McDermott rattling in a hat-trick.

A 7-1 aggregate victory, which resounded around Europe, was all the more gladdening because some Hamburg players had undergone respectectomies, bragging about what they would do to us. No paragons in the cordiality stakes, the Germans also made KK's early days difficult because they resented his bank-busting salary.

"I found everyone so cold," he said. "I was trying to learn the language but when I spoke to team-mates in German, they just turned away."

Goaded by these snubs, Kevin bust a gut to prove he was worth the money, winning over doubters with a string of terrific performances that culminated in Hamburg's first Bundesliga title for 19 years. "Mighty Mouse" became a megastar and fans christened their baby sons Kevin.

Now that Bob Paisley had made history as the first manager to take the UEFA and European cups in consecutive seasons, he faced the challenge of winning the premier trophy again and no one was more conscious that the tortuous road to football's summit is littered with skeletons of so-called wonder-teams.

He also needed to identify a replacement for Keegan. While some supporters deemed him irreplaceable, fearing his exit concluded a golden era, they could not have known another superstar was walking in.

"I'd played for Celtic against Dunfermline on the Tuesday," said Kenny Dalglish. "Spoke to Liverpool after the game. Up early in the morning. Jock Stein took us down to Moffat and John Smith and Bob Paisley drove us to Anfield. Had a medical. Signed. Came in for training Thursday morning. Travelled Friday. Played Saturday.

"But I felt comfortable. They'd just come straight off two trophies – European Cup, the League – and got to the FA Cup final. And they said, 'You get nothing for last year'. The attitude was magnificent."

Paisley had paid a bargain-basement £440,000 for Kenny but this wasn't the first time the Glaswegian had travelled to Merseyside with the intention of joining Liverpool. As a 15-year-old, he came down for a trial in 1966 and, having lit up Melwood with his skills, was driven by Shanks to the Mount Pleasant YMCA, where he was staying. In the end, Kenny thought he was too young to leave home and signed for Celtic.

Now, 11 years later, he had signed on the dotted line. Once the deal was done, Jock Stein, Celtic's manager, said he was looking forward to seeing the Kop's reaction to Dalglish's boyish grin when he got the ball in the net. In years to come, Anfield was to fall in love with Kenny's inimitable enthusiasm, for just as every baby and every bride is beautiful, so every one of his goals was accompanied by that trademark smile, even when he'd been clobbered by some lump of a stopper.

Wearing Keegan's No 7 shirt, the newcomer took minutes to demonstrate he'd replaced his predecessor's pace and power with poise and finesse; Dalglish fired home in the seventh minute of his debut game, away to Middlesbrough, and found the sweet spot again on his Anfield bow.

Paisley knew this football wizard was suited to Liverpool because "he did the simple things" and before turning out, Kenny was struck by the instructions: "Just play – that's all they said."

In 1977-78's campaign, he went on to appear in all 61 matches, scoring 31 goals, aided by two other Scottish arrivals, Graeme Souness, who joined from Middlesbrough, and Alan Hansen, recruited from Partick Thistle.

The squad's depth was brought home in September when England manager Ron Greenwood picked Clemence, Neal, McDermott, Ray Kennedy, Hughes and Callaghan to turn out against Switzerland at Wembley, the most from one club since the war. Nonetheless, Cally's Anfield days were drawing to an end. Since signing in 1959, he'd helped the club progress from Second Division also-rans to European champions but in early 1978 he moved to Swansea on a free transfer after a record 856 senior appearances for the Reds. Booked only once during his long career, he was immortalised in an ingenious newspaper headline after he notched up three goals against Queens Park Rangers. Refining the Mary Poppins song Supercalifragilisticexpialidocious, the headline read: "Super Cally scores a hat-trick, QPR atrocious".

Atrocious was the only word to define a key decision against us in the League Cup. Having reached the Wembley final and drawn with Nottingham Forest, the Reds replayed at Old Trafford where the stalemate was broken when Thompson brought down O'Hare, a yard outside the box. I know it was a yard because I was directly in line with the tackle. Despite this, a penalty was awarded, Robertson scored and Liverpool were robbed of a trophy.

Afterwards Thommo groaned to a TV interviewer: "I'm sick as a parrot." With this sentence, its first known use over the airwaves, a phrase entered football's lexicon, to be called on by distressed players and coaches alike. Are parrots perennially sick? Where does this phrase originate? Is it a truncated variant of the Scouse saying, "As sick as a parrot with a rubber beak"? Is it another instance of the Mersey vernacular that stresses a point through deliberately implausible exaggeration, like "as rough as a bear's arse", used to describe any dive of a pub or club?

Show me the man who's had the temerity to examine the texture of a bear's backside and I'll shake his hand.

Perhaps not ...

While Thommo was parroting his despondency, we were in a traffic jam on Old Trafford's industrial estate, brooding on the evening's iniquity. It was pouring and the four of us sat in silence. Through our car window, another motor snailed past, a boy in a Liverpool shirt inside, crying. His big night had ended in tears.

Chin up, lad, I felt like telling him. Injustice is part and parcel of the game and should always make you stronger. But he and I could never have suspected the Reds would go on to collect an unprecedented four League Cups in a row.

They also had their Continental campaign to look forward to. After disposing of Dynamo Dresden 6-3 on aggregate, a taxing quarter-final pitted them against Benfica who had gone 46 matches without defeat in the Stadium of Light. Hughes silenced the 70,000 crowd in rain-lashed Lisbon, scoring the clincher in a 2-1 downing of the Eagles. The return leg was a formality – a 4-1 exhibition – to set up a semi with old foes Borussia Mön-chengladbach.

Although the Germans nicked it 2-1 over there, Dalglish, who was marked by one-eyed Wilfried Hannes, netted in a 3-0 victory in L4 to book our second European Cup Final, at Wembley.

Our opponents were other old acquaintances, Bruges, but they did not have to grapple with Smithy, who had postponed his departure from Anfield. He was ruled out, a hammer having fallen on his foot and broken a toe during DIY work in his house. Despite this blow, Liverpool dominated the Belgians in front of a 92,000 gate.

Paisley had once told his forwards, "If you're in the penalty area and don't know what to do with the ball, put it in the net and we'll discuss the options later", and now Kenneth Mathieson Dalglish showed precisely what to do. When Souness passed to him, Kenny caressed the ball over the keeper – an exquisite chip – before running to our fans behind the goal. The four of us grabbed each other in a dancing scrum, without the teeniest tear from Crawfie, while other lads toasted victory by pulling out a bottle of Liverpool FC Scotch, labelled "This is Anfield".

As in the previous year's final, Reds had conquered Whites to capture the 18lb silver and gold grail and, another coincidence, they'd defeated Borussia Mönchengladbach and Bruges in UEFA Cup and European Cup finals. Yet within minutes of quitting Wembley's turf, the winners' thoughts were being focused on next season. In the dressing room, a glass of Champagne had barely touched Hansen's lips before Joe Fagan, the coach, was insisting in no uncertain terms that our League form had not been good enough. Runners-up wasn't satisfactory. That had to be improved on.

But Kenny's piece of skill had turned a dream into reality. Becoming European champions once is the easy part; the real challenge is retaining your title and we were the first British team to do that, laying to rest the cant of can't – that strength-sapping, hoary old English lament: "It can't be done, it's not possible. We might win once but we can't match those crafty Continentals, winning again and again."

Tommyrot. Paisley had repudiated the hand-wringing and head-shaking and made his Liverpool into Europe's monarchs in successive years, like Real Madrid, Ajax and Bayern Munich. His squad had emulated the Continent's best with steely determination, unrelenting hard work and simple tactics: when the opposition had the ball, every Red became a defender; when we had it, the whole team became attackers.

Bob had an ace up his sleeve, too: after studying physiotherapy, he was expert at assessing injuries, *as they occurred*. No other manager possessed his knack of judging how badly hurt a player might have been and how long it would take to recover.

Hansen singled out another reason for our supremacy. "Everyone was treated the same. There were no prima donnas," he said, while Sir John Smith, the chairman, put his finger on one simple principle: "Liverpool have always been a personal club, a family club, and we have always believed people matter most."

People matter most. Anfield's golden rule, underpinned with European silver.

* * * * * * * * * *

That summer of 1978, the World Cup was staged in Argentina but England were absent, having failed to qualify because of a 2-0 defeat by Italy. Before Brazil's first game, their coach, Claudio Coutinho, gave an interview to the international media about his team's prospects, during which he made a point of heaping praise on the European champions. "If Liverpool played in the World Cup," he said, "they would finish in the top three." This from a Brazilian. Could there have been a greater accolade for Paisley's heroes?

11
A Threesome In Rio: Pelé, Ursula Andress And Me

Life is nothing but a series of sensations.
– Francis Bacon

ONE lunchtime in my third year at Alsop, I slipped into its most tranquil haven, the library in the Rectory. Across the playing field from our classrooms, this Victorian mansion acted as an annex where boys could escape the playground's hurly-burly during their breaks.

From the shelves of its Geography section, I pulled out a book about South America and, leafing through it, a black-and-white photograph caught my attention: a three-master, accompanied by the caption, "A Liverpool sailing ship off Iquique".

Iquique? Where in the name of Mercator …?

Before you could say Phillips' World Atlas, I pinpointed it as a town in Chile's distant north. Up the Pacific coast of South America. Other side of the world from Liverpool. What an obscure place to get to! The picture was undated but must have been 1870, 1880, 1890, something like that.

I slid into a chair and scrutinised this ancient, atmospheric monochrome, visualising the Scouse crew in Dock Road boozers on a Saturday night and then, with hungover heads, setting sail for Cape Horn on Sunday morning's tide.

What a voyage, hanging on grimly in tempestuous seas off South America's tip, knowing so many crews had been shipwrecked and drowned. What would it have been like for a cabin boy from Marmaduke Street on his maiden passage, surviving Cabo de Hornos, docking in Iquique, knowing you had to endure it all again to get back to your Ma and Da on the Mersey?

This murky photo bound me in its spell, sowing a seed of fascination with Latin America, its history, its peoples, its cultures, that was to grow and bear fruit. From that moment in the Rectory, I consumed books about this distant continent, unearthing them on Alsop's shelves and, more so, in Rawdon public library down Breck Road, where I pored over chapters about Conquistadores, Indians, the Amazon, the Andes, the wildlife and wild life, football, fiestas, cities. Perhaps I was rediscovering one strand of my family's seafaring roots, since Liverpool's maritime links with the Latin West have long been strong. Why else would there be a branch of BOLSA, the Bank of London and South America, in Cook Street in the city centre?

Naturally, Uncle Len had circumnavigated South America and his anecdotes fanned my interest. He told me that cities worth seeing fall into two categories: those whose attraction resides in their setting, such as Vancouver, with beautiful bays and mountains, or those that depend on antiquity and architecture, such as Venice, with its squares, palaces and churches. Mulling over places to berth in, he'd reel off Cape Town, Hong Kong, San Francisco and, top of his manifest, Rio de Janeiro, which slumbered in the "Must Visit" section of my memory bank until 1978, year of the World Cup in Argentina.

By this point, I'd decamped from the *Express* to the *Mirror* in Manchester and during a symposium with three colleagues in Mad George's cocktail lounge, we romanced about this, that and the other, meandering into faraway places, exotic destinations, Rio's carnival. In that order. As alcohol lubricated our conversation, shunting mouths into turbo mode, brains into reverse, we committed ourselves to seeing Rio and the following February, inebriated reverie became eye-popping fact; Pete Donlan, Pete Kilner, Jim Seddon and yours truly flew over the Maracana stadium and down into Santos Dumont airport where our Kuoni representative was waiting to greet us.

On the coach journey to our hotel, he gave a few words of welcome, followed by several sentences of warning: Get back to the safety of your hotel by 10.30pm every night; be on constant alert for robbers and pickpockets; don't wear watches or jewellery in the street; don't walk about with a camera; don't take any belongings, even towels, on the beach; only carry small amounts of cash. To underline his message, he informed us a thief with a revolver had robbed a bus conductor of £11 worth of coins the previous night in Copacabana.

Why's he telling me all this? I've been to New Brighton loads of times, you know.

Anyhow, our rep concluded his spiel: "Enjoy your holiday in Rio." You bet.

São Sebastião do Rio de Janeiro embraces any European with an all-out assault on the senses, the nearest approximation to which is probably a saunter down Scottie Road on Saturday night at chucking-out and chucking-up time. Sight, hearing, smell and taste are overpowered by potent sensations, the like of which the most vivid imagination could never prepare you for. A Wow! city, bar none.

Descending into the airport, a blinding landscape greets you, an unmatched amalgam of ocean and skyscrapers, islands and urban sprawl, beaches and factories, jungle and shopping malls, mountains and motorways. An hors d'oeuvre for the sensual banquet at ground level.

After checking in to your hotel, you go out and are immediately conscripted into a samba band parading down the street. Stroll into the tunnel linking the city centre with Copacabana and almost expire from car fumes before coughing your way out at the other end. Get the beach vendor to slice a fresh pineapple with his machete and allow juice from a celestial plantation to trickle down your parched throat.

If Britain can be termed bland – and that *does* have numerous blessings – then without question Brazil is outrageously voluptuous. Yet within hours of bimbling around Rio, your strongest impression is the gulf between have-a-lots and have-nots in a place exhibiting obscene wealth cheek by jowl with abject poverty.

In Ipanema, the mega-rich descend from chauffeur-driven Rolls-Royces to be escorted into their apartments by armed guards – while a stone's throw away the destitute glare from their favelas, vast shanty towns clinging to the dizzy mountain slopes that barge into chic residential zones.

If you live in a tin and wood hovel, though, you're laughing. Slumped outside the front door of our hotel, the Florida, was a Ford Falcon wreck, wheels missing, windows broken, door panels stove in – the home of three chaps who curled up inside each evening for a night's sleep. They didn't even have a shack in the poorest favela. Meanwhile, in smart restaurants close by, American tourists were tucking into sizzling sirloins, washed down with chilled Antarctica beer.

Across the promenade from the grillrooms, bars and dossers' den lay Flamengo beach which by day resembled a seaside sculpture park, reclining bronzes positioned on a white sandy floor. Not everybody was a tanned Adonis in budgie-smuggler Speedos or an Aphrodite in her cheek-splitting thong; older, sun-wrinkled gents padded along the waterline in black, elasticated swimming trunks, pulled up to their armpits and exposing long articulated legs, like gargantuan Mato Grosso frogs.

On the beach, the four of us joined in a football game with a dozen Flamengo lads, marvelling at their subtle barefoot skills. Before flying to Brazil, I'd visited Anfield's souvenir shop. Souvenir shop! How times have changed. There I bought pin badges as little gifts for my trip and mentioned to the salesman that I was off to Rio. Wait a mo'. He presented me with a bundle of colour prints of the squad with the European Cup and once we'd run out of puff in the inaugural beach footie tournament, I distributed these to our Carioca pals. From their gratitude, you'd have thought I was handing out dollar bills. As for the badges, they were soon shared among a group of Argentinians in our hotel. After all, Argentina were now world champions, so their nationals deserved mementoes of the European champions.

During the evening rush hour of our second day, the Kuoni rep's crime alert was given substance. Returning from a trip up Corcovado, the mountain crowned with the statue of Christ, I was standing in the aisle of a jam-packed single-decker which began approaching our stop. I needed to reach the door, so attempted to push past a tank of a bloke who was clasping the overhead rail, his back turned to me. Even though I asked him to budge, this 18-stone boulder pretended to be deaf.

I applied pressure with my shoulder but could feel other burly brutes forcing themselves against me, from behind. The pickpocket gang had set their mark up nicely, wedged between their immovable bodies.

As the bus was drawing to a halt, hands probed the pockets of my trousers and fingers slid along the inside of the waistband. A right going-over and if it went on much longer, they would soon be fondling my jewel pouch.

No time for Lake District manners. Mustering all the force I could, I kneed Fatso where the sun don't shine. He let out a squeal like a stuck pig – I must have cracked his coccyx – and, Timberrr! he keeled over onto a woman sitting at the side who was forensically filing her nails.

She let out a yell, flinging her file in the air, but my knee-jerk reaction had unblocked the blocker.

Path clear, I galloped through commuters and dived out the door onto the pavement.

Quick! With the bus pulling slowly away, I nipped into one of my socks to retrieve the couple of notes stashed there. As Grease-Ball Godzilla scowled down, I flourished my wedge in his face through the window.

There! Not quite so smart, bugalugs. If canny lads in the Boys' Pen couldn't crack the Bank of Wolsey's safe deposit system, I'm sure you couldn't either.

That same night we went for dinner at a pavement café in Copacabana, located at a semicircular road junction, the base of which was Avenida Atlantica, that famed boulevard skirting the beach. While we savoured the inner warmth of Brazil's liquid dynamite, cachaça sugar-cane liquor, and the caress of the cooling sea breeze, we could observe the nubile bodies, female and male, gliding past on the mosaic pavement.

Suddenly our attention was diverted by a drum roll, an invitation to a show. On a corner across the street, two black chaps, each holding a drum, were talking to a couple of girls. As they nattered, they were tapping out beats on their skins.

While our feijoada bean stew was being served, five more drummers emerged from a side street, accompanied by sundry wives, girlfriends, children, chums. After greeting the first-comers, they gabbed away to a hubbub of diverse samba rhythms and over the next half-hour, others arrived in dribs and drabs until about 30 drummers and 60 followers stood around in several groups.

While they chinwagged, the percussionists continued tapping. Gradually, though, drumming took precedence over conversing, with three or four cliques exploring different musical avenues, watched by their adherents.

Anyone would expect this to create a racket but the cadences ebbing and flowing, dominating and declining, were hypnotic. In time, imperceptibly, these disparate harmonies blended together until, as I sliced into my barbecued beef, a deafening bang from all the drummers hurled them into a single frenetic beat that resounded across the junction.

For someone like me, whose favourite musical instrument is the drum, this was spellbinding. Throughout our long wait between cachaças and courses, we had been a captive audience for a musical Amazon, minor tributaries gradually merging to create one irresistible river of Afro-American harmony.

Listening to the beat pulsing across Copacabana, you could appreciate why the drum is Rio's cardiac monitor, a barometer of wellbeing for a bewitching city. You hear it in the streets and bars, on the beaches and buses, everywhere. However, *the* place to catch professional samba music is Oba Oba nightclub, renowned for spectacular dancing by ravishing mulattas, Rio's counterparts of Merseyside's Chilli Whackers, that alluring blend of European and African blood.

On our visit, we were categorised, quite rightly, as men of means and allocated a table in front of the stage from where we watched an extravaganza worthy of the Paris Lido, at one tenth its price, dancers supple as pieces of string shimmying away to the accompaniment of virtuoso drummers.

Oba Oba also tried to entice us with unanticipated extras. During the intermission, I was sipping my caipirinha, cachaça with lime juice, when a mulatta drew a chair up alongside me. A divine creature, a beguiling fusion of compatible genes, with a quivering bosom.

Wilson Hall, opposite Garston bus depot, this was not.

Fixing me with winsome brown eyes, she flashed a teeth-perfect smile, drew a fingertip down my cheek and pleaded: "Buy me some wine."

Although Brazilian Portuguese was designed for poetry, love songs and seduction, this was one occasion to turn a deaf ear. Those boobs were certainly up for grabs but buying her a sherbert might land me with more than I'd bargained for.

"Sorry, no."

"Some cigarettes, then? Please ..."

"No."

Earlier that evening in our hotel bar, a ratted German had treated us to cringe-making accounts of his carnal relations with Rio's prostitutes. When I inquired whether he was married, he grunted: "Why keep a cow when you can buy a glass of milk?"

I ruminated on this for a few seconds before countering with: "If you keep your own cow, you can make sure the milk's pasteurised and the bottle's clean."

Boom, boom.

The Frankfurter was not persuaded.

Now my personal goddess in Oba Oba was aiming to tempt with a late-night tub of yoghurt that might be rancid and precipitate a calamitous malady – not a titbit I'd wish to gulp down my gullet, particularly as our little floor show was attracting people's attention.

I wanted rid of her and, being a battle-scarred traveller, man of the world, Old Alsopian, St John's Market Saturday boy, lad from Ullswater Street, I knew how to send her packing.

This always used to work in the Standard and should do the trick here.

"Oye," I said. "Listen. I'm not interested – I'm maricón, gay."

With a glance of withering pity, my temptress shrugged and flounced away.

Sorted, Neil. You can settle down for the second-half entertainment.

Till I felt someone snuggling in beside me.

Uh-oh! To my disquiet – and the audience's audible titters – it was a geezer, in long blond wig and sequinned ballroom gown, looking like Julian Clary on a bad hair and bad make-up day.

A confusion of lip gloss, false eyelashes, nasal hairs and 10 o'clock shadow, the real giveaways were his muscle-bound arms.

Good grief, he must have rushed straight from the docks after unloading bags of cement all day.

Get out of this one, buster.

Jim and the two Petes were chortling but I didn't consider it quite so comical, especially when I felt the befrocked docker's calloused hand on my thigh. His gaze locked on to me, searching for reaction.

Sod this for a game of soldiers. Straight to the kill.

I gave daggers to his nibs and informed him in no uncertain terms that I did not, repeat, did NOT, desire his companionship.

Exhaling a snort of disdain, he upped and wobbled off on his high heels to the bar, leaving in his wake a trail of Revlon face powder – or Castle cement dust.

My reputation, or the remnants of it, had been salvaged.

After these cameo performances, I could absorb myself in the real show at Oba Oba, whose second half offered prodigious dancing and drumming, bereft of any knee-clasping distractions.

An even more celebrated spectacle awaited us, though: carnival.

Through a friend on the *Mirror* in London, our foursome had been put in touch with Alfredo Machado, one of Rio's well-to-do who offered to be our chaperon for the festivities. The five days and four nights of this Brazilian publisher's beano opened with a cocktail party, for which we planned to enter into carnival spirit by donning fancy dress hired from a shop near Man City's ground. Its proprietor had the inspired idea of turning us into emissaries of the home countries: Donlan became an Irish leprechaun (emerald green tights, jerkin and jester's hat), Kilner was kitted out as a Welsh rugby player (complete with, no bull, a triffid-size leek), Seddon lorded it in a suit sewn from Union Jacks (England!) and Dunkin was done up as a Scottish Highlander, chalky knees protruding beneath Royal Stuart kilt.

Posing in all our glory outside the hotel before Machado's thrash, taxis gave us a wide berth, either because of Kilner's leek or my bony knees, but we lay in the road until one driver capitulated, ferrying us to swanky Lagoa.

At the address, a mansion block, we showed our invitations to a pair of pistol-packing doormen and were conducted into a private lift whose attendant whisked us to the top floor.

The lift doors opened and we stepped directly into Alfredo's penthouse, bulging with la crème de la crème of international gossip pages … Brazilian TV moguls, Argentinian film actresses, German publishing magnates, Italian directors, American editors.

Our entrance was a sensation. No shrinking violets, we absolutely stole the show.

We charged into the room … and our comedy costumes cut conversations dead.

Whoops! All the other guests were resplendent in white dinner jackets and long evening gowns.

Monty Python gatecrashes Monte Carlo!

Obviously someone hadn't read the dress code in Portuguese on our invites.

To this glitzy gathering, we must have looked like refugees from the nearest circus, rather than pillars of the jet set. Nonetheless, having composed themselves after their initial shock at this irruption of riotous clowns, they gave a sympathetic ripple of applause and Alfredo combined diplomacy with delight, complimenting us on upholding the image of eccentric Englishmen out on the razzle in Rio. Which, of course, we were.

What a location to kick off our frolics. After admiring the Modiglianis and Picassos in our host's opulent salon, we gravitated towards a terrace as big as a tennis court and drooled over the breathtaking view of Christ's floodlit statue on Corcovado, above a shimmering lake.

Cariocas contend that this immense monument (the head alone weighs 30 tons and the fingertips are 28 metres, 91 feet, apart) is usually swathed in cloud during carnival, to spare Jesus any glimpse of the widespread debauchery below. On this occasion, his statue was pin-sharp against the night sky, perhaps because our shenanigans had yet to begin. Give us time, Lord.

A couple of hours mingling and imbibing with the guests, who included Rio's mayor and a congenial Robert Stigwood, and it was soon 10pm, time for the headline event. Feeling rather mellow, we handed our crystal whisky tumblers and caviar dishes to the waiters and vacated Alfredo's pad. In the street, a fleet of minibuses was lined up, our transport to the baile, a lavish ball organised by the Rio city authority in a concert hall to mark the formal inauguration of carnival's high jinks.

Outside the venue, a broad red carpet dissected massed ranks of celebrity-spotters, flash-bulbs popped, TV cameras zoomed, radio reporters gabbled. Patently word had circulated that a camp Scouser was on the prowl in a kilt.

All those evenings in the Magic Clock were about to stand me in good stead.

Playing flagrantly to the gallery – why let my new and few admirers down? – I sucked in my cheeks and, knobbly knees clacking, tartan swishing, minced along the walkway ... to the visible consternation of a Newcastle couple who'd chatted to me on the plane out and were now positioned behind the barrier at the front of the crowd.

Incredulous that this Scouser was attending such a prestigious event, the husband, a marine engineer, shouted: "What're you doing here?"

"Having fun," I lisped shamelessly as I pranced past.

Inside the hall, Alfredo escorted us to his capacious box above the dance floor where we were soon topping up our alcohol levels, until a kerfuffle to our right distracted us. People were congregating below another box, gesturing to a diminutive black man who leant over the balustrade, waving back.

Pelé!

How fortunate can you be? Pass the smelling salts, Nobby!

I hadn't seen him since Goodison Park in '66 and now, on his first visit to Rio's carnival, I was there too.

A throw-in from our box stood O Rei, The King, whose record reigned supreme: a grand total of 1,363 matches and 1,281 goals, including 92 hat-tricks and four or more goals 36 times; 77 goals in 92 internationals between 1957 and 1970; and World Cup winners' medals, in 1958, 1962 and 1970.

All this, of course, I knew off by heart. And there he was, His Royal Highness, metres away.

Alfredo, a lofty figure in Rio's stratospherically high society, dashed out to say hello. Since he'd met Pelé once before, he persuaded minders to allow him access to the sacred conclave where he enjoyed a convivial conversation with the master.

On return to our box, however, Alfredo was infuriated to find three intruders, a couple of teenage girls and a boy, brazenly wolfing canapés from *our* buffet table.

What cheek!

"Out! Out!" our host yelled, scorning their protests as he manhandled them through the door.

Only when he slammed it and turned to see faces gawping at him did he realise: wrong box!

His account of this howler caused considerable merriment for us, adding to an indelible all-nighter at the city of Rio ball, a merry-go-round of band after band on the revolving stage, non-stop samba and relentless rhythms, nearly-nude showgirls, brawny men in lavish carnival costumes, Dior-clad society ladies, white-tuxedoed Don Juans, scandalous transsexuals and transvestites (they adored my Scottish *miniskirt*), kaleidoscopic cocktails, and strenuous rumpy-pumpy by ghostly figures in the hall's murkiest recesses. Not to mention Jim Seddon getting in on the action once we put aside our glasses to join the gymnastic, hip-dislocating shindy down on the dance floor.

As he partnered me for the Gay Gordons with Can-Can variations, a raver grabbed our attention – a stunner in microscopic silver-lamé bikini, samba-ing on a chair, arms extended sexily above her head. Drop-dead gorgeous, and she knew it.

While she was rollicking away, her boyfriend/husband poured red wine down her glistening brown torso ... and started licking it off.

No prior invitation was required for Liverpudlian Jim (all unexpurgated verses of Maggie May during any pub sesh, by appointment or otherwise). Jaw on floor, his expression said everything: I fancy some of that.

Before I could restrain him, he heaved into action. Shouldering the chap with the bottle to one side, Jim snapped: "My turn, pal."

His tongue popped out and, hands planted on the girl's writhing hips, he licked away as if his very existence depended on it.

For some reason arguably associated with his exuberant consumption of Glenmorangie, he must have presumed he was back on Merseyside at the free 'n' easy, "bring your banjo" amateur night in Bowring Park Bowls Club.

What's more, the snake-hipped bird was lapping it up, Jim's rough tongue inflaming her randiness, stoking her sensuous samba.

As for her companion, he appeared as turned on as she was. Refusing to take umbrage, he gazed voyeuristically at this vicarious vinolingus, the half-full carafe dangling from his hand.

One genuine Brazilian gentleman.

Only when Jim's tongue got sore did the Scouse interloper desist. Abandoning the human lollipop, he toddled away unsteadily for further stimulation amid the tangle of interlocking bodies on the dance floor.

Watching this whole escapade, I thought: Only in Rio during carnival ... or in Bowring Park on Monday nights.

The rest of the hours we danced and drank ourselves silly – well, that's my story and I'm sticking to it – until, at 8 in the morning, the minibus decanted us back at our hotel. We were dead on our feet but, after a few hours in our battery-charger beds, we were raring to go again. A day's sightseeing set us up nicely for another venue and another ball – with notoriety a regular on its guest list.

Alfredo had warned us that jollifications at the Monte Libano club were best avoided as they invariably ended in a riot. Clearly he'd never been on Bismarcks in Yates's Wine Lodge on King Billy's birthday.

A riot? What greater incentive could we have?

Our taxi driver refused to pull up directly outside the club's door, dropping us a distance away on dimly-lit Avenida Borges de Medeiros.

"Walk down this side of the road," he cautioned. "Don't go on the other side. Muita violência! Lots of violence."

Glad we came. Admonition given, the cabby did a rapid U-turn and tore away into the night.

Nice to know natives in apartments on the west side wouldn't molest trusting tourists whereas those in the slums to the east weren't so hospitable.

Having discarded our clown outfits for Northern casual, we scurried down the eerily deserted street to reach Monte Libano without taking any casualties.

Outside the venue's high walls, clusters of Cariocas were begging doormen to allow them in but we were granted immediate access; white faces bring certain advantages.

Unsure of what lay inside, we entered a kind of smart country club, with tennis courts and swimming pools, not your run-of-the-mill setting for public disorder. Alfredo must have got his wires crossed.

From the noise, you could tell all the action was taking place in a ballroom, so we shoved through its doorway. The place was jumping to a band and the party spirit was catching. In spite of the crush, the four of us started showing off our exaggerated samba technique, a bracing hybrid of jive, twist, conga and hokey-cokey straight out of any Hogmanay party in Hunts Cross.

There was a distraction, though.

In one of the private boxes, yet another enchantress, busting out of a sparkly, two-piece dental-floss outfit, was cavorting on a table. No wine-tasting – just a doll with another figure to die for.

As she pranced away, blokes massed on the dance floor below, goggling at her provocative, bouncy routine until she gave them what they were aching for: she dropped her top strand of floss to flash her nipples.

Phwoar! The lads were aroused. Notwithstanding the fact we were already well juiced, the heavy scent of sex was befuddling.

Deftly the teaser covered up and resumed her girations, until chants of "Mais, More!" incited her to flash again. And again ... until all of a sudden heavies wearing red XXXL T-shirts printed with the word "Segurança, Security" stormed into the box, yelling angrily for her to stop.

The audience of horny, hyperventilating young men was less than gratified. In fact they were livid. A barrage of lager cans rattled around the box, driving the bouncers out.

The security force couldn't disregard such an affront. Machismo grievously insulted, they massed outside the ballroom with hastily sum-moned reinforcements.

Just as we tried to get a chant of "Spoilsports, spoilsports" going, Whoomf! double doors whammed open and a phalanx of enraged bouncers charged onto the dance floor, lashing out with fists at one and all.

Shut your eyes and visualise every black heavyweight champion of the past few decades – Ali, Lewis, Holyfield, Foreman, Frazier, Tyson, Williams, Witherspoon and the rest – taking on 200 testosterone-saturated lads and you've got the picture ... the mother, father, sister and brother of all brawls.

Marching away from Old Trafford in 1972 after we'd won 3-0, Warwick Road had degenerated into a Scouse v Manc freestyle slapping zone but this Monte Libano malarkey was far more brutal. Everywhere antagonists were going hammer and thongs, trading punches, hurling chairs, sprawling among tables, while the band played on at a markedly quicker tempo to accompany the maelstrom.

Yee-haa! Shades of a Liverpool engagement knees-up.

In the eye of this havoc, we were left untouched, conceivably out of deference to our seniority and pale, touristy complexions, more likely because the bouncers didn't fancy taking on more than they could chew. Like bystanders mesmerised by an accident as it happens, we stared at the chaos until, quite irrationally, we elected to defuse the situation. In a surreal interruption defying logical explanation, unless it can be attributed to all those sundowners swigged in our hotel, we linked arms and began belting out "Should auld acquaintance be forgot ..."

The strains of Auld Lang Syne wafted across the dance floor as the four of us ushered in the New Year ... any New Year.

During a mass fist fest. In a country club. In Rio. In February.

Monty Python meets Monte Carlo meets Monte Libano.

You couldn't make it up, and I'm not.

Our insanity had a strangely tranquillising effect on the madness. Across the room, pugilists froze in mid-punch and gaped at this huddle of deranged Englishmen performing their esoteric religious rite.

Everyone forgot what they were scrapping over, clenched fists dropped to hips, hands were shaken, hugs were exchanged.

A slight misrepresentation. As a matter of fact, a sizeable one. But as suddenly as it kicked off, this rip-roaring ding-dong subsided, the security wazzocks withdrew and the party resumed.

To the best of my knowledge, the tabletop titillator kept the floss on her threepenny bits, no more wallopathons enlivened the night and we boogied into oblivion well before dawn.

This horseplay at Monte Libano provided an uproarious appetiser for Rio's lavish carnival parade on the Sunday night. After dinner in one of Copacabana's most exclusive restaurants, Alfredo's guests were conveyed to his cavernous box alongside the parade route, a broad boulevard lined by stands seating 70,000 spectators.

At a sticky 10pm, the procession of escolas de samba, samba schools, began, dancers and drummers creating a riot of colour, choreography and music in "o maior show do mundo, the greatest show on earth".

And across the road, on the top tier of the stand, who was watching? Pelé!

Blimey! I've only been in Brazil five minutes and already the blighter's stalking me!

That kilt has a lot to answer for.

Once more Mr Football caused a stir. Throughout the night-long pageant of 24,000 carnavalistas, people were shouting and whistling to him, yet patient and amiable to the end, he acknowledged their calls, smiled for galleries of photographs and signed an electoral roll of autographs. If evidence were ever needed of the dignity and decency that has coursed out of Old Africa to the New World, from Mandela and Biko to Martin Luther King and Muhammad Ali, then Pelé afforded it.

What a man and what a night as celebrities – "beeps" to Brazilians, VIPs to you and me – promenaded from private box to private box during pauses in the parade, reacquainting themselves with old friends and quaffing refreshments, served in our temporary lounge by Alfredo's butler.

Fancy a bit of brazen name-dropping? Why not? This Ullswater laddie will never have a better opportunity.

Your starters for one: Ursula Andress, Beth Carvalho, Franco Zeffirelli, Martha Anderson, Candice Bergen, Silvia Bandeira, Albert Finney, Lamartine Babo, Liza Minnelli, Odile Marinho, Anita Ekberg, Fernando Resky, Frederique Aragon, Petula Clark, Vanuza Bardot, Tessa Kennedy, Ivo Pitanguy, Michael Medwin, Silvinho Cabeleireiro, Gary Wright, Guy Laroche, Regine, Epimetheus Woodcock ...

What do you mean you've never heard of half of them? I knew who they all were – at least once I'd seen their photos days later in Manchete, Brazil's glossiest magazine.

After decades sharing pork scratchings with pop idols in the Standard, I felt at ease in such glittering company. I knew my place ... and at 10 next morning, I found it.

In my hotel bed. With Ursula undressed in my arms

My starry, starry night to remember had come to a close with the Sixties' sexiest woman snuggled up beside me. I kid you not.

All right then, I do. Let me fantasise ...

However, another of my fantasies was about to turn into fact.

The instant we made our decision all those months before to visit Rio, I vowed to worship at one particular altar, a temple any football fan would give their right arm to visit – the Mario Filho Stadium, universally known after a nearby river, the Maracana.

On our last evening in Brazil, a Sunday, the derby of derbies was scheduled between bitter rivals Flamengo and Vasco da Gama, and the whole city was going.

After a long wait on Avenida Atlantica, we hailed a taxi, a beat-up VW Beetle which, judging by its deformities, had been losing stock-car races for 50 years.

To make space for luggage, the front passenger seat of this automotive equivalent of the Elephant Man had been removed so I squatted on the floor, straining to peer over a dust-coated dashboard, while my three mates were shoehorned into the back.

During the five days of carnival, newspapers reported 360 people had died – stabbed, shot, overdosed on drugs, drowned while swimming in the treacherous Atlantic swell – although the highest number of fatalities resulted from car crashes.

Vibrating on the taxi's corroded floor, with no seatbelt and just the flimsy boot lid between my legs and amputation, I was rather mindful of Rio's accident statistics. By a long chalk, traffic is the city's worst mass murderer and in the event of any head-on with another vehicle, I could kiss goodbye to my lower limbs, if not the rest of my body.

While I was ruminating on this eventuality, we started losing momentum. I glanced at our driver and, to my horror, saw his eyes were shut, his head listing. He was dozing off.

I shook his shoulder and he woke with a jump.

Minutes later he nodded off again.

"Hey!" I bawled. He opened his eyes and smiled.

"You're falling asleep. What's wrong? Tired?"

"Não," he giggled. "Estou bebado. No. I'm drunk."

That's all right then, I don't think. We'd already viewed the aftermath of horrific crashes at crossroads, where juggernauts had flattened cars like cardboard. Now we were lumbered with a driver who was mullered. And hazards lay ahead.

Since footpads can be lurking at night, Cariocas rarely halt at traffic lights – they edge through, eyes skinned for other vehicles.

Now it was daytime. Robbers should be resting.

Hold on, though.

Approaching a red stop sign, our intoxicated cabby gripped the wheel firmly ... and put his foot down. Without the briefest once-over, he barrelled straight through. In shock, I was too paralysed to react.

Japanese sumo wrestlers are physically incapable of reaching round their voluminous hindquarters to wipe them, so they employ personal hygienists to do it. At this laxative juncture, hunkering down in the Beetle, I could have done with just such an associate to my rear.

Further on, our narcoleptic chauffeur blundered through another red light at a crossroads where candles burned in the gutter around a plate of rice and bottle of beer, gifts placed by a local for deities of the Afro-Brazilian Candomblé religion.

Shutting my eyes, I prayed to his gods: keep us safe, please.

Congestion came to our rescue. Usually Rio taxi drivers live way out from the city and, having no knowledge of its streets, dump passengers kilometres from their destination because they don't want to lose face asking directions. On our journey to the Maracana, even this bladdered chappie couldn't get lost. As traffic built up, he was forced to go with the heavy flow and, more critically for my life expectancy, to slow down.

Providence and Candomblé smiled on us; we reached the stadium where I flopped out the Beetle like a wet rag after my white-knee ride. At least we'd arrived undamaged at the Maracana – Nirvana, Mecca, Zion for me and any true football lover.

In the street, I bought a red-and-black Flamengo flag for £2 and then we all tagged on to a line of fans, many in nothing but shorts, to queue beneath the stadium's 100-foothigh, overarching walls.

Turnstile negotiated, a gloomy corridor led into the ground.

Out of the shadows into the sun.

We emerged at pitch level in the Templo do Futebol, the Temple of Football, twin tiers sweeping round to form a prototypical concrete bowl, like a giant saucer. Above the roof opposite, Corcovado thrust into the sky; Christ was watching from his royal box.

Thinking this was make-believe, I sat down.

Go back to 1950. After 11,000 construction workers had laboured night and day for two years, using 40,000 lorryloads of materials, the Maracana opened for the World Cup in Brazil. The host nation stormed through the tournament, inflicting 7-1 and 6-1 humiliations on Sweden and Spain and meeting Uruguay in a final ordained to bring the Brazilians' first world title. Even though 199,854 spectators turned up for this formality, Uruguay spoilt the storyline, winning 2-1 and plunging Brazil into mourning.

Now I was in that very stadium. Behind one goal, Flamengo supporters were describing figures of eight in the air with flags as big as billboards while the Vasco hard core at the opposite end brandished theirs in this battle of colours. A music contest was also going full throttle. Amid both sets of fans, samba drummers competed for the loudest noise, deviating abruptly from one rhythm to another to wrongfoot their musical adversaries.

The fixture was Rio's biggest derby, with the added spice of class conflict. Flamengo regard themselves as the people's club, champions of the starving, guardians of the favelas, working-class. In contrast, middle-class, establishment Vasco were founded by Portuguese expatriates who cherished their European roots.

With kick-off approaching, I handed my last two pictures of the Reds with our European Cup to a couple of lads alongside. A Flamengista studied his before muttering, "Cope".

He meant Kop. I nodded. He knew his football.

Around the edge of the lower stand, a moat encircled the pitch and beyond this, on our side of the arena, lay steps that descended into the turf. Up these, Flamengo and Vasco's teams appeared, to tumultuous acclaim. In a frenzy of drumming, rival percussionists had lost the plot, yet their faces were blank as they banged away. No emotion, no smiles. While they gave it the bifters, they were in a trance.

Among Flamengo's players, I picked out Zico, the White Pelé and South America's Player of the Year, legendary for the free kicks he practised two hours every day. How many overrated, overhyped, overpaid English stars could be bothered to do that?

Nah. Off to the snooker club, mate. New barmaid.

Once the game began, both sides' skills were so exemplary you'd be forgiven for believing they had hands on the ends of their limbs, rather than feet. On receipt of a pass, they caressed the ball, controlling it instantaneously even though the surface was ropy, bare earth in places, because two or three matches were being played on it every week. Back in 1970, when Brazil were crowned world champions for the third time in Mexico to become outright winners of the Jules Rimet trophy, an astonishing 214 games took place at the Maracana during that single year.

And who can we credit for the Brazilians' dominance of the international game? Take a bow, Charles Miller, a 19-year-old São Paolo lad who, as his name denotes, was of British descent. After returning from university in England in 1894 with two balls and a copy of the rules, he introduced football to his South American homeland and out of those seeds the game's most exotic orchids grew.

They were blossoming again down on Maracana's pitch where Flamengo and Vasco (top scorer ever, no fibbing, Roberto Dinamite) indulged in some languidly balletic movements, a synthesis of the sluggish slow and mercurial quick that made you marvel at their switches of tempo and injections of pace. As they shuffled this way and that to wrongfoot opponents, it was child's play for them. What should we expect, though, when toddlers are taught to dance the samba and teenagers work at their soccer techniques on sandy beaches or rock-strewn wastelands? Out of second nature come first-class footballers

Pelé demonstrated to the world that o jogo bonito, the beautiful game, is more art than sport, embellished by graceful movement and delicate control. And the springboard for the sublime has to be offensive play. As he put it: "The game's complete beauty is best seen in the inventiveness, ingenuity and skill of the players, both individually and in teamwork, and this is only seen in an attacking style of football." Now Vasco were about to comply.

On the scoreboard, the temperature was showing as 27C when the attendance flashed up: 109,545. My biggest crowd ever! Not bad for a confrontation between city rivals but well behind the 180,000 for one league game in 1969.

The stadium was supposedly half-full but you'd never have believed it once Vasco, who exult in the nickname Bacalhau, dried cod, after Portugal's national dish, netted their first catch. The black and whites scored.

While Saturn rockets irradiated the duskish sky, Vasco's drummers raised the volume with a furious pounding that continued unabated until the referee whistled for the break and both sides scooted down the stairs.

They were off to the suite of five dressing rooms, all kept at the same temperature as the pitch. One room was for referees and the rest for teams, since two matches were often staged back to back. Other stadium facilities included 46 bars, 30 radio booths for different stations, five TV studios and 300 private boxes. A rather imposing venue which since 1950 has accommodated 75 million spectators.

After the teams came out for the second half, Arthur Antunes Coimbra, Zico to you and me, gave an exhibition of the art of aggression befitting Flamengo's craque, star player. He orchestrated a siege of the Vasco goal and laid on the through-ball that enabled his side to equalise.

If anything, the jubilation was louder and more dramatic now than when Vasco had gone ahead. With night fallen, fireworks and flares illuminated the heavens, lighting flags that billowed across the stands. Meanwhile, Flamengo's drummers, impassive to the last, were rupturing multiple blood vessels as they out-thundered their opponents at the other end.

What a setting for a game. They say architecture is music set in concrete. Well, the Maracana is music and sport set in concrete.

Once the final whistle shrilled, it remained honours even in the Clássico dos Milhões, Classic of the Millions, named in recognition of the clubs' fan bases, and both sets of supporters shuffled out, heads held high.

In the street, the four of us stood around, weighing up how to get back to our hotel. Few white faces and no police could be seen, but by this point in our stay we were scornful of Rio's false sense of insecurity. After such a fierce contest, we didn't detect the faintest whiff of aggro, just like Merseyside derbies, apart from the odd verbals. Although our footballing set-tos are famous for their intensity, fisticuffs have been a rarity at Anfield or Goodison, despite historians telling us that Liverpool used to be Orange and Protestant, Everton Green and Catholic. At White Hart Lane in the Sixties, I do recall a couple of Reds bellowing a smutty ditty about the Pope but since then any sectarian distinction has faded away, leaving a rivalry as deep-rooted as Celtic and Rangers', without their political and religious hostility. At the end of the day, we are all Scousers and childish abuse can never alter that.

How much worse in Buenos Aires where the barras bravas, the wild terraces, who follow Boca Juniors and River Plate, have engaged in gun battles before and after their hate-filled Superclásico. So when a couple of River fans were killed in the wake of a 20 triumph for their team, graffiti celebrated their deaths with a 2-2 scoreline and if any Boca aficionado dies, he must meet his maker in a coffin in club colours of blue and yellow, the conclusive declaration of loyalty on sale at the Bombonera stadium shop.

Here in Rio, peace reigned. Minibuses crept through the throng, touting for custom, and we boarded one bound for the city centre via the Maracanazinho, or Little Maracana, a roofed clone of the football arena next door, seating 20,000 for boxing, basketball, volleyball and pop concerts.

Inside our bus, we were in the mood for a nightcap. Out of his knapsack, Jim pulled some cachaça, in a bottle with a jink, a metal cap, and looked around for a sharp edge to prise it open.

Our driver gestured; hand it over.

Did he have a bottle-opener? 'Course not.

He inserted it in the side of his mouth and gave a twist.

Crack! The cap was off.

No broken wisdoms, just a bloke with a crocodile's bite.

After giving Jaws a swig, Jim passed the bottle around, oiling the fans' animated discussion of the game.

While they jabbered away, I drifted off ... back to the Maracana ... goals ... dribbles ... tackles ... drums ... flags ... rockets ... once again I was floating in God's football ground.

12

Tarnished Silver

It is not a calamity to die with dreams unfulfilled; but it is a calamity not to dream.

– Nelson Mandela

LIVERPOOL had won the European Cup in 1977 and 1978 and if they made it a hat-trick in 1979, they would keep the trophy, just as Real Madrid, Ajax and Bayern Munich had already done.

The draw threw up a tricky opening tie, an all-English collision with League champions Nottingham Forest who played the first leg at home. Doing live commentary at the City Ground for Merseyside's Radio City was Clive Tyldesley, assisted by Shanks for analysis.

When Forest's new signing, Garry Birtles broke the deadlock with a goal, Tyldesley remarked: "Cup-holders Liverpool are trailing 1-0 and a few minutes ago nobody had heard of Birtles. What do you think, Bill?"

Furious, Shanks couldn't curb his tongue.

"Well you've f****** heard of him now," he snapped.

Oddly, Radio City didn't receive a single complaint.

A 1-0 reverse would have been a reasonable outcome but Liverpool went in search of an equaliser, conceding another goal. Although they had Forest under siege in the Anfield return and shuddered the woodwork twice, the Trent men's resolute defence held on to keep a clean sheet.

The champions were out, our treble dream extinguished – and Granada TV closed its match coverage by playing The Party's Over, a tune that seemed to gloat over our defeat.

Kopites would not forget.

For days I felt gutted by our dismissal, but what could you do about it? Nothing, except take it on the chin. Then logic lifted me. Face facts. We have been given so much – just try pushing open our trophy room door. European glory will return.

The Forest reverse had an acute effect on one Liverpool veteran. In both matches, Hughes laboured to cope with the pace and intensity, his body paying for years of punishment. Paisley acted, telling him: "Em, I'm going to have to leave you out the team."

Honest as ever, Emlyn replied: "I can't handle playing in the reserves."

After a career bedecked with cups and caps, he couldn't stomach mouldering in the stiffs. Later that season, the only British player to lead two European Cup-winning sides signed for Wolves, bringing to an end his near-13 years at Anfield, during which he played 657 games, second only to Callaghan's 857.

In the Twenties, Paavo Nurmi, Finland's middle-distance runner who won nine gold and three silver Olympic medals, said English athletes were admirable because they could push themselves to total exhaustion and ultimate collapse. Roger Bannister bore this out in 1954 when he entered record books as the first sub-four-minute miler, slumping into supporters' arms the instant he crossed the finishing line. To me, Crazy Horse also lent substance to Nurmi's opinion, giving his all for our cause in every game.

As Emlyn left, Souness told him: "If I can do a tenth of what you've done at this club, I'll be a proud man." Em stated: "That's the nicest thing anyone's ever said to me."

Liverpool's European ambitions might have been over – for the moment – but in the FA Cup they advanced to the semi-final, meeting Manchester United at Maine Road. That finished 2-2, after McDermott missed a spot kick that would have taken us to Wembley.

Standing in the Gwladys Street end during the replay at Goodison, I sensed the tie was slipping away and, true enough, Greenhoff netted the winner.

The Reds were left to pursue the biggest domestic trophy, the League. They had already set their stall out in September at Anfield in a 7-0 trouncing of a Spurs side gilded with Argentinian World Cup winners Osvaldo Ardiles and Ricardo Villa, mere spectators at one of the performances of that or any season.

The standout goal began in the Kop penalty box after a Spurs corner was cleared to Dalglish. He flicked on to David Johnson, who passed to Heighway on the halfway line. Big Bamber hared along the touchline before sending over a pinpoint centre to Terry Mac who'd gone like the clappers all the way from the other end. He bulleted a header in.

Three passes taking the ball from one goal into the other.

Another satisfying victory came just before Christmas. The sweet aroma of revenge for our European exit wafted around Anfield as a McDermott brace saw off Nottingham Forest, ending an unbeaten run that stretched back 13 months.

By the New Year, Liverpool were already reaching out for the League pennant. After going top in December, they were never overtaken, with their best away performances coming in 3-0 conquests of the Uniteds in Manchester and Leeds. The Elland Road victory came in the Reds' last match, giving them 68 points, eight ahead of runners-up Forest and overhauling the previous First Division best set by the Yorkshiremen.

In 1969 I had applauded Leeds when they won the title at Anfield. Now, 10 years later, as I clapped our lads on their parade around the pitch, some Tykes fans inside their ground weren't over-enthusiastic. Perhaps the F-word is complimentary in broad Yorkshire.

Undefeated at home, the Reds achieved 30 victories, suffered just four away reverses and let in a miserly 16 goals, including four at Anfield. Their 68 points came in 42 matches (two points for a win), while they had a record number of goals for, 85, and the lowest goals against, 16, conceding none in 28 games.

Hansen called this the finest team he played in, while Paisley designated them "the best of the Liverpool Championship sides I have been associated with". He used just 14 players, including a superb midfield of Case, McDermott, Souness and Ray Kennedy, who took the Goal of the Season award on BBC's Match of the Day. Receiving a long, diagonal pass outside the area, he ghosted between two defenders, rounded the keeper and tapped home.

One unsung stalwart of the office staff was pivotal in the Reds' ascendancy. After working in club administration at Stockport, Scunthorpe, Brighton and Crewe Alexandra, Peter Robinson was appointed Anfield's secretary in 1965 on the recommendation of Reg Drury, the veteran Fleet Street football reporter. Known to colleagues by his PBR initials, Robinson worked with Sir John Smith on reforms that revolutionised the game. While Shanks and Paisley enjoyed absolute control of coaching and managing, the boardroom partners devoted themselves to commercial operations, negotiating transfers and contracts and ensuring the business operated efficiently and profitably.

Well ahead of the pack in appreciating TV's significance, PBR's far-sightedness paid dividends in 1979 when he sealed the deal with Hitachi for British football's first shirt sponsorship. His long-term impact on our club can never be overstated and every Kopite should be indebted to him.

For 1979-80's campaign, Liverpool were back on their biggest stage, the European Cup. In the first round, they shaded Dynamo Tbilisi 2-1 at Anfield but the Georgians, most of whom appeared tiny, exhibited sumptuous skills and with better finishing would have won.

They did not make the same mistake on their own turf, assisted by "impromptu" support. In a Soviet police state where you couldn't cough in public without official authorisation in triplicate, hundreds of their supporters congregated outside Liverpool's hotel at 4 in the morning of the game, chanting "Dynamo", which had the desired effect of disrupting our players' sleep.

Although Tbilisi would doubtless have won without this organised commotion, they coasted to a 3-0 win in a stadium holding 80,000 vocal Georgians and a few hundred adventurous Scousers. Our vision of a third European Cup had vaporised.

The following Saturday, a chap in front of me on the Kop was flicking through the Tbilisi programme, printed in three alphabets – Russian, Georgian and Roman, for a few paragraphs in English welcoming our fans.

Tbilisi did not progress much farther in the competition. Peter Robinson warned their next opponents, Kevin Keegan's Hamburg, what was in store in the away leg, so the Germans rearranged their schedule, going to bed at 5pm. That way they were well rested by the time the demonstrators arrived and Hamburg knocked the Georgians out.

On the domestic front, Liverpool subdued Grimsby 5-0 in the FA Cup before facing Nottingham Forest, something of a cup bogey side for us. Despite this, driving to the City Ground with Bill, Dave and Crawfie, I sensed this was going to be our day and had two packets of King Edwards in my coat, leftovers from our Christmas festivities. Sooner or later, Forest's luck would run out and, when it did, I would celebrate with a cigar, even though I rarely smoked. Liverpool were going to blow our opponents away in the cup.

On the contrary, it was the same old story. We were the guv'nors on a ploughed field of a pitch but Brian Clough had his team so well organised that goalscoring chances were virtually nil. Once Case hit the post, vague misgivings started needling me, until justice was done when Dalglish pulled the trigger and Terry Mac added a second. The King Teddies came out, to be distributed among my mates, and a few others besides. As the closing minutes ticked by, we evaporated in a grey fug of nicotine, our smoke signal of victory.

A mate back on the *Mirror* in Manchester wished he could have been puffing merrily away with us. Eddie Cummins was working frantically on that night's edition when he ran out of his favourite cigars and craved one quickly. Summoning a messenger, he gave him a fiver and, in broad Geordie accent, rasped: "Go to the canteen and get me five Hamlets."

The teenager disappeared and was gone ages. Soon Eddie was gasping for some therapeutic nicotine, looking at his watch, drumming his fingers, glancing at the newsroom door.

At last, it flew open and the messenger walked in … carrying a tray overloaded with plates.

Baffled, Eddie inquired: "What's this?"

"What you asked for," the lad replied indignantly. "Five omelettes!"

Eddie was convulsed with the first recorded seizure by Tourette Syndrome in the *Mirror*'s Withy Grove office.

After our disposal of Clough's boys, the FA Cup's sixth round gave us another exacting draw – Spurs at White Hart Lane. McDermott settled it with a cracker at our end, straight out of the top drawer. Beyond the angle of the penalty box, 25 yards out, Ardiles gave the ball away to Terry, who flicked it up and volleyed home. A consummate display of skill.

Now the Reds took on Arsenal in the semi-final. At Hillsborough, it ended 0-0 while the replay at Villa Park remained 1-1 after extra time and a second replay there had the same scoreline. Normally, win or lose a semi, the crowd leaves in animated mood, but walking away from Villa's ground with other Liverpudlians, silence muffled the streets – everyone was deep in reflection about the third replay. Finally, on May 1, after four games and seven hours of play watched by 168,000 spectators, Brian Talbot put the Londoners through at Coventry's Highfield Road.

That day, the Reds signed Ian Rush from Chester City for £300,000. Paisley's rating of the teenager: "He's dynamite in the box." Praise indeed for this unpolished gem that was to hold good over the years.

The League's final furlongs saw a two-horse race, Liverpool versus Manchester United, with our match of the season coming against Norwich at Carrow Road. In a seesaw encounter, the score went 1-0, 1-1, 1-2, 2-2, 2-3 (Fairclough hat-trick), 3-3, 3-5 (Dalglish and Case).

In their last match, the Reds would be champions if they saw off Aston Villa at Anfield. David Johnson put them ahead with a simple tap-in and Avi Cohen deflected a ball into his own net (1-1), then made amends by scoring at the Kop end with a long-range shot. After Johnson nicked his second and an own goal made it 4-1, the title was ours, won by 17 players, three of whom turned out in every one of the 42 fixtures.

When Cohen arrived at Anfield back in July, dressing-room fable maintained that Liverpool's first Israeli player stumped Dalglish with the statement: "You, me, same." Unsure how to respond, Kenny nodded. Next day, Avi said this again to the Glaswegian, who had to ask: "What are you talking about?" "You, me, same," replied Cohen. "Both learn English."

Now Avi had learnt the most important word for any footballer: Champions.

While Liverpool had been focusing on the bigger picture, the League Cup represented the minor star waiting for a Hollywood director's call. It came during the 1980-81 season when Dalglish passed a landmark, his 180th consecutive game for the first team, a sequence ended by an injury that kept him out of the League Cup's second round at Bradford City.

He was back for the return leg at Anfield, netting twice, and scored in every round to put the Reds in the final with West Ham. So we're all off to Wembley, self-proclaimed Venue of Legends but more appropriately Venue of Listeria, the noxious ingredient offered in some less-than-hygienic food shacks outside, charging exorbitant prices for reconstituted gristleburgers and mangey hot dogs. Wouldn't you rather starve?

"Wembley is a public toilet in the wasteland of North London," wrote Michael Henderson in *The Daily Telegraph*. Couldn't sum it up better.

Inside we were at the top of a terrace, heads almost stuck in roof girders, and once the whistle blew, we were churned in a tumble drier of bodies, left, right, up, down, backwards, forwards, sideways. I feared I'd break an ankle, stumbling over steps not shallow like the Kop's but a foot high.

After years at Anfield, I was used to crammed stands but this was painful.

Within minutes, my pals had been swallowed up and I was on my own, rupturing myself to watch the game. Then, when Alan Kennedy put the Reds ahead, the crowd went bonkers, jumping in unison, and you could feel the concrete beneath your feet moving with the leaping thousands.

Scary. That's never happened on the Kop.

At the break, I propelled myself through the crush to an overflowing Gents where I was 97th in line to the throne, allowing plenty of time to chat to an Irish Red, from Cork. When I inquired how he got his ticket, he answered. "We pay at the gate."

Interesting, because the final was supposed to be an all-ticket sell-out.

"How come?"

"We pay for every Liverpool game," he said. "Always get in. Just ask coppers outside which gate is letting people in, pay the gateman and climb over the turnstile. Been doing it years."

This nice big earner for bizzies and gatemen in on the fiddle explained why our end was brimming over. But with hundreds of extra fans admitted to a full house, conditions on the terraces were bound to be unpleasant, if not downright dangerous.

The second half brought no relief from my compulsory steeplechase up and down the steps and West Ham put the top hat on a drab final, equalising through a penalty in the dying minutes. A replay was ordained. At the end, bruised and deflated, I swore never to set foot in this sporting slum again.

What a relief to go to Villa Park for the replay, as exciting as the first clash was dull. Compared with Wembley, the Holte End was sheer luxury and we nailed the Hammers 2-1, a Dalglish special and Hansen header landing our first League Cup.

Remember that lad crying after Forest beat us with a non-penalty? He'd feel a lot happier now.

* * * * * * * * * *

For five years, John Lennon had found contentment in a life of domesticity with wife Yoko and son Sean in his Manhattan apartment, putting music on the back-burner. In November 1980, however, he did release an album, Double Fantasy, which a fan was holding as the Beatle came out of his home, the Dakota Building.

Could he have his autograph? John obliged.

When he returned six hours later, the fan, Mark Chapman, was still waiting outside. Before the 40-year-old singer could enter, Chapman drew a gun and fired five bullets into his back.

John bled to death in the entrance.

"My love of New York is something to do with Liverpool," the Beatle had remarked. "There is the same quality of energy in both cities." Yet his love of his birthplace was growing stronger by the day; Yoko said hearing Liverpool mentioned on BBC World Service Radio would bring tears to his eyes and, just before he died, he wondered if a ship sailing out of New York was heading for the Mersey.

"Time I went back," he sighed.

So John had been contemplating going home.

Within hours, on December 8, 1980, he was no more.

* * * * * * * * * *

Between January 21, 1978, when they lost 3-2 to Birmingham, and January 31, 1981, when Leicester won 2-1, Liverpool totted up a record total of 85 unbeaten matches at Anfield, comprising 63 League fixtures, nine League Cup games, seven European matches and six FA Cup ties. Nonetheless, by the close of the 80-81 League campaign, 17 draws meant they lay in fifth place.

Despite this, they already had the League Cup on the sideboard and were on course for another, the European Cup.

Our Continental crusade opened with a landslide victory. Liverpool pulverised Palloseura 10-1 at Anfield, making the Reds the only side to have bagged double figures on three occasions in the European club championship, after they'd caned Dundalk 10-0 in 1969 and Stromsgodest 11-0 in 1974.

The second round gave our lads a ticklish pairing with Aberdeen, Scotland's wonder team who had confounded both Glasgow clubs by doing the double. During the first minute of his bouts, Muhammad Ali would always go into a clinch to gauge how strong any challenger was. In the away tie with the Granite City men, Liverpool sized up their opponents and struck swiftly in the fifth minute, Terry Mac executing a delectable chip over their keeper to give us a 1-0 victory.

The return leg was a romp for the Reds, who flattened the Aberdonians 4-0 as Kopites sang in a mock Scottish accent, "Oh why are we so gid?" Hansen, who got one of the goals, admitted: "I had a point to prove to those Scots critical of players earning their living in England. I never performed with so much fire and aggression."

After wresting the championship from Celtic and Rangers, Aberdeen manager Alex Ferguson had expected to make his mark on Europe, so his side's summary ejection represented a blow that, according to one or two commentators, was to leave him with a certain sensitivity and fragility in his dealings with Liverpool.

Our home game with the Dons was watched from Kemlyn's stand by my mother, attending her first Anfield match ever, with a friend. Because her nerves were jangling so much, she had to rummage in her handbag on two occasions for valiums to calm herself and she decided her constitution wasn't robust enough for another game.

After 30 years in the Lake District, Mum had relocated to Cantril Farm, an overspill estate on the city's outskirts for people moved during slum clearances. Across district after district of inner Liverpool, terraced houses were being demolished, creating rubble-carpeted spaces. Upstanding at the junction of Islington, Brunswick Road and Prescot Street, the end wall of one derelict property served as a broad canvas for a Christian with a Biblical message of hope and an aptitude for signwriting. On the brown bricks, he used a tall ladder to paint in neat white letters: "Tear down the slums of your life and rebuild them with Jesus in your heart."

Within 24 hours, some cynic not possessing quite the same expertise with a paintbrush scrawled his incisive opinion beneath this exhortation, in crude splashes of red: "The vicar is all my arse."

Perhaps our ambassador to the United Nations was using up some home leave on Merseyside.

Once European competition resumed in March 1981, the quarter-final draw set Liverpool against CSKA Sofia who had knocked out the champions, Nottingham Forest. In L4, the Reds were a different proposition for the Bulgarians, outclassing them 5-1, as Souness cracked in a hat-trick and Sammy Lee and McDermott grabbed the other two. A David Johnson tap-in made the return in Sofia even more of a formality.

Now four giants were through to one of the most competitive semi-finals; Liverpool, Real Madrid, Bayern Munich and Inter Milan had won the trophy 13 times between them. Despite drawing the short straw, Bayern achieved what they came for at Anfield, a 0-0 stalemate that enabled Germans in the Sandon afterwards to express confidence about reaching the final. I'd have felt the same. However, before the second leg, their superstar, Paul Breitner, who had won the World Cup with Germany, gave the Reds added motivation, branding them "unintelligent", "predictable" and "technically inept". So confident were Bayern of going through that leaflets with information about the Paris final had even been put on every seat, a fact that our fans quickly brought to the Liverpool team's attention when they went for a stroll on the pitch beforehand.

German arrogance was about to receive its retribution.

Watched by a 78,000 crowd, FC Hollywood encountered our ace in the pack. In October 1980, Howard Gayle had become the first black player to turn out for the Reds, to the disgust of Anfield's resident racists, and now, in one of Europe's biggest arenas, he replaced the injured Dalglish minutes after kick-off.

Gayle thought it was a wind-up when coach Roy Evans told him to get on the pitch but the youngster wasn't fazed, playing a blinder on the left wing, from where he dragged Bayern's defence inside out. Seven minutes remaining, Ray Kennedy volleyed in and Howie had helped grab the jackpot. Even though Karl-Heinz Rumenigge equalised in the dying seconds, we were through.

This match represented the pinnacle of Gayle's Liverpool years. After five first-team appearances, he was transferred to Birmingham and then Blackburn and didn't get another opportunity to show off his talent at the game's highest level. But as Joe Louis, spending his twilight days as a greeter in a Las Vegas casino, pointed out: "Better to be a has-been than a never-been." Well, Howie will always be a star for what he did in Munich and for defying Anfield's white bigots. Has any other player left as deep an imprint in such a short span of time? I can't think of one.

The victors in the other semi were Real Madrid, who had already won the European Cup six times. With the showdown taking place in Paris, no Kopite could have wished for a more mouth-watering prospect but the first requisite was a ticket and here I'd been given a leg-up.

Through a Wigan businessman, I'd met Alan Kennedy and partaken of a few scoops with Barney Rubble, Alan's nickname after the Flintstones cartoon character who charged through stone walls. Once the Reds booked their Paris berth, Barney offered to supply a couple of tickets, so that was me sorted and Crawfie got in early for the spare.

A week before the final, some press pals and I wound up in the Land O' Cakes in Manchester's Ancoats Street for the latest round of our pro-celebrity pint-pot challenge, celebrity coming in the shape of Tom Dobney, an *Express* journalist with a rare claim to fame.

Born in May 1926, Tom gave his age as 15 years 5 months, instead of 14, to join the RAF during the Second World War and became the youngest military pilot ever, flying bombing missions over Germany. This fib was only rumbled after his father, who was divorced, spotted a newspaper photo of his son being introduced to King George VI at an airfield in East Anglia.

Dad contacted the Air Ministry to ask what the hell was going on and the youngster, to his considerable annoyance, found himself discharged from the RAF ... until he reached 17. Immediately he rejoined but was gravely injured when his plane crashed with engine failure on a raid.

During his press career, Tom kept his war service well camouflaged and only because someone mentioned an entry in the Guinness Book of Records did I learn about it, otherwise I'd never have suspected. By the by. Now Tom and the rest of us were having an invigorating reunion in the Land O', one of those evenings when the fellowship of your fellows makes you glad you're a fellow who has fellowship.

With a couple of United fans in attendance, the subject of Liverpool's Continental campaign was broached, repartee about our teams whipping between us while pints were swallowed and points scored.

Plainly I was excited about Paris and later that night, a-slumber in my sack, this graphic vision came to me. In the Parc des Princes, the clock's ticking away, the crowd's roaring, the Reds attacking – and Barney snatches the winner! Brilliantissimo!

If only it were true...

On the Monday before the game, as arranged with Alan, I parked my grey Cortina on Skelmersdale's by-pass and a few minutes later he rolled up from Rainford in his red E-type Jaguar to deliver my pair of tickets. As he handed them over, I enlightened him: "I've had a dream, Al. I know your goals are as rare as hen's teeth but you're going to score the winner."

He shook his head. "No. I've done well this season. I've got a couple and that's my lot."

A few more words on the game ("It'll be hard," Barney said), then we went our separate ways.

Next day, Crawfie and I winged from Speke to Paris where, after dropping our bags in the hotel, we set out to find a present for his wife, languishing back in Lancashire while the boys made whoopee in Gay Paree.

Along the Rue Rivoli, tourists are spoilt for choice for something to buy and we window-shopped – léchant les vitrines, licking the windows, as the French put it – until a lingerie boutique gave us the come-on, its windows adorned with slinky lace undergarments.

Inside this perfumed boudoir, we were greeted by a saleswoman, late-40s but figure of a 19-year-old, sheathed in a body-hugging white shift dress. Immaculately coiffed and glowingly tanned, the epitome of Parisian elegance. Once Crawfie had disclosed he fancied a gift for his wife, our sales adviser suggested a negligee and selected three from a rack, laying them side by side on the counter with a sensual swirl of her wrists.

In that shy, self-conscious way men exhibit in such situations, Crawfie held each of them up to the light, picturing his missus in it, assessing its aphrodisiac efficacy, until he selected the one that appealed most, a silky black number.

The saleswoman, oozing sexuality as only the French can, set about folding the selected item in a slow, deliberate fashion that acted as a form of retail lap-dancing. As she smoothed the silk, you knew this woman could handle herself, and any man, big or small. That fragrance in the air wasn't just Christian Dior, it was her libido.

She reposed the negligee within a veil of diaphanous tissue paper, laid this package delicately inside a black presentation box and sealed everything with a yellow satin ribbon, teasing out a perfect bow.

Lastly, she slid the box carefully, precisely, into a silver carrier bag with tasselled handles.

Voilà! Titillation and penetration. An erogenous shopping zone. Forget Kirkdale Co-op first thing on a Monday.

Back to reality. As she wrote out Crawfie's bill, she inquired: "Are you here for the football?"

Naturellement.

Raising her big brown eyes, she stared in turn at each of us, toying with our imaginations. "Messieurs," she said, tapping the carrier bag with a long, red-varnished fingernail, "Messieurs, this is the best sport."

At that instant, she was almost right.

With a breathy "Au'voir" and "Bonne chance", she opened the door and my mucker and I tumbled out, unzipping our jackets to cool off in the shaded colonnade.

This seductive lady's "Good luck" was something my team might require to get the better of Real, a special club. If you travel a bit, you soon appreciate that for people everywhere they have genuine style and glamour, not the self-deluding pretensions of others, and these qualities were conspicuous when we arrived at the Parc des Princes for the big game. Outside, Madridistas flaunted their elegance and affluence, walking fashion statements in gear straight out of the Spanish edition of Esquire magazine. Not a pair of faded denims in sight. How fitting that many were topped off with white bowler hats. The crowning touch.

Before the final, Paisley the psychologist had used his habitual ploy: he complimented Real, gave them "a little bit of toffee", to take the edge off their performance. It worked. On the pitch, their players were cautious, lacking ambition, and each side neutralised the other. In the second half, with no goals and the clock ticking away, I grew a mite apprehensive that Real's winger, Laurie Cunningham, could exploit our tiring defence but in the 82nd minute came the passage of play substantiating that sleep can be prophetic.

Kennedy (R) took a throw-in to Kennedy (A), who diverted the ball with his chest, toed it towards goal and set off like a bullock bursting out of an abattoir pen.

Into their 18-yard box Barney rampaged, barging between two defenders and charging towards Real keeper Agustín. From an acute angle, our left-back raised his hoof – and booted the ball into the onion bag. Gooooooooooal! I went bananas, hugging Barney's brother Keith and sister Beverley alongside me and yelling that I'd dreamt he'd score. "Oh, yeah," they humoured me.

The stadium remained in uproar until the ref blew.

We were Kings of Europe again and the Reds had beaten the Whites once more.

Quite a turnaround for Barney, whose Liverpool debut in 1978 had not been auspicious. At the interval, he returned to the dressing room to be greeted by Paisley with "They shot the wrong Kennedy". Now, the right Kennedy was on the Parc des Princes turf, showing *his* European Cup to family and friends in the stand as Kopites chanted to Granada, "The party's only just beginning".

Sitting directly in front of me were Clemence's parents and from the periphery of his dancing team-mates on the pitch, he gave them a wave. None of the fans was to know he had played his last match for the Reds. After taking every honour in the game, he would seek a fresh challenge, joining Spurs in the close season.

For the Madrid media, Liverpool's coronation as Kings of Europe turned them into la negra bestia, the black beast; for Paisley, their triumph made him the first manager to win three European Cups, something gifted coaches such as Fabio Capelli and Helenio Herrera never accomplished. Bob stood head and shoulders above them all, the principles he taught at Melwood – pass and move, never lose the ball, never waste it – bringing glory in the most prestigious competition. And each time we won the cup, we deserved it because we'd been the better side.

Once Crawfie and I got out of the Parc des Princes, we kept to the rule usually guaranteeing slick escape from any venue in a major city: head in the opposite direction to the crowds. Five minutes' away, we chanced upon a bar where we received a friendly reception from locals, including a couple of St Etienne fans who insisted on buying Kronenbourgs and joined in our throaty YNWA. While thousands queued hours for a train in the Métro, the two of us got pleasantly plastered with Parisian chums.

Meantime, because they had to give urine samples, Souness and Neal were late for the victors' banquet, missing the dinner. "It took Graeme and me two-and-a-half hours to produce a wee drip," Phil revealed. "Afterwards we flagged down a police car and got a lift back to the hotel."

When the squad returned to Merseyside next night, captain Phil Thompson transported the European Cup in the boot of his Capri to his local. Wednesday: Parc des Princes, Paris. Thursday: Falcon boozer, Kirkby, where congregations of residents came to worship and have their photos taken with our latest silverware.

* * * * * * * * * *

The summer of 1981 on Merseyside offered a vicious antithesis to our Parisian bliss. Riots raged with such ferocity in Toxteth that police resorted to CS gas and the Rialto ballroom, where I'd listened to Merseybeat bands, was burnt to the ground.

Liverpool might have been stomaching unemployment, economic decline and serious social problems but that did not warrant terrorising children and pensioners, destroying shops and pubs. Once the disturbances began, yobs in other parts of Merseyside joined in, wrecking whatever they could lay their hands on. Out at Cantril Farm, Mum watched one mob smashing shop windows in the nearby precinct until police arrived and inflicted some vigorous kerbside justice. Peace returned.

More anguish came on September 29 with news that Shanks had died of a coronary thrombosis in Broadgreen Hospital. Throughout the city, supporters wept, a grief shared by people who hadn't the least interest in football but regarded him as one of their own.

For the funeral at St Mary's in West Derby, thousands lined the streets and Ron Yeats, Emlyn Hughes, Ray Clemence and John Toshack acted as pallbearers, flanked by Ian St John, Ian Callaghan and Kevin Keegan.

At the end of the service, You'll Never Walk Alone filled the church as Shanks was borne away to Priory Road crematorium, across the park from his beloved Anfield. No finer resting place for a man who deserved all the tributes that poured in.

Sir John Moores, Everton's millionaire backer, said: "Bill Shanks made Liverpool. Before he became manager, they were a very ordinary club. With Shanks in charge, they became a great club."

That great endeavour unquestionably exacted its toll. Johnny Giles declared: "I believe Shanks died of a broken heart after he saw Liverpool go on to even greater success without him. Giving your whole life to a football club is a sad mistake."

But Bill was a man who gave his all in everything he undertook, whether running a team or cleaning the cooker. He could never change because it was in his blood. And what a legacy he left us, achievements engraved in full on his memorial in Glenbuck, with this expression of gratitude: "The legend. The genius. The man. From Anfield with love. Thanks, Shanks."

After retiring, Bill said: "I was only in the game for the love of football and I wanted to bring back happiness to the people of Liverpool." Now his statue outside the Kop bears this simple inscription: "Shanks – He made the people happy". Could anyone, anywhere, wish for a finer epitaph?

＊＊＊＊＊＊＊＊＊＊

By Christmas 1981, the European Champions found themselves in alien territory, 12th in the League, and every day players had protracted discussions about why they were faring so badly.

Bruce Grobbelaar, our new goalie, shouldered some of the blame. When Clemence went off to Tottenham, the Zimbabwean was summoned unexpectedly into the first team and the defence had to adjust to his more adventurous style, which sometimes created uncertainty.

Thompson had also suffered a dip in form that led Paisley to make Souness skipper, initially unsettling the team but ultimately proving a master stroke as the Reds notched up 11 straight victories to challenge for the title by Easter. They also struck silver again in the League Cup, now the Milk Cup, when they eclipsed Spurs 3-1 at Wembley.

However, our European Cup advance was halted by CSKA Sofia. After spanking Finland's Oulu Palloseura 7-0 at Anfield and then disposing of AZ Alkmaar 5-4 on aggregate, we were knocked out by the Bulgarians, 2-1 over the quarter-final's two legs.

With all eyes trained on the League, Manchester provided the setting for two decisive victories: United succumbed to a Craig Johnston humdinger and City were tonked 5-0. After that, the Championship was settled in our last home fixture when Spurs – and Clemence – were the visitors. For this, I abandoned the Kop in favour of the Main Stand because my Wigan businessman pal had got hold of two tickets, courtesy of ... Alan Hansen.

I know, name-dropping again. Does he have no shame?

In this instance, actually, I do not.

In a full-blooded encounter with Tottenham, Hoddle nicked one during the first half for the Londoners who tried out-muscling us to protect their lead and conceded a succession of fouls. Taking full advantage of these invitations to score, Lawrenson, Dalglish and Whelan rattled goals in. After lying below mid-table in December, we were champions again.

A due period of celebration marked in the stand, it was time to crack out the Tetley's and I accompanied my mate Geoff Bigg to the players' lounge where Alan had invited us for a toddy. Me, in the players' lounge, at Anfield. Jammy lad.

After 20 minutes, the man himself, immaculately besuited, joined us at the bar, bought beers, talked about the game as though we'd been mates for years, bought more beers, listened attentively to our unsophisticated opinions and insisted on filling up our pints again. Then he asked to be excused as he had to meet someone else in the room. Did we mind?

Mind? I was in awe of this great footballer, this superlative centre-half, this Liverpool icon.

Feel free, lad.

While Geoff and I were sipping our ales, parents pushed children in wheelchairs into the lounge for photographs with players, principally Rush and Dalglish, who made a fuss of these kids, some of whom might have had terminal illnesses.

Forget celebrity and wealth – the capacity to give so much pleasure to sick youngsters has to be beyond price.

Alan returned, more beer flowed and we talked again like old friends.

Call me a sad, simple Kopite, I don't care – I was chuffed to be spending these moments in this magical place with this Anfield idol, and when we had to leave, I gushed my thanks for his hospitality. A day to cherish: winning the Championship and meeting Alan Hansen.

Paisley now had his fifth title and he admitted: "I am proudest of this one because there was so much to do. Back in January, a lot of people were shouting at us to bring in new players. Any idiot can do that. It's a matter of bringing them in at the right time and place."

The League and League Cup double wasn't a bad opener for our new skipper, Souness.

"He would fight for 90 minutes every match he played in," Hansen said. "He and Dalglish were the same. If they were playing tiddlywinks, they wanted to win."

An opponent's viewpoint was offered by Frank Worthington: "Souness is the hardest, most ruthless player I've come up against in 15 years of top-class football."

Roll on, next season.

Before it began, Paisley announced he would retire the following May, after nine years as manager. With another European Cup topping the team's list of retirement presents, they progressed to a quarter-final tie with Poland's

Widzew Lodz. In the dressing room before the away leg, Bob had a spasm when he spotted Hansen sipping a cup of tea.

"It'd been put in our dressing room by a Widzew official," Alan said. "Bob swept it off the table, shouting, 'What have I told you? Drugs! Don't drink anything!' "

Drugs or no drugs, the Reds came unstuck 2-0 and, despite winning 3-2 at home, they were out.

The full-time whistle at Anfield showed Kopites at their fairest. As they clapped, Widzew Lodz walked down to the Walton Breck end, applauded our fans and then lined up for photos, the Kop as a backcloth. A picture for the Poles to prize.

In the FA Cup, TV requirements dictated that the lads turned out for their first game on a Sunday, going down 2-1 at home to Brighton, a reverse that ended 63 cup games without defeat. We still got to Wembley for the Milk Cup final, Paisley's 11th and last trip to the Twin Towers as manager. After Alan Kennedy levelled for the Reds against Manchester United, Ronnie Whelan snapped up the pot with a 20-yard curler past Gary Bailey in extra time.

At the presentation of the trophy, Paisley's third League Cup in three years, the lads insisted on him going up the royal box's 39 steps to receive it, the first instance of any manager given this honour.

That evening, I rang Mum to wallow in our triumph and she asked: "Did you hear? There was loads of trouble in pubs around Wembley before the game.

"Landlords barred all Manchester United fans – they said they'd only serve regulars."

Quite right, too.

On the League front, Dalglish appeared in every fixture for his fifth season out of six at Anfield, while Rushie grabbed four goals at Goodison, including the first derby hat-trick since 1935, in a 5-0 conquest of Everton, acknowledged as one of the Reds' finest away performances ever.

At the finishing line, Bob had his second retirement present, the title, leaving runners-up Watford 11 points behind.

After 44 years at Anfield, Paisley stepped down with a brace of trophies in his arms, In nine seasons, Britain's most successful manager had won six League championships (1976, 1977, 1979, 1980, 1982, 1983), three European Cups (1977, 1978, 1981), three League Cups (1981, 1982, 1983) and one UEFA Cup (1976).

Manager of the Year in 1976, 1977, 1979, 1980, 1982 and 1983, he knew precisely how good his Liverpool were, confessing: "I've been here during the bad times, too. One year we came second."

After Paisley finished his last shift in L4's silver mine, Kopites were surprised to learn his deputy had got the top job.

Joe Fagan had never been a high-profile figure, preferring to stay in the background and carry out his duties without any fuss, but like Paisley before him, he agreed to move up because the club wanted him to.

He was an excellent choice because nobody knew as much about European football, while Anfield's players and coaching staff regarded him as a decent, honourable man.

A product of the Boot Room where he'd been a fixture for 26 years, Joe rose from reserve team trainer to first team trainer to chief coach when Paisley took over from Shanks in 1974 and since being promoted to assistant manager in 1979, had fulfilled the vital role of Bob's understudy during his era of supremacy.

With such world-class players as Dalglish, Rush, Hansen and Lawrenson in the side, our new boss was convinced he could follow in Paisley's footsteps but his first trophy, the Milk Cup, required 13 matches, including five replays.

To conclude this long journey, the Reds drew 0-0 with Everton at Wembley in the first Merseyside final but won the replay 1-0 at Maine Road, through a Souness grass-cutter from the edge of the area. Liverpool had picked up the trophy four years in a row and set a new mark for the longest undefeated cup run, 25 rounds since 1980.

The League campaign permitted Dalglish to add more lustre to his coruscating record. When he scored in the Ipswich fixture in November 1983, it was his 100th League goal for Liverpool, making him the first player to score a century in both England and Scotland for just two clubs. While the main man was in sparkling form and Rushie found the net for fun, the Reds swept on to their 15th Championship, leaving rivals in their wake from November as they became the only team since Arsenal in the Thirties to take the title three years on the bounce.

Joe had his second trophy.

In the European Cup, Liverpool faced a hard road to the final. The campaign started sedately with a 6-0 aggregate victory over Denmark's Odense, including two goals by Dalglish to overtake Denis Law as Britain's highest scorer in the competition, with 15.

After a goalless tussle with Athletic Bilbao on our turf, the Reds won the away leg with a strike by Rush and were applauded off the pitch by the Basques at full-time.

The next round paired them with old friends Benfica. At Anfield, our lads won by the only goal but in Lisbon they put on a show, trouncing the potent Portuguese 4-1, a result that made Europe sit up. Now any tie with Liverpool aroused trepidation in Continental sides who, like boxers freezing with Gardenitis at Madison Square Garden, would suffer crippling attacks of Anfielditis at our place.

The last barrier on our road to the final was bulldozed aside with home and away dismissals of Dynamo Bucharest, 1-0 and 2-1 respectively.

Now we faced a challenge that could not have been more intimidating: Roma on their own patch in front of tifosi with an unshakeable conviction they would become champions for the first time. Regrettably, the Reds could not look to me for support, since I'd had an operation on my cornea and had to miss the trip.

One-eyed in Standish, I viewed events in the Stadio Olimpico from afar, with a growing sense that the Italians' overconfidence might prove their undoing.

In the Eternal City, banners covered whole buildings proclaiming Roma as Campioni, people flourished red and yellow scarves bearing the statement, in English, "Roma, Champions of Europe", and minutes before kick-off, the home end unfurled a definitive declaration of intent: an enormous European Cup and the words "Ultra Roma".

The final was a done deed. That was how sure they were of getting their hands on the trophy, although a Scouse banner begged to disagree: "Shanks marmalized Milan, Paisley munched the Gladbachs, now Fagan's making Roman ruins".

The match itself had an eccentric overture. After the Liverpool squad had inspected the pitch, they went back into the main stand and, on the way to their dressing room, Dalglish, Michael Robinson and a few others started warbling Chris Rea's song, I Don't Know What It Is But I Love It. Soon the tune was picked up by the rest of the team who belted it out.

In their sanctum on the opposite side of the corridor, Roma's players could not believe their ears.

These English are crayzeee! Minutes before the biggest game of their lives, they are having a pub singsong. Have they taken drugs to calm their nerves? Are they too stupid to know what is riding on this match? Not just glory, prestige, global recognition and commercial spin-offs but also £64,000-a-man bonuses for the Italians, compared with Liverpool's piffling £6,000 a head.

No, to the Romans, the Inglesi had no comprehension of what was at stake. Perhaps the singing was to disguise their fear that they were on a hiding to nothing. And yet, and yet …

Once both teams walked out, the noise was ear-popping and smoke from dozens of flares drifted across the ground. Not the least intimidated, the Reds held their own until the 15th minute when Neal snapped up a loose ball to notch the vital opening goal.

Pruzzo headed an equaliser just before the break, Liverpool weathered a flurry of Italian attacks in the second half, and the score remained 1-1, a deadlock extra time failed to break.

After 120 minutes, all down to penalties.

First up, Steve Nicol fired over the bar, sending home fans into paroxysms of glee. However, Neal, Souness and Rush all outfoxed Roma keeper Tancredi whereas Conti and Graziani missed the net completely, boggled by Grobbelaar's jelly-legged antics.

The tally was 3-2 to Liverpool when Alan Kennedy stepped up. If he pinged it in, Ol' Big Ears was ours. For seconds Barney waited, 12 yards from eternity, as most of the 70,000 fans shrieked and whistled to put him off.

The racket didn't unnerve him. He ran up and coolly sidefooted the ball into the righthand corner. The Scouse sector of the ground went doolally as Barney embarked on an insane run, topped off by a manic two-footed jump into the ground. Yes, crayzeee!

In a millisecond, he was buried beneath a heap of ecstatic team-mates.

Back at the BBC studios in London, a Liverpool diehard, John Robert Parker Ravenscroft, lay on the floor, weeping uncontrollably after hearing the closing seconds on radio. John Peel – for it was he – felt so choked that a colleague, David Jensen, had to introduce his show.

Once again, as with Borussia Mönchengladbach, Bruges and Real Madrid, the Reds had overcome the Whites to take their fourth European Cup in eight seasons, all won in knockout tournaments for champion clubs, not a competition watered down to accommodate three or four teams from the elite leagues.

Liverpool's feat was memorable for other reasons. They had become the first to prevail over a team playing the final on its home ground; the first to win on penalties; and the first to take three major trophies in one season, all in Joe's debut year as manager.

Brasso's sales rep on Merseyside was rubbing his hands.

Barney also entered Kopology as the only Briton to score winners in two European Cup finals. Yet before the Roma game, a somewhat unpromising training session had been held at Melwood when the squad practised a shoot-out, the five who would take penalties competing against youth players. The youngsters won 4-2.

Barney proceeded to take dozens of kicks, repeatedly putting the ball to the goalie's right. Exasperated, Joe told him that, in the event of a penalty, "you must, MUST, shoot to the keeper's left". Conveniently, Barney forgot in the Stadio Olimpico, drilling the ball to the right.

For Roma, the defeat was a humiliation that triggered a bloody sequel.

Final four: Outside Lime Street station before catching a train to Rome, Dunkin, Wakefield, McMath and Crawford take part in a line-up with that flag and those flagpoles.

Red Roman legion: The Stadio Olimpico is a-flutter with flags, but my state-of-the-art poles are in a heap outside.

Monster bash: Middle of the night at the city of Rio's prestigious ball and Seddon has one of his Jekyll-and-Hyde moments.

Holy vision: The statue of Christ looms out of cloud shrouding Rio's Corcovado mountain.

Maracana overture: The lull before the storm of a derby between
Flamengo and Vasco da Gama.

Happiness before the horror: That flag puts in another appearance,
this time outside Heysel.

Home comfort: A welcoming pub in Mexico City where the Liverpool name features prominently.

Bird's-eye view: The Azteca before all its lights go out and a pair of laser eagles begin hunting for prey.

Science fiction stadium: The San Siro spaceship has landed
in Milan after its inter-galactic journey.

Band of hope: Our Inca Trail group at the start of the four-day slog,
with me in a funny Peruvian hat at the front and Russ directly behind.

Fantasia in rock and stone: The classic panorama of Machu Picchu
during early morning.

Capricious beauty: Cotopaxi seen from the Pan-American Highway
as it runs through Ecuador's Avenue of the Volcanoes.

Lost cause: With daylight breaking, it dawns on one Kopite
that he isn't going to make it to Cotopaxi's summit.

Euro zone: Ferrett and Davenport, in the foreground,
savour the atmosphere before our game in the Camp Nou.

Kings of all we survey: The Mighty Reds are crowned
Champions of Europe yet again in Istanbul.

Together for ever: On their way out of the Ataturk, Dad and lad
celebrate a Liverpool triumph that will echo through eternity.

Their hooligans exacted revenge in streets around the stadium, where Italian police displayed a reluctance to intervene.

Tifosi bombarded Liverpool fans and their coaches with stones and bottles while Howard Foy, a mate of mine, witnessed Romans speeding along on scooters, their pilion passengers slashing out randomly with stilettos at Scousers. Many received lacerations and when Howard reached his bus, one lad had been stabbed in the stomach. At least he had found safety; other supporters endured a fearful night because their transport drove off without them.

A year later, this violence, unreported by Britain's national media, was to have deadly repercussions.

After the final, football writers conferred the laurel of best English side since the war on Liverpool, who also boasted Europe's deadliest striker, Ian Rush, winner of the Golden Boot for European goals and Footballer of the Year in votes by both fellow professionals and sports reporters. During the season, he scored 48 goals: 32 in 41 League games, eight in 12 Milk Cup ties, two in the FA Cup and six in European games.

The Rome decider also gave Neal his fourth European Cup winners' medal, the first and only Englishman to win that many. "Now we felt invincible," he said.

During the season, Frankie Goes to Hollywood had been advising everybody to relax and Kopites could certainly do that, given Joe's wondrous trio of trophies. His treble also supplied heavy-calibre ammunition against those Jeremiahs moaning that nice guys don't win things. Give them both barrels, two names: Fagan and Paisley.

The lads' playing style won praise on the Continent, since the team adapted so readily to the muddy, badly drained pitches that blighted our winter season. These poor surfaces made it more difficult for skilful teams to impose themselves on scrappers; both sides could be reduced to the same level.

Among Red enthusiasts was the future England coach, Sven-Goran Eriksson, who in December 2000 recalled: "I always admired the great Liverpool, how they played football, and their lack of interest in what rivals were doing, even when those rivals were doing well.

"I remember being there one January when they were fighting for top place with another team, Ipswich, maybe, or Manchester United. And after the game at Anfield I asked Joe Fagan how the other leading teams had got on. He said he didn't know, didn't even know who they were playing. Impossible in Italy!"

Eriksson added: "Everyone liked Liverpool a lot. I liked the easy way they played. One touch, two touches, simple but effective."

By attaining greatness in Rome, Joe had put up a ginormous marker for our rivals. Year after year the Reds were filling their boots with silverware, setting new yardsticks for excellence. Now they were the most respected, most revered, most feared team in Europe.

* * * * * * * * * *

"Look at that!" A fan on our coach picked out the Atomium, Brussels' sky-scraping representation of an atom, and everyone craned their necks to see this steel and concrete totem.

Alongside lay Heysel Stadium, to where I was travelling from the airport with Howard Foy for Liverpool's latest European Cup adventure, a meeting with Juventus billed as the Dream Final.

Two of the continent's most glamorous sides, the demand for tickets had been so feverish that UEFA could have sold 200,000 when only 58,000 were available – and we had ours for a game that might guarantee our slot in the following season's competition.

After the Stadio Olimpico epic, Souness had left for Sampdoria, bearing a portfolio of medals, and the Reds had laboured without him during their 84-85 League campaign, finishing second to Everton. Now they had to win this final to qualify again for the premier competition.

Just as importantly, if we did collect Ol' Big Ears, that would make our fifth European Cup, meaning we kept the trophy, ours for ever and a leaving present for Joe, who was retiring after the match.

As the champions, Liverpool had plenty of backers and swept past Lech Poznan, Austria Vienna and Benfica in earlier rounds without too much difficulty. The tie with the Portuguese brought Dalglish's first sending-off but, once he'd completed a three-match ban, he returned for the semi, helping us to an aggregate 5-0 victory over Panathinaikos. Now, on May 29, 1985, our path to glory was blocked by Juventus, who were out to bag their first European Cup.

As our coach drove up to Heysel, Liverpool and Juve fans were having kickabouts, sitting in mixed groups on the grass, nattering, singing, exchanging scarves and badges. Everything was relaxed and friendly, no hint of bother. Given the disturbances in Rome, this was how football should be, even though the choice of stadium had met with reservations a couple of weeks before.

After Peter Robinson and other Anfield officials inspected the ground, they expressed concerns about its suitability for a showpiece game because, in their opinion, it was obsolete and rundown. They also told UEFA and Belgium's Football Association that the allocation and sale of tickets had not been thought through properly, since a corner section of our end had been set aside for neutral Belgian fans. The fear was touts would sell those tickets to opposing supporters who might confront each other.

Liverpool's apprehensions were noted but Europe's football authorities declined to act on them.

Now, easing past in our coach, the stadium appeared tolerable from the outside and no one viewing how rival supporters mingled amicably could have had the faintest idea what lay in store.

Our driver drove slowly past, onto a boulevard leading to the town centre. Brussels is a city bristling with beer pumps and he soon pulled over alongside a bar to allow everyone off. With the sun cracking the flags – jolly brewers' weather – Howard and I didn't wait for an invitation to enter for our first glasses of Gueuze beer. Merveilleux.

Once we'd sated our thirsts, our stomachs were agitating for nourishment so we dived into the Grand'Place, surely Europe's most handsome square and a stately setting for a pre-Heysel dinner.

In one corner of this masterpiece, a courtyard of civilised living lined with bars and restaurants, we came across La Rose Blanche, whose menu offered a fine selection of dishes at reasonable prices.

Outside broken glass glinted on the cobbles. I asked the waiter if there'd been any trouble. "No," he answered. "People were having beers and some bottles got knocked over."

Good. After last year's final, this one had to be peaceful.

We ordered steak, accompanied by a mountain of chips smothered in mayonnaise, and Kwak lager, in its idiosyncratic bulbous glass, shaped like an inverted skittle. Since the bottom is rounded, this glass will not remain upright, so it comes in a wooden stand with a handle.

The amber liquid did not disappoint and neither did the Rose Blanche's food, fit for an emperor's birthday.

With an hour to kick-off, we settled our bill and jumped on a Métro train rammed with Scousers who entertained commuters with We Love You Liverpool and the inevitable YNWA.

This early-evening entertainment had the Belgians smiling and as a finale for our French-speaking fellow travellers, a chorus of "Allez les Rouges, Allez les Rouges" resounded through the carriage.

What an atmosphere, like Rome '77.

What fans – and what a game to come.

Heysel was next to a tube station and we soon got in the ground where our seats lay at pitch level, beside the Liverpool end. Walking down the steps, I sized up the arena and was puzzled by smoke or dust rising from the far corner of the goal stand to our right.

What's all that about?

The atmosphere was uncomfortable, strained, without any chanting or singing, only a background hum as people discussed what was going on.

Sitting down, I became aware that where the smoke was drifting into the air, aggro had broken out. In a large space on the terrace, a handful of police were flailing around with batons, driving Reds supporters away. Meanwhile, down on the touchline, gendarmes were dragging people out of a mêlée next to the corner flag and laying them on the pitch. Juve supporters, in zebra-striped shirts.

What's happening? The bloke next to me, an Australian, put me in the picture. "There's been a ruck," he said. "Liverpool fans attacked Italians, in that corner."

I stared, trying to grasp what was going on. We didn't have any previous in finals, so why had Scousers attacked Italians? It didn't make sense.

Now, with the trouble subsiding, casualties were being carried away on stretchers, dozens of them. Howard and I watched in disbelief until, desperate for the Gents, I couldn't wait any longer. I skipped up steps to the top of the terrace where a man in an English coach driver's jacket spotted my Liverpool shirt. Nodding towards the far side, he said: "Thirty people have been killed over there."

No!

I raced into the toilets. Couldn't be possible. If there'd been a fracas, a few fans might have got hurt, but 30 dead, that wasn't credible. Yet ... My blood ran cold at the thought.

I legged it back to Howard and told him what the driver had said. He was stunned.

Never, never, never had we expected anything like this.

An announcement came on the PA system, in Italian, which I don't speak, but from the few distinguishable words, it sounded like an appeal for a representative of a Juve supporters' branch in Torino to go to the main stand.

Another appeal followed for someone from Genoa, then Roma, Pisa, Napoli, Bologna ... on and on the announcer went, naming city after city, town after town in Italy. That's for casualties, I thought. They must be members of those branches.

Isn't this wonderful? You fly from Speke to Brussels, enjoy some beers and a meal, go to a football stadium and watch people dying. People like you. People who love their club.

My lifetime worshipping the Reds has been reduced to this: seeing another team's supporters perish in front of my eyes.

Now, while I contemplated ambulancemen clearing up the mess of soiled humanity, I slid into a volatile mind set, a mixture of shame and hatred welling up inside.

I felt deeply ashamed of the vile minority who'd latched on to my club – *MY* club! – and used it as a pretext for gratuitous violence that had caused deaths.

And I felt a hatred that ached for revenge on the perpetrators.

I had gone into a dark place and an ugly stranger had emerged from this shadowland. Someone I didn't recognise. Someone who frightened me. Someone capable of anything.

And I do mean anything.

For 30 years, Liverpool had been the love of my life and she'd returned my love unconditionally. Now *MY* Liverpool had been raped and I was seething with a murderous rage.

Vermin! Vermin! *Vermin!*

The Tannoy crackled again and Phil Neal came on, saying something about "the match will go ahead ... tragic circumstances ... just behave".

You couldn't hear distinctly but once he'd finished, the Liverpool terrace gave a muted cheer.

Moments later, a red-shirted Joe Fagan appeared out of the tunnel on the far touchline and, face down, trudged across the grass to our side. When he reached the fence, he looked ghastly, tears glistening on his cheeks. He shouted to our supporters, begging them not to get involved in any trouble, but I couldn't catch everything, although "my last game" did register.

His brief appeal over, he plodded back to the main stand, face streaked with sorrow, shoulders hunched, the embodiment of desolation.

How could anyone do this to such a lovely man? One of Anfield's most loyal servants, he should have been savouring his finest hour before retiring. Instead, he was being gutted by a madness transmitted by TV into living rooms across the world.

By this stage I hadn't any interest in the game. I feared the worst – that many Italians had been killed – and all I wanted was to get home. Surely the final would be abandoned. But no, the PA announcer came on: "Le jeu aura lieu. The game will take place."

Two hours late, the teams walked out and the final kicked off.

Action on the pitch was an irrelevance, even more so when Juve fans charged down the running track, hurling bottles into the crowd. Some tried to rip open a gate in the fence in front of us but a police baton-charge forced them back to their end. After that, the only incident I can recall was Juventus being awarded a penalty for a Gary Gillespie foul yards outside the box. Platini scored.

Game over, thank God.

At the whistle, Howard and I hung on to watch Juve's celebrations. Whether they should have won was neither here nor there; on such a frightful day, after such horrendous events, they had to be given that trophy.

The team embarked on their lap of honour, reaching our corner where Italians piled down to the bottom of the terrace to greet them. We found ourselves surrounded by families sharing the Zebras' joy.

Suddenly, an explosion, then another and another. Wine bottles, dispatched from on high, were smashing around us.

Everybody cowered, peeping up the terrace, from where the missiles had been lobbed. Silhouetted against the skyline, three figures, teenagers, were scarpering after conveying their congratulations to the Italians.

Given everything that had gone before – the deaths, the injuries, the panic – what putrid brains did those kids have? For crying out loud, the mankiest maggots have more pity.

But why should anyone from England be horrified by such behaviour? Within hours, those same scumboys would be back in their own fetid cesspit, throwing bricks at trains, setting fire to schools and persecuting pensioners. What little heroes you are. How proud your parents must be.

The Italians had had enough. Arms around their youngsters, they hastened away. We'd had enough, too. Get back to England and let's try to come to terms with this black night.

I knew my wife and my mother would be fretting over whether I was all right but police outside the stadium wouldn't let anyone go hunting for a phone box. Herded straight onto a coach, we were ferried to the airport, directly onto the apron where we stewed in stifling heat, awaiting our plane.

After an hour, a policeman got on to speak to the driver and gave the latest news: 39 Italians had been killed. Thirty-nine! I could have wept. Thirty-nine people go off to a match and die!

The Dream Final had turned into a nightmare.

At last, around 3 in the morning, our Aer Lingus plane taxied alongside and we took off for Speke. There, an Italian TV crew was conducting interviews in a corridor next to the arrivals hall.

I like Italians – a lot – and I hesitated, wanting to say how sorry I felt, but the reporter was surrounded by fans clamouring to give their accounts.

Forget it. Home to Standish – fast.

Back at Heysel, Grobbelaar *had* managed to communicate his feelings to Juve's players, clambering on their coach after the game to speak from the heart about that evening's events.

Unlike the 39, I returned safely, but my rage within simmered for days as the tragedy's facts gradually came to light.

At our end, most tickets for neutrals in the corner block, sector Z, had been bought by tifosi Juventini from touts. Consequently, the volatile situation had been created of several thousand Italians separated from the huge mass of Scousers by the cordon sanitaire of a wire fence guarded by a handful of gendarmes. Possibly because of overcrowding on the Liverpool terrace, fans climbed this fence into Juve's section where taunts were hurled, then bottles and stones – confusion persists about who launched the first missiles.

What is beyond dispute is that our supporters got into the wrong area, menacing Italians who implored police to intervene. Their reaction: to laugh. Then, about 7pm, a mob of some 100 from the Anfield contingent charged and their quarry fled to the perimeter wall which collapsed, killing 39 and injuring 580, 42 seriously.

These were the basic facts, although a full inquiry into the tragedy was never held. Nonetheless, after Belgium's FA was pilloried for bad organisation and crowd control, two of football's top officials were convicted on criminal charges. Negligent policing was also blamed for allowing a bad situation to deteriorate, since gendarmes could have nipped any problems in the bud by intervening earlier, and UEFA were deemed culpable, too, for ignoring Liverpool's pleadings about inadequate segregation.

Despite this, the blame should be laid squarely on the guilty. Whether Heysel was a crumbling stadium or not, people lost their lives because of hooligans. An argument can be made that the seeds of what became known in Italian eyes as the accursed cup were sown the year before when Liverpudlians suffered attacks in Rome. On the other hand, Bianconeri, White and Blacks, could hark back to the Battle of Turin during the European Championships in 1980 when English thugs assaulted Italians after England's match with Belgium in the Stadio delle Alpi. Riot police used tear gas to suppress that savagery and the guilty were identified – UEFA fined our FA.

Yes, *some* Roman fans did stab and terrorise *some* Scousers in 1984 but how can that justify revenge attacks on blameless parties who happen to speak the same language as the original assailants? What moronic logic.

Someone from Breck Road jumped you so now you're going to jump anyone you come across from Breck Road? How clever, a guaranteed formula for blood and tears.

Jean Genet wrote that "only violence can put an end to man's brutality", a reasonable sentiment when you're taking on dictators like Margaret Thatcher's torturer chum, General Pinochet, or the dear old Queen Mum's pet war criminal, General Franco. But in most societies, thuggery simply begets more thuggery, revenge spawns more revenge, and only sense can break the spiral of violence.

In my view, a small group of our so-called fans were the villains in Brussels. They may not have set out to kill Italians but their charge did lead to deaths, adding another chapter to an inventory of English bestiality.

Over and beyond the Battle of Turin, make a cursory inspection of entries in our criminal record on the Continent, as far back as 1974 when Tottenham fans rioted in Rotterdam at the UEFA Cup final with Feyenoord. The following year Leeds supporters wrecked the Parc des Princes as they lost to Bayern Munich in the European Cup final, while in 1977 Manchester United were ordered to play a home game in Plymouth after their fans ran amok in St Etienne during the Cup Winners' Cup. In 1984, English vandals caused £700,000 damage to the Parc des Princes – again – after France beat England 2-0 and in Brussels a Spurs supporter was shot dead before a UEFA Cup decider with Anderlecht that resulted in 200 arrests. We could go on and on.

Yet these are simply incidents on the Continent. Those on home soil would require volumes, because so many of our clubs attract puerile specimens who cannot control their aggression. Why else would bookshops have sections devoted to – makes you proud to be English – "Football Violence"?

Quick, boys. Form a disorderly queue here, y'know, for the f****** Nobel prize for litcheratcha, and stuff.

When it came to attributing responsibility for Heysel, a Brussels court gave suspended three-month sentences to the police chief in charge of ground security, the Belgian FA's president and UEFA's general secretary. It also used video footage to find 14 Red fans guilty of involuntary manslaughter, jailing seven for three years and handing down suspended terms to the rest. In addition, UEFA banned Liverpool from Europe for six years and all English clubs for five, denying champions Everton the chance to compete in the elite competition.

So hooliganism's scourge had banished Reds and Blues to football isolation. Tragically, it had also condemned 39 Italian, Belgian, French and Irish families to mourn their loved ones, day in, day out for the rest of their lives.

Let's give the last word to a relative of one victim, Roberto Lorentini, a doctor who dragged himself out of the crush but went back onto the terrace to resuscitate an 11-year-old girl. Both were trampled to death, along with the girl's father.

In 2005, Roberto's father, Otello, president of the Association for the Families of Heysel Victims, said: "I blame the people the official tribunal blamed: UEFA, the Belgian FA, the Belgian state, the Mayor of Brussels and the police who didn't call reinforcements. And I blame the English hooligans.

"Some talk of forgiveness but I'm not in a position to forgive. I still suffer."

* * * * * * * * * *

Heysel, May 29, 1985
The innocents who died because of English hooligans

Rocco Acerra, 29
Bruno Balli, 50
Alfons Bos
Giancarlo Bruschera, 21
Andrea Casula, 11
Giovanni Casula, 44
Nino Cerullo, 24
Willy Chielens
Giuseppina Conti, 17
Dirk Daenecky
Dionisio Fabbro, 51
Jacques Francois
Eugenio Gagliano, 35
Francesco Galli, 25
Giancarlo Gonnelli, 20
Alberto Guarini, 21
Giovacchino Landini, 50
Roberto Lorentini, 31
Barbara Lusci, 58
Franco Martelli, 46
Loris Messore, 28
Gianni Mastroiaco, 20
Sergio Bastino Mazzino, 38
Luciano Rocco Papaluca, 38
Luigi Pidone, 31
Bento Pistolato, 50
Patrick Radcliffe
Domenico Ragazzi, 44
Antonio Ragnanese, 29
Claude Robert
Mario Ronchi, 43
Domenico Russo, 28
Tarcisio Salvi, 49
Gianfranco Sarto, 47
Amedeo Giuseppe Spolaore, 55
Mario Spanu, 41
Tarcisio Venturin, 23
Jean Michel Walla
Claudio Zavaroni, 28

13
Better Than The Brazilians

I have a dream that my four little children will one day live in a nation where they will not be judged by the colour of their skin but by the content of their character.

– Martin Luther King

BEFORE the Heysel final, Liverpool's directors had settled on Joe Fagan's successor but their choice of Kenny Dalglish surprised supporters, most of whom had been tipping Ronnie Moran.

Kenny agreed to act as player-manager at the most difficult juncture in Anfield history, facing the challenges of rehabilitating our supporters' image and adjusting finances to lost European revenue. Soon, though, he imposed his will and his working methods on the club of the people, as he fondly described it. "His transition to manager was so smooth," Gillespie said. "He combined being your mate and your boss at the same time."

One early decision was to recruit Aston Villa's Steve McMahon, a combative replacement for Souness, who slotted in smoothly and helped Dalglish's side to continue their phenomenal Milk Cup run, defeating Oldham, Manchester United, Brighton and Ipswich to reach the semi. There they lost 3-2 on aggregate to Queens Park Rangers; the four-times champions were out.

During nearly all the season, the League appeared a lost cause, especially when Manchester United were 10 points ahead of the pack, but Everton overtook the Mancunians to top the table, inflicting a 2-0 defeat on Liverpool at Anfield in March 1986.

That night Hansen went to dinner with Dalglish and told him this was the worst Reds' team he'd played in. Extra-large portions of bouncebackability should have been on their menu. Eight weeks later, the worst had taken maximum points from 11 of their last 12 League games and done the double.

On the road to these twin triumphs, they grabbed crucial victories at Stamford Bridge, knocking Chelsea out in the FA Cup's fourth round and then Kenny clinching the title with a princely goal in our last League game.

After Jim Beglin shanked the ball forward, it arced across the field from behind Dalglish. In a flowing movement any supporter would treasure, he swivelled his shoulders, cushioned the ball on his chest, allowing it to drop onto his right foot which then volleyed home, sending 10,000 Scousers into raptures.

In every football generation, a handful of players have a presence on the pitch that spectators can feel. At the Bridge, Kenny verified once again that in his pomp he was one of those gifted few.

Our genie in studded boots had won the League; the FA Cup was next, in an all-Merseyside final.

After 93 years' competition, Red and Blue met for the first time at Wembley in a rendezvous that turned Liverpool into a ghost town.

Over in Wigan that day, a clash of a different kind brought the town to a halt, all because of a typographical error in a paper. These have always been a source of merriment for readers everywhere, like the notice in a Kent weekly publicising a talk on glovemaking at the Women's Institute, which a typesetter turned into a lecture on "lovemaking with leather accessories". They were queuing round the block for days beforehand.

In Wigan, another newspaper advert was meant to promote a psychic fayre in the Grand Hotel, with "tarot readings, palmistry, clairvoyance and demonstrations". Oops! Instead the ad promised "tarot readings, palmistry, clairvoyance and demons".

On the Saturday morning of the event, the hotel was invaded by Bible-brandishing zealots from churches throughout Lancashire, a pack of Ian Paisleys on steroids who drenched the place with holy water, bellowed hymns and recited from the Scriptures as they cast the Devil out.

The fayre had to be abandoned.

A day to remember in Wigan – and also for 98,000 spectators down at Wembley.

In the first half, Everton took the lead when Grobbelaar pushed a Lineker shot away, only for the centre-forward to follow up and score. On the restart, Molby threaded a pass through to Rushie, who dribbled beyond keeper Bobby Mimms, slotting home from a narrow angle. 1-1. Next Molby crossed to Johnston who banged it in. 2-1. Now the Reds were rampant. Whelan passed to Rushie at the angle of the eight-yard box and he fired a low shot into the net. 3-1.

The FA Cup was Liverpool's, the double was done.

After the dejection of being ignored for Scotland's squad for the World Cup in Mexico, a beaming Hansen held the trophy aloft. Equally elated in the VIP seats were Liverpool's directors, whose policy of promoting from within had been vindicated once more.

As the baton passed from Shanks to Paisley to Fagan to Dalglish, the Anfield dynasty had consolidated their status as the kings of football and Kenny had become the first player-manager to do the double. Bob Paisley, the new boss's adviser, voiced his admiration: "Of all the players I have played alongside, managed and coached in more than 40 years at Anfield, he is the most talented. When Kenny shines, the whole team is illuminated."

The Kop's raucous backing had also spurred our lads on, inducing Simon Inglis, the authority on football stadia, to select Anfield as "probably the most exhilarating and unnerving experience in the English game".

During the close season, Rush, who clubs across Europe had wooed, signed for Juventus for £3.2 million, a good financial return for the Reds and also an attempt at bridge-building with the Italians after Heysel. As part of the agreement, he was to spend the next year on loan at Anfield but the team were still losing one of their most lethal strikers ever.

As he looked ahead to a new life in Turin, you could have understood Rushie taking his foot off the pedal for 1986-87's campaign. No way. In our opening fixture, away to Newcastle, he was on fire, getting both goals in a 2-0 victory that set the tone for his farewell season.

In our 2-1 home defeat of Arsenal, he netted again but Mark Lawrenson was my man of the match, snaffling the ball with immaculate interventions.

Filing out at full-time, I noticed the playwright, Alan Bleasdale, and pleaded: "Why don't you write a play about Lawro's tackling?"

His response: "That ain't no play – that's poetry!"

Yessiree. At times, the lads were poetry in motion and their eminence was underscored during a stopover I made in Zurich. In a pedestrian mall, I paused at a sport shop's window – full of Liverpool kit and players' photos. This when we were banned from Europe.

Back home, in the Littlewoods Cup, the League Cup's latest manifestation, we demolished Fulham 10-0, our biggest home win, but hope springs eternal – the programme for the return at Craven Cottage stated that "should the aggregate score be level after 90 minutes, extra time will be played". Since the Reds won 3-2, the crowd left on the dot.

Further victories over Leicester, Coventry (Molby bagged a hat-trick of penalties), Everton and Southampton sent Liverpool to Wembley where Arsenal came out on top, 2-1, ending a notable sequence: in 143 games, when Rush got on the scoresheet, the Reds did not lose.

As one record ended, another was set. Dalglish came off the bench to replace Paul Walsh, laying down a benchmark of 15 Wembley appearances with a single club.

Luton curtailed our FA Cup run in a third-round replay on their notorious plastic turf. The Hatters were accustomed to the high bounce on its firm surface – we weren't. As for the League, the Mersey duo led the field until Everton nabbed the title, even though Rushie amassed 30 League goals, including the only one against Watford at the Kop end on his farewell.

At the final whistle, he hurled his shirt into the terrace and departed to ply his trade in Serie A.

Now Dalglish was masterminding his super team. In June 1987, he paid Watford £900,000 for Jamaican-born John Barnes, who three years earlier had been gripped by the long arm of racism after England took on Brazil in Rio.

The Hornets' winger fashioned a wonder goal – his first for his country and one of the finest ever at the Maracana – dribbling past seven Brazilians before slipping the ball beyond the keeper. He wasn't finished, putting over the cross for Mark Hateley to seal victory with a header.

The morning after this seismic result, which Rio's newspapers marked with black borders, the England squad caught their plane to London, only to find National Front boneheads on board. Throughout the flight, four of these tosspots jeered Barnes and chanted 1-0 to indicate his goal for "In-ger-lund" did not count because he was black. Welcome home, John.

Throughout my childhood, Mum raised me to abhor prejudice and across from us in Ullswater Street we were fortunate to have a black family, the Lake District's only "darkies". You couldn't have wished for better neighbours than the Williamses, always on hand to help anyone.

Their children, Barbara and Alvin, were my playmates and on Sundays they used to take me by bus to visit aunts and uncles in Toxteth, homely people who greeted this little lad with kindness and plentiful supplies of cream soda and dolly mixtures.

As we grew up, I became friendly with some of Alvin's black mates who gave me an insight into juvenile behaviour patterns. In mid-teens, some Scouse lads regarded swearing as big, use of the F-word somehow singling them out as tougher, more grown-up.

Afro-Caribbean kids never descended to effing and blinding. While their parents had brought them up not to use expletives, they also did not have to "prove" their toughness through bad language; any black lad in the Fifties and Sixties had no choice but to be hard, not least when cornered in a back jigger by a gobbet of racists.

One Saturday night, journeying down to the Cavern, I heard the everyday voices of bigotry. On the top deck of a crowded bus from Breck Road, Mr and Mrs Williams sat alongside me.

We were talking quietly when a couple of loudmouths at the back started making snide remarks: "Niggers ... Could do with a good wash ... Taking our jobs ... Niggers ... Send 'em back ..."

I was incensed.

Harry Williams, an amateur boxer who could punch above his weight, was listening to nothing original. He tapped his lips with his index finger, indicating I should ignore it, but this provocation pointed up how Afro-Caribbeans were treated on a daily basis. What strength they must have had to turn the other cheek. I couldn't have done it.

Given this ground swell of racism, black footballers were easy prey for opposition supporters. In the Sixties, Leeds had a talented winger, Albert Johansen, who became the first African to appear in an FA Cup final, against the Reds in 1965, and was ridiculed at many grounds, including Anfield where imbeciles chanted, "Go back to Africa" and "Oh, Oh, Oh, Coco Pops", the advertising jingle for a breakfast cereal.

Such bile gobbed out in stadia across the country would undermine anyone's mental stability and poor Albert ended his days as an alcoholic, dying alone in squalor in a Leeds block of flats.

How the hateists would have gloried in that. Sorry souls racked by low self-esteem, they channel contempt for themselves into hatred of anyone who may appear different: Cockneys, Scousers, Mancs, Geordies, blacks, Pakis, Jews, Catholics, Moslems, French, Germans, Italians, Argentinians, gays, lesbians. You name them, they'll loathe them.

The trash on our terraces had not made Howard Gayle welcome, so they were not about to acclaim Barnes's arrival in L4, spewing out their animosity with graffiti on Anfield's walls, of the "NF" and "Wogs out" variety – short, silly words even knuckle-dragging Neanderthals are unlikely to mis-spell.

His first appearances were not without incident, either. When Liverpool met Everton in the Littlewoods Cup, he was the butt of retards who spat, threw bananas, made monkey noises and chanted "Niggerpool" and "Everton are white".

Barnes refused to be provoked. With the intellect to use insults as motivation to perform better, he knew any racists would have succeeded if you betrayed any weakness or retaliated. Later in his Anfield career, he even poked fun at bigots by attending a fancy-dress party in white Ku Klux Klan robes.

Our new winger's performances energised a scintillating 1987-88 season during which Dalglish concentrated on his managerial role, turning out just twice as substitute. The blow of Rush's departure was softened by the arrival of Oxford's John Aldridge and Ray Houghton, while Peter Beardsley joined from Newcastle for £1.9 million, the highest fee between British clubs. Many fans reckoned the side would struggle to score without Rushie but they grabbed four goals in four fixtures on the trot, against Newcastle, Derby, Portsmouth and Queens Park Rangers, who were

League leaders. On a flying visit, Rushie watched the encounter with the Londoners at Anfield, a spellbinding exhibition as Barnes (2), Johnston and Aldridge found the net.

From the opening day of the season, the Reds went 29 matches without defeat – 22 victories and seven draws – equalling Leeds' 1973-74 record. Although Everton ended the run at Goodison on March 20, Liverpool lost just one more League game and were never beaten at home, conceding only 24 goals during their campaign.

Their defence was majestic, marshalled by Hansen who neatly dispossessed opponents and strolled forward to launch attacks. Down the left wing, Barnes was flying, skinning defenders, whipping crosses in ... and making the Kop lopsided. In the Fifties, fans used to migrate from one end of the Kemlyn stand to the other, so as to be close to whichever goal the Reds were besieging. Barnes had a similar influence on Kopites in the Eighties, drawing them to the right of the terrace from where they could admire his seductive skills.

In the penalty area, Aldridge was the gifted goal-poacher, supported by Beardsley who would drop a shoulder to send a defender the wrong way, then embark on a meandering dribble through the opposition.

Commanding the centre of the park, McMahon and Whelan offered another formidable pairing while Johnston, the madcap, skateboarding Aussie who went on to invent the Predator football boot, was like a metronome, speeding up and down the right touchline.

In Barnes's view, this was Liverpool's team of all the talents. Their intuitive, one-touch passing lit up the pitch, a fluency so hypnotic that sometimes it stilled the crowd, apart from audible intakes of breath as the ball moved telepathically from player to player.

The most breathtaking showcase of their mastery came in a 5-0 rout of Nottingham Forest, an exposition of attacking football Sir Tom Finney judged the most complete performance he'd ever witnessed, "better than the Brazilians".

"Liverpool must be the best team of all time," he concluded. "It was the finest exhibition I have seen in all my time playing and watching the game."

In April, with four fixtures to go, they sewed up the Championship when, from the corner of the 18-yard box, Beardsley swerved the ball around Tottenham's new keeper, Bobby Mimms. However, our chief provider of goals was Aldo, who rattled in 26, scoring in nine consecutive games.

The Reds' superiority was not appreciated by everybody, particularly Alex Ferguson who had switched from Aberdeen to Manchester United. TV reporter Clive Tyldesley recounted how, after the Mancunians drew 3-3 in L4, their manager complained about intimidation of referees.

"I can understand why clubs come away from Anfield choking on their own vomit and biting their tongues," he told Tyldesley. "You need a miracle to win here".

Once Ferguson had finished, Tyldesley passed his comment on to Dalglish, who was about to address the media.

When Kenny came out of his office holding his six-week-old daughter, another journalist was interviewing Ferguson. As Liverpool's boss walked past, he nodded at little Lauren and advised the reporter: "You might as well talk to my baby daughter, you'd get more sense from her."

Ferguson responded with a colourful character reference for Kenny who countered: "Careful, Alex, the baby's a wee bit young for that."

Anfield might have been a sickener for Old Trafford's gaffer but Liverpool were in rude health, bidding for their second double. In the FA Cup semi, they topped Nottingham 2-1, Aldo grabbing a brace, the second a sumptuous volley with outstretched leg that was voted BBC Goal of the Season.

At Wembley, the Reds would lock horns with Wimbledon and, to mark the occasion, they released a Craig Johnston composition, Anfield Rap, which swept to the top of the charts. Out on the pitch, though, they had an unwelcome hit.

Five days before the big showdown, they met Luton in the League and as Gillespie and Nigel Spackman went for a high ball, their heads clashed, causing gashes that required stitching. Perhaps the pair should have been on the bench at Wembley but they did turn out, protected by "ridiculous headbands", according to Vinnie Jones.

The game started well for the Reds when Beardsley rode a foul by Andy Thorn to dink the ball over opposition keeper Dave Beasant. Frustratingly, referee Brian Hill had already blown for the foul and he disallowed the goal, awarding a free kick. If he had played advantage, Liverpool would have been ahead.

The Dons grabbed their chance when Lawrie Sanchez headed home a free kick. Although the Reds could have levelled through an Aldo penalty, Beasant saved, an inconsequential miss when weighed against all John's other goals which had helped earn the biggest prize, the League. So Wimbledon's set-piece skill snapped up the trophy, not the way some tabloids reported it. "Insiders" told them that Bobby Gould's Crazy Gang had won the psychological battle in the tunnel, screaming and intimidating their opponents. Paper tales; the Dons hadn't prevailed because they psyched out the Reds but because fortune favoured their free kick. End of story.

Liverpool might not have got their double but Barnes had two reasons for satisfaction – the professional footballers' and football writers' associations both picked him as their Footballer of the Year. Albert Johansen and Howard Gayle would have been so proud of you, John.

Before 1988-89's campaign, Kopites received surprise news: Rush was returning from Juventus. Used as a lone striker in Serie A's defensive quagmire, he had still notched up eight goals in 29 outings, making him top scorer, ahead of Michael Laudrup who didn't find the net once. Juve's fans were restive, enduring their worst season since 196162, so the Zebras sold Rushie back to Liverpool for £2.8 million.

Before putting pen to paper, he received an urgent call from deep within the bowels of Old Trafford's vomitorium: Alex Ferguson, summoning up all his persuasive powers to entice the Welsh hero to Manchester.

Rushie listened, promised to consider the offer and put the phone down. An eye blink later, he'd made up his mind. It had to be Liverpool because he could never wear any other club's red shirt.

On his return, papers quoted Rushie as saying: "I couldn't settle in Italy – it was like living in a foreign country." He dismissed this as a joke, probably thought up by one of the lads in Melwood's dressing room and entering sport mythology, on a par with the remark attributed to Southampton midfielder Mark Draper, "I'd like to play for an Italian club, like Barcelona", or American reporter Joe Thiesmann's verdict on one star, "Nobody in football should be called a genius. A genius is a guy like Norman Einstein."

Rushie's comeback season coincided with a slump in Reds form. Because of injury, he played irregularly and, despite Aldo being in fine fettle, Liverpool lagged 19 points behind leaders Arsenal at Christmas, prompting some authorities to write them off. After losing on New Year's Day, though, they set off on a winning stretch that was to continue until the season's closing fixture.

During this topsy-turvy campaign, I faced upheaval in my domestic arrangements.

Defining moments occur throughout life, like the first time you coughed on a ciggie in a shop doorway, the last time you witnessed a British Rail toilet roll unfurling on a football pitch or the day you learnt that Ayds is no longer a food supplement from the chemist's but a killer virus.

I remember when and where one of my tipping points came. When: 1.11am. Where: Platform 11 at Crewe.

Some 18 months previously, the Withy Grove complex, that haven of professional and social fulfilment, had ceased to be a publishing centre for national newspapers, ending my two decades of happiness in the marvellous city of Manchester and converting our busy branch office, alias the pub, from the Swan With Two Necks into the Swan With Two Customers. Since the Grove's demise, I'd been commuting by train to London every week, doing freelance work as a sub-editor and staying in a B & B in West Hampstead. Until, one Friday night, I conceded this disjointed existence was unsustainable.

At 10.45pm I caught the last service from Euston to Wigan, which entailed a change at Crewe – all the aforementioned 1's, Platform 11 for my connection at 1.11am. Only it didn't arrive. Cancelled, and I was stuck until another service chugged in at 3 in the morning.

As birds twittered for the dawn, I put my key in the door in Standish, knowing I had to bite the bullet: move south where the work was. My B & B days and Crewe BR platform nights must end.

So the family – wife Anne, daughter Helen and son Russell – followed the footpath trodden by Scousers for years, migrating in quest of employment. We uprooted from Lancashire to St Albans in Hertfordshire, from where I continued grafting as a sub in the metropolis. Aided and abetted by good fortune, I was able to keep my head above water, using what limited abilities I possessed, and did not fall back on other personal attributes, like the pair featuring in a tale that circulated in the North-West. As recounted in Fleet Street, the northern editor of one Manchester tabloid took on a handful of young journalists who answered an advert in a trade magazine. One evening, he entered the newsroom, sighted this fresh female face and asked a colleague who she was.

"The new sub you appointed," came the reply.

"No, no, no," the executive groaned. "I wanted the one with the big tits!"

On such vagaries of sexism can our futures depend.

For me, Crewe's Platform 11 had become a memory but now the Reds were a hard act to follow. No longer could I sprint through West Lancashire lanes to Anfield in 45 minutes; it had turned into a 200-mile marathon by car along the M1/M6 umbilical cord joining St Albans to Liverpool.

Before one trip north in March 1989, I decided eight-year-old Russ should be initiated into the Kop's secrets, at a midweeker with Derby under those floodlights that always bathe the ground in an atmospheric, pearly glow. After parking in Pinehurst Avenue, we hurried up Arkles Lane and I noticed he had become white-faced, sickly, as he saw the crowds, heard Anfield's excited buzz, smelt the fried onions … Entering the Kop from Walton Breck Road, he couldn't credit how big everything was, his gaze roving around the stands, adjusting to their scale and the brilliance of the setting.

Dads who were regulars on the terrace took beer crates for their lads to stand on, not something I normally carried in my back pocket, so to give some elevation to Russ, I sat him on a crowd-barrier and when the teams ran out, his little eyes were wide with wonder, beholding Barnes, Aldridge,

Beardsley, Grobbelaar and the rest. Heroes he'd only ever seen on telly were now before him in the flesh; his instant of Kop revelation had arrived.

Ten minutes into the match, physical reality deflated this period of illumination; I had to lift him down from the barrier because he felt uncomfortable.

Peering around for a spot with a view of the pitch, I felt a tap on my shoulder. A bloke in his 40s, unshaven, in a greasy donkey jacket, pointed. "Here, lah," he said. "A spec here. Stick him in – he'll be able to see."

I positioned Russ in the space in front of a pillar, from where he was able to watch through a gap and jump about when Barnes grabbed the points. Just what the team craved, since Liverpool were now fourth in the table, above Derby.

Russ had been inducted into the Kop and we both shuffled out on a high.

Never could we have imagined that, within days, people around us on that very terrace would have drawn their last breaths.

14
Death In The Afternoon

*Do not go gentle into that good night, rage, rage, against the
dying of the light.*

– Dylan Thomas

SATURDAY, April 15, 1989. A date no Liverpool fan can forget. A day
radiant with spring sunshine that turned into the blackest in British
sporting history.

The day I visited the council tip in St Albans.

Just as everyone remembers where they were when news broke of
President Kennedy's assassination, Princess Diana's death or the 9/11
attacks, so every Red supporter remembers where he or she was when the
Hillsborough disaster unfolded.

That morning, April showers had yielded to blue skies, ideal for me to
springclean the garden and perfect for the FA Cup semi-final. With Dalglish's
men coveting another League and Cup double, they faced Brian Clough's
Nottingham Forest at Hillsborough that afternoon in a rerun of the previous
year's semi when Liverpool won 2-1.

Naturally, Cloughie had other ideas. Fixated on reaching his first FA Cup
final, he was going for a different twin set, having already won the
Littlewoods, while Kopites were burning incense for an all-Merseyside final,
since Everton were confronting Norwich in the other semi at Villa Park.

At home in St Albans, I had my day planned. An early assault on the back
garden with lawnmower, garden fork and secateurs, a few hours' intense
effort to impress the wife, then radio on for the game.

It went well. I beavered away until 1.30pm when I took the wireless
outside for BBC Sport on 2. Peter Jones, the commentator at Hillsborough,
was previewing the tie, saying it could be a classic and that Hansen was in
our starting line-up after a nine-month layoff through injury. Yes, this should
be a good day.

Kick-off 10 minutes away, I began filling bin bags with grass-cuttings,
weeds, stones and leaves, ready for a brisk drive to the council tip and back
home to listen to the commentary. While I was compacting the bags, Jimmy

Armfield enthused: "As always, Hillsborough looks a picture." Then he drew attention to something that did not really register but hinted at problems ahead. After saying how great the atmosphere was, he remarked that although the Forest terrace was full, some spaces remained at Liverpool's end.

Spaces? Among Reds at an FA Cup semi-final? Just before kick-off? As always, there'd been a stampede for tickets and demand was impossible to satisfy because our lads had been allotted the smaller Leppings Lane stand, rather than the capacious East terrace. Now, with minutes to go, there were gaps at our end. Odd.

Just before 3 o'clock, I put three plastic bags in the car boot, flicked the radio on and drove towards the tip in Sandridge Lane. Edging into traffic in King Harry Lane, the news summary was being broadcast. A proposed dock strike had been called off and the victim of an IRA bomb in Ulster was being buried. Oh, yes – British fugitive Ronnie Knight had been released by Spanish police.

These headlines were followed by a race at Newbury but all I was interested in was the semi. Had there been an early goal? Had Aldo banged one in? How was Jocky Hansen doing?

As I reached Batchwood Drive, the race ended and Sport on 2 returned to Hillsborough, not for the football, rather "a major incident". The calm but concerned voice of Jones came in, reporting that six minutes into the semi referee Ray Lewis had taken both teams off after up to 300 fans got on the pitch at the Liverpool end. Police were trying to hold them back but more were clambering over the fence as St John Ambulance men treated people lying on the grass. The match was suspended.

With that, Jones finished for cricket. I had reached the lights at the Ancient Briton pub and was mystified. What was going on? Why were people climbing on the pitch?

Jones resumed, saying there was still chaos and he had seen three stretchers being carried away. But he stressed there was no disorder among spectators, although one Liverpool supporter had run down the field, making V-signs at Forest fans.

Now it was over to Villa Park for Everton's match, then reports from around the country on League games. As I turned into Sandridge Road and joined the file of cars entering the council depot, Jones was back on air, talking in a sombre tone about sirens ... an ambulance on the pitch ... police pleading with people ... a very serious situation.

I couldn't take it all in. What was the trouble?

Cricket came on again as I applied the handbrake in the tip. I opened the boot, grabbed the bin bags, and joined people on a metal staircase leading up to the oversized skip. While I waited to drop my bags in, a council worker pulled a lever to squash rubbish in the compactor alongside us.

Amid the debris of consumer life – cardboard boxes, mattress, polystyrene packaging, bundles of magazines – lay a couple of dining chairs. As the machine's hydraulic rams flexed their muscles and compressed this junk, the wooden chairs were slowly contorted, writhing and resisting the remorseless mechanism, until gradually their legs and backs arched and splintered.

Within seconds, they were reduced to firewood.

I tossed my bags in the skip and hurried back to the car. Some rugby, Llanelli versus Bath, was on the radio before they went back to Hillsborough. Jones said he'd seen 15 stretchers being carried away. A nurse was giving the kiss of life to one youngster. The problems were being caused by congestion, not hooliganism.

I drove out of the tip into Sandridge Road as the BBC moved to a dressing room in Sheffield, to Alan Green, who mentioned unconfirmed reports about a door being broken down and fans flooding in. Someone else said: "People are running across the pitch." Then: "There's no way this game can go ahead."

Now I was driving through an endless tube. Something terrible was unfolding at Hillsborough.

I reached home without any recollection of the journey. It could have taken two minutes or two hours. In the kitchen, I turned the radio on and sought reassurance in a cup of coffee. Alan Green was interviewing a Liverpool fan, Glyn Phillips, a GP from East Kilbride.

"There's no doubt that this crowd was too big for this ground," Dr Phillips said. "Liverpool just filled the end they were given. The police allowed the fans to fill the middle terracing section to the point that they were crammed in like sardines. And yet the two outside portions of the terracing were left virtually empty and I stood and watched police allowing this to happen.

"It got to a point where they lost control completely. Lads were getting crushed against the fence right down near the pitch and there were so many people in that part of the ground that nobody could even move to get out. I climbed sideways into an emptier section and then made my way on to the pitch to try and help.

"Now unfortunately there are guys who have died down there on that pitch. I've seen about eight to ten, I don't know how many there are. There was one chap I went to, he was clinically dead. He had no heartbeat. Myself and another guy – I think a nurse – we resuscitated him for about 10 minutes. We were just about to give up when we got his heart beating but I don't know what the state of his cerebral function's going to be like.

"We asked for a defibrillator. I've been informed there isn't a defibrillator in the whole ground, which I find appalling for a major event like this. We were given an oxygen tank to help with our resuscitation and it was empty. I think this is an absolute disgrace."

With that damning indictment, Dr Phillips ended his testimony.

I turned the radio off and, stirring my coffee, walked into the living room. I put the telly on. A clearly shaken Des Lynam was saying there had been "a tragedy at Hillsborough ... many dead".

Many dead!

They showed chaotic scenes outside Leppings Lane before the game: a mass of fans pushing towards turnstiles, a couple of mounted police wedged helplessly in the middle. Then coverage switched to the inside of the ground: people being dragged out of the pens by supporters in the upper stand, dead and dying on the pitch, fans attempting to give resuscitation, others shrieking, a solitary ambulance moving indolently along the by-line, blokes running with casualties on makeshift stretchers of advertising boards to the Forest end.

After that, the TV newsreels, journalists' reports, growing toll – 15 dead, 20 dead, 30 dead, 50 dead – everything coalesced into blackness until early-evening news exposed the disaster's true enormity. Now fatalities were put at more than 70.

Inside Leppings Lane, desolation: crowd barriers bent grotesquely, bulging fences, abandoned scarves, clothes, shoes. Worst of all, pictures of weeping parents who'd travelled across the Pennines to identify their children in Sheffield Wednesday's gymnasium, now a mortuary.

That evening I phoned Mum. In the afternoon, she'd been downtown, shopping in Church Street, when clusters of people passed on news of some "incident" at Hillsborough – crushing, fans injured, even fatalities. She took the bus home to Cantril Farm where TV laid bare the disaster. Since then, neighbours in Whincraig, her block of flats, had been going back and forth, knocking on each other's doors, inquiring if anyone they knew had been in Sheffield.

I asked how people were feeling and Mum said quietly: "Everyone up here's very upset."

"Very upset".

Two simple words defining a city's pain, while families went through torment.

"Up here" – that got me, too.

Liverpool was my home, one of the reasons for my being. I should have been "up there", where people needed help.

How could I have helped? I might have wanted to be "up there", standing in the Barley Mow with fellow Scousers, shaking my head, emotion trickling down my cheeks, but I could do nothing to ease the suffering of those who were mourning.

My sensibilities were typical of any outsider, an urge to console that would amount to intrusion in private grief. At that moment, you could not soothe the stricken. You could do nothing, except think, and share the tears of Hillsborough's heartbroken mothers.

And I kept going back to that game with Derby, Russ's baptism on the Kop, and the people standing nearby. The two lads dipping into a bag of pear drops ... teenager with a crew cut ... grey-haired gent reading the *Echo* during half-time ... chap in a greasy donkey jacket who steered Russ into that spec by the pillar ... Were any of them dead?

After a night staring at TV, I went to bed about 2am. Sleep, "the twin of death", was a long time coming for me but God only knows how hundreds of grieving families across Merseyside shut their eyes for one second that night, or the next, or the next, or the next.

Early the following morning, I went to the newsagent's for papers, their front pages covered with images of fans in extremis. One showed two girls, faces against the fence, mouths open, gasping for breath. In another, a man had his arm around a hysterical woman, struggling to protect herself from the wire mesh with her arms.

Human beings at a football match, lives being squeezed out of them.

One September, from Lake Ontario's shore, I beheld a pathetic spectacle: as far as the eye could see, the surface of this inland sea was sprinkled with thousands of butterflies, dragged into the water by brutish waves as they fluttered above the surface.

Now Hillsborough's photos reminded me of those drowning butterflies. Like them, our trapped supporters had no chance against a merciless force.

For the latest accounts of the tragedy, I listened to the radio, which offered clues to the causes and effects. Because roadworks delayed traffic across the Pennines, a build-up of fans in the half-hour before kick-off meant turnstiles couldn't cope – 23 gates for 24,000 spectators at our end, compared with 60 for 30,000 on other sides. Early reports maintained ticketless Liverpudlians broke down a door to get in but it transpired that, to relieve crowding, police ordered exit gate C should be opened to afford entry.

This created a death trap. With the Leppings Lane terrace divided by iron railings into seven pens, numbers 3 and 4 behind the goal were already full while the side ones had plenty of space. Once gate C opened, the absence of stewards led to thousands streaming into a tunnel that sloped down to the middle pens. Soon they held double their capacity and, since a high fence along the perimeter blocked escape, people next to the pitch were strangulated by vice-like weights that buckled a steel barrier and killed them where they stood.

Watching events unfold, most spectators around the ground did not appreciate the gravity of the situation, except for those seated at the rear of Leppings Lane who hauled dozens to safety. One gate in pen 3's fence offered an outlet for overcrowding but when it sprang open, police slammed it shut and even pushed back Scousers clambering over the top.

While people were fighting for their lives, the teams kicked off, heedless of the mayhem until a couple of supporters ran to Hansen who, fearing a pitch invasion, asked them to get off. They told him people were dying in the stand. Soon afterwards, the referee sent both sides back to their dressing rooms and confirmation of fatalities came at 4 o'clock.

Despite this, the full horror did not register with Aldridge until later that evening when he got home and watched the news with his wife Joan. Then the magnitude sank in. "That was when we broke down, as one, in tears and hugging each other. We cried most of the night and slept little," Aldo revealed in his autobiography.

Next day he took his daughter Joanne to lay roses at Anfield's Shankly Gates and stood in silence amid dazed supporters as more and more people arrived with flowers. Men, women, children, whole families wanted to be at the ground, and when Peter Robinson saw how many were outside, he asked for Annie Road's gates to be opened.

Immediately fans walked round the touchline to the Kop goal, attaching bouquets to its net, floral tributes that spread rapidly into the goalmouth, onto the turf and up the terracing, where loved ones had once stood.

On cold, concrete steps, people sat beside their flowers, weeping, and throughout that Sunday, the Kop and the pitch gradually filled with carnations, roses, tulips and daffodils, creating a tear-stained tapestry, a perfumed garden of remembrance, a fragrant memorial to lost Scousers. If anyone required proof football *is* a religion on Merseyside, then the way our ground became a shrine that day offered it.

Those paying their respects weren't just Liverpudlians. Supporters came from clubs near and far. Everton, Tranmere, Wigan, Chester, Wrexham, Preston, Blackburn, Bolton, Burnley, Manchester United, Manchester City, Leeds, Villa, Arsenal, Chelsea, Tottenham, Celtic, Rangers – scarves, caps, rosettes and flags of every team in the land could be seen among Liverpool's colours.

By this time, more members of the team had arrived and they consoled people out on the pitch, until someone invited the sorrowing into the players' lounge for some privacy. Here in the Main Stand, a steady stream of distraught fans was met by Marina Dalglish and other wives and girlfriends, offering cups of tea and shoulders to cry on. The pain became so acute, though, that after a while players and partners were being comforted by the bereaved, like one widow who joked with Kenny: "My husband was a miserable old sod. He'll be quite happy in Heaven watching all the games for nothing." Laughter in the midst of tragedy.

Next day, Monday, the team faced a harrowing task, visiting casualties in Sheffield's hospitals. In a single room, five supporters were in comas, and two regained consciousness while players talked to them. One asked: "If you get to Wembley, can you get me a ticket?" "Unbelievable," said Hansen.

After whispering in 14-year-old Lee Nicol's ear, Aldo asked a doctor about his chances of recovery, only to be told he was clinically dead. Aldo broke down.

His grief was shared across the land. That evening, John Peel abandoned the introduction to his Radio 1 show and opened straightaway with Aretha Franklin's Gospel version of You'll Never Walk Alone. As her haunting interpretation went out over the airwaves, John sat at his studio console, shedding silent tears.

Hospital visits over, Liverpool's squad returned to Merseyside and steeled themselves for another ordeal, going to funerals. A total of 95 supporters had died, the youngest aged 10, the oldest 67, while Anthony Bland was to lie in a coma for four years until his life-support machine was shut off.

Hansen was present at 12 funerals and Kenny attended four in one day.

Aldo was shattered to see a pair of coffins being carried into church. He hadn't known: it was father and son.

As a Scouser, the lifelong Red took the tragedy particularly badly, admitting he was in trauma for weeks. Forcing himself out on a training run, he pulled up after a few strides, overpowered by thoughts of his own children, and he withdrew from Ireland's squad for a World Cup qualifier with Spain.

During the fortnight after Hillsborough, more than 1,000,000 people visited Anfield, a place of pilgrimage where half the grass and the entire Kop became covered with mementos of the dead.

When Kenny went on the terrace, he spotted a pair of boots and two oranges placed precisely beside a barrier, which he found terribly affecting. The whole spectacle was "the saddest and most beautiful sight", he said.

As well as funerals, players went to memorial services in the Anglican and Roman Catholic cathedrals, attended by people of every persuasion, and none. Reflecting on this palliative process, David Sheppard, the Bishop of Liverpool, said: "Liverpool has always had a real sense of belonging where in other cities everything feels terribly individualistic. Hillsborough was in some ways the most profound coming-together of the city, of the feeling of grief together and the feeling, as far as we could, of helping to hold one another in healing afterwards."

Not only did the disaster represent a watershed in Liverpool's history but it also confirmed this wasn't a mere football club, it was a family. The instant people cried out for help, that family pulled together. Craig Johnston flew in from Australia, John Toshack returned from Spain and many other former players rushed to Anfield, while famous fans responded too, like Jimmy Tarbuck who wrote personal letters to families of victims.

But it wasn't only Merseyside's Red half that was hurting – Evertonians felt the heartache, too. Aldo said: "I will never forget the support that Liverpool as a club and our fans received from Everton and their fans."

For me, the tragedy's enormity hit home when Mum sent a copy of the *Echo*, with page after page of death notices for victims, as well as messages of sympathy from every corner of the globe. Regardless of where they lived, a part of every Scouser seemed to have perished that Saturday afternoon.

Then the St Albans paper landed on our mat, its front page all about a local lad, 15-year-old Kester Ball, who went with his father to Hillsborough where the cold hand of death reached out to touch him.

This story of someone who lived nearby moved me. Instead of Kester, it could have been my Russ who hadn't come home. Instead of Kester's dad walking through the front door that night, alone, it could have been me.

There but for the grace of God ...

I had to let Kester's family know they were in our thoughts. I found their address in the phone book and wrote a few inadequate sentences on a card from my family, "Anfield exiles who can but grieve with you". Then I drove down Watford Road, past the Three Hammers, turning into their street. It was full of parked cars, knots of dark-suited people.

The funeral was about to take place.

I asked a mourner if she could pass the card on to Kester's family and sped away.

Of all the days to choose ...

In the following weeks, moving stories emerged, like how Asian families around Hillsborough took distressed fans into their homes and shared their tears. Then there was the pub en route to Sheffield that has always offered hospitality to Liverpudlians. Before the game, a party of Reds settled down for a few gills, noted the licensee's wife was missing and were told she'd just had a miscarriage. A quick whip-round covered the cost of flowers for her. That afternoon, she heard about Hillsborough and anguished over which of those Scousers would never walk into her pub again.

Over in Germany, Borussia Mönchengladbach supporters, whose hearts we'd broken twice in European finals, collected thousands of pounds for an appeal fund. Ron Yeats and Trevor Hicks, who lost his daughters Sarah and Victoria in the disaster, went over to accept the donation, a token of sympathy that has forged unbreakable bonds. Since then, groups of up to 150 Gladbach fans have journeyed to Merseyside, staying with families and shouting for the Reds at Anfield, and Kopites have made return trips to watch the German side.

Across the British Isles, Hillsborough's victims were remembered with a minute's silence, respected at grounds everywhere, apart from one where a handful could not curb their mouths. In response, visiting Sunderland fans sang You'll Never Walk Alone at the end of the 60 seconds.

Our anthem also resonated at stadia across the Continent, like the San Siro. There, a European Cup semi between Milan and Real Madrid was halted by the referee after six minutes when 80,000 rose as one to give voice to YNWA. A spontaneous gesture by strangers, rival fans who felt for Liverpool.

Bless them all.

* * * * * * * * * *

For the rest of their days, families and survivors will have to cope with Hillsborough's agony, incapable of drawing a line under an event that eventually claimed 96 lives, injured 766 and traumatised thousands.

Although a public inquiry, inquest and judicial review investigated the circumstances, families believe the full facts have never been disclosed and one mother, Anne Williams, has gone to the supreme European tribunal, the Court of Human Rights, submitting a dossier of evidence about her son Kevin.

They fight on because of all the unanswered questions: why police officers' statements were altered to make them consistent with each other; why many documents vanished; why video tape from the stadium's camera control office went missing; why only one ambulance was allowed on the pitch when 42 more were parked outside; why the door in pen 3's fence was kept shut; why cutting tools weren't used to alleviate the crush; why no emergency medical equipment was stored at the ground; why lessons from previous tragedies had not been acted on; why Hillsborough's safety certificate was 10 years out of date.

In his excoriating book, Hillsborough: The Truth, Phil Scraton brings to light many damning truths, including a change of police command that had disastrous ramifications. One senior officer from South Yorkshire Police, Chief Superintendent Brian Mole, was usually tasked with responsibility for semi-finals and, the previous year when Liverpool also played Forest, he threw a police cordon around the ground for tickets to be inspected. Yet for this match he was delegated to other duties, his filtering system was abandoned and people massed outside the turnstiles.

His replacement, Chief Superintendent David Duckenfield, had hardly any familiarity with spectator control, believing stewards should take the lead role. As a result, the police failed to organise queues properly and to direct supporters' entry.

Warning signs about Leppings Lane should have been read earlier. When Wolves met Spurs in another semi in 1981, fans were routed into Sheffield in a police operation designed to keep rival factions apart, a plan that ensured Wolves supporters had the extensive open bank while Spurs, despite a bigger following, were allocated the smaller Leppings Lane. Well before kick-off, Tottenham supporters were being squashed, compelling police to allow hundreds to watch along the touchlines. In all, 38 people sustained injuries, including fractured legs, arms and ribs, and the FA halted semis at the ground for six years.

Alarm bells rang again four years before Hillsborough when the dangers of fencing were underlined in a report on the Bradford City fire, which claimed 56 lives. Mr Justice Popplewell wrote: "The importance of allowing full access to the pitch where this is likely to be used as a place of safety in an emergency should be made plain."

Why wasn't that advice heeded at Hillsborough? Why didn't police react like at the Spurs semi? Why was a police inspector ignored in 1986 when he warned about access problems creating a potential for disorder in Leppings Lane?

To find some explanations, Lord Justice Taylor held an inquiry which heard that PC Michael Buxton grew uneasy about crowding outside Hillsborough and sent a radio message to Chief Superintendent Duckenfield, pleading for the kick-off to be delayed. A precedent had been set in 1987 before a Leeds-Coventry game when Chief Superintendent Mole put off the start because of traffic congestion.

Notwithstanding the fact Duckenfield could monitor the crowd from his control office and enjoyed the benefit of five CCTV screens, he refused. Yet while people lay dead and dying, he summoned extra officers to quell "a pitch invasion", did not implement the emergency plan and did not call ambulances. Finally, at 3.15pm when Graham Kelly, the FA's chief executive, sought out the police chief to discover what had happened, Duckenfield maintained that Liverpool supporters had forced open exit gates.

However, in his report, Taylor concluded: "The real cause of the disaster was overcrowding. The main reason for the disaster was the failure of police control." Deciding to open gate C but not to close the tunnel amounted to "a blunder of the first magnitude". Despite "a drunken minority of fans", alcohol was not a significant factor in the tragedy, while Liverpool supporters acted more decisively than emergency services to save lives.

Discarding Margaret Thatcher's panacea of identity cards for the sport's ills, Taylor said clubs and police had exacerbated conditions that sustained bad behaviour; squalid grounds fostered squalid conduct. All-seater stadia would ease this, he concluded, while the FA and Football League had to meet their responsibilities for safety.

The next stage in the judicial process was an inquest, which disregarded Taylor's report because his witnesses had not taken oaths. Dr Popper, the coroner, also limited testimony by imposing a cut-off time for accounts of 3.15pm on the fateful day, directing that later events were inadmissible because any "real damage" had been done by then. This despite incontrovertible submissions that some of the dead, including Kevin Williams, were alive after that time. Within these arbitrary parameters, the jury returned verdicts of accidental death in 1991.

Unwilling to accept this outcome, the Hillsborough families campaigned tirelessly for a no-holds-barred investigation into what they perceived as failings on the authorities' part. Their pressure became such that Home Secretary Jack Straw allowed a judicial review under Justice Stuart-Smith in 1997 but a year later he announced a further public inquiry could not be justified.

Even though the Taylor report castigated police failings and culpability, no one was charged with negligence or maladministration, no prosecution took place and no officer faced disciplinary proceedings.

All other avenues of redress blocked, families launched a private prosecution of the men responsible for Hillsborough's crowd control, former Chief Superintendent Duckenfield and former Superintendent Bernard Murray, charging them with manslaughter of two victims and wilfully neglecting to carry out their public duty.

During the trial in 2000, the prosecution said Duckenfield had changed his account three times but Justice Hooper directed the lesser charge of wilful neglect should be abandoned "because it does not really add anything in this case". The jury deliberated for four days before acquitting Murray of manslaughter and failing to agree on Duckenfield. Both were discharged by the judge who declared there should be no retrial.

Having spent 11 years trying to unearth the facts about Britain's worst sporting disaster, the families felt betrayed, sacrificed in a cover-up that suppressed the truth.

Imagine if your daughter or son went to a football match and was brought home in a coffin. You'd damn well want some explanations, some answers to the Why? question. Surely you have a right to that.

Move on? How can you? Closure? Forget it. And if there was the slightest hint of incompetence, negligence or downright culpability, you would not rest until the guilty parties were called to account. You owe that to your lost loved ones.

Imagine what Trevor Hicks went through. While Victoria was being placed in an ambulance at the ground, he was straining to revive Sarah with mouth-to-mouth resuscitation and for six months afterwards the only thing he could taste was her vomit.

Imagine that.

Now Trevor regards Hillsborough as two disasters: the one on the day and the miscarriage of justice persisting to the present. No parent should be left to live with that.

Somehow, he and his wife Jenni have drawn strength from Scousers, not so much the salt of the earth, more its gold dust.

Through the tears, Trevor expressed their feelings: "All this has done is reinforce our love for Liverpool and its people."

* * * * * * * * * *

Two weeks after the tragedy, Liverpool took part in a charity match at Celtic Park for the victims. As both teams walked out, 60,000 fans, many wearing our colours, sang You'll Never Walk Alone with a fervour that gave me goose pimples and when the players stood around the centre circle for a minute's silence, the sorrow was palpable. At the whistle ending those 60 seconds, the roar must have reverberated in Heaven.

Ties between Glasgow and Liverpool have always been close but the Bhoys' outpouring of sympathy that day made them stronger than ever.

Thank you, Celtic.

As Hillsborough's families had agreed the Reds could start playing again, our League programme resumed with a visit to Goodison where Evertonians had been deeply affected by the tragedy, too, since many had relatives and mates caught up in the events.

In a solemn atmosphere, both teams went through the motions for a goalless draw that signified their thoughts were far away.

Now Liverpool faced the FA Cup replay at Old Trafford, a match they had to win for those who had suffered. With the country, even Nottingham fans, rooting for them, they did the necessary, going through 3-1.

In the final, we met our neighbours from across Stanley Park and never in Wembley's annals could there have been a more uplifting occasion as Reds and Blues stood shoulder to shoulder, arm in arm, on the terraces.

A year before, Aldo had missed that penalty against Wimbledon and within four minutes of this kick-off, he clanged home a McMahon cross to erase his bad memory. Buoyed by this early breakthrough, Liverpool controlled play but could not find the net again.

That trophy had to be ours. Seconds remaining, however, Grobbelaar was unable to hold a ricocheting ball and Everton substitute Stuart McCall slotted it in.

Our fingers had been ripped from the silver.

After the draining weeks they'd been through, the Reds must have dreaded extra time, so Kenny summoned fresh legs, Rush replacing Aldo. His stage set, Rushie responded with the performance of a lifetime. A cross from Nicol, a nimble half-turn and a shot past Southall. 2-1. Trademark Rush effort.

When McCall hit back to put Everton level, Rushie was adroitly positioned for his riposte. Barnes flighted the ball over and our super marksman headed home. 3-2.

The cup was ours.

Inside Wembley and back on Merseyside, more tears were shed for the Hillsborough souls. This was for them. And once again, despite their defeat, the Blues showed your colours were irrelevant. We were all Liverpudlians.

Thank you, Everton.

The silver secured, Liverpool could think about the double. At the end of February, they had been eighth in the League, trailing Arsenal by 19 points, but since then they had got stuck into the fixture backlog caused by the Hillsborough mourning, hauling themselves up the table with 13 wins in 14 matches.

This prodigious effort meant they'd be crowned Champions if they didn't lose their last game, at Anfield against the Gooners, who for their part needed to win by two goals for the title.

When the teams met on Friday, May 26, the first half ended goalless, so the Reds had one hand on the trophy. After the break, however, the tension mounted once Nigel Winterburn took an indirect free kick that ended in the net. Waving away Liverpool protests about a foul on a defender, the referee judged the ball had hit Alan Smith's head on the way in and the goal stood. Then, in injury time, Michael Thomas stole into the box to strike again for Arsenal through the last kick of the season's last match. Both teams had the same points and goal difference but the Londoners clinched the title because they had scored more times.

At the end, Kopites applauded them so warmly that football writer Patrick Barclay praised "this sportsmanship of the highest order" while Smith said the fans' reaction meant Anfield would always remain special for him.

With hindsight, this game, our third in six days, was one too many. After Hillsborough, its paralysing aftermath and two hours on Wembley's energy-sapping pitch, Liverpool were spent. Yet they'd won the trophy that mattered most during this hideous period: the FA Cup.

* * * * * * * * * *

On Merseyside, the memory of Hillsborough can never be divorced from contempt for *The Sun*.

In Fleet Street bars, hearsay maintained that Kelvin MacKenzie, the paper's editor, had never exactly placed Liverpudlians high on his Easter card list and once the disaster occurred he wasn't about to dash off a sympathy note to the city.

Wallowing in his reputation as one of the more infamous denizens of the media zoo, MacKenzie was the intellect behind such Pullover Prize-winning fantasies as "Freddie Starr Ate My Hamster" and now Hillsborough gave his organ of sleaze and scandal an opportunity to excel itself.

Initially, South Yorkshire police refused to bear any responsibility for the tragedy, condemning the fans instead. Paul Middup, a Police Federation spokesman, set the agenda with his observation: "I am sick of hearing how good the crowd were. They were arriving tanked-up on drink and the situation faced by the officers trying to control them was quite simply terrifying."

London's *Evening Standard* echoed this: "The catastrophe was caused first and foremost by violent enthusiasm for soccer, in this case the tribal passions of Liverpool supporters. They literally killed themselves and others to be at the game."

The city's grieving was even mocked, one *Sunday Times* writer scoffing at "the world capital of self-pity".

But the editorial stances of these publications amounted to dinner-table chitchat for Kensington's twittering and tittering classes compared with what *The Sun* published.

Police officers had leaked stories to selected papers and Irvine Pannick, the MP for Sheffield Hallam, repeated claims made by the South Yorkshire Police Federation. The Tuesday after the tragedy, MacKenzie had persuaded himself of the facts, laying out a front page that plumbed new depths for the gutter press when it hit the streets next day.

Beneath a stark headline, "THE TRUTH", subsidiary lines stated:
"Some fans picked pockets of victims"
"Some fans urinated on the brave cops"
"Some fans beat up PCs giving kiss of life"
Below *The Sun's* masthead name was its thought for the day: "Kop of shame". The story itself stated that "drunken Liverpool fans viciously attacked rescue workers as they tried to revive victims" while one

anonymous policeman said Scousers further up the terrace "were openly urinating on us and the bodies". The report went on to charge that thugs went through injured fans' pockets as they lay unconscious and Pannick disclosed that a gang of fans spotted the blouse of a dead girl had risen above her breasts. As a policeman laboured to resuscitate her, the mob jeered: "Throw her up here and we will **** her."

While MacKenzie designed the edition, jettisoning an alternative headline of "YOU SCUM", colleagues in Fortress Wapping felt distinctly uneasy. One reporter, Harry Arnold, had the guts to warn the editor that he could not print allegations as facts but he refused to listen.

In Stick It Up Your Punter!, a dissection of The Sun, Peter Chippindale and Chris Horrie wrote: "As MacKenzie's layout was seen by more and more people, a collective shudder ran through the office [but] MacKenzie's dominance was so total there was nobody left in the organisation who could rein him in except [Sun proprietor] Rupert Murdoch. [Everyone] seemed paralysed, 'looking like rabbits in the headlights', as one hack described them.

"The error staring them in the face was too glaring ... It obviously wasn't a silly mistake; nor was it a simple oversight. Nobody really had any comment on it – they just took one look and went away shaking their heads in wonder at the enormity of it ... It was a 'classic smear'."

The Sun's front page was a pack of lies. There was no hooliganism. While police stood and watched, Scousers carried wounded and dying out of the ground. One doctor who gave first aid said: "The supporters were fantastic ... helping each other and trying to resuscitate people."

The death toll soared because senior police officers failed to recognise that fans inside the pens were fighting for their lives, not trying to "invade" the pitch.

The catastrophe was triggered by a failure of admission control by police who were now seeking to divert blame, assisted by newspapers who required no encouragement to put the boot into Liverpool. Just as Hollywood, led by John Ford, exulted in portraying the English as monsters and cowards, so some residents of Fleet Street drew on prejudice and ignorance to sustain the notion of Merseysiders as dole cheats, muggers and burglars.

But ripples from The Sun's fiction spread far beyond British shores. Wapping's falsehoods were disseminated across the world, doing incalcul-able harm to Liverpool Football Club and the city. Worse still, they com-pounded families' grief, just as they were struggling to cope with the loss of their loved ones.

Merseyside's retaliation for this "journalism atrocity", as Chris Horrie branded it, devastated The Sun. Overnight, sales plummeted as people refused to buy the paper. Newsagents in Liverpool put notices up, "Sun boycotted here", copies were burnt in the street and the verdict heard most frequently was, "I wouldn't wipe my arse on it".

Referring to MacKenzie's blunder, media commentator Roy Greenslade said: "It led to the biggest and most effective boycott of a newspaper ever in Britain – an immediate, definite loss of 200,000 sales, newsagents refusing to stock *The Sun* and the whole of Merseyside up in arms."

Aghast at the nose-diving circulation, MacKenzie rang Kenny Dalglish to ask how he could defuse the furore. Kenny told him to put a headline on the front page, the same size as "THE TRUTH", admitting "WE LIED". When the editor pleaded that couldn't be done, Kenny said he was unable to help and put the phone down.

The Press Council went on to denounce the fiction, so Murdoch ordered publicity-shy MacKenzie to eat humble pie. He told BBC Radio: "It was my decision and my decision alone to do that front page in that way, and I made a rather serious error."

Four years later, he expanded on this to the House of Commons national heritage committee. "I regret Hillsborough," he said. "It was a fundamental mistake. The mistake was I believed what an MP said. It was a Tory MP. If he had not said it and the chief superintendent [David Duckenfield] had not agreed with it, we would not have gone with it."

Now analysts estimate that MacKenzie's splash has lost *The Sun* more than half a billion sales since 1989 and the influential Media Week magazine reported in 2003 that, as a consequence of "the most disastrous publishing decision in the paper's history", the boycott had cost £125 million. David Yelland, who succeeded MacKenzie as editor, said: "Everyone associated with the paper then and now will admit the Hillsborough story was a significant error which cost us dear and continues to cost us dear."

That cost is borne out by the circulation: 4,200,000 when "THE TRUTH" appeared, 3,000,000 now, even though the paper has tried to pander to Merseyside by publishing "Salute to the Kop" specials and the like when Liverpool have won trophies.

Hillsborough signalled a sea change in *The Sun's* popularity with the British public and, as sales declined in the Nineties, a "knackered" MacKenzie was transferred to the Sky organisation. He lasted six months there.

So The Lies had signalled the beginning of the end of Wapping's despot. They had also proved that ordinary people, so often patronised and despised, can punish cruel, callous Big Business.

* * * * * * * * * *

AN FIELD OF DREAMS

Hillsborough, April 15, 1989

You live for ever in our memories and in our hearts

John Alfred Anderson, 62
Colin Mark Ashcroft, 19
James Gary Aspinall, 18
Kester Roger Marcus Ball, 16
Gerard Baron Snr, 67
Simon Bell, 17
Barry Bennett, 26
David John Benson, 22
David William Birtle, 22
Anthony Bland, 22
Paul David Brady, 21
Andrew Mark Brookes, 26
Carl Brown, 18
Steven Brown, 25
Henry Thomas Burke, 47
Peter Andrew Burkett, 24
Paul William Carlile, 19
Raymond Thomas Chapman, 50
Gary Christopher Church, 19
Joseph Clark, 29
Paul Clark, 18
Gary Collins, 22
Stephen Copoc, 20
Tracey Elizabeth Cox, 23
James Philip Delaney, 19
Christopher Barry Devonside, 18
Chris Edwards, 29
Vincent Michael Fitzsimmons, 34
Steve Fox, 21
Jon-Paul Gilhooley, 10
Barry Glover, 27
Ian Thomas Glover, 20
Derrick George Godwin, 24
Roy Hamilton, 34
Philip Hammond, 14
Eric Hankin, 33
Peter Andrew Harrison, 15
Gary Harrison, 27
Stephen Francis Harrison, 31
Dave Hawley, 39
James Robert Hennessy, 29
Carl Hewitt, 17
Nick Hewitt, 16
Paul Anthony Hewitson, 26
Sarah Louise Hicks, 19
Victoria Jane Hicks, 15
Arthur Horrocks, 41

Gordon Horn, 20
Thomas Howard, 39
Tommy Anthony Howard, 14
Eric George Hughes, 42
Alan Johnston, 29
Christine Anne Jones, 27
Gary Philip Jones, 18
Richard Jones, 25
Nicholas Peter Joynes, 27
Anthony Kelly, 29
Michael Kelly, 38
Carl David Lewis, 18
David William Mather, 19
Brian Christopher Matthews, 38
Francis Joseph McAllister, 27
John McBrien, 18
Marion Hazel McCabe, 21
Joe McCarthy, 21
Peter McDonnell, 21
Alan McGlone, 28
Keith McGrath, 17
Paul Brian Murray, 14
Lee Nicol, 14
Stephen Francis O'Neil, 17
Jonathon Owens, 18
Roy Pemberton, 23
Carl Rimmer, 21
David Rimmer, 38
Graham John Roberts, 24
Steven Robinson, 17
Henry Charles Rogers, 17
Andrew Sefton, 23
Inger Shar, 38
Paula Ann Smith, 26
Adam Edward Spearritt, 14
Philip John Steele, 15
David Leonard Thomas, 23
Pat Thompson, 35
Peter Reuben Thompson, 30
Stuart Thompson, 17
Peter Tootle, 21
Christopher James Traynor, 26
Martin Kevin Traynor, 16
Kevin Tyrrell, 15
Colin Wafer, 19
Ian Whelan, 19
Martin Kenneth Wild, 29
Kevin Daniel Williams, 15
Graham John Wright, 17

And in remembrance of those who have succumbed since that day.

15
Twilight Of The Gods

Where there is no vision, there is no hope.
– George Washington Carver

AT THE end of a decade that brought the highest honours to Liverpool, Hillsborough marked the lowest ebb in our club's history.

During the Eighties, Anfield's roll call of trophies was: European Cup, 1981, 1984; League Championship, 1980, 1982, 1983, 1984, 1986, 1988; FA Cup, 1986, 1989; League Cup, 1981, 1982, 1983, 1984. With a consistency never equalled in these isles, Liverpool were rated one of football's greatest, joining Real Madrid, who won five European Cups in the Fifties, and Ajax and Bayern Munich, who completed hat-tricks in the Seventies.

Now, in 1989-90's season, the Reds did not just have to overcome opponents, they had to cope with the Hillsborough trauma while playing in front of smaller crowds, since a reassessment of stadium regulations after the disaster brought the Kop's licensed capacity down to 16,400 standing spectators, a drop of nearly 9,000.

The lads dug deep to get results, initially lagging in the League until Ronny Rosenthal was parachuted in from Standard Liege. Trailing 2-1 at home to Southampton, our recruit was summoned off the bench and his bustling runs rattled Saints' defence. We won 3-2.

A fortnight later, in his first full game, he became the only Liverpool player since Bobby Graham in 1964 to score a hat-trick on his debut, against Charlton at Selhurst Park. Despite this, Dalglish did not select the Israeli international for an FA Cup semi with Crystal Palace, presumably because a newcomer mightn't be prepared for the high tempo and harum-scarum. In one of the competition's most exciting ties, Rush, McMahon and Barnes scored, making it 3-3 after 90 minutes, but Alan Pardew snatched an extra-time winner for the Eagles.

This outcome was all the more surprising because Liverpool had already routed the South Londoners 9-0 in the League at Anfield, eight names going on the scoresheet and Nicol netting twice. In response to a Kop chant of "We want 10", the small knot of Palace fans pleaded, "We want one", and Steve Coppell, their manager, summed up his side's trouncing, the First Division's heaviest for 26 years, as like 15 rounds with Mike Tyson.

Having agreed a move to Real Sociedad, Aldo marked his swan song by converting a penalty and at full-time threw his shirt and boots into the Kop.

During the League campaign, Barnes and Rush garnered 40 goals, while Rocket Ronny, as fans dubbed Rosenthal, managed another seven in eight appearances, so that after lying 13th on Boxing Day, Liverpool lost just once during the rest of the season to bag the title. By dint of this, they became the first club to be champions in four successive decades. With 78 goals in 38 League fixtures and 104 in all competitions, they finished nine points above Aston Villa to give Dalglish his eighth League winner's medal, three as player-manager and five as player.

Kenny's days at the cutting edge were over, though. On May 1, at the age of 39, he graced the turf for the last time in a 1-0 home win over Derby.

The following season, 1990-91, the Reds picked up where they'd left off, winning 12 and drawing two of their first 14 League games, including a 4-0 drubbing of Manchester United at Anfield in which Beardsley grabbed a hat-trick. They progressed into the FA Cup fifth round, a goalless stalemate with Everton in L4, before a Goodison replay in February that turned into a blockbuster.

Gordon Lee, the former Blues boss, once said: "I love derby games. Three tackles have gone in before you can even bring the ball down." Well, he'd have loved this dingdong battle.

Beardsley scored and the Toffees equalised. Beardsley popped another in, only for Everton to peg level. Rush put us ahead once more but the Blues got back to 3-3. Then, in extra time, after "Digger" Barnes made it 3-4 with a curler, Cottee grabbed the fourth equaliser in the last minute.

Two days later, on Friday morning, with Liverpool topping the League and still in the cup, Dalglish shocked football by announcing his retirement. At a press conference, he admitted: "The biggest problem was the pressure I was putting myself under. The pressure is incredible. I can cope during the week but on match days I feel like my head is exploding."

Beneath such frankness lay one major factor: Hillsborough had put an intolerable strain on him and his wife Marina. How many couples attend four funerals in one day? What long-term emotional wounds could Hillsborough inflict? What was it like for Kenny knowing his own son Paul was somewhere inside the ground?

Since that horrific day, he had coped manfully; now he was quitting for the sake of his health. For an insider's perspective, listen to Gary Gillespie: "You have to respect the fact he was physically and mentally drained. When Kenny left football, the transformation was night and day – he looked so much healthier."

Dalglish was a professional to his bones, striving for perfection and always setting the highest standards. After the disaster, he might have accepted football was no longer paramount, life had been put in its rightful context. When people had died, how could perfection matter?

In Tommy Smith's eyes, "Dalglish was the best player I ever lined up with" but genius comes at a price and no one can overestimate the demands placed upon such a high-profile figure. Among the crockery in his kitchen was a mug printed with a warning: "We interrupt this marriage to bring the football season." Kenny's resignation signified he was putting his family, and himself, first.

The day after this bombshell, Russ and I were at Kenilworth Road to see Luton playing the lads, with temporary manager Ronnie Moran holding the reins. Although Molby stroked a penalty in, the Hatters got three goals during the second half for a win that knocked us off top spot.

Despite vociferous backing from travelling Scousers, one Sunday paper reported that our supporters had booed the team off. As if. Since I'd heard nothing, I sent a letter to the sports editor, pointing out this inaccuracy, but he wrote back, insisting both his reporter and an agency journalist had heard abuse. Weird how my hearing-aid batteries briefly went on the blink.

As the season came to the boil, Hansen announced he planned to hang up his boots after 14 years at Anfield, leaving behind a huge hole in our defence. Later, Barnes would maintain we never replaced the unflappable centre-half, of whom David Johnson said: "He gave the impression he could play with a gin and tonic in one hand and a book in the other."

Alan's decision was a downer, just as crucial games still lay ahead. After losing the toss for second Cup replay venue, Liverpool met Everton at Goodison, where Dave Watson got the Blues' winner, a reverse followed by another as the Reds went down 1-0 at home to Arsenal in the League, giving the Londoners a three-point lead in the table.

The title race wasn't over, though. While a 7-1 annihilation of Derby at the Baseball Ground, one of Liverpool's best away results ever, capped a run that leapfrogged them over Arsenal, two defeats and one draw at Easter put the Londoners in pole position again.

During this seesaw period, ever-reliable Moran was still holding the fort as caretaker manager while the board weighed up candidates for a permanent appointment. Some supporters wanted Hansen, who appeared committed to his media work and gave no hint that he fancied Anfield's hot seat. Another contender, unknown to most people in England, was a highly regarded French coach, Gérard Houllier, who had stood on the Kop while teaching on Merseyside. Now assistant to France's national supremo Henri Michel, Houllier was fixated on one objective and responded to Liverpool's overtures by telling them: "I'd rather wait until the 1998 World Cup is over."

A third name in the frame was John Toshack but Liverpool's directors plumped for Graeme Souness, the Rangers' boss who had binned Ibrox's ban on signing Catholics. After filling his boots with medals at Anfield, the Scot favoured a return to the scene of so many triumphs and accepted the board's offer, "the perfect choice" in Rushie's view.

While supporters gave the thumbs-up to Britain's highest-paid boss, they understood silverware north of Hadrian's Wall did not guarantee trophies in England and Souness's five games in charge concluded with Liverpool in runners up spot.

As Arsenal took the Championship pennant, Kopites could never have foreseen that King Kenny's League title in 1990 was the last hurrah of a golden age.

* * * * * * * * *

Souness's reign opened with a timely turn of events. Juventus's directors had been lobbying for the Reds' European ban to be quashed and soon after our new boss moved in, UEFA announced it would end for the following season, 1991-92. Since Liverpool had finished second, they would compete in the UEFA Cup. The glamour of international competition was back.

Faced with this prospect, Souness decided the team needed a shake-up. He believed he had inherited an ageing squad, with some older members lacking commitment, so they had to be yanked into the Nineties through lots of running – long, exhausting laps around Melwood – to reach modern levels of fitness. Souness was a man in a hurry; players would have to get their fingers out.

The UEFA campaign got off to a flying start as Dean Saunders rattled in our first European goal since the ban, against Finnish side Kuusysi Lahti in a 6-1 Anfield stroll. After that, in a match rekindling memories of glory nights, the Reds ran out 3-0 winners over a talented Auxerre team who'd undone them 2-0 in France. Molby and Mike Marsh levelled the score, leaving Mark Walters to wrap up the tie seven minutes from time.

In the next round, Liverpool disposed of Austria's Swarovski Tirol 6-0 on aggregate to reach the quarter-final with Genoa, who played out of their skins in both legs. They won 2-0 in their Luigi Ferraris stadium and, before a raucous contingent of supporters in L4, controlled a game that ended 2-1 to them, only the Reds' fourth home reverse in all European competitions. Our Continental excursions were concluded.

The standout League game came in April when Manchester United visited Anfield seeking points for a title they had waited 25 years to win. Rushie's first ever goal against the Old Trafforders, followed by another from Walters, sent the visitors away emptyhanded and eased Leeds's path to the title. The Yorkshiremen finished 18 points above Souness's side, who lay in sixth place. So Liverpool's last chance of a trophy came in the FA Cup final, reached after disposing of Crewe, Bristol Rovers, Ipswich, Aston Villa and Portsmouth, in a penalty shoot-out.

Before their Wembley date, I had a personal showdown, my first London marathon. Once Greenwich's gun triggered this journey into the unknown, I was dissolved in a river of humanity flowing remorselessly between banks of people, a river that carried me along.

Few endeavours can compress so many images into such a short space of time. (In my case, at 4 hours 25 minutes, a bit longer than most.)

Whether it's a rampaging rhino, the Invisible Man trailing white bandages or a gorgeous woman athlete (hundreds!), your eyes savour rare vision after rare vision. If you could compile a log of all these bizarre and beautiful apparitions, it would contain 1,000 entries, including the T-shirt that overtook me, bragging, "Marathon men make the best lovers – but not tonight".

Past halfway, you headbutt the first bricks in the wall, drawing strength from hidden depths to smash through, until you reach the finishing line at the uttermost end of your physical limits but in a state of euphoria that would gratify saints. Race ends, endorphins rage.

Wallowing in the opiate rush, amid funky chickens and Teenage Mutant Ninja Turtles, what you cannot visualise are the victories over adversity and illness that motivate many entrants. To take part, some have clawed their way out of the Valley of the Shadow of Death and for them and every competitor the crowds' unflagging encouragement is a shot in the arm. I was running for the Multiple Sclerosis Society and along the course shouts of "Come on, MS!" were both rousing and humbling.

Forget the finishers – every spectator deserves a medal. Without them, I couldn't have finished.

Thank you, London.

A week later, when the lads met Sunderland in the Cup final at Wembley, I'd already sworn to do another marathon, even though I was still recovering from my first ordeal. If I wasn't 100 per cent, Souness felt a lot worse; he was convalescing after emergency cardiac surgery. Ronnie Moran, who had been in charge for the semi, led the lads out, watched from the bench by our manager who had left hospital 24 hours before.

His rehabilitation was aided by Steve McManaman, who unlocked the Mackems' defence, dribbling down either wing, sliding past tackles and laying on the chances that Michael Thomas and Rush fired home to take our fifth FA Cup. Unusually, a gaffe occurred at the presentation of the trophy when the Reds were handed losers' medals while Sunderland got the winners', an error rectified in the dressing rooms.

Now Souness had his first silver, Kopites hoped for more success and a stronger squad. In the close season, he signed a fresh keeper, Watford's David James, who played his debut in front of the spanking new Kemlyn Road development. Renamed the Centenary Stand in recognition of the fact Liverpool Football Club held their inaugural match on September 1, 1892, this 12,500-seat extension, complete with upper tier, was built after terrace houses were demolished behind the ground.

Since a Cup Winners' Cup would fill the only gap in the continental line-up on Anfield's sideboard, Kopites kept their fingers crossed for 1992-93 to complete our full set. That hope evaporated before Christmas with losses in both legs to Spartak Moscow, while Bolton and Crystal Palace terminated our FA and Coca-Cola campaigns.

In the League, the Reds finished sixth to wind up a drab season. "I'm glad Bill's not here now," Nessie Shankly confessed. "He'd have been devastated."

Our style of play was not particularly endearing, either. Some theorists contend that, like dogs and their owners, teams mirror their manager and Souness was building a side in his own likeness: physical, abrasive, hard, personified by Neil Ruddock and Julian Dicks. Whelan attested to this, saying that "Graeme Souness as a manager was just like Graeme as a player".

Once the 1993-94 campaign began, Kopites yearned for some flair and Toxteth lad Robbie Fowler offered that, scoring on his Coca-Cola debut at Fulham and rattling in all five goals during the home leg.

After this nap hand, the media pleaded for the 18-year-old to leave the dressing room for an interview. Souness had to disappoint them, passing on the message: "He's not coming out. He says he wouldn't know what to say."

And how did Robbie mark his feat? "I went round the chippy," he revealed, "and got a big kiss from my mum when I got home." The teenager would enjoy many more celebratory suppers of special fried rice and barbecue sauce.

The Co-Co cup run was ended by Wimbledon, winners on penalties on their own patch, while Bristol City of the First Division wiped away our last glint of silverware in an FA Cup replay at Anfield. At the end of their 1-0 victory, Kopites gave them a standing ovation.

In the League, lack of consistency bedevilled the Reds, although they showed how to raise their game in the clash with Manchester United in L4. After 23 minutes, the Mancs had taken a 3-0 lead but Nigel Clough replied with a brace before the turnaround and Ruddock sent the Kop berserk with an equaliser in the second half.

Alex Ferguson was not happy. Since complaining about what he perceived as pressure on referees at Anfield, this past master of motivation had added the media, led by the BBC, to his roster of bogeymen. When the Beeb's Jimmy Hill criticised Eric Cantona for a stamping incident, Fergie was miffed.

"Jimmy Hill is verbal when it suits him," he complained. "If there's a prat in this world, he's the prat. I am not interested in Jimmy Hill. Four years ago he wrote us off in the warm-up. That's how much he knows.

"The BBC is dying for us to lose. Everyone is from Liverpool with a Liverpool supporter's flag. They'll be here every time until we lose, that mob – Barry, Bob, Hansen, the lot of them. Liverpool supporters' association."

The Reds' fightback for a draw did not mollify United's boss – and it also could not safeguard Souness, who upset Merseysiders by selling the story of his heart operation to *The Sun* on Hillsborough's anniversary. Asserting in mitigation that he had been unaware of the depth of feeling about Wapping's lies, his fate was finally sealed by indifferent results. In January 1994, he was sacked, a dismissal hastened by his squad's catalogue of injuries, more than under any other manager.

On his return to Anfield, Souness had been dismayed by the fitness levels, so training programmes dating back to Shanks's days were revamped. The result: queues outside the physio's room.

Superior fitness had long been a vital factor in Liverpool's dominance, 20 or fewer players being used in the first team and a lowest total of 14 in 1965-66. However, a flurry of sick notes in 1993-94 meant the line-up had to be rejigged for every match.

The squad's overhaul was also too radical and Souness admitted: "The biggest mistake was shipping people out when it suited them, not the club. Changes needed to be made but I tried to do it too quickly."

Among those allowed to leave were Beardsley, Houghton, Whelan, Gillespie and Saunders, while McMahon, the only one to captain both Liverpool and Everton, was also handed his P45. A well-tried club policy of evolution, rather than revolution, was abandoned, causing top internationals to be replaced by the likes of Paul Stewart, Torben Piechnik and Istvan Kozma.

During his three-year tenure, Souness sold 18 players, including veterans who could still do a professional job, and brought in 15, several of whom were not good enough, although to his credit he did develop youngsters such as Fowler, McManaman and Jamie Redknapp.

Now Liverpool's board believed a trusted Scouser could succeed where the Scot had failed.

16

Eagles Over The Azteca

*Throw your dreams into space like a kite, and you don't know what they
will bring back: a new life, a new friend, a new love, a new country.*

– Anaïs Nin

IN April 1994, my second London marathon turned into a punishing
prelude for my latest flirtation with Latin America.

Perhaps because of overtraining or the cold, windy weather, the 26 miles
were a killer, far more exhausting than my initial attempt, and at mid-point I
ran into a wall that made me consider throwing in the towel. Thoroughly out
of sorts, I decided that if a station lay on the route, I'd take the tube to
Charing Cross where my car was parked.

There was no station, though. Dragging one foot in front of the other, I
resorted to the cyclists' maxim in the Tour de France: I can't go on, I must go
on, I will go on. With the assistance of the marvellous crowds, I did go on,
surviving my rough patch and collapsing over the finishing line in a similar
time to my first effort. The winner was a Mexican, Dionisio Cerón, and
coincidentally on the following Tuesday I caught a KLM flight to his home
town, Mexico City.

As we took off from my favourite airport, Amsterdam's Schipol, I was
physically equipped for the objectives I'd set myself: exploring the tourist
sites; walking on the volcano of Popocatépetl (try saying that while stuffing
your chops with salted peanuts); and watching a game in the Aztec Stadium.
However, from my window seat on the plane, I was not prepared for the
dirty, grey pollution blanketing the streets of the Mexican capital, with one
solitary skyscraper peeking out. Once our pilot had plunged into this
miasma, he contrived to land on the airport's sole runway, an uneven
concrete strip that jarred the fuselage and set the wings waggling ostenta-
tiously.

Despite the stresses, our engine bolts did not shear off and soon I was
through immigration. Outside the arrivals hall, I commandeered a taxi to my
hotel, a journey along congested roads that authenticated the definition of a

nanosecond in Mexico: the period between lights changing to "Go" and the first car horn blaring.

Caramba! In this land of earthquakes and volcanoes, patience is not a virtue.

One agreeable observation I did make was a bus with Liverpool on the front. Liverpool? Why? My cabby informed me it was a prominent street, in addition to being the country's biggest chain of department stores.

He dropped me off in the Zona Rosa, the Pink Zone – not a reference to the sexual predilections of its habitués, that's what the tourist district is called – where I had booked a room in the Casa González, a rosetted entry in any compendium of great little hotels and a hideaway for businessmen and backpackers, academics and actors, amid the ferment of metropolitan life.

That evening, its proprietor, the eponymous Señor González, presided over a communal dinner of chicken in dark chocolate sauce, fortunately not spiced with the chilli strengths offered to a mate in a San Antonio Tex-Mex takeaway: Hot, Very Hot and El Scorchero. Actually, no chilli was required for our chicken and chocolate, which complemented each other very well. Recommended.

My 10 fellow diners around one large table consisted of a miscellany of travellers of all ages, with riveting tales about remote Latin America regions, from Patagonia to Paraguay to Paramaribo. You name it, they'd been there.

I'd done my research but Señor González offered personal insight into Mexico City's must-do's, invaluable recommendations I profited from during my nine-day stay.

As promised by him, the National Anthropological Museum was astounding, a treasure house of mankind that I felt compelled to visit twice.

Leon Trotsky's fortified villa, with bullet-riddled rooms, is like no home I have been in. Alone in the study, I visualised Stalin's assassin raising his ice-axe, then burying it in the back of the Russian fugitive's head as he sat reading at his desk. It happened, in that very room, at that very desk in 1940.

If Teotihuacán, the 2,000-year-old City of the Gods, were situated in Europe, it would be one of the wonders of the world, luring millions. Here, in unearthly stillness, a handful sauntered down the mile-long ceremonial Avenue of the Dead, past the Pyramid of the Feathered Serpent and the Pyramid of the Moon, to the gigantic Pyramid of the Sun.

The capital's baroque cathedral remains an ornate monument to the Conquistadors' barbarity and greed after they subjugated New Spain. On entering, a poster grabbed me, "En caso de sismo. In the event of an earthquake", which advised leaving the building promptly and calmly. How perplexing that in a house of the Lord, the advice failed to recommend kneeling down and praying for deliverance, although any such prayers would have gone unanswered in 1985 when an earthquake did wreck the cathedral and killed 20,000 in the capital.

Another threat to la Catedral Metropolitana has been posed by its irresistible weight, forcing one end of the nave to settle 10 foot lower than the other, so that the floor slopes down and pews tilt. With the combined effects of earthquakes and sinking foundations, it was a miracle the pillars could still support the roof and arch after arch was clad in scaffolding. Despite this, the vista through darkness to the main altar, carved out of solid onyx, was something to behold.

Stepping through the cathedral's main entrance, you find yourself in the Zócalo, the largest public square in the Western hemisphere and a vast stage for official parades, political demonstrations, philosophical debates and street theatre, as dancers and drummers in regal plumed head-dresses put on a folk show next to the excavated Templo Mayor, the Aztecs' great temple.

In the National Palace which occupies one side of the Zócalo, expansive murals by Diego Rivera portray the country's turbulent history, and a caption lists the natural bounty bequeathed to our world by Mexico: maize, cocoa, cotton, tomatoes, tobacco, peanuts, chilli, pineapple, to select a few.

After a week exploring the capital and adjusting to its altitude of 2,240 metres (7,200 feet), I was ready to take a hike on Popocatépetl, or Popo as Mexicans have the good sense to call it.

To reach this ice-domed peak, I began by travelling on the metro, a revelation to any user of London's tube. On the surface, Mexico City is urban chaos: go underground and you alight upon a fast, clean, efficient and cheap transport system worthy of the most modern, ordered society. As sparkling trains sped along the tracks every couple of minutes, I asked myself which was the Third World country, the United States of Mexico or the United Kingdom. Our capital has had to try very hard to get it so very wrong.

My journey to the metropolitan boundary at Pantitlán was enlivened by a man of Mayan countenance who delivered a political speech to our carriage. Trigger Happy TV this wasn't as he spoke with conviction about the Zapatista movement in the jungle-clad southern state of Chiapas, their campaign for indigenous rights, arguments for autonomy, the 150 peasants killed by the army in January and his charismatic leader, Subcomandante Marcos.

Several stations farther on, he thanked passengers for their attention and got off. Not the sort of diversion you get in rush hour on the Jubilee line.

At Pantitlán, a coach was waiting to convey passengers to the sleepy town of Amecameca, where we switched to a minibus that hauled this solitary gringo, a gaggle of giggling Indians and their baskets of aromatic lemons and earthy potatoes up the Paso de Cortés, the Pass of Cortés. From here in 1519, the Spanish invaders gazed down in wonder at Tenochtitlan, a city on islands in the middle of a lake. That Aztec capital of 200,000 inhabitants grew into present-day Mexico City, with 30 million, a rough estimate because no census has been carried out in its boundless shanty towns which testify to a 21st-Century paradox: across the continents, country-dwellers are flocking to cities; meanwhile, city-dwellers are escaping to the country.

Beyond the Pass of Cortés, signposted by a graffiti-scarred stone block, our minibus trundled up to a bunkhouse for climbers, the start of my hike on Popo. Map in hand, I surveyed the route for my stroll across the flanks of the Smoking Mountain. High above, on a mantle of ice blanketing its summit, black dots were crawling, painfully slowly.

Climbers. Ordinary people with an extraordinary love of their sport, putting their lives on the line without regard for fame or money.

Wishing I was up there with them, I set off across grey sand cleared from the volcano's throat over centuries, along a path walked by Conquistadors to the crater where they were lowered on ropes into the fiery abyss to collect sulphur for fresh gunpowder and fresh conquests.

I knew my limitations, though. Popo is a serious mountain, its 5,452-metre (17,880feet) summit reached after an exhausting eight-hour slog, so I was looking forward to an afternoon's ramble.

Trailed by a pair of wild dogs that must have sniffed food in my backpack, I walked for a couple of hours to a spot known as Las Cruces, The Crosses, at about 14,000 feet, and sat down to goggle at the spectacular view of Iztaccíhuatl, Popo's sister volcano. A drink of orange juice, a taco, some slivers of chicken for my canine companions, and time to call it a day.

My descent was a breeze and within little more than an hour I was back at the climbers' hut. On a knoll alongside this, a Japanese woman was sitting cross-legged, contemplating Popo's beauty, and in Spanish I asked her when the minibus was due. She responded in American-accented English that she was visiting Popo with her family and, if I wished, they could drive me back to Mexico City. I was also welcome to share a picnic with them. Estúpendo.

It transpired this day marked the anniversary of the passing of her grandfather, the first generation of the family to emigrate from Japan to Mexico. Since Popo was shaped like a surrogate Mount Fuji, his ashes had been scattered here and every year the extended family would drive out to pay homage to their forebear.

The woman, Gloria, had studied at a Californian university, hence her fluent English, and she accompanied me to the car park where I met a group of about a dozen relatives waiting by their 4x4s. Introductions completed, our convoy of Jeep Cherokees and Nissan Patrols bounced down a potholed track to a forest glade, a pine-scented setting for an alfresco spread of delectable Japanese specialities and thirst-quenching Corona lager, supped while we sat on jute mats.

The Japanese had engrossing anecdotes about life in Mexico. Crime and corruption, earthquakes and eruptions were everyday topics for people who had legitimate seismological anxieties when they asked: "Did the earth move for you?"

One story they related concerned a chief of police who financed the construction of a Parthenon-style and -size mansion in the capital's millionaire enclave, its sweeping grounds guarded not by a pack of Rottweilers but a pride of lions. All on a salary that would not buy a bungalow in Burscough. The whole city knew he was financing this property with drugs money but the authorities turned a blind eye until, stupefied with his own self-importance, Mr Top Cop went a tad too far.

One Friday evening, he commanded traffic police to close a motorway leading into the city centre so his chauffeur could drive an open-top limousine down the empty carriageway while the gold braid reclined in all his splendour in the back.

That was not all. As a permanent memento of this exercise in narcissism, his limo's progress was dutifully filmed from the force's helicopter, which had been requisitioned for the job.

The upshot of such a preposterous ego trip was the worst gridlock ever – and grudging acceptance in high places that this out-of-control scuffer had to be reined in before the spotlight of justice spread wider. Substantiating the Latin American belief that all police are criminals in uniform, he was charged with involvement in narcotic trafficking and Mexico City's traffic was permitted to revert to its habitually sluggish tempo.

My new-found friends could have regaled me with tales like that for hours but the sun was sinking behind the conifers and they had a duty to perform: they spread out to collect rubbish abandoned by previous picnickers, which was piled into a mound and set alight. In accordance with their philosophy of life, the Japanese had to leave a place or a person better than they found them. As their maxim explains: What we have done for ourselves alone dies with us. What we have done for others and the world remains and is immortal.

Within half an hour of completing our Popo litter pick, we were snared in heavy traffic on the capital's outskirts, the highway hemmed in by mile after mile of a shanty town you smelt long before you saw.

All at once, our speed was reduced to walking pace. Ahead in the middle of the road lay a bundle of rags, around which vehicles were manoeuvring before accelerating away.

"Está muerto. He's dead," Gloria murmured.

As we drove around this heap of clothes, I could see it was the broken, bloodied body of a boy, about 10. Must have been run over. Yet no one was with him, no one was doing their damnedest to staunch his bleeding.

What's going on? Dead or dying, the lad had been abandoned on the carriageway.

"Where's the driver who hit him?" I asked. "Why's no one stopped to help?"

"No," Gloria emphasised. "Never, ever, stop after accidents. Too dangerous. If you did, the boy's family could kill you with knives, axes, pistols. No. Always drive on – if you don't want to die yourself."

How awful. Back home, people would be queuing up to offer assistance. Like one Saturday night when my last Corpy bus from town was overflowing because the conductor wouldn't leave anyone behind. The open platform at the rear where you got on was jammed with revellers and, as the double-decker slewed off Kirkdale Road into Everton Valley's gradient, this flat area began bouncing like a diving board, catapulting a chap head first into the road.

The bell tinkled in alarm, the bus juddered to a halt and conductor, driver and most of the bottom deck rushed to the casualty, unconscious, face down on the tarmac, blood trickling from a deep scalp wound.

While somebody dashed to a phone box to dial 999, a bloke in a suit calmly removed his jacket, took his white shirt off and tore it into long bandages which he started binding around the victim's head.

"Is he a mate of yours?" the conductor queried. "No" came the answer.

A first-aider, probably someone who'd been in the Forces, was doing his best for a stranger. That was Liverpool then, this was Mexico City now, and a little lad had become another road kill statistic, if anyone bothered to keep them.

We sped away from the scene, back to the genteel surroundings of the Casa González where my Japanese mates dropped me off.

Tucked up in my comfy bed that night, my mind was dancing with disbelief: that bundle of rags could have been my son. And if we'd got out of our Jeep, perhaps we could have helped the poor boy, even saved his life. But ...

After my thought-provoking return from Popo, I had one more mission: a match at the Estadio Azteca, the Aztec Stadium, the only ground to have hosted two World Cup finals.

I had already read a fair amount about this structural colossus. Opened in 1966, some 100,000 tons of concrete – enough for four old Wembleys – was used to build the two-tier bowl, separated by a circle of 850 double-decker private boxes. Boasting a 115,000 capacity, most beneath a concrete roof covering the highest number of seats in any sports arena, the construction technique left it unscathed by 1985's cataclysmic quake.

Apart from the national side, three league teams play there – Atlante, Necaxa and América, the country's most successful club. Since América are looked upon as the team of the government and establishment, they are despised by their biggest rivals in the capital, the UNAM university side, whose home is the 70,000-seat Olympic Stadium, the athletics venue for 1968's Games.

Football was introduced to Mexico in the early 1900s by Cornishmen working in Hidalgo's silver mines and now it is the No 1 sport, the most eagerly anticipated duels pitting América against any team from Guadalajara, the industrial powerhouse where 4 million live. By pure coincidence, my Azteca visit coincided with a clásico, a match between the capital's kingpins and Tecos, Guadalajara's university team, to determine who would go through to the championship final.

Reputedly Mexicans are only punctual for football and funerals, and on my arrival at the ground for the evening kick-off, crowds were milling around in something of a fiesta atmosphere.

Seeking a quiet turnstile, I walked leisurely around the stadium.

Outside one gate, 30-or-so Américanistas had gathered, hard-core supporters in blue and yellow colours, some holding long poles adorned with flags, but one ultra stood out because he had a bird of prey clamped on a leather gauntlet on his right arm.

Even though I'd slugged a couple of beers and a tumbler of boot-melting mezcal in a cantina near the ground, I wasn't hallucinating. What a bizarre sight. Conceivably its owner didn't feel too happy with the team and planned to give them the bird.

As I stared at this magnificent creature's beautiful head with a hooked beak, it was startled by something, rattling its chains and flapping its wings. No angler's tale – the wingspan was about four feet.

Musing on why anyone should take that into a match, I strolled to an entrance where nobody was queuing and paid to go in. Hauling myself up a long staircase, I found myself in the Azteca's top tier. Above, its roof flowed seamlessly around the stands, without beginning, without end, while below, the oval of turf offered an emerald counterpoint to the elliptical grey sky.

Poised high over the centre spot lurked a monstrous spider, with splodgy black body and straggly legs: the loudspeaker console for the public address system. Despite being suspended from steel cables at a considerable height, I speculated whether a ball had ever hit it and, if so, what the laws stipulated for such an eventuality. Dropped ball? Free kick?

Towards the summit of the terrace, I sat down on the edge of a precipice, staring around this awesome arena. Even though it was getting dark, my thoughts slipped back to a brilliantly sunny afternoon in 1970 when I watched a stellar game on telly.

Here on this lush pitch, in the first World Cup final broadcast in colour, Brazil gave a master class in attacking football, a 4-1 demolition of Italy, to become champions for the third time and outright holders of the Jules Rimet trophy. In their green and yellow jerseys, Pelé, Jairzinho, Rivelino, Tostao, Gerson and Clodoaldo, the planet's six finest footballers, conspired with their team-mates to destroy the Italians.

Pelé opened the scoring in the 18th minute, leaping like a black salmon to head Rivelino's cross. After Boninsegna equalised, the game was on a knife-edge until the 67th minute when Jairzinho and Gerson carried out a scissor move that finished with Gerson smashing the ball in from 18 yards. Next, Pelé headed to Jairzinho, who slotted home, and with four minutes on the clock, Carlos Alberto capped the afternoon with his first goal of the tournament. In a move involving nine Brazilians, their skipper ran on to a deliciously weighted lay-off from Pelé and drove the ball past Albertosi.

The maestros of futebol had given their art's purest performance. From thereon, every football addict, apart from Argentinians, was a Brazilian.

Here, too, England came up against Argentina in the 1986 World Cup quarter-final, their first meeting since the Falklands War, and in front of a jury of 114,000, Maradona condemned himself with his "hand of God", then went on a wondrous dribble from his own half to score again.

Despite these body blows, England mounted a stirring rally, Barnes sending over a pinpoint cross for Lineker to head in and delivering another centre which our striker narrowly failed to nick in. England packed their bags while Argentina moved into the Azteca's second final, defeating West Germany 3-2.

Now in that same stadium, a setting for high drama and perpetual disgrace, I was looking forward to the teams coming out.

Until someone pulled a plug; all the lights went out.

Must be a failure in the electricity grid, I thought. Happens in Latin America.

The Azteca, about two-thirds full, was black and the crowd fell silent.

Not for long. From directly behind each goal, a laser beam lanced into the air, striking the underside of the roof where it began to swell. As these pinpoints of light expanded, they metamorphosed into two gigantic birds, wings outspread, hovering over both ends of the ground.

Having assumed form, they took flight, moving slowly at first around the roof and picking up speed until, like pursuit cyclists on opposite sides of a track, they were chasing each other.

By now, music was blasting out of the spider and 70,000 fans – Camisa 12, in Spanish parlance, Shirt No 12 or the 12th man – were singing lustily, interspersing their choruses with cries of "América!" It was the Azteca's YNWA.

With the birds sweeping above my head in pursuit of quarry, I now grasped thesignificance of the eagle on that character's arm; a mascot for the team, the Águilas, or Eagles. But Selhurst Park this was not.

When a thunderous roar of "América!" ended the song, the Azteca's floodlights turned night into day, the laser eagles flew back into their electronic cages and both teams ran out.

Because of travel difficulties in a vast country like Mexico, away support at games is negligible but 20 or so Tecos aficionados were sitting nearby. When these Guadalajarans chanted, there was no animosity, no hint of tension, and I couldn't spot any police either, testimony to the absence of hooligans in Mexican football.

This laid-back mood was enhanced by a civilised refreshments service for every seat, cheap or expensive. No hustling for a Bovril deep in the stand, missing a penalty. White-coated waiters were awaiting your call. Put your arm up to attract attention and they'd bring whatever you requested – beer, taco, pizza, chocolate, chewing gum, ice cream, the full enchilada...

The visiting team's complete title was Club de Fútbol Tecos de la Universidad Autónoma de Guadalajara and their knot of supporters knew better than to launch into a chant of "Give me a C, give me an L, give me a U ..." Anyway, Tecos did not require interminable vocal backing. Way down, down, down yonder on the turf, they plucked the Eagles 3-1 and were a step closer to their first championship.

By the final whistle, that yardstick of boredom, the Mexican wave, had not rippled through the crowd and once both sets of fans had saluted their sides, the Guadalajaran faction ambled out with the Américanistas as if they'd all been watching Toy Story at the multiplex.

With justification, the Azteca can take pride in its motto, "Estadio seguro, estadio amable, Safe stadium, friendly stadium". Long may it remain so.

17
Back To The Boot Room

I'd rather be a failure at something I love than a success at something I hate.
– George Burns

AFTER Graeme Souness's departure in January 1994, Liverpool's directors gave notice of a return to Boot Room principles by naming a club stalwart as manager. A member of the backroom staff for 20 years, Roy Evans had won the Central League title no fewer than seven times while running the Reserves between August 1974 and May 1983 and now his brief was to re-create the Liverpool Way that had brought so many trophies.

Even though the Boot Room had been demolished during Souness's regime when the Main Stand's interior was rebuilt to accommodate a media centre, the new appointment meant Anfield's blood line of Shanks, Paisley, Fagan and Dalglish had been restored.

If anyone was steeped in the club, it was Evans. After a scout watched him playing for Bootle Boys and England Boys, he joined Liverpool straight from school in October 1965 and his first-team debut came at left-back against Sheffield Wednesday in March 1970. In all, though, he only turned out 11 times before retiring in 1973 because Shanks thought he should become a coach.

The boss's advocacy of a fresh career path was shrewd, as the bright novice progressed from first-team coach to assistant manager to the top job. But even wildest optimists were not expecting a quick fix under our new boss and the season ended with the Reds eighth, their worst League position since 1964-65.

The closing fixture signalled the end of an era. Since the Kop was being turned into an all-seater, April 30, 1994 marked the last day for standing on our hallowed ground and it was packed for the farewell party. Norwich threw cold water on our festivities when Jeremy Goss pecked one for the Canaries, sparking a chant of "You're supposed to let us win", with encores of "We only sing when we're losing" and "We only sing when we're standing". City refused to lie down and, at the end, Kopites hailed them as victors.

Some 45 minutes after the whistle sounded, police shepherded reluctant Kopites from their Boer War monument.

As another page was turned in Anfield's journal, our concrete steps might be disappearing but all those glorious memories would remain.

So 1994-95's season brought an all-sitting, all-singing Kop and renewed hope that Evans could restore Liverpool's prestige, anticipation that increased when Robert Bernard Fowler leathered in the Premiership's fastest hat-trick, in four-and-a-half minutes, against Arsenal.

With Robbie and Rushie leading the line, the Reds suffered one defeat in 25 games and supporters' spirits rose, only for the campaign's second half to initiate a slump that left our lads off the pace. Blackburn and Manchester United were vying for the championship until the last Saturday when Rovers came to Anfield seeking a win, while the Old Trafforders took on West Ham.

Well before this decisive day, the mindless games had started – tabloids sniped that Liverpool wouldn't break sweat against Rovers if it handed the title to Manchester and might even serve the points on a blue and white platter to Blackburn. Twaddle. Professionals to the tips of their toes, Liverpool battled for every ball, snatching a 2-1 victory in the last minute through Redknapp's curler of a free kick. Blackburn's support and their boss, Kenny Dalglish, were downcast. The title had gone.

Hang on. News spread that the Hammers had held Manchester, meaning Rovers were champions. In an outburst of delirium, home and away fans made merry with Kenny who had now taken two clubs to the title.

This victory's three points placed Liverpool fourth in the Premier League while in the FA Cup they reached the quarter-finals, where Jurgen Klinsmann netted in the 88th minute at the Kop end to send Spurs through. At the close, Anfield gave him a standing ovation – the "greatest moment at Tottenham" for this quiet, self-effacing star who was content to trundle around London in an ancient VW Beetle.

Evans did steer the Reds to the Coca-Cola final with Bolton, Man of the Match McManaman bagging both goals to win the trophy and take us back into Europe in the UEFA Cup. The club also earned one commendable double: the team and its supporters were awarded the Premier League's Fair Play awards, based on the number of red and yellow cards and the fans' behaviour.

In his first full season in charge, Evans had a cup. The question preoccupying Kopites was whether he could move up a level to win the League.

Paisley and Fagan had shown it was possible to be caring, thoughtful bosses who landed the game's biggest trophies but the megabucks sloshing around football in the Nineties had eroded old-fashioned values of loyalty, sacrifice and hard work. Now millionaire players barely out their teens could smirk at these traditional virtues as they took delivery of their 12-cylinder Ferrari posing pouches.

Evans's trusting approach to his squad provoked accusations he was too soft and tabloids slapped the Spice Boys label on one group, bandying various names around: McManaman, Fowler, Redknapp, Ince, James, Ruddock, Stan Collymore, Jason McAteer and Phil Babb. Stories circulated that some were too preoccupied with modelling and clubbing, governed by their motto, "Win or lose, first on the booze", and according to columnists in the red-tops, that explained why Liverpool weren't in the frame for the title.

For Barnes, a handful of youngsters did warrant criticism for their time-keeping, lack of respect and casual attitude in training and he put his finger on the solution: "We needed more professionalism and discipline." As a senior player, John passed on his concerns to Evans and criticised coaching methods such as five-a-sides, which he considered unsuited to the modern era.

Despite this, April 1996 brought an Anfield game that Sky's Martyn Tyler described as "the most thrilling match I've had the privilege to broadcast in 25 years". In a pulsating contest with fellow League contenders Newcastle, Fowler opened the scoring in the second minute, only for Les Ferdinand to equalise and David Ginola to put the Magpies ahead. After the turnaround, Fowler levelled but Faustino Asprilla restored the Geordies' lead. Now it was end-to-end stuff as Liverpool hurled themselves forward, creating gaps in their half which Newcastle threatened to exploit. Urged on by the frenzied crowd, Collymore got a richly deserved equaliser and, two minutes into injury time, he lashed the ball into the Kop net again. Final score: Liverpool 4, Newcastle 3.

Jimmy Hill once said: "What makes this game so delightful is that when both teams get the ball they are attacking their opponent's goal." If any match bore out that observation, this was it and Tyler included it in his top five sports events ever on television, along with England's World Cup victory in 1966 and Jim Laker's 19 Australian wickets in the 1956 Test. Newspapers were unanimous in nominating it as the best match of the millennium while later the Premier League voted it their Game of the Decade.

This corker ended Newcastle's title challenge, although Liverpool reverted to erratic form in their next fixture, losing away to lowly Coventry. A couple of lacklustre draws followed, meaning they finished third.

In one competition, they were victorious, winning the FA Youth Cup with a line-up that featured trainees who would become stars: Steven Gerrard, Jamie Carragher and Michael Owen, scorer of 11 goals in five games.

On the senior stage, the club's UEFA ambitions foundered against Brondby, leaving the last glint of silverware in the FA Cup. On the road to Wembley, Rushie scored against Rochdale to overtake Denis Law's record of

41 goals in the competition and the lads cruised home 3-0 in the semi against Aston Villa.

The final with Manchester United turned into a tame affair, both teams neutralising each other. Liverpool had released a record, Pass and Move (It's the Liverpool Groove), but getting into the groove was easier in a studio than on the pitch. Fowler and Collymore posed little threat to the Manc goal, even though McManaman ran himself into the ground, while James made some fine saves, apart from one Cantona shot that snaked through defenders to take the spoils.

This no-show showpiece was followed by a favourite's exit. Seeking regular first-team football, Rushie moved to Leeds after 16 years at Anfield, during which he played 658 times and chalked up 346 goals. Not just a striker, he acted as our bonus defender, tackling back, closing down, feigning fatigue, making a token effort as he lolloped after an opponent who was also chasing the ball. Suddenly, Rushie would put a spurt on – and nick the ball away.

He always worked his cotton socks off, affirming the value of defending from the front. A player worth his weight in Machynlleth gold.

After the FA Cup reverse, critics opened fire on Evans, saying his selection had shown too much deference to United, but Fowler rejected this: "I don't think either side deserved to win. Manchester scored a late goal but it could have gone either way." Liverpool were also slated for the way they dressed, walking out before kick-off in white Armani suits and dark sunglasses, which did reinforce the Spice Boys image, although McManaman took a contrary view. "It doesn't matter what suit you wear," he said. "We didn't play well enough and that's why we lost."

While the Spice Boys stories undermined Evans's reputation, Collymore posed his biggest challenge. After signing in August 1995, the target man had developed into an effective foil for Fowler but problems arose during his second year. He refused to buy a house close to Merseyside, preferring Staffordshire to be near his mother. He refused to play in the reserves. He refused to train. When he went missing, Kopites suggested that Stan, who had an eye for the ladies, was hiding from an irate husband in the Williamson Tunnels, that vast labyrinth hewn out of Edge Hill in the 1800s. From sexual folly to the world's biggest underground folly.

Asked about our spluttering star, Tommy Docherty was unequivocal; he would never have touched him because the striker had been trouble at so many clubs. A rumour even surfaced that the Cannock man was going through a quarter-life crisis, assailed by psychiatric ailments like those that had put the mockers on Rangers' keeper. After he was diagnosed with mild schizophrenia, Kilmarnock fans sang: "Two Andy Gorams, there's only two Andy Gorams."

For lots of public figures, from A to Z list, fame and fortune are the wardens of a prison and Collymore wouldn't have been the first to learn the greater your success, the smaller your cell. Freddie Mercury, who warped from enjoying stardom to enduring it, hit the nail on the head: "The more money you get, the more miserable you become."

Although the English are loyal by nature and ever ready to prop up wobbling idols, Kopites got cheesed off with Stan's wayward behaviour. For them, he was taking advantage of the club and its fans and ultimately he would destroy the trust they put in him.

* * * * * * * * * *

The second half of 95-96's season was overshadowed by the loss of a legend: Bob Paisley passed away in a Merseyside nursing home, at the age of 77. As he was laid to rest, the minister characterised him as "an ordinary man of extraordinary greatness" and Kopites reflected on the precious gifts he'd lavished on them and their club, a roll call of prizes without equal. Verily, the Fates smiled on us when Bob became our boss.

Not only a great servant of Anfield, putting others before himself, he was also a patriot, a soldier who fought his way through North Africa and Italy during the Second World War. Yet, despite the achievements of the only manager to win three European Cups, our betters did not consider him worthy of a knighthood. Doubtless the arbiters of such awards pooh-poohed Scouse grumbles about this snub as yet another example – yes, Ma'am – of Merseyside's victim syndrome but the reasons Bob wasn't honoured were plain: wrong man, wrong club, wrong city.

Surveying some recipients of this accolade, any fair-minded person might conclude the title of Sir wasn't worthy of him, better suited to lesser mortals. No, Bob, you were far, far superior to them.

A chap of humility, our boss would never shoot his mouth off, preferring to think before he uttered his words of wisdom. Some of his most enlightening were: "My headmaster told me that if you want to tell anyone anything, speak softly. They'll try to listen to find out what you're saying. If you shout, they probably won't be interested."

Unlike other managers with big smiles and dead eyes, Bob was a kind, honest, human being whose down-to-earth nature was exemplified by a story told by an Old Alsopian, Alan Doddridge, now a doctor in New Zealand. On a trip to his parents in Stoneycroft, he popped round to Anfield where he explained to the receptionist that he was a Scouser on a flying visit and wondered if it might be possible to see inside the stadium.

She picked up the phone, passing on this request to the person at the other end of the line.

Seconds later, Bob Paisley bounded into the Main Stand foyer, welcoming Alan like an old friend and accompanying him on a tour of the ground.

The boss of the European champions showing around a stranger, from the far side of the world. Would any other manager have deigned to do such a thing? Dream on. But Bob was behaving in accordance with the Liverpool ethos: fans are the club's life force. They should never be dismissed as mammon fodder for batteries of cash tills, herded unceremoniously into the maw of the super-hyper-mega merchandising warehouse.

For Bob, everybody counted, be they big or small, important or menial, and he treated them right. As he put it at a board meeting: "We couldn't survive in this job without the support of everyone pulling in the same direction, from the chairman to the tea lady."

Yes, the chairman and the tea lady in the same breath. Doesn't that say everything about warm, humble Bob Paisley?

* * * * * * * * * *

Despite losing at Wembley, Liverpool took a slot in the 1996-97 Cup Winners' Cup, reaching the quarter-finals where they saw off Brann Bergen 4-1 on aggregate. In the home leg, Fowler toasted a goal by pulling up his jersey to display a T-shirt supporting Merseyside dockers who'd been locked out for 18 months. UEFA fined him £900 for this gesture.

From a lockout to a knockout: in the semi with Paris St Germain, the Reds lost 3-0 away and could only pull two goals back in L4. Kopites' passports were put away again.

I fished mine out, though, for a pop at getting the work-wife balance right. I hadn't quite reached the stage of one colleague, dearest Syd, who informed me: "There are only two things my missus doesn't like about me: what I say and what I do." However, Anne did deserve a treat, so I took her for a weekend in Amsterdam, where we scrutinised the cultural sights, from the sumptuous Rijksmuseum to the hilarious red-light district. There my attention was grabbed by a sign outside an erotic theatre, promising, "Live sex show – with audience participation and free Heineken".

Yabbadabbadoo! I was up for it, if you'll forgive the expression. What more could a couple desire on a romantic getaway? What better location to corroborate for a captive audience that I was growing old disgracefully? No bit part for me, none of your half an inch and 16 wrinkles – I'd inherited a rather sizeable endowment from my forefathers and was ready, willing and capable of extending my largesse to the disadvantaged. It's showtime, babe!

"Come on," I said to Anne. "Let's give it a whirl. Should be a laugh."

A laugh? My soulmate didn't get the joke. Never seen her so angry. Well, not since one January dusk when, hurrying across Standish rec, she spotted some headbanger in the bushes. She couldn't miss him – he was sticking out a mile, a grinning exhibitionist, shining a torch on his drilling tackle.

Yes, I know. If I've heard it once, I've heard it 100 times. A real flasher.

Now here in Amsterdam, my Judy was even more outraged.

"I am NOT going in THAT place," she spat, storming away.

I chased after her.

"Lost your sense of humour?" I pleaded. "Only joking."

"Joking?" she squealed. "Call that joking? How dare you! How dare you! How long have we been married? Don't answer that! You'll get it wrong – again! No! No! No! How many times do I have to tell you? I – CAN'T – STAND – HEINEKEN!"

Ouch! Point taken. Despite tramping Amsterdam's streets, I found no cabarets serving free flagons of her tipple of choice, Cuarenta y Tres, that liquor mirabilis, and my last chance to attend an orgy vanished.

So what? I've always preferred Carlsberg to Heineken.

Back to more pleasurable issues. In the League, Liverpool's sparkling form put them five points ahead of the pack in December but a rocky spell threw that away by early February when I drove with Russ to Selhurst Park for the Wimbledon fixture. We arrived minutes before kick-off ... as the car radio announced play was impossible because of a rain-logged pitch. A wasted six-hour journey for us – Scousers could at least double that.

March opened with a classic, the Reds coasting into a 3-0 lead over Newcastle at Anfield. The Mags dragged themselves off the floor, finding the onion bag three times in 17 minutes to level, until in the dying seconds Bjornebye fired over one last cross and, sweet as a nut, Fowler headed the winner. A groundhog game, repeating the previous year's 4-3.

By this stage, Collymore's Anfield days were ebbing away. As and when he made himself available, he was substituted time and again. More frustration was caused by James, who struggled between the sticks because – his explanation – he had been spending hours tinkering with a hand-held computer. "I now realise," he confessed, "that computer games have affected my performances badly."

Our rearranged game with Wimbledon in May brought a ray of hope: at the age of 17 years and 144 days, Michael Owen came on as substitute. He had averaged a goal a game in the reserves and now, as the Reds trailed 2-0, the first team's youngest ever player got on the scoresheet to make it 2-1.

At the season's close, Liverpool were fourth. Could we improve on that in the new campaign? Owen would certainly be an asset but, in my inexpert opinion, the squad as a whole seemed lacking in belief. As a French proverb puts it: To believe a thing is impossible is to make it so. Evans had to make the impossible possible.

18
Spaced-Out And Star-Struck

To live without hope is to cease to live.
– Feodor Dostoevski

IN August 1997 I was having some rehab amid the Great Outdoors, on a family holiday in Chamonix. After a walk through pinewoods in the Valley of the Arve, we were watching a sports channel on TV in our apartment when the French announcer began discussing a match on the Wednesday, the Coppa Berlusconi between Milan and Juventus in the San Siro.

Preview completed, Russ, who was 16, asked: "Can we go?"

Spiffing idea. Any run-in between AC and the Vecchia Signora, or Old Lady, is a biggie, up there with Liverpool versus Everton, and this curtain-raiser to the Italian season would enable me to see the San Siro, high on my stadium want list.

Scrutiny of the map indicated Milan was about 150 miles away on the other side of the Alps. Go for it. Berlusconi or bust.

On the morning, we set out at 9 o'clock, drove through the Mont Blanc tunnel into the Valle d'Aosta and along motorways to enter Milan's outskirts. As we got nearer to the ground in the San Siro district, ticket touts waited at almost every traffic light. Noon, eight hours before kick-off, they were already touting for business.

For them, the giveaway was our British number plate. Tourists! They must be interested in going to the match. The instant we halted at one red light, they were tapping on the window, welcoming us to Milano, brandishing the best tickets in the house. They appeared kosher, with watermarks, but I wasn't convinced. "No, grazie" and we cracked on towards the stadium.

Minutes later, turning into a dual carriageway, we caught our first glimpse of it, directly ahead, unlike anything I'd ever seen.

The San Siro has been likened to an aircraft carrier looming over the city but to my eye it looked straight out of Stanley Kubrick's 2001: A Space Odyssey. After a two-year journey from Klemola 44 galaxy, 400 million light years away, a gargantuan spaceship had landed in the middle of a residential neighbourhood.

The magnitude of Milan's other cathedral was jaw-dropping. Massive, colossal, enormous, gigantic, monumental, titanic ... flick through a giant's dictionary to convey its impact.

Along the sides, round towers spiralled up, solid-fuel booster rockets supporting mahussive steel girders, with air locks sticking out where replenishment vehicles could dock with supplies. Sloping walkways linked these towers and, as we got nearer, a couple of astronauts could be spied near the top of one ramp.

This inter-galactic craft had alighted in the midst of a vast open area, big enough for another San Siro, across which buses and trams were trundling. A Space Age stadium with boundless amounts of space. Obsolete, cramped Wembley this was not.

Driving past the concourse, I spotted the Biglietteria, or ticket office, but when I turned into the access road next to the booths, a security guard approached. Parking not allowed.

He directed me to the far side of the dual carriageway, to a street of shabby maisonettes and mansions within high walls.

As I pulled up, an old man indicated I should not leave our motor because Albanians and zingari, gipsies, would break in. Thanks, mate.

Car crime is an Italian growth industry, especially during summer when foreign tourists migrate to the sun, and those ticket touts had attested to how a number plate made your vehicle stand out. Delegating sentry duty to Anne, I hurried with Russ to the Biglietteria, purchasing three seats for £11 each. Extortionate Wembley, this was not.

Now that everything was tickety-boo, we could take a look at Milan. A policeman on traffic duty at a junction alongside the stadium offered a modicum of security so we abandoned our car there, catching a tram to the city centre for visits to the divine cathedral, il Duomo, and august Vittorio Emanuele shopping gallery, before appeasing our hunger with pizza.

At 6.30pm, another tram conveyed us back to the San Siro, formally the Stadio Giuseppe Meazza, in honour of the inside forward who played for both Milan teams and the Italian national side that won the World Cup in 1934 and 1938.

By this time, the concourse had become the venue of not so much a car-boot sale (Just who is buying all these car boots?) but a lorryload sale. Through rear doors of a dozen juggernauts, traders were unloading racks and boxes of football gear, merchandise for every Italian club you could think of, as well as Liverpool jerseys – counterfeit, unquestionably.

Russ settled on a Juve shirt with Del Piero's name for all of £15. Did Alessandro know his side's black and white colours were adopted from Notts County?

One hour before kick-off, we passed through our gate and walked into the San Siro at pitch level.

We were at the bottom of a man-made gorge, a concrete canyon, smudge of sky high above, mountainous stands all around.

Gobsmacking.

At each corner of the stadium, circular cliffs formed load-bearing buttresses for the girders visible from outside, a steel latticework extending over most of the pitch. You could see the problem this has caused. Bare patches of grass signified how lack of sunlight has stunted growth and made Europe's leading turf technologists tear their hair out. Yet the Serie A season had yet to begin.

Beneath the upper stand's overhang, our seats were to the left of the Curva Sud, the South Curve, San Siro's Kop, where AC's hardcore tifosi displayed banners proclaiming Commandos, Tigres, Fossa dei Leoni (Lions' Den) and You'll Never Walk Alone. All around, flags trumpeted where fans came from – Milan Club Pisa, Milan Club San Remo, Milan Club Bar Seveso and elsewhere – but no one was wearing an AC shirt. Suits were de rigueur for men, the principal players being Versace, Armani, Moschino, Ferre and Dolce e Gabanna, while beautiful women competed in a fashion parade that even encompassed fur coats. In summer! What a reception they'd get in the Sandon's public bar.

Spectators were seemingly dressed for a night at La Scala rather than the San Siro, perhaps accounting for the ground's nickname of L'Opera del Calcio, Football's Opera House.

Style was evident too in the handsome flags being swung back and forth. No one designs and waves flags like Italians, world standard-bearers of these pieces of cloth combining art and sport.

In the midst of a red and black blizzard, one superlative example stood out, an artist's depiction of Che Guevara, Christ raising his eyes to the Father, but with nothing to identify which team the freedom-fighter was endorsing.

Why should any supporter fork out for a custom-made flag that does not show his club? This non-partisan image brought to mind an American, a professional organiser of protests, whether against the building of a new airport in Phoenix, closure of a factory in Detroit or relaxation of gambling laws in Louisiana.

He criss-crossed the States, earning hefty consultancy fees from pressure groups and becoming noted for the placard he ensured got TV coverage on every march or picket.

It featured one word applicable to just about any conflict or quarrel: "Shame."

A canny choice, as with Che's flag. You could flourish that revolutionary emblem at any ground without causing offence, except possibly in Bolivia.

Che was shaking his head vigorously as Milan and Juve strode out through smoke from flares that shrouded half the ground. Because of this, the early action was hazy but all was clear when Juve scored, setting off a hail of bottles that landed on the pitch, despite high netting to protect the goal. Now the few hundred Zebra supporters made themselves heard, as would fans of Milan's other half, Inter, when they saw their hated foes conceding a goal on TV.

Behind our seats were some carabinieri and I asked how many people were present. Ottanta mil, one estimated, 80,000. I'd researched the stats and this wasn't bad for a stadium whose full capacity was 85,700 – 30,785 in the bottom tier, 33,914 in the second, 19,890 in the nosebleed seats as well as 302 places in the VIP tribune, 200 in the press box and 609 places for disabled people, with carers.

As the game grew more intense, spectators stood up, gazing at the far end where Juve's contingent was caged. In a gap in the terrace, riot police were whacking supporters with batons. Home fans responded with eardrum-melting whistles, then at the behest of a bloke with a megaphone, sang such diverse ditties as Roll Out The Barrel and Yellow Submarine, which must have inspired the Rossoneri to fire torpedoes. They scored thrice to win 3-1 and Silvio Berlusconi's cup was remaining in the Starship San Siro, to a YNWA soundtrack from the Curva Sud.

Operation Coppa over, we hastened back to our car, which had not been looted by zingari tribes, and lingered for a last glance at the stadium.

From the interior, a super-size shaft of light punched into the black ether while the towering booster rockets shimmered as they were primed. With seconds ticking away, astronauts were scurrying along walkways to their command posts.

Mission accomplished, Starship San Siro was about to blast off on its return voyage to Klemola 44.

* * * * * * * * * *

During our Chamonix summer, moody Collymore was offloaded to Aston Villa for £7 million and feisty ball-winner Paul Ince was enlisted to fill the central midfield slot of Barnes, who was offered a free transfer. The star who had dazzled us with pace, grace and power had no wish to leave, hoping to see out his days at Anfield. Now he accepted his illustrious Liverpool career was over and joined Kenny Dalglish's Newcastle.

Off the pitch, there were alterations, too; the Annie Road stand was rebuilt with two tiers, increasing ground capacity to 45,000, barely half the

San Siro's. As fans weighed up prospects for 1997-98, their verdict on Evans's teams was adventurous and dangerous going forward, vulnerable in defence at set-pieces because of a lack of height and strength. In general, his players appeared lightweight compared with their opponents' all-round athleticism.

The manager knew where his priorities lay when Richard Keys of Sky Sports asked: "Do you think you'll have to finish above Manchester United to win the League?" "You have to finish above everyone to win the League," Roy flashed back.

Topping the table proved unattainable, even though Owen shone. On the season's opening day, facing Wimbledon again at Selhurst Park, the 17-year-old was handed the ball after the Reds were awarded a penalty. Coolly he tapped it in to earn a 1-1 draw.

In the UEFA competition, he scored in the seventh minute of the tie with Celtic in Glasgow, letting the keeper dive before chipping him. The Bhoys hit back twice, keeping their lead until the 89th minute when McManaman set off on a mazy dribble that ended with him rifling home. At Anfield, the second leg was goalless, putting Liverpool through on away goals, only for them to come unstuck against Strasbourg.

Like in Souness's time, their campaign was not aided by a slew of injuries. At one Melwood media briefing, an exasperated Evans responded to questions about the number of crocked players by listing specialists and consultants who ministered to his squad.

"We even have a bloody paedophile," he told the gentlemen of the press, who momentarily assumed they were on to the story of the decade.

The club's podiatrist was mortified.

Hamstrung by their casualty list, the nearest Liverpool got to a trophy was the League Cup semi-final, losing 3-2 to Middlesbrough, while they finished third in the League, one spot higher than the previous season, thanks to Owen's tally of 18 goals. Now outsiders were taking notice of our boy.

* * * * * * * * * *

When the greatest footballer ever visited the greatest football team in Greater Manchester, it was meant to be an unforgettable day and it was ... for the wrong reason.

In April 1998 Pelé called in at Old Trafford, giving a press conference at which he answered questions with his customary grace. Then he was asked: "Who's your favourite Manchester United player?"

"Michael Owen," he replied, inducing audible groans from the ranks of spin doctors and publicity consultants. Nonetheless, this party pooper showed how Owen's renown had spread way beyond Europe, to no Kopite's surprise since they'd watched him mature from boy to teenager and appreciated the diamond Liverpool had unearthed.

I was a hesitant convert to his legion of admirers, heedful of one wise journalist's counsel. Reviewing youngsters tipped to become superstars (usually by their uncles who are also their agents) and subsequently failing to make the grade, *The Guardian's* Jimmy Holland told me once: "The moral is don't go overboard." If you do, you can fall into the trap of one hack who turned a "teen sensation" into "an instant legend" – *on his debut*. Oh, yes ...

I'd remembered Jimmy's advice, applicable as much to life as to sport, so I hadn't gone overboard about young Michael, only allowing my cynicism to fade when I learnt about his footballing childhood.

Born in Chester in December 1979, his inherent ability was soon spotted by his father, Terry, who had played for Everton, Chester and Bradford City. "Michael's coordination and eye for a ball were exceptional for a five-year-old," he recalled. "Most lads of that age were toe-punting the ball but he was tucking shots into the corner of the net with the side of his foot."

As a seven-year-old, he scored nine goals in 20 minutes for Mold Alexandra Under10s and was relegated to keeper because his coach, Howard Roberts, reckoned it wasn't right to slaughter the opposition.

"I made him go in goal," Roberts said. "Know what he did? Sat on the edge of the box complaining no one was giving him any back-passes."

County rules decreed that boys had to be at least eight to turn out for under-10s but Michael's mother Janette gave written permission for him to play at the age of seven. Even though bigger lads roughed him up, Michael never squealed for protection or asked to be substituted. He just laughed and carried on with the games, said Roberts.

Aged eight, he was selected for Deeside Schools' Under-11s, pipping Gary Speed as the team's youngest player ever, and, at nine, he was made captain, amassing 97 goals in two seasons to exceed Ian Rush's total by 25.

Scouts were soon drooling over him. Dave Nickless, secretary of the Flintshire Schools' FA, said; "We played Trafford in Manchester and I was talking to Brian Kidd about Michael. He hadn't thought much of his first-half. I told him to hang on because he always did something."

After the break, Owen grabbed every goal in a 6-0 win for Deeside.

By the age of 11, he was being wooed by a host of clubs, including Everton, Tottenham, Chelsea, Nottingham Forest, Manchester United, Manchester City and Arsenal, who were the first to give him a trial. Impressed, the Gooners sought to nab him but Terry Owen opted to assess all the suitors' personnel and facilities.

In this process of appraisal, Michael spent two weeks at Old Trafford before visiting Melwood where immediately he fitted in, reassured by Steve

Heighway who was now in charge of youth development at the Centre of Excellence.

Coming from a close-knit family, the lad and his dad recognised Anfield's values and, years later, Michael wrote in his autobiography: "Liverpool has always been a club of decent people who understand what really matters in life." This innate decency had a strong effect on Terry, who said: "I knew the first time he went there that it was the place for him."

Contract signed, the youngster was nurtured in Melwood's training scheme, playing 90 games for the under-13s and under-14s, until Heighway encouraged him to apply for the FA School of Excellence, which received hundreds of applications every year. He was accepted as one of 16 trainees and on their first day, a coach told them that out of each year's intake, only two would be recruited by clubs. Michael ran his eyes around the group, wondering who the other one would be.

After two years at Lilleshall, he rejected tempting offers from numerous clubs and returned to Liverpool, where he was a key member of the FA Youth Cup winners in May 1996, netting 11 times, including a hat-trick in the final against Manchester United. Club success was accompanied by international recognition – eight caps for England Schoolboys and a record 12 goals out of the side's 20 in 1995-96.

Soon after his 17th birthday, he signed professional forms at Anfield and in May 1997 became the youngest player to turn out for the first team, in the League fixture with Wimbledon at Selhurst Park, scoring one goal.

On his European bow in September, he found the net once more, against Celtic, and two months later he grabbed his first senior hat-trick, in the Co-Co Cup against Grimsby. After he scored on his debut for England Under-21s in December, Glenn Hoddle, manager of the senior international side, called him into the squad for a friendly with Chile in February 1998 and, at 18 years and 59 days, he replaced Duncan Edwards as the youngest player this century to turn out for his country.

Three days later, he notched up his first Premiership hat-trick against Sheffield Wednesday. Come the end of his opening season, he had 30 goals in all, of which 18 were in the League, making him joint top striker and PFA Young Player of the Year.

At every level, Michael's boots had blazed trails on the pitch. Having hit the bull's-eye on his debuts for England's Under-15s, Under-16s, Under-18s, Under-19s, Under-20s and Under-21s, he became his country's youngest scorer in a senior international when he snatched the only goal against Morocco in Casablanca in May 1998.

Now his eyes were focusing on the World Cup in France. Before the tournament, Four-Four-Two magazine brought out an edition featuring him on the front and a headline, "The teenager who'll shock the world", but Hoddle wasn't so keen, justifying a reluctance to use our lad up front with the comment, "I'm not sure Michael Owen is a natural-born goalscorer."

Quizzed on this, England's boss pleaded he had been misquoted (Where've we heard that before?) and intended to say Owen was not just a goalscorer but also a goal creator. Certainly Michael could fill both roles but his short period as a pro bellowed out that he was one of the most instinctive hitmen around.

Hoddle also made an eccentric reference to the teenager having to watch his "lifestyle", this when the lad had always been a consummate professional. When Owen saw this warning splashed all over the papers, he couldn't fathom what the manager was getting at and a phone call from Hoddle sought to clarify his remarks. "He told me he'd been talking about the dangers to young players in general," Owen said, "and it had been taken out of context." (Again, where've we heard that before?)

Nonetheless, Hoddle began the World Cup with twin strikers, Alan Shearer and Teddy Sheringham, who had no inkling the death knell was about to toll for their SAS pairing. Brought on as substitute, Michael netted in a 2-1 defeat by Romania but victories over Tunisia and Colombia steered the team out of their group into the second round, facing Argentina in St Etienne.

That evening I was working in a City of London office, catching glimpses of the game on a telly in an adjoining room whenever opportunity arose, as it developed into an electrifying confrontation, albeit in juicy, dislocated segments for me.

After Simeone was brought down by Seaman and Batistuta buried the penalty, Michael announced his arrival. As he tore through the Argentine defence, Ayala nudged him over. Penalty!

Shearer hit the trawler net, leaving the arena primed for a moment of artistry.

By pure chance, I had just nipped back to the box when Michael received the ball in the centre circle and set off towards goal. ITV's Brian Moore painted a picture of the unfolding drama: "And here's another Owen run. He's going to worry them again."

Petrified of Michael's explosive pace, a defender tried to block him with an arm, failed and, as a last resort, stuck his foot out in an attempted trip. Michael's balance and ball control enabled him to slide past, shrugging off the brutality with contempt.

"It's a great run by Michael Owen," Moore said, as our wunderkind sped past another Argentinian and cut across to the right of the 18-yard box. "And he might finish it off."

From the start of his impudent charge, Michael's face had said it all: No fear. Now he was about to confer ecstasy upon us all.

From the edge of the box, at an acute angle, with the keeper blocking the goal, he rifled a shot into the far corner.

I gave a scream the whole Crooked Mile must have heard, and Moore echoed it. "Aaaaaaah!" he shrieked. "That's a wonderful goal! What an amazing moment in Michael Owen's young career."

While England supporters exulted on the terraces, Michael ran with palms open, as though bearing a gift, a golden goal on a silver salver, to his parents in the stand. In one breathtaking act, the 18-year-old had expressed the bravery and beauty of youth. "Il bambino fenomenale, The phenomenal baby", as one Italian newspaper termed him, had announced his coming.

Hoddle, the judge who questioned Owen's natural scoring ability and off-field activities, said: "When it hit the net, it was a stunning moment and one I'll never forget."

An earlier remark by Michael gave an insight into his mentality and how he sliced through Argentina's stoppers. "Sometimes you look at a defender," he said, "and think, yeah, he's a big lad. But when I see a big defender, I think, great, he can't turn."

Life is a succession of moments. Seize the ones that count or they're gone for ever. Michael grabbed his with both hands, and feet. Even though England drew 2-2 and were squeezed out 4-3 in a penalty shoot-out, that goal resounded across the continents.

Next day I bought *L'Equipe*, France's daily sporting bible. Beneath two-inch-high letters stating, "On s'en souviendra, We will remember this", the broadsheet front page was filled with a colour print of the teenager leaving an Argentine in his wake. Alongside, the caption read: "Young Liverpool prodigy Michael Owen, shown battling with Chamot, was one of the heroes of a crazy night, because of his superb goal and exceptional runs. A star is born."

Michael thought this goal failed to surpass one straight from the restart in a schoolboy international against Scotland. "They'd just equalised," he said. "From the kick-off, my strike partner passed to me and I can't remember how many players I beat but it was a lot, most of the team. When I got to the box, I just smashed it into the top corner."

His goal-in-a-million against Argentina, five seconds, 25 strides, catapulted him into the headlines and reaped fans across the planet. While Roy Evans noted: "You can't talk about potential with Michael any more, he's there already, the full player", Kevin Keegan observed: "Michael Owen has made as big an impact on world football as Cruyff, Maradona and Pelé."

The country rhapsodised over its new pin-up, the housewife's choice, the boy-next-door, the son or brother you'd like to have. Michael was a normal, healthy teenager, his very ordinariness captivating. He could have been the model for Pelé's advice to any young footballer: "Keep being yourself. Don't change your ways or put on a mask, trying to be someone else. Be nice, be happy, be humble."

About his upbringing, Owen said: "Mum and Dad always stressed a right way of doing things. They brought us up to be considerate and polite to others, especially our elders, and those early habits have lasted us through to our adulthood."

Michael's marvellous goal turned him into a prized commodity. Back home from France, companies queued up with contracts to endorse such products as Jaguar cars, Walker's crisps, Tissot watches, Nationwide insurance, Umbro boots and Pepsi Cola.

An advertiser's fantasy had come true; Liverpool's teen star was delivering the goods on and off the pitch.

* * * * * * * * * *

After four years at Anfield's helm, Roy Evans had still not won the Holy Grail of the League and directors had come round to the view that fresh input was required. They knew who they wanted, an earlier target who had been otherwise engaged: Gérard Houllier, technical director of the French Football Federation.

Once France had won the World Cup in the summer of 1998, he agreed to move to L4 and was introduced to the media in July as joint manager with Roy.

Evans professed happiness with the dual approach, saying: "I am delighted to have Gérard on board because we feel we can work together as a team ... the decision was made with my full blessing." Truth be told, the Frenchman's arrival was a tacit admission by the board that Roy had failed to make the transition from coach to boss; the Boot Room concept of appointments from within was no longer suited to the modern era. Nonetheless, once the season began, this system of power-sharing did not click smoothly into operation.

After early results were discouraging, including home reverses by Derby in the League and Tottenham in the League Cup in November, papers carried stories about Roy moving upstairs or even leaving altogether. They were on the right scent.

The Friday after our Spurs reverse, he resigned, leaving Gérard to take full responsibility for the team.

Evans had spent 33 years as player, coach, assistant manager and manager, helping make Liverpool into the giant it was. A member of a dynasty stretching back to Shanks's heyday, he had followed Paisley, Fagan, Dalglish and Moran into executive positions but his departure, coupled with Moran's retirement in the summer, represented the severing of the last links with Shankly.

At the press conference to announce the news, a visibly upset Roy revealed: "I have felt over the past three or four weeks that things have not been working out. You feel it's not the right formula for players. They don't know who the boss is but the players have always tried."

Wishing Houllier "the greatest success with this fantastic club", he went on: "This club is dear to me. I love the bones of the place. I have loved every minute of it but it must be back up there with the best."

Houllier said: "I feel sorry about Roy's departure. I would have liked him to have stayed longer. I regret his decision but I respect it. The objective now is to get back to winning ways."

Watching glumly over the press conference was the club chairman, David Moores. A true Kopite who cherished the rich seam of loyalty running through the bedrock of Scouse character, he said: "This is one of the saddest days of my life. Roy is a Liverpool man and his dedication to this club can never be questioned."

Dedication could not save his job. In the long tradition of Anfield taking care of its own, he reportedly received a £500,000 settlement and, as he drove away through the Shankly Gates, Doug Livermore, his assistant, also left, to be replaced by Phil Thompson.

Holding strong opinions wherever the club was concerned, Thommo was sacked as reserve team coach by Souness in 1992 because he was so outspoken and since then had been working in the media.

"I thought my time had passed," he admitted. "I thank everyone for having faith in me. My passion and love for Liverpool have never been questioned. Gérard will get my 100 per cent support."

Evans fell on his sword because of defensive weaknesses that signings such as Babb and John Scales failed to eradicate and James's crisis of confidence did not help. The outgoing manager had also been condemned for being too close to his players when the opposite style, Souness's aggressive, abrasive manner, had alienated squad members.

Roy had to be true to himself. Throughout his life he abided by principles of fairness and decency; do unto others as you would have done unto yourself. Yet, after his resignation, stories surfaced that one player indulged in dark sarcasm in the dressing room, mimicking the boss's leaving speech.

Houllier was alerted to this crass behaviour. Disruptive elements would face a rude awakening.

19

The French Kopite Comes Home

If it were not for hopes, the heart would break.

– Thomas Fuller

IN September 1969, a French lover of football stood on the Kop and fell head over heels for Liverpool. Gérard Houllier, a teacher at Alsop High School, was watching a UEFA cup tie that would live in his memory.

"We beat Dundalk 10-0," he recalled, "and the players kept going, hammering the opposition right till the end. The score was 5-0 at half-time but the team kept attacking, kept going forward. A French team might have taken it easy."

This newcomer was so smitten with the Reds he vowed to become their manager. "Watching those great players and mingling with fans whose passion and knowledge swept you along made a lasting impression," he revealed. "I always wanted to be a top coach and I could think of nowhere better than Anfield to fulfil my dream."

As well as teaching French, Houllier had arrived on Merseyside to research his master's thesis, Growing Up In A Deprived Area ... and to sample the city's football mania, evident the instant he stepped into an Alsop classroom.

In 1999, he told the BBC's Football Focus: "When you come to a school, the first question is who do you support? Are you for Liverpool or Everton? I was a Red one, so that was my choice. I came here in 1969 and spent a very good year. I stood on the Kop. Well, I swayed on the Kop. If you wanted to see the game, you had to stand on your toes to watch it. But it was enjoyable.

"Liverpool had an outstanding, still now an outstanding aura all over Europe and many people wanted to see where the Beatles started and where the football was."

Within days of arriving on Merseyside in 1969, this soccer fanatic left his digs in Toxteth and took the bus to Melwood to inquire if he could study Shanks's coaching techniques. Beguiled by the Frenchman's charm and boldness, Peter Robinson agreed, activating a friendship that was still flourishing when Houllier's contract as technical director of the French Football Federation (FFF) drew to a close in the summer of 1998.

As a 26-year-old sociology graduate, teacher and ex-Alsop Old Boys forward, Houllier entered football management in 1973, becoming player-coach of Le Touquet and then youth trainer at Arras. In search of a fresh challenge, he rode on his moped in 1976 to Noeux-les-Mines, a coalmining town near Lens in the Pas-de-Calais region of Northern France, where he was interviewed for the post of head coach of a side dozing in the Fifth Division. He got the job.

Noeux's little ground had one similarity with Anfield – its own Kop, a slagheap behind one goal which players ran up and down to boost stamina and which locals used as a free terrace if the match was a sell-out. Under Houllier, it often was. Even though the town's population was only 13,000, some games attracted gates of 5,000 in temporary stands erected along the touchlines.

The coach blended discipline with democracy; he discussed training and tactics not just with the squad but also supporters and his inclusive methods propelled Noeux into the dizzy heights of France's Second Division, transforming them into cup giant-killers. They knocked out big guns Nantes in front of a 15,000 crowd at First Division Lens's stadium where the tie was switched because of ticket demand, and in the next round lost narrowly to Paris St Germain before 30,000 spectators.

A part-timer at Noeux while teaching English to sixth-formers in Lille, Houllier was spotted as a rising talent by Lens who headhunted him in 1982, an astute choice since their new boss and his assistant, former Polish international Joachim Marx, piloted them to fourth place in the league and UEFA Cup qualification.

Looking back on their partnership, Marx identified one match at Anfield as a turning point for Houllier.

"We wanted to sign a Polish player, Smolarek, of Widzew Lodz, who were playing the return leg of a European tie against Liverpool in 1983," Marx told David Barnes of *The Observer*. "I got tickets and could see from the start that something was getting to Gérard. He seemed very excited. Liverpool won 3-2 but it was not enough because they had gone down 2-0 in Poland.

"We went to a pub afterwards and drank a few beers. No one knew who Gérard was, even though he was a top coach in France. But what really impressed him was that, whereas an eliminated team got whistled in France, these supporters were still solidly behind them.

"As we left the pub, Gérard said, 'You know, Joachim, I would love to be coach of this club one day'. I honestly believe Gérard never lost that dream."

Lens's steady progress caught the eye of Paris St Germain, who made an offer Houllier could not refuse. Their faith was repaid in his opening season of 1985-86 when he led PSG to their first league title and became a hero for the Boulogne Kop die-hards in the Parc des Princes stadium.

Having tracked his steady rise, the FFF asked Houllier to become technical director and assistant to national coach Michel Platini in 1988 with one priority, a youth programme, and one objective, the creation of a crack international side.

Houllier implemented a five-point plan: nominate the best young prospects; provide them with world-class facilities; introduce leading-edge programmes to develop physical, mental and technical capabilities; ensure all youth coaches have undergone an exhaustive course of instruction and passed compulsory exams; and help youngsters pursue their careers.

To those ends, the FFF opened six regional training hubs and a national centre, the Institut National Francais de Football, at Clairefontaine, near Paris, while top clubs were prodded into building academies by a rule that restricted every team to 21 senior professionals. Since there was no limit on youth players, clubs had an incentive to develop them and Monaco's academy alone supplied Henry, Petit, Trézéguet and Thuram to the national side.

At Clairefontaine, Houllier mentored a Who's Who of stars such as Henry, Papin, Trézéguet, Ginola, Lizarazu, Anelka, Gallas, Blanc and Silvestre, and by the start of Euro 2000, some 50 French professionals were plying their trade with top European teams outside their homeland. The FFF's talent-spotter had helped create more millionaires than anyone else in football.

In 1992 he succeeded Platini as national coach but resigned in November 1993 after France failed to qualify for the World Cup in the USA because of a lethal error by Ginola. Playing Bulgaria at the Parc des Princes, les Bleus needed a draw and, with 23 seconds to go, were on course at 0-0 when Ginola received the ball. He should have wasted time, holding on to it, but instead put in a cross, which was intercepted by Kostadinov. The Bulgarian raced up the other end and scored. Afterwards, beside himself with rage, Houllier lashed out: "David Ginola is the murderer of this team."

Although the FFF accepted their coach's resignation, they retained him in his former technical role at Clairefontaine from where he guided the under-18s to a European title in 1996. The following year, at an FA symposium in Birmingham, he used videos to expound his rattlesnake theory of attack, according to which the ball is passed back abruptly towards your own goal before another lightning assault is launched on the opposition.

This quicksilver forward move was employed with deadly effect by France's World Cup winners, prompting Aimé Jacquet, Houllier's successor as national coach, to say: "We owe our victory to him." In appreciation of this contribution, an extra winner's medal was minted for him.

World Cup on his CV, Houllier opted for a change of scenery, in club football, and there could be no more suitable place than the UK for this incorrigible Anglophile. At first, Sheffield Wednesday were linked with him, then Celtic opened negotiations. News of this reached Peter Robinson who grabbed the phone to ask his old friend if he would consider moving to Merseyside. Oui!

Given this green light, an Anfield delegation led by David Moores flew to Paris and the deal was done. Arsenal's Arsène Wenger backed Houllier's decision, saying: "Gérard was quite advanced in discussions with Sheffield Wednesday. I told him Liverpool were like a Ferrari ... and Sheffield Wednesday did not have the same potential. My opinion was it was better to go to Liverpool."

After Houllier's appointment as joint manager was announced, one of his mates, Alain Tirloy, said: "Gérard must be in Heaven. He's always been completely crazy about Liverpool."

Although a total of 15 clubs across Europe had wooed him, this foreign professor of Kopology was drawn back to a city he loved, to a club whose roots in the community he admired. What he did not foresee was the difficulty job-sharing with Evans might cause.

"Maybe players didn't know who was the boss, who they had to refer to," Houllier admitted.

Within months of arriving at Anfield, the Frenchman judged the trouble with English footballers was not ability but attitude. Talented players did not mature like their Continental cousins principally because of a lack of application and discipline, illustrated by tabloid tales of inebriated, loutish behaviour.

Now the iron fist in a French velvet glove was to make some telling blows. Houllier banned mobile phones, those aural dummies, at Melwood, instituted three periods of training a day under new coach Patrice Bergues, called the squad in for coaching on Sundays and prohibited alcohol in their Anfield lounge after matches.

They were also instructed to be punctual. If training was scheduled for 10am, that meant 10am, not 10.15 or even 10.30, and Melwood was not somewhere to wind down, relax after a hard match. Houllier demanded total professionalism there, as well as at Anfield where the team now completed methodical warm-up exercises on the pitch, something rarely seen except by players testing injuries.

One squad member did not appear in these pre-match workouts. Ince was keeping to a personal superstition; he had to be last out the dressing-room and any warm-up broke that tradition. Houllier was already setting his stall out, warning: "I won't let anybody raise a finger against the togetherness of the team, otherwise I chop it off immediately."

Underlining this message, he placed a poster summing up his philosophy on the wall of his Melwood office, alongside a photo of Shanks: "Respect. Be a winner. Always be a top pro. Think team first." To that end, the dressing room was rebuilt with curved walls so no one was marginalised in the corners.

On November 14, 1998, Houllier flew solo, selecting his first team without Evans, and they lost 3-1 to Leeds at Elland Road, a discouraging debut for the boss who stressed qualification for the Champions League within two years was "imperative".

After their Leeds setback, the Reds mastered League leaders Aston Villa 4-2 at Villa Park but were beaten 3-1 in a UEFA Cup away leg by Celta Vigo, who prevailed again, 1-0, at Anfield. Even though his side had been knocked out, Houllier took positives from the crowd.

"We played Celta with half a side because of suspensions and injuries and lost," he said. "But the fans were very supportive. Everywhere I went, they said, 'Keep the good work going, it will come'. It was like, 'You belong to us, so we believe in you'. The fans were far more patient than the media."

He also pointed to what was required from his squad: "I believe in individual responsibility. Are you a man or not? For 10 years players have to live for the job. After that, they'll live thanks to it."

He added that if players wanted to go to nightclubs, they could buy one when they retired.

With these words, Houllier was warning that changes were imminent.

* * * * * * * * * *

The afternoon of Christmas Eve, 1998, and a party for Anfield staff in the trophy room. As festivities get into their swing, four people slip away.

Gérard Houllier, assistant manager Phil Thompson, executive vice-chairman Peter Robinson and chairman David Moores walk down the corridor, enter an office and close the door quietly.

Within these four walls, to distant sounds of music and laughter, they hatch Houllier's revolution, listing players who will leave and those who will replace them. Agreement reached, they open address books and phone clubs across Europe. It is 4 o'clock. Five hours later, their blueprint for the future has been inked in.

"We decided on the positions that needed strengthening, the players we wanted and what we could afford," said Robinson. "There was one period around 8 o'clock when we were all on different phones."

Houllier took responsibility for Continental players, Thompson dealt with English clubs and Robinson drew on his far-reaching network of friends and contacts.

Sometimes calls were brief; if someone was not available or a price was silly, the phone was put down. Other feelers were welcomed, enabling serious negotiations to begin, so that by the time the quartet walked out of that office to resume their Christmas holiday, they'd laid the foundations of a new team. Over the next seven months, they would spend £29 million on fresh blood; meanwhile, those squad members viewed as unsuitable would be persuaded to leave.

The first acquisition in January was an unknown, Jean-Michel Ferri, for £1.5 million from Istanbulspor. Along Anfield's corridors, the French midfielder was rumoured to have been enlisted as the manager's eyes and ears in the dressing room, watching and listening to how players responded to the new regime.

Controversy surfaced about Robbie Fowler, who mocked his England colleague, Graeme Le Saux, by bending over and pointing at his backside in the game with Chelsea at Stamford Bridge. Then, after netting against Everton at Anfield, our striker pretended to snort the goal line as if it were cocaine, a riposte to jibes about him being a user. Even so, a blot on the Reds' 3-2 win, their first derby success in 10 attempts.

For Robbie's misdemeanours, the FA imposed a £34,000 fine and six-match ban, depriving the club of their ace goal-poacher.

Faith healer Eileen Drewery, who had been recruited by Glenn Hoddle as an England adviser, identified Fowler's trouble after a session with him. He had three demons, she warned, and there wasn't much she could do.

This diagnosis didn't ruffle Robbie; he admitted he wasn't worried because he'd heard Paul Gascoigne had five.

Capitalising on his knowledge of French football, Houllier could have turned his squad into a team of Gallic imports but he pledged "to keep a Liverpool heart beating in the club" and, to that end, a welcome signing came when Owen put pen to paper on a five-year deal. The day before his 19th birthday, Michael was also voted BBC Sports Personality of the Year, even though he had spent months in the treatment room since his Argentina cracker.

Despite constant therapy, his hamstring and tendon frailties could not be cured, so the club announced in April that he would be out for three months. In Houllier's season of reorganisation, the teenager had netted 28 goals, including 18 in 30 Premiership starts, to make him the League's joint top scorer. He had had two hectic years; now an enforced break would allow his body to recuperate.

Kopites were realistic enough to accept Liverpool couldn't be turned around overnight; the most we could hope for was to hang on to the leading pack's coat tails. A pointer to their potential came in a 7-1 trouncing of Southampton, every goal smote by Melwood graduates – a Fowler hat-trick and singles for Carragher, Owen, Matteo and Thompson.

Another yardstick of progress was put up in the match with Manchester United in L4. The visitors were leading 2-0 when the referee, David Elleray, awarded a penalty to the Reds and sent Dennis Irwin off for time-wasting because he humped the ball away before a throw-in. Liverpool fought back to 2-2, causing Alex Ferguson to have a quiet word in Elleray's ear afterwards.

Martin Edwards, United's chief executive, also spoke out, saying that if Arsenal or Chelsea took the League, they could give a winner's medal to the referee. Yet one or two

individuals have occasionally argued that officials favour the Mancs, like Sam Hammam who during his Wimbledon era commented: "I have to hand it to Manchester United; they have the best players and best referees."

Houllier's period of reconstruction brought no victory parade with a trophy and the Reds wrapped up their League programme in seventh place, seeing Wimbledon off 3-0 at Anfield. Before this fixture, Kopites held up cards in a mosaic of the European Cup, League Championship trophy and Milk Cup – a reminder to anyone forgetful of their facts that Liverpool were the first to achieve a treble in 1984.

The lads had one more engagement, the Football League's 100th Championship Challenge on Wearside, pitting Sunderland, 100th winners of the League, against the club with the most titles. The Reds won 3-2 but because the Mackems had moved from Roker Park to their new Stadium of Light, local papers were unable to sum up this result with that sub-editor's favourite, "Roker Choker". England's heritage of headline-writing had lost an old friend.

The same night Liverpool signed Sami Hyypia from Holland's Willem II, the Finnish international giving up a Champions League place to join his boyhood heroes. As a result of a tip-off from a TV cameraman who filmed matches across Europe, Houllier had secured a commanding centre-back.

During 1998-99's campaign, one bone of contention had been McManaman's contract, which was due to terminate in July, making him a free agent under the Bosman ruling. No agreement was reached and during the summer he signed for Real Madrid for £67,000 a week. A player who'd progressed through the ranks, from schoolboy to first-teamer, quit without a penny of his £12m value going into Anfield's coffers.

For Kopites, the talks had been allowed to drag on far too long. A deadline should have been set months ago. Now Macca had left for nothing.

Another player moving to pastures new was David James, who had betrayed a lack of judgement with crosses, tending to dither, then making a hash of catching the ball. Houllier, suspecting the keeper was being distracted by external interests, warned him to concentrate on his game but the advice did not bring a satisfactory outcome. Once Brad Friedel was installed between the posts, James's days were numbered and he was sold to Aston Villa.

Rob Jones and Paul Ince were other high-profile departures. Joachim Marx, Houllier's Polish pal, said: "I knew Gérard was having problems with Ince and there would be one outcome. When I joined Gérard at Noeux, another player from Lens came with me. He kept telling Gérard he was a pro and knew better. He disagreed with Gérard in the dressing room. It was not long before he was no longer there."

One player slipped away unnoticed: at the end of his short stay in L4, Ferri joined Sochaux. Now that Le Boss had enough inside information on his squad, he made clear Fowler, Redknapp, Owen, Gerrard, Carragher and Berger would form its nucleus.

Starkly, Houllier summed up his attitude to those who wouldn't conform: "The players who did not want to change we got rid of."

Among his recruits was Blackburn's Stephane Henchoz, victim of a painful instance of mistaken identity in a League Cup tie against Chelsea in 1997. With the score at 1-1 after 90 minutes, the tension boiled over in extra time when Patrick Valéry, Rovers' right-back who was on loan from Bastia in the French league, flung an arm at Gianluca Vialli during a tussle for the ball.

Even though the Corsican was shown a yellow, Vialli was seething and at the first opportunity, he floored his assailant with a haymaker. Before the ref had even pulled out his red card, the Italian hit-man strode off, not suspecting his error: he had poleaxed Henchoz, not Valery.

Once the Swiss international repossessed his faculties, he was mystified why he'd been the victim of such an unprovoked attack – until Vialli entered the home dressing-room to apologise for his mistake.

Now Houllier had Hyypia and Henchoz as central defenders, he sought another goalie.

In 1998-99, statistics showed only 71 per cent of shots on target were saved by Liverpool keepers, the Premiership's second-worst tally, whereas in attack the Reds were second for goals scored, 68. The manager addressed this discrepancy by signing Sander Westerveld from Vitesse Arnhem for £4 million. The Dutch shot-stopper, who had just won his first international cap against Brazil, told reporters at Anfield: "This is an unbelievably big club. It's been the English club of the century. They, for me, have played the best football in England for many years."

Referring to the defensive wall he was creating with Westerveld, Hyypia and Henchoz, Houllier said: "The concrete is poured and the foundations have been laid."

Would this defence signal a new dawn, another delivery of silverware to L4 where the Visitors' Centre was finally getting replicas of our four European Cups? Would more space be needed for more trophies?

* * * * * * * * * *

On the eve of 1999-2000's season, the media met Houllier's summer signings, an all-international line-up of Hyypia, Henchoz, Westerveld, Germany's Didi Hamann, an £8m recruit from Newcastle, Czech midfielder Vladimir Smicer from Lens, Titi Camara, Marseilles' Guinean forward, and Erik Meijer, Bayer Leverkusen's Dutch striker.

On the financial front, Granada also put their signature on a contract to pay £22m for a 9.9 per cent stake in the club. With a mission to promote Liverpool's "brand" across the continents, the media group was investing in a global fan base, unrivalled pedigree and enough icons to make any sozzled adman shake his San Lorenzo swizzle stick: The Kop, Anfield, Liver bird, You'll Never Walk Alone, Shankly and a single name that speaks volumes. Football might be cluttered with Cities, Uniteds, Rovers and Athletics but there's only one Liverpool.

Houllier's new-look team kicked off their home campaign by losing 1-0 to Watford, who were applauded off the pitch by the Kop, to the delight of their manager, Graham Taylor. Fillips came with victory over Leeds at Elland Road and a 2-0 defeat of Arsenal in L4 that brought a substitute's appearance by Owen, back after his three-month lay-off.

October closed with a poignant moment at Anfield: hours after being told his father had died, Camara grabbed the winner against West Ham. Once the ball hit the net, he dropped to his knees, hands clasped in supplication, and lifted his face to the sky in memory of his dad. Tears were rolling down his cheeks, and those of some Kopites. Eventually Titi was substituted, the ground rising to him.

After eight full games, Owen was ruled out again by another hamstring injury but the Reds were handily placed fourth in the League by Christmas, although the turn of the year brought setbacks: in January, they were put out of the Worthington and FA cups.

One reason for their disappointing form: during the season so far, 13 players had been suspended or laid-up, including long-term injuries for Owen, Fowler, Redknapp and Hamann.

In February, a Camara smasher at Highbury enabled us to leapfrog over Arsenal into third place but the side was crying out for a top-notch goalgetter. Meijer had been a letdown as an out-and-out banger so Houllier went for a big prospect, using £11 million of Granada's cash to sign Emile Ivanhoe Heskey from Leicester in March.

Le Boss had first spotted him playing alongside Owen at the UEFA under-18 tournament in 1996 and expressed his admiration to Andy Roxburgh, UEFA's technical director and former Scotland manager. "Gérard was coach to France then but he was taken by the partnership of Owen and Heskey," Roxburgh recalled.

With Owen and Redknapp off the sick list, Liverpool rose to second in April, leaving Houllier to wish the campaign had begun late. "It must be remembered," he said, "that at the beginning of the season we were 12th, so we have worked very hard to be in this position now."

The Reds lost just twice in 25 games from October but their concluding five fixtures yielded three defeats and two draws, without a single goal scored.

The last game brought a 1-0 reverse at Bradford, guaranteeing the Bantams' Premiership survival and consigning Liverpool to fourth spot, out of the Champions League places.

Chief executive Rick Parry was still bullish. "If you leave aside the way it finished and judge the season as a whole, it was ahead of schedule," he said.

Seven Merseyside lads had turned out for the first XI and most of the time Hamann, at 26, was the oldest player, statistics that encouraged Houllier.

"The team is 85 to 90 per cent there," he said. "But one factor no one seems to take into account is its youth. The average age is 23.9 years, youngest in the Premiership."

Time would tell if youth was on his side.

* * * * * * * * * *

At the season's end, a Kop hero took leave of Anfield: Ronnie Moran retired with a testimonial against Celtic that attracted 33,000. In a Liverpool career stretching from the Second Division to the European Cup, he had served under Taylor, Shanks, Paisley, Fagan, Souness, Evans and Dalglish.

As player, coach and caretaker manager, Ronnie had given his all for the cause, inspiring Jim Beglin to say his influence on the Reds for nearly half a century was beyond price. Every Kopite would second that.

20
Our Incredible Treble

The future belongs to those who believe in the beauty of their dreams.
– Eleanor Roosevelt

SINCE all those lunchtimes in Alsop's library, macheteing my way through the Latin American shelves, a dream had lain dormant within me and in July 2000, I realised it: I walked the Inca Trail to the mystical Andean city of Machu Picchu.

For this latest foreign jolly, my companion was Russ, taking a summer break from his computer science course at university in Aberystwyth. How generations go full circle. In 1958, I'd spent a week cycling and youth-hostelling in Wales with three Alsop pals and we'd pedalled through sun and rain as far as Aberystwyth. Now my son was studying in that same town and making the most of 99p treble vodkas in his eventide haunt, the Glen public house. (Cymru am byth! Lloegr am byth! The money *I* saved on *his* bar bills.)

Heavy intoxication – not of the alcoholic sort – was free on our Iberia flight from Madrid to Peru. After winging down North Africa's west coast and vaulting across the South Atlantic into Brazil, the pilot poured an extra-large one for passengers, announcing: "The Amazon is on your left."

A wake-up call to end all wake-up calls.

World travellers slumbering in their seats, drunks snoring in a stupor, people hallucinating on chocolate bars, everybody jumped out their seats and flocked to windows for the mind-blowing view.

At 37,000 feet on the 747's altimeter, 1,000 miles from the Atlantic, the Amazon filled the landscape, a vast lake extending beyond the horizon, marshes and wetlands spreading for miles on either side as far as the distant green jungle.

A river all of 30 miles across, the width of the English Channel.

This nostrils-squashed-against-the-window moment was an eye-opener – and Peru still awaited us.

Two hours after our Amazonian Epiphany, we cruised across the sun-lit Andes before plunging into thick cloud on our approach to Lima. Out of the sunshine, into the night.

As we descended into the Peruvian capital, it was still afternoon but street lamps shone below, cars drove with headlights on and homes winked in the gloomy Garúa, a grey mist caused by the Pacific's Humboldt current. Six months of the year, this obscures the sun and mires Lima in a wearying melancholy. Not a place to tarry in.

Two days were ample: Plaza de Armas, presidential palace, cathedral, San Francisco's catacombs, the gold museum ... and McDonald's because Russ wanted a burger. Swamped with teenagers, its walls were adorned with black-and-white photos of pop stars.

Nirvana? REM? Oasis?

No. The Beatles.

Here in faraway South America, 30 years after Liverpool's finest split up, they remained idols for Big Mac consumers, straddling the ages, from grandparents to parents to children.

A couple of statistics: the year we visited Peru, a compilation of their hits, 1, became the fastest-selling album ever, 23.5 million copies in a month, and pushed total sales of their records way past the one billion mark, giving more substance to the opinion that the Beatles and Elvis are popular music's greatest figures, everyone else is secondary.

While Lennon pronounced, "Before Elvis, there was nothing", Liverpudlians can declare, "After the Beatles, there was everything" and during our holiday those McDonald's pictures would not be the only pointers to my Mathew Street muckers' enduring appeal.

From sea-level Lima, Russ and I managed to catch our morning flight – sometimes they take off early if the weather window is closing – over the blustery Andes to Cuzco, where the airport provided just what my GP would have ordered; sticking out of her mound of petticoats in the refrigerator of an arrivals hall, a Quechua girl served complimentary maté de coca, coca leaf tea, to deaden the overbearing altitude of 3,360 metres (11,000 feet).

Three cups and Russ and I were ready to take on the world, or at least the taxi to our hotel where, before we'd even signed in, the receptionist guided us to a shaded patio, a Cammell Laird canteen urn of maté de coca was installed on a table and we sipped away contentedly once more.

A pint of class-A Typhoo later, we had conquered the world, without moving from our cosy armchairs.

Bolstered by this Andean refresher, we rapidly acclimatised to Cuzco's high life, exploring its tourist sites for a couple of days without any ill effect. The Inca capital – its name means Navel of the Earth – was laid out in the shape of a mile-long puma whose teeth were still visible, 22 sharp zigzags in the monumental walls of Sacsayhuaman fortress, as well as its humongous penis, formed from stone blocks in the city centre.

Why didn't Skelmersdale's town planners let their imaginations rip? They could have had a monstrously cocky badger constructed below Beacon Hill.

Cuzco was a convivial city, where we frequented the Cross Keys pub in the Plaza de Armas and a backstreet bar serving wicked Pisco sours and stomach-churning chicha. Fermented using women's saliva, this maize beer looked and tasted like coagulated dog sick, even making Watney's Red Barrel palatable. Try some from its putrescent dustbin and shimmy into dark alleys to tackle "strangle robbers", Cuzqueño gangs who choke lone tourists into unconsciousness, stripping them of everything, right down to their Y-fronts.

After exploring, walking and eluding throat-fingerers to reach our hotel, Russ and I felt fit for the Inca Trail challenge, so we booked a four-day trip through an agency who organised a guide, cook and porters to carry the requisite tents and cooking gear. At 5 in the morning, off we set.

Our band of 16 trekkers comprised nine nationalities, from Ireland and Germany to Peru and El Salvador, a genial group who all got on, whether they were young or old.

Take Flavia Rima who lived for travel but loved travelling home to Mantua in Italy. She would work in the Banca Agricola Mantovana for a year, saving every lira to finance a month in Asia, Africa or America, after which she would return to the bank for another year, accruing funds for her next destination. Now she was exploring the Andes and whenever exhaustion sapped my energy on the trail, she would dip into a chuspa, a textile pouch dangling from her belt, to give me the Quechuas' livener, a wad of coca leaves to chew.

Radiant, generous Flavia. As we toiled along the path, her tinkling laughter lifted my mood.

After the staggering beauty of Dead Woman's Pass (admire the beauty while staggering up the vertical track), Flavia and the rest of us arrived at our goal of Machu Picchu, the Lost City of the Incas. Lost, of course, only for Europeans, because locals knew of its existence for centuries, but once Hiram Bingham blundered upon it in 1911, the eyes of the outside world were opened to its awe-inspiring prospect. Overcome, the American explorer wrote: "In the variety of its charms, the power of its spells, I know of no place which compares with it."

During our trek to this promised land, we had been frozen and fried, soaked and poached, exhausted and exhilarated. Ever vigilant for venomous spiders and deadly three-metre-long bushmaster snakes, we had to avert our eyes from yawning chasms alongside shoelace paths, wade through piranha-infested puddles, curl up in anaconda-sheltering sleeping bags, sneak past poison-dart-puffing peasants – and that's just the script for the trailer for Channel 5's documentary.

Yet danger and discomfort counted for nought when, having set out by torchlight at 4am on our last day, we stood high up at Intipunku, the Gateway of the Sun, and watched dawn's golden light descend over Machu Picchu, a glimpse into the Inca soul that moved some trekkers to tears.

"Vamónos! Let's go!" A yell from our guide shattered our reverie. Freddie wanted to show us the city before the first load of tourists galloped off their train. Urged on by him, we sprinted through the cloud forest to the ruins, which were deserted apart from a handful of other adventurers. For a couple of hours, this celestial place was ours alone as we trod in the footsteps of Andean gods until Japanese and American hordes began intruding.

Even so, I had achieved my boyhood ambition: I had seen Machu Picchu. And, finally, I could understand why Che Guevara had termed it "the place that drives dreamers to ecstasy".

The French have a saying, one day's walking, one week's health. After my thrutch through the mountains, I must have been good for at least a couple of months because I was positively glowing as Russ and I took the train along the raging Urubamba river back to Cuzco.

Next day we caught another train across the desolate, empty altiplano to Lake Titicaca, perpetual instigator of friction between Peruvians and Bolivians since its waters are divided between the pair of them. In Spanish, titi calls to mind the word tit whereas caca means shit, so the citizens of both countries goad each other with "We have the tit, you have the shit". High-level diplomatic arbitration has failed to resolve this squabble; the Pope's intercession is now being sought.

During a day's sail to Taquile, an island where men sit around knitting scarves for tourists while their women tend the fields, we were informed the water level had gone down two metres in 10 years, as a consequence of global warming. You have to ask: How loud does the Earth have to scream before we take notice? Is anyone listening out there?

After Titicaca, we flew to the white city of Arequipa, departure point for a mini-bus ride to the Colca Canyon, which is twice as deep as the Grand Canyon. Our bone-shaking journey into the mountains ratified regulation number 7 of the Peruvian Highway Code: any public transport vehicle worming its way up a steep hill is only ever permitted to overtake slower-moving traffic on blind bends.

Because of this, Russ and I always commandeered seats at the rear but why our bus didn't meet a lorry head-on I'll never know.

As we wheezed over a 16,000-foot-high dirt track, bottomless gorge directly below the nearside wheel nuts, I sought distraction from impending doom by striking up a conversation with our Arequipan guide, Daniel, sitting in front. A swarthy desperado straight out of a Hollywood Western, with gnarled face, Pancho Villa moustache and cigar-stained Panama hat, he asked where I came from. "Liverpool," I responded.

Daniel stared, assessing the truthfulness of this answer, then jabbed an index finger. Don't utter another word.

On his lap rested a khaki knapsack and he thrust his upper body within its confines. Like the Scouse Houdini striving to extricate himself from that chained sack in the Lake District, he wrestled with its contents until one object had been retrieved: a music cassette.

Grinning, he pushed this into the mini-bus's console and pressed, "Play". "Can't buy me love ..."

Lyrics I'd first heard on the radio in Ullswater Street in the Sixties filled our vehicle. I could but smile back at Daniel. Here, in the high Peruvian Andes, the Beatles were performing for our little band of tourists and, along with those McDonald's photos, our guide was attesting to their unflagging popularity. New Orleans has jazz, Chicago has the Blues, Liverpool will always have its Beatles, as well as a multitude of other stars.

Fact: The Guinness Book of Hit Singles has designated our city as the World Capital of Pop because it has produced more No 1s than anywhere else on earth.

Farther along the canyon road, we pulled up at roadside stalls to buy syrupy Inka Cola and eccentric varieties of fruit. One of our party, an American from Denver, had been roaming south of the border for ages and had spent much of his time living with the long-suffering indigenous peoples of Latin America. He contemplated a Quechua woman sitting behind a pile of vegetables, a baby swaddled in a thick blanket on her chest.

"You know," he remarked to me, "I've spent months in the Andes and I've never seen an Indian baby cry. Why?"

In fluent Spanish, he explained this intriguing fact to the mother, who appeared embarrassed, bowing her head, lips sealed. Perhaps she didn't understand, but this time-served traveller was on to something. If indigenous children do seem happy, the explanation must lie in the way their parents dote on them, for those who have least love most, whether it's their family or their country.

The poorest Britons are comfortably-off compared with Andinos who share their daily lives with destitution's cruel brother, poverty *with cold*. A sun-kissed pavement in Rio? Sheer bliss. But for those facing old age amid South America's hypothermal, infertile mountains, every newborn child offers hope of warmth and sustenance to come. Bless all their contented babies.

Our visit to Colca's awesome canyon had a major selling point: the chance to see condors, the biggest flying birds, whose wing span can reach 10 foot. A few miles beyond the mini market we arrived at the most promising observation post, Cruz del Cóndor, the Cross of the Condor, near where the Amazon begins its 3,900-mile passage from source to Atlantic.

At the Cross, we waited patiently until a single condor yielded to our pleading. From out of the gorge's dizzying emptiness, it rode a bubble of thermal air into our view, outstretched wings tipped with whopping finger feathers. Soon afterwards, others followed on updraughts until a dozen hovered effortlessly above our heads.

Some spectacle. Although these enormous creatures are under threat and declining in numbers along the Andes' length, we were seeing 12 in one place, a soaring finale to our South America adventure.

A belief is held that once a condor enters your life, it never leaves. Well, Colca's condors won't leave my memory and neither will Peru.

As independent travellers who organised everything ourselves, Russ and I had expected hitches and hiccups but all our arrangements had gone like clockwork. Essentially, we had followed our dreamline, experiencing the mana of Machu Picchu, one of the most magical spots on earth, and I had fallen in love with the spectacular land of Peru.

I would return.

* * * * * * * * * *

In Lima's departure lounge, I sat beside Henk, a Dutch tourist who'd spent a month travelling around, and we compared notes, swopping anecdotes and stoking the ardour we both felt for this country. For two hours, we nattered until boarding was called and our plane took off for Madrid.

Some four hours later, Henk, who was sitting near the front, ambled down the aisle to chat after our meal.

"You know we agree Peru is great," he began. "I've just been talking to a compatriot of mine and he has a different story."

This is what he had told Henk.

After arriving in Lima from Amsterdam, the Dutchman was going round tourist sites when, out of the blue, plainclothes police arrested him on suspicion of being involved in the drugs trade.

He wasn't.

Utterly innocent, he was flung into infamous Lurigancho jail, which Henk said was one of the worst prisons anywhere, a penal institution that made Midnight Express look like Hi-de-Hi!

Built to hold 1,500 inmates, it contained about 8,000 in steel cages – cells would have been a luxury – and unless prisoners had relatives who could bring food, they existed on pig-swill which they fought over.

But the extreme violence occurred at night, between 5pm and 8am when warders withdrew from the interior of the jail. With no one in charge, homosexual rape provided entertainment and rival gangs settled scores in gun battles that claimed numerous lives. Yet most prisoners had not been found guilty of any crime – they were waiting for Peru's archaic legal system to grant them a court hearing.

During the days after his arrest, the Dutch tourist received visits from his country's consul who assured him the detention was a misunderstanding that would soon be sorted out.

It was ... seven months later.

After that stretch in Lima's appalling hell hole, he was freed and was now flying home. To think I was relieved to get out of Walton Jail after a couple of hours' visiting.

This story was so ghastly that, after mulling it over, I decided to get the facts straight from the victim.

I found him sitting next to Henk but one glance at his haggard face told me he should not be disturbed. Emaciated, hollow-cheeked, black-eyed, he appeared traumatised, as if he'd just seen a phantom. I left him alone with his nightmares.

* * * * * * * * * *

Back amid the peace and tranquillity of England, changes were afoot at Anfield, off and on the field. During the summer of 2000, Peter Robinson announced his retirement after 35 years with the club. Having joined as secretary and risen to executive vice-chairman, "Mr Anfield" could take enormous pride in his pivotal role in establishing Liverpool's empire.

Meanwhile, Granada revealed it was investing £20 million in a joint venture with the club to show matches and clips on the web for subscribers who would also get live audio commentary and online shopping and betting. Now supporters worldwide would be able to watch the action and monitor developments in L4.

Amid reports that Barcelona had 35 first-teamers, Gérard Houllier was investing in his squad, snapping up Nick Barmby (Everton) for £6 million; Bernard Diomede (Auxerre), £3 million; Gary McAllister (Coventry City), free; Pegguy Arphexad (Leicester City), free; and Markus Babbel (Bayern Munich), free.

Babbel said: "At Bayern we were always first or second and I've come here to Liverpool to win. I could have gone elsewhere but it was always my dream to play for Liverpool.

"As a kid, I was always watching them on television in the great times of the Eighties, so I was very honoured when I got an offer and didn't have to think much about it. I just signed. It was mainly the tremendous atmosphere I wanted to experience."

Jurgen Klinsmann, recalling the Kop's sportsmanship, supported Babbel's decision; he advised his mate to shun a £5 million deal with Real Madrid, the European champions, and also a sizeable pay rise from Bayern.

With these new boys being put through their paces at Melwood on the eve of the 2000-2001 season, Houllier laid down his objectives: "To consolidate, to make sure that we continue to build on our concrete base. I feel that a good target for everyone would be to step up a little bit from where we are and that means the top three."

In terms of rebuilding, 80 per cent of the job had been done but "the other 20 per cent you won't change in a year". Refusing to be discouraged by last season's sorry start and finish, he underlined the 25 games that brought just two defeats. "We need to mature a little, just like wine," he said.

The League campaign began with a stormy confrontation at Highbury where Liverpool went down 2-0, with red cards for McAllister, Hamann and Arsenal's Patrick Vieira. Then, although the lads gave away a three-goal lead to Southampton at the Dell and could only draw 1-1 with Sunderland on their own turf, victories over Aston Villa and Manchester City lifted them into fourth spot. Perhaps Gérard was gradually producing a vintage to satisfy any Kopite's palate.

While the Reds were on the up, I renewed acquaintance with Germany, a country I'd first bumbled around as a student in 1964.

Nowadays, young and not so young embark on journeys of discovery, filling a gap in their lives by backpacking through Australasia or Latin America. During the Sixties, that insular epoch when the BBC did not even show the Continent on TV's weather maps, a rite of passage for students and jobless youths did not demand long-haul jumbos to distant destinations but a mode of free travel exploitable both at home and across the Channel: hitch-hiking.

Many times in that decade of promise, I stood at the roadside on the outskirts of Calais or Ostend, rucksack on my back, international youth hostels' card in my pocket, thumb at the ready, hope in my heart, and went on to traverse thousands of miles of France, Belgium, Holland and Spain.

One country I always felt a strong impulse to visit was Germany, the origin of so much grief for my mother. Not only had Germans striven to slaughter her and other Liverpudlians by blitzing them to bits but they had also killed her brother, Uncle Ron, who was torpedoed in a Royal Navy patrol boat off the South Coast. His body was never recovered, although amid the vessel's flotsam, rescue crews did find his accordion, which was presented to his fiancee.

Mum kept his Record of Active Service, detailing ships he served on from September 30, 1939, his character and efficiency, marks, wounds and scars, up to the terminal entry, "October 7, 1942: Discharged Dead". So as a student bumping across the German border for the first time in 1964, in a Belgian lorry hauling bricks to Cologne, I was conscious of the enigma that had caused so much horror in Europe and snatched Uncle Ron's short life away: a people of culture, sophistication and civilisation, the Germans' nationalism, militarism and racism perverted them into provoking the Second World War.

However, once I began exploring this cradle of wanderlust, any misgivings I might have had quickly faded, because teenagers in Koblenz or Dortmund's youth hostels were not that dissimilar in outlook and aspirations to those back home. Let slip in die Jugendherberge in the Sixties that you came from Liverpool and strangers would soon be picking your brains about the city's music scene.

Since I did mention the war, Germans in their teens and twenties were also genuinely mindful of the Nazis' dark deeds, having lived through the repercussions for their fatherland: economic disintegration, urban devastation and the shame of occupation by umpteen foreign armies, not something you readily forget. After my initial visit in 1964, a couple more expeditions left me feeling that what unites us is far more important than what divides us and I came to admire the way modern Germany has embraced the ideal of a Europe committed to peace and prosperity.

Long after those hitch-hiking forays, my daughter Helen trotted off to study in Bavaria in 1992, presenting me with a chance to see Germany again and offering a Teutonic taster for Anne and Russ.

On our drive south along the autobahn to Augsburg, Russ was astonished by the myriad signs for one city, Ausfahrt, a sprawling megalopolis – until after 100 kilometres, I enlightened him: "It's German for exit."

The motorway was a marvel, quiet for a major artery from west to south, surface as smooth as a Formica table top, and we bowled along. On one straight, as I overtook a Trabant with East German number plates, someone tossed a beer can out and it bounced beneath our car.

I pulled over into the inside lane, where my concentration was interrupted by a beeping horn. Shadowing our motor was a Mercedes, man and woman in front, teenage girl holding up a sheet of paper in the back. In Biro, this bore the admonition: "Don't drop litter."

Fair enough, when you see how tossers in grotty Britain have turned our roads into ribbons of filth. However, it was the Trabi's can, not mine.

I put my hand up in acknowledgement of their message, the Merc steamed away, but this injustice began to rankle. The record needed putting straight … so I told Russ to get his own piece of paper on which to write in fibre tip, "It was the other car".

Now all that remained was to retrieve the Mercedes.

By excessive use of the whip on the horses under my bonnet, I did catch it after 15 minutes and, with a honk, the explanation was displayed to the German family, who peered at it and exchanged a few words. The driver gave a wave and dropped behind. The record had been put straight.

A couple of minutes later, the Merc overtook us again, displaying one word: "Sorry."

To which we responded with "Don't mention it!" Producing another reply of "But we must because we are polite Germans", followed by a series of "No you don'ts" and "Yes we dos".

Donner und blitzen!

After this exchange, we'd driven past our turn-off and were well into Austria! [Editor's note: The sentences after "Sorry!" can be attributed to journalistic exaggeration. Don't believe a word of them. Rest is fact.]

This paper chase enlivened our journey to Augsburg, from where Helen accompanied us on our exploration of Munich, the German Alps, bierkellers and the subtleties of Swabian cooking.

Our trip was not all beer and skittles, though. Far from it.

For a lesson in modern history, we drove to Dachau to see the Nazis' first concentration camp, opened days after they swept into government in the 1933 elections. Our guidebook contained a map of the pretty town of the same name but, having lost our bearings in its one-way system, I pulled up outside a corner shop for Helen to ask the way.

She went inside, seeking directions to our destination, Alte Romerstrasse. "You want the concentration camp?" the woman behind the counter inquired matter-of-factly, as though referring to the nearest Alton Towers, rather than a prison where upwards of 70,000 perished and doctors carried out experiments freezing inmates to death.

On reflection, her attitude was understandable. Some half a century afterwards, you would be immunised to the atrocities.

We soon reached Alte Römerstrasse, the backdrop to a sombre regression into mankind's black past as we walked silently around the barracks, gas ovens and museum, which contained a letter to Hitler from the chief scientist. This condensed years of horror into a single page; it requested relocation of the camp to Poland because screams were disturbing the neighbours.

Perhaps the apocalyptic evidence of one prisoner, Pastor Martin Niemöller, offers the most compelling lesson about this hideous era:

When the Nazis arrested the Communists, I said nothing. After all, I wasn't a Communist. When they arrested the Social

Democrats, I said nothing. After all, I wasn't a Social Democrat.
When they arrested the trade unionists, I said nothing. After all,
I wasn't a trade unionist. When they arrested the Jews, I said
nothing. After all, I wasn't a Jew. When they arrested me, there
was no one left to say anything.

Even though we only spent one week in Bavaria in 1992, the mostly pleasant memories lived on and in September 2000 I revisited this land of peaks and castles, wursts and steins. Before setting out, I decided to indulge my lust for fussball with a game in Munich's Olympic Stadium, logging on to the internet for all the gen. Once I'd found Bayern's website, I discovered they were playing Wolfsburg in the Bundesliga on the Wednesday, in what Germans call an Englische woche, or English week – three league matches in seven days.

Using Bayern's online booking system, and my Liverpool FC credit card, I paid £15 for a seat high up in the main stand, to the left of the directors' box in the website's graphic. I could have purchased a seat in the Sudkurve, the Kop, for £8 but preferred a central position, high up, from where to survey the stadium. Five days after reserving my ticket, the postman delivered it in St Albans, along with a multi-coloured map of the ground and directions for car, metro, bus or tram.

A fortnight later, I arrived in Munich and made tracks for the Olympiastadion on the super-efficient U-bahn underground train, along with hundreds of Bayern fans and a couple of dozen Wolfsburgers in green and white, merrily singing away. All in the best of humour with no sign of die rowdies, hooligans.

A quarter of an hour after leaving the Hauptbahnhof, the main railway station, I was walking to the stadium amid a straggle of Bayern Kopites in their mandatory uniform: jeans with denim waistcoat covered in assorted team badges and Sudkurve patches.

Several sported Gerry Francis/Chris Waddle mullet hairstyles which, contrary to popular belief in Sloane Square, did not die out in the Seventies. Grey, pointed felt hats garnished with the Bayern crest were also conspicuous, as were scarves emblazoned with "You'll Never Walk Alone". Most striking, though, were the family units, including grandparents and teenagers, considerably more than football attracts in England.

Located within a capacious park, Bayern's stadium was constructed for the 1972 Olympic Games and above a screen of trees I glimpsed its acrylic spider's web of a roof, as emblematic of Munich as the Opera House is of Sydney. Punctuated by steel pillars, this transparent cover bounds around the arena in peaks and troughs, which are all you can see from the outside, since its concrete superstructure was deliberately buried within a huge bowl excavated out of bare earth.

Nearer the ground, stalls were selling lager, popcorn, sweets, sausages and brezen – figure-of-eight bread pieces scattered with rock salt – and one vendor even displayed a varied selection of cigars. Cigars! Scousers only get a whiff of them at Christmas, from seafarers who've just returned from the Caribbean. Munich's Olympiastadion was not Oakfield Road on a Wednesday night in April.

At one stall, I bought a programme for 2.50 Deutschemarks, or 75p – terrific value given that pages double the dimensions of your average Premier League product made it more a magazine than the pocket booklet sold back home.

Farther on, in parkland girdling the stadium, tables and chairs were set out for eating and supping. Less than 400 metres from where families now sat peacefully, the bloodiest chapter in Olympic annals had been written during the 1972 Games: Palestinian gunmen from the Black September faction took Israelis hostage in the athletes' village, shooting two of them dead, while another nine perished during a botched rescue by German police at the city's military airport, as they were about to be flown away.

Outside the present-day ground's entrances, security constraints made themselves felt. At a fence barring access to turnstiles, everybody was frisked and any beverages, alcoholic or not, were confiscated.

Past this barrier, I entered the stadium and found my seat, facing the 290-metre-high Olympic Tower and BMW's headquarters, which towered above the far terrace. Bizarrely, police vans drove slowly across the top of this stand, confirming the arena is below ground level.

While a pair of mascots named Bazi, with elephantine wooden heads, waddled around in leather shorts, a jumbo TV screen showed a reporter interviewing fans and conferring the Player of the Month award on Alex Zickler, selected by captains of all 18 Bundesliga teams. As Zickler waved to the crowd, a banner was hoisted aloft in the Sudkurve, "Leeds, danke, Leeds, thanks", gratitude for United knocking out Bayern's rivals and ground-sharers, Munich 1860, in the Champions League preliminary round. Quite sad, really, almost as pathetic as, say, the Kop applauding Leeds for turfing Tranmere out of the FA Cup.

To the strains of "I will survive", both teams ran out while four large Bayern flags billowed away in the Sudkurve, which now bore a warning, "Red Sharks", along its perimeter. Once Gloria Gaynor had sung the final bars of her survival plan, the crowd burst into Yellow Submarine, that favourite in Continental stadia, to the accompaniment of drums and bugles which sounded out loud when play kicked off, even more so when Mehmet Scholl netted a penalty.

After Carsten Jancker made it two, the PA announcer gave the score: "Bayern 2, Wolfsburg ..." He hesitated to permit the crowd to holler "Nul! Nil!", whereupon he said "Danke", to which the supporters shouted "Bitte! Don't mention it". Such manners, like driving along the autobahn to Augsburg.

At half-time, the crowd of 41,000, two thirds of the 63,000 capacity, were treated to match highlights on the TV screen while I browsed Bayern's Fankatalog, 100 pages of replica kit, scarves, badges, keyrings, flags, tracksuits and products rarely encountered in English club merchandising. Here's a selection for your Christmas stocking: snow sleds, sunglasses, toy cars, cameras, watches, lighters, fountain pens, suitcases, briefcases, hairdryers, toothbrushes, doormats, babies' dummies, snuff, bike locks, temporary tattoos and complete suits of lederhosen for men and women – trousers, waistcoats, shoes and shirts, as worn by the squad in a line-up on one page.

I reflected how they'd go down a bundle on Heskey and Camara.

Once the second half kicked off, the match became a nail-biter for the Sudkurve when Wolfsburg scored. That made it 2-1 but, a quarter of an hour to go, Fink calmed nerves with a "Tor! Goal!" acclaimed by a pair of clapping hands on the TV, and at the whistle, it remained 3-1, putting Bayern top of the Bundesliga.

As I hurried for the U-bahn, Munich's players were being interviewed on the big screen but I had another match on my mind. The lads were playing Aston Villa that night and I'd already done research at my hotel to locate the nearest cybercafé, behind the Hauptbahnhof, although it took some finding because a deluge had driven everyone off the streets. A policeman put me right and after a few minutes' plod, one drowned Kopite snuggled down in the café. A glass of Kulmbacher by my keyboard, I searched for the Reds' score.

No clickety-click. Liverpoolfc.tv refused to download, the BBC's website was off air, ITV were on a commercial break, Reuters had dropped off the radar, Teamtalk had lost their tongue.

By this time I was getting almost as frustrated as a mate who'd just bought a new telly back in St Albans. He pressed a button on his remote control to change channel but nothing happened. He thumbed it several more times, without a flicker of response from his £800 box of tricks.

Exasperated, he prodded other combinations of buttons, to no avail, and was about to hurl the zapper at the screen when, alerted by howls of rage, his wife darted into the living room.

She put him right; it wasn't the remote control he was using, it was his mobile phone.

Well, here in Munich, I was becoming almost as peeved as my pal. Where was Liverpool's score?

Had the downpour shortcircuited the mainframe? I tried again. Eventually, Football365 chugged into action: Owen 3, Villa 1. Wunderbar! My bill settled, I slopped happily away in squelchy shoes to the hotel.

On my return to England after Bayern's table-topper, Michael and the rest began rattling cages, ramming Derby 4-0 away. In the 17th minute, Heskey bulleted a header into the rigging and was putting himself about so much that at the break Houllier predicted: "You're going to score a hat-trick."

In the second half, Emile won the treble chance, firing into the top corner and tapping in at the near post.

After the lads achieved only their second victory in 13 derby games, 3-1, Berger made favourable noises about the club's new professionalism, training methods, gym workouts, match preparation and tactics. But the French revolution was not confined to coaching; Houllier was laying down standards of behaviour that applied 24 hours a day, like when he learnt a player was being disrespectful to canteen ladies.

Le Boss acted. That budding talent received a gentle nudge on his wonky tiller and within days he was conducting himself as he should, even presenting bunches of flowers to the canteen lasses. Manager's message received and understood.

In the League, Liverpool had gone down 3-0 to Chelsea at Stamford Bridge but gained revenge in November by dumping the Pensioners out of the Worthington Cup, 2-1.

Houllier praised Hamann and Babbel. "My English players had gone down," he said. "The ones who really put us in charge were the Germans. They looked tired but still went forward, still went on doing their job. I think you need character in England. You can't have softies."

In December, Owen reached 21, turning his back on a year of stop-go, stop-go because of hamstring injuries, groin pains and cranial scans. He was a goer, though, at Old Trafford, where Phil Neville committed a two-handed slam on the ball to concede a free kick that Murphy drilled into Barthez's net. Then Michael should have added another, striking the bar. Next Smicer embarked on a 60-yard run, only to be wrestled to the deck by Luke Chadwick, who was punished with an early bath.

After the statutory amount of added time for Manchester to find the net, the final whistle brought an explosion of glee in the Scouse sector which the *Daily Telegraph's* Paul Hayward described as resembling the inside of a boiling kettle.

As well as ending a five-year wait for a win over the Mancunians, Muffin's goal gave Liverpool their first victory in a decade at Old Trafford and inflicted United's first defeat in 37 home League games, nearly two years. In his 100th fixture in sole command, Houllier's men had provided a centenary gift and the following Saturday they tonked Arsenal 4-0 at Anfield, courtesy of Gerrard, Owen, Barmby and Fowler.

Sluggish start over, Liverpool remained fourth in the table at Christmas and were eyeing a berth in the Champions League, son of the European Cup and a UEFA gambit to nobble plans by the G14 group of major clubs to launch their own competition.

Now what Reds yearned for was silverware … any silverware.

Ask any Kopite and he would contend our best chance of success lay in the League Cup, our annual property in the early Eighties, since when sponsors throwing budgets at football had variously rebranded it as the Milk, Littlewoods, Rumbelows and Coca-Cola trophies. In its current apparition of the Worthington Cup, Liverpool did reach the final, sailing past Chelsea, Stoke (8-0 away win), Fulham and Crystal Palace in the semi (5-0 at Anfield, 6-2 on aggregate).

One week before our big day, L4 laid out the red carpet for prestigious visitors. On the eve of a European tie with Manchester United, Valencia undertook a tour of "el mítico Anfield", the legendary Anfield, because, their coach driver explained, "they wanted to see England's greatest football club".

Since – crack out the bubbly – bulldozers had been let loose on crumbling Wembley, the Worthington final with Birmingham was relocated to Cardiff's Millennium Stadium where Growler Fowler netted a cracking volley. As the clock ticked down, the Brummies scored a penalty to bring extra time, which failed to break the impasse. A penalty shoot-out would determine the winners and Westerfeld was spot-on, saving Andrew Johnson's kick to grab the trophy for us on a 5-4 decision.

Watching the action from the stands was a foreign observer, Sven-Goran Eriksson, who had quit Lazio to succeed Kevin Keegan as England coach. After his appointment, this long-time admirer of the English game met the media at Sopwell House Hotel in St Albans and recalled that his football education incorporated classes in our Boot Room.

Looking back on his early years in management working with an assistant, Tord Grip, at Degerfors and Gothenburg in Sweden, Eriksson disclosed: "We were both Liverpool fans. In 1984 I met Bob Paisley and was invited into the Boot Room. I went to see others but I liked – and who didn't? – the way Liverpool played. They won the European Cup every year, or second year.

"The Liverpool of that time were one of the best teams in Europe. I liked the easy way they played, one touch, two touches, simple but effective."

Although it had been no walkover against Palace, the Reds had their first trophy in six years and were also advancing on other fronts. Having knocked out Rapid Bucharest, Slovan Liberec and Olympiacos in the UEFA Cup, they were drawn against Roma, the Serie A leaders who were unbeaten on their own grass all season. Owen did the business in the Stadio Olimpico, a brace of fine strikes sending 5,000 Scousers potty.

Despite losing 1-0 at Anfield to the Gialorossi, the Yellow and Reds, Liverpool moved through to the next round where they eclipsed Porto 2-0 at home and 0-0 in the Das Antas stadium to set up an exacting semi with Barcelona.

In April they put on a thoroughly professional performance to neutralise the Catalans and a Camp Nou crowd of 90,000, although the Spanish press deplored the Reds' defensive tactics, their refusal to use two attackers who might have made it more of an open contest. In truth, these gripes were reassuring; away from home, Liverpool had adopted methods which Italian and Spanish clubs had capitalised on for decades.

Veteran McAllister had added fresh ingenuity, directing moves from midfield with clever touches and probing passes, and he pinged in a peach against Barça in L4 to put the Reds in their first European final since 1985.

During the home semi, Anfield's atmosphere had been reminiscent of heady European nights in the Seventies and Eighties and even Barcelonistas joined in YNWA, the words having been printed in Catalan papers.

Around the ground, signwriters had been doing overtime on banners that proclaimed the Scousers' aptitude for aphorisms: "Unparalleled history, glorious future", "If Houllier was at Waterloo, we'd all be speaking French" and – the longest, just fitting inside the Centenary Stand – "There is a tide in the affairs of Red men which taken at the flood leads on to great fortune". But the swashbuckling command that warmed the cockles of any Kopite's heart was, "Wine for my men, we ride at dawn".

As well as advancing to the UEFA final, the Reds were homing in on the FA Cup, amazing Babbel with the crowd for the 3-0 defeat of Third Division Rotherham United. "There were 30,000 at Anfield," he said. "If that game had taken place in Germany, there would have been 500."

The Merry Millers out of the way, Liverpool thumped Leeds 2-0 at Elland Road, Manchester City 4-2 at Anfield and Tranmere 4-2 at Prenton Park to move into a semifinal with Wycombe at Villa Park. Beforehand, Houllier had the Wanderers watched seven times and this respect for his opponents paid off; a Heskey header and a curling free kick by captain Fowler put the Reds into their second final of the season, greeted by the travelling Kop with the message, "Tell me ma, me ma, to put the champagne on ice, we're going to Cardiff twice".

In the League, Liverpool's priority had been qualification for the Champions League and in March they took a giant stride towards that by completing the double over Manchester United, their first since 1979. After Gerrard loosed off a blistering shot from 35 yards that left Barthez grasping at thin air, Fowler wrapped it up with another ripper of a goal, guiding the ball down and lashing home a fierce shot.

Another must-win contest came in April. At Goodison, the crowd couldn't draw breath as Heskey scored, Duncan Ferguson equalised, Babbel rifled home, then Robbie missed a penalty. If that had gone in, it should have sewn matters up but after Biscan's sending-off for a second foul, the Blues were awarded another spot kick for a Hyypia challenge. Unsworth hit the mark to make it 2-2, and 10-man Liverpool would have to settle for a point.

Now, though, the accuracy of a comment by Trevor Brooking was borne out: "Merseyside derbies usually last 90 minutes and I'm sure today's won't be any different."

Seconds remaining, McAllister conjured up a big one, bending a free kick all of 44 yards into the bottom righthand corner of Everton's goal. Houllier had said, "Macca is a diamond," and this gem guaranteed three vital points.

Asked the secret of Liverpool's resurgence, Le Boss explained that Anfield's Boot Room of the Shanks-Paisley-Fagan-Dalglish era had been replaced by Melwood's Bunker, a place where staff could bond, a room where people such as Phil Thompson, Patrice Bergues, Sammy Lee and Joe Corrigan could chat.

"Every morning we'll have a cup of coffee and a discussion," Houllier said. "What we're going to do and who we need to talk to, one on one. Sometimes it'll be formal. Other times we'll just have a laugh, tell a few jokes."

The bunker boys must have enjoyed a good chuckle when they heard about an incident before Millwall's Division Two fixture with Bristol City at Ashton Gate. According to a report by the police's National Criminal Intelligence Service, "at 6.45pm the Millwall supporters were taken under escort towards the stadium. As they passed a public house, a group of 30 to 40 males came out and bottles and glasses were thrown and pub windows smashed. After a short while it became apparent both groups were from Millwall and each thought the other were City supporters."

No such disorder blighted Liverpool's bid for their second trophy in Cardiff, a ground-breaker for two reasons: the first FA Cup Final since 1923 not at Wembley and the first outside London. On Welsh turf, this fulminating drama fitted an occasion which 43 TV cameras, the most for any British match, transmitted to hundreds of millions.

Even though Arsenal dominated, they had to wait until the 72nd minute to take the lead through Fredrik Ljungberg and squandered other chances to secure victory. Waste not, want not.

With eight minutes to go, Owen dragged the Reds off the ropes. In a goalmouth mêlée, Babbel sprang high in the air to nod the ball down to Michael who, pivoting athletically on his left foot, lashed it home with his right.

Next came a strike worthy of winning any final. In the 88th minute, substitute Berger lofted a long ball into space in the Gooners' half where Michael outpaced Lee Dixon to snatch it and sped like a greyhound towards his target.

Not once did he glance up. Fixated on speed and control, he knew precisely where he was going, what he had to do.

Just as acting is all about eyes, so football is all about angles; they can dictate victory or defeat. Before Tony Adams could flatten our attacker with a sliding tackle, Michael's size 6-and-a-half left boot angled the ball diagonally across Seaman into the onion bag's bottom corner.

Houllier's rattlesnake pass out of defence had been used with maximum venom; Liverpool had not only wrenched the silver out of the Londoners' hands but they had also avenged their 2-1 defeat on a comparably sweltering day in 1971.

Michael, still only 21, said: "This goal was better than scoring in the World Cup. People talk about the fact I had a good World Cup and scored a good goal but it didn't win us anything or get us anywhere."

Originally he had intended wearing brand-new Umbro boots, until Houllier persuaded him to stick with his old pair. The marksman, who had netted six times in three previous outings, revealed: "The manager saw me putting them on for the final training session. He questioned whether I should be discarding lucky boots that were bringing all my goals. I did as I was told and the old boots kept on scoring."

The 1953 showdown between Blackpool and Bolton will always be remembered as the Stanley Matthews final; Michael's two goals in six minutes meant 2001 would go down as the Owen final.

Houllier put his finger on one of the striker's virtues, "he's a winner in his soul", while Thierry Henry blamed Arsenal's reverse on "a god protecting Liverpool". "We need a player who will be the fox in the box and on the pitch," Henry pleaded. "We need a player like Owen is for Liverpool."

Our boy had become one of the most famous sportsmen around, through deeds in matches, not outlandish pictures in the tabloids. In fact he'd run a mile at the slightest suggestion he was a publicity junkie, the kind of hair-gel wholesaler and designer clothes horse whose performances on the super-rich's Quai d'Honneur catwalk at St Tropez are more eye-catching than their dead-ball posturing on the park.

After his Cardiff brace, Michael wasn't going to be distracted by any off-field ballyhoo; his gaze was fixed on a third trophy, the UEFA Cup in Dortmund, and fans were beginning to feel our team were on the brink of greatness. They could not lose.

Their relentless momentum, their aura of invincibility brought to mind the comment of Kevin Summerfield, Shrewsbury's coach who visited Anfield on a spying mission. After watching a 5-0 shellacking of Leeds, he remarked: "The gaffer sent me to see if I could spot a weakness and I found one ... the half-time tea's too milky."

To take their third trophy, however, Liverpool would need to overcome the unheralded but dangerous Deportivo Alavés, from Vitoria in Spain, site of Wellington's rout of the French army commanded by Napoleon's brother, Joseph Bonaparte. The Basque side had enjoyed a meteoric rise from nonentity, drubbing Inter Milan 2-0 in the San Siro and reaching the final with a 9-2 aggregate annihilation of Kaiserslautern. Teams just do not score nine goals in semi-finals of any European competition, yet overall Alavés had totalled 32 in a dozen UEFA ties.

John Toshack, coaching in Spain, knew what they were capable of and declared they would win. "I can't see any way of beating Alavés," he said. "You score one against them and they score two. You score two and they get three. And on top of all that, it doesn't matter who's in their side that day."

An Anfield scout watched them in the quarter-final and reported back to Houllier. "He told us we would probably be playing Alavés in the final," the manager said. "That's how highly he rated them. He predicted this final back in March."

Before the teams came face to face, the Basques' hard-man coach, José Manuel Esnal, was angered by a disparaging comment from one of his defenders. "Liverpool lack imagination," Oscar Tellez said. "All they do is belt the ball forward."

Once Esnal heard this, he rebuked the international: "No one has the right to say such things about such a club, with such a tradition, such a European pedigree. Liverpool have been a marvellous team and I have the greatest respect for the club. I demand the same from my players."

The Reds had another admirer in Alavés's ranks; captain Antonio Karmona disclosed that, as a boy, they were his team. "There's something noble in the way Liverpool play football, a nobility that resembles the Basque people's," he told a Spanish newspaper.

Well, if ever opponents merited the adjective noble, then Liverpudlians and Basques did in Dortmund's Westfalenstadion on May 16, 2001. In this archetypal English ground, enclosed by stands hard up against the pitch, three German tenors sang You'll Never Walk Alone before kick-off, its opening line, "When you walk through a storm", fitting the weather as a cloudburst drenched supporters on their way in.

They had barely had time to begin drying out than this roller-coaster match slammed into motion. Babbel, the Bavarian Scouser, nodded the ball in from a McAllister free kick and Gerrard ran onto an Owen pass to slot home. Sixteen minutes and 2-0.

Alonso pulled one back for Alavés but after their keeper Herrera tripped Owen in the area, Macca restored our two-goal lead with a penalty that made it 3-1 at the interval.

Within five minutes of the restart, the Basques were on level terms. Moreno headed past Westerveld, then notched up another with a low free kick that went through the wall. 3-3 and Fowler's moment had come. In the 64th minute, he replaced Heskey and announced his entrance with a splendid goal, dribbling across the box before firing in 4-3

It wasn't over yet. Two minutes remaining, Westerveld failed to collect a corner and Jordi Cruyff headed home. 4-4. Despite having one of Europe's stingiest defences, Liverpool were conceding goals from set-pieces. Full-time and we're still drawing. What a bummer.

Bobby Robson once said: "The first 90 minutes of a football match are the most important." Not always, Bobby. Extra time counts for everything when two teams are going hell for leather for a golden goal to guarantee a trophy.

Drama upon drama. In the 99th minute, French referee Gilles Veissière sent Magno off for a second foul and four minutes before the whistle that would have signalled penalties, the crux of this rip-roaring final arrived.

Smicer, racing down the left, surged past Karmona, who'd lost his legs.

As the Czech hared towards goal, the Basque skipper resorted to brute force. In a double wrist lock straight from the World Wrestling Federation training manual, he strove to tear Vladi's arm out of its socket. Smicer crashed to the ground, limb considerably elongated, and retribution loomed. A second red card dismissed Karmona, the admirer of noble Liverpool.

A free kick to the Reds, on the left, 20 metres from goal, tailor-made for Macca.

All nine Alavés players were in their box as the old warhorse stepped up to the oche, took stock and curled the ball into the goalmouth.

Herrera was a home banker to fist it away but as he leapt from his line, Geli also jumped, aiming to head out to the far side. Instead, he deflected the ball past his keeper. 5-4!

A golden goal transmuted by Liverpool's alchemists into more, precious silver.

Pandemonium convulsed the Westfalenstadion, as 35,000 Reds celebrated our first European trophy for 17 years.

While the press pack were spitting feathers on the phone, straining to fit every incident into late-running reports, Liverpool's squad walked to the Alavés end to clap their supporters. Then they joined hands on the touchline with Anfield's coaching and medical staff for a ground-shaking YNWA, orchestrated by a euphoric Elvis Costello in the stand and applauded by the gracious Basque contingent. Not only had they shared their leather flasks of red wine with Liverpudlians before the match, now they were joining in our party. An admirable race, the Basques, like the peoples of our isles.

In the year's understatement about this nerve-shredder, Hyypia commented, "I think it was a nice game to watch", but Houllier put events in context.

"We have written our own history for a new generation," he said. "Liverpool has a great tradition of success and now we have added our names to that long list."

He also praised his coaches and the supporters. "I want to dedicate the win to my backroom staff who have all been magnificent – you don't win anything without them – but also to the fans.

"Three years ago I remember us losing to Celta Vigo in this tournament. Beaten 3-1 away, we ended up with virtually a reserve team for the second leg and lost 1-0. But I have never forgotten how the fans received the lads that night, how well they treated them regardless of the defeat. This is our way of paying them back for that support."

The treble of trophies had been wrapped up in a European final featuring more goals than any other, apart from Real Madrid's 7-3 trouncing of Eintracht Frankfurt in Glasgow in 1960.

Each of the three cups went to the wire: the Worthington was decided by penalties after extra time; the FA was won by a two-goal comeback in the dying minutes; and the UEFA was bagged with a golden goal, the first to decide a European final.

Liverpool had been reinstated on the Continental roll of honour, drawing tribute from FIFA president Sepp Blatter, who wrote to the club, acclaiming its hat-trick and its fans who "once again set standards for the rest of football to follow".

Even hard-bitten hacks ran out of superlatives to define a final that Spanish newspapers termed a nocáut, a knockout, while *France Football* talked about "une saison bénie, a blessed season" for the Reds. Beneath a headline across two pages, "Triomphe total pour Liverpool, Total triumph for Liverpool", the magazine said our treble symbolised "the awakening of a legend, of a club that makes whole generations fantasise". You'll Never Walk

Alone, resounded around the Westfalenstadion, "seizing the hearts of all those who love, sometimes without really knowing why, English football".

Couldn't have expressed it better myself.

Our blessed season was not over. One more League fixture remained, against Charlton at the Valley, and if the lads took the points, they would secure a Champions League place. A true game of two halves. Outplayed in the first 45 minutes, Liverpool walked off 4-0 winners, to an ovation from Addicks fans.

Houllier knew they would qualify for Europe's top competition when McAllister zinged in his last-minute free kick against Everton. "After that, I told the boys I was certain they could win all the rest," he said.

He was almost right; in six matches, they notched up five victories and one draw to complete a season of 63 fixtures, including 25 cup ties, and a tally of 127 goals for.

Once past New Year, two facts had stood out: we were sweeping aside struggling teams, whereas previously we would have lost; and we were nicking results in the last 15 minutes or so.

Houllier pinpointed one Anfield secret: "The atmosphere is different here from other clubs. We have a community feeling. The groundsman has a meal with the pros. The lady who does the cooking and the people who clean the place all have a bond with the club."

He went on: "The mutual faith between fans and the team dates back to Shanks. His charisma helped that relationship to develop and that relationship is still valid now. Even when the team went through a difficult period, the fans were very supportive."

He added: "Liverpool are a club who mark people for life."

And they have left an indelible mark on Merseyside, for if the Almighty created alcohol to stop the Irish ruling the world, then he surely devised football to keep impoverished Scousers from emigrating.

On the Sunday after the Charlton clincher, 500,000 people filled city streets to greet Anfield's dream-weavers on a 17-mile parade with their three trophies, moving Jamie Redknapp to say, "I have never seen anything like it", and Sammy Lee to observe: "These people are what it is all about."

Another crowning moment came in August at UEFA's grand gala in Monte Carlo where, in front of a glittering audience of dignitaries, Liverpool and Alavés fans were lauded as supporters of the year and Gerry Marsden reprised YNWA with a choir of Scousers and Basques.

Earlier in the campaign, Houllier had summed up his philosophy: "In football, you must compete, you must run and fight until you have nothing left."

During this momentous season, the Reds had given their all.

21
Cotopaxi 2, Kopites 0 [Match Abandoned]

He who can no longer pause to wonder and stand rapt in awe is as good as dead; his eyes are closed.

– Albert Einstein

I JUST couldn't take any more. I'd reached breaking point. Incapable of filling my lungs with sufficient air to breathe, I was drawing on my body's last faint reserves of oxygen.

I'd used every ounce of strength and strained every sinew until they were snapping, but the altitude was destroying me.

No, I wasn't crawling up Everton Brow after a gallon in The Slaughterhouse. This was summer 2001, more than 17,000 foot up a mountain in the Andes, and I was losing it.

How did I get in this state?

A week before, as UEFA were honouring Liverpool and Alavés in Monte Carlo, Russ and I were taking off on our latest Latin American jolly, a trip to Ecuador to climb one of the highest active volcanoes.

For me, "do it now" time had arrived. As more and more body parts began heading south, I peered into the not-so-distant future – the age when you don't have birthday parties, you have rehearsals for a wake – and concluded this was the moment for a dream expedition.

To Ecuador. To Quito. To Cotopaxi.

In 1802, Alexander von Humboldt undersold this 19,388-foot, 5,911-metre white pyramid: "The most regular of all the colossal peaks in the High Andes, it is a perfect cone covered by a thick blanket of snow which shines so brilliantly at sunset it seems detached from the azure of the sky."

Landing at Quito airport at midday, I caught the German explorer's drift. I stared in awe at the horizon. There it was, a white ogre skulking beyond the runway perimeter but still 50 kilometers, away. Cotopaxi was big, very big, giving credence to stories that the view from its summit could extend as far as 200 kilometres into the Amazon basin.

This was going to be quite a challenge but my son and I had it all planned. Using a Quito hotel as our base, we spent a week adjusting to the city's altitude of 2,850 metres, 9,405 feet, toning up on puny peaks that encircle its sprawl and bulking up in Adam's Rib, an American-owned joint where Meg Ryan held somewhat frosty court during filming of Proof of Life with Russell Crowe.

On our third visit to this restaurant promising "the best barbecues south of the Equator", we polished off succulent T-bones in pepper sauce and decamped to the lounge for post-prandial mojitos and some satellite telly.

Joining us with a coffee, an American woman introduced herself as Mary, owner of a ranch near Loja in the south of Ecuador. Since getting divorced and vowing to make a complete break from the past, she'd sold her New England farm and begun a fresh life on a 5,000-hectare estate close to the Peruvian border.

While we swopped anecdotes, Russ was absorbed in Cheers, chuckling at the jokes.

Mary gazed at him, a wistful expression on her face, until finally she disclosed her thoughts.

"I'll never see my son like your son now," she whispered to me. "He died a month ago. He was 18."

After a pause, she told his story.

Gary loved riding along trails that wriggled through the hilly jungle on his mother's land but one day his horse lost its footing on a muddy slope, throwing him to the ground.

In his belt, he was carrying a loaded revolver which went off. He was shot dead.

I had to ask: Why didn't he have the safety catch on?

"There were poisonous snakes and he kept the gun ready to shoot them," Mary explained.

When he did not come home, it was she who went searching and discovered his body lying in the mud, dead from a single bullet fired by his own pistol. What could I say that she hadn't heard before? Words fail you.

After one week in Quito and workouts on surrounding summits, Russ and I felt prepared for our attempt on Cotopaxi, so we hired a mountaineer from a trekking agency to accompany us up the Rotary Club ramblers' route. At 21, Alejandro was Ecuador's youngest guide and most arrested climber, all because he trained by shinning up office blocks, to the alarm of secretaries whose typing was interrupted by his grinning mug at 15th-floor windows.

One in 10 climbers reaches Cotopaxi's crater, so it would be no cakewalk, but we aimed to give it our best shot; we would spend two days and nights on the volcano, acclimatising to its higher altitude, honing our rudimentary snow and ice skills with Alejandro and sleeping in the José Ribas mountain hut. At 4,800 metres, 15,748 foot, this refuge is known far beyond Latin America, ever since an earthquake on Easter Sunday, 1996, destabilised the ice cap covering the summit and dispatched an avalanche onto its stone walls. Thirty climbers were buried, of whom 11 died. In their infinite wisdom, the Ecuadorian authorities rebuilt the ruined hut in the same spot, below a gully shaped by nature to smooth the path of any more avalanches.

However, whenever Cotopaxi has really felt in the mood for demonstrating she's a fully paid-up member of the Pacific's Ring of Fire, she has staged eruptions, flattening towns and villages and propelling mud flows as far as 320 kilometres, 200 miles, away. Eat your heart out, Helvellyn.

Our first day and night as guests of this feisty lady went well, the altitude neglecting to cause physiological problems for we volcano virgins. That was about to change.

During late afternoon of the second day, after going on a snout of the glacier to practise handling our ropes and braking with an ice-axe while sliding down a slope, we returned to the refuge for a snooze. Within an hour of hitting our bunks, Russ was racked by acute mountain sickness – severe headache, nausea, persistent vomiting, hallucinations, as a knot in the wooden headboard uncurled into a worm that wriggled around.

To combat altitude malaise, our GP had prescribed Diamoxin tablets which raise your red blood cell count, but despite this medication and our structured week of acclimatisation and six-month fitness programme, Russ had been laid low by AMS, a condition that taxes the minds of medical researchers. Why can it reduce Olympic athletes to blubber while leaving pensioners as fit as butcher's dogs? Nobody can explain.

Alerted by me to Russ's condition, Alejandro came right away, scrutinising the colour of his lips, eyes and fingernails and taking his pulse. Over a period of two hours, he returned every 30 minutes to monitor him and then gave the prognosis we feared: the AMS had reached a critical juncture and, if Russ were to lose consciousness, he might not recover.

The priority now was to get him to a lower altitude.

"I'll go down, too," I said. "That's the end of Cotopaxi."

"No, I'll be OK," Russ insisted. "Go up without me."

Our guide made his casting vote. Let Russ descend, Alejandro assured us, and the AMS would ebb away. So we agreed my boy would return to Quito, I would stay.

Since people avoid driving in Ecuador at night, the challenge for Alejandro was finding transport to collect Russ and return him to our hotel.

Using the hut's radio telephone, contact was made with a driver willing to make the journey from Quito to the bottom of the mountain and at 11pm I watched through a window of the refuge as Alejandro assisted a seriously unsteady Russ to stumble down the ash path to meet the Land Rover.

Once blackness had snuffed out their head lamps, I felt as though I'd been cut in half.

Our dream of father and son reaching the summit together was over.

An hour later, with Russ conveyed away, Alejandro was back in the hut. Now it was me and him against the elements.

To climb Cotopaxi, you set out at the latest by 2 in the morning, and return by 10am, before the tropical sun melts snow and ice, creating volatile conditions. After Russ evaporated into the darkness, I lay in my sleeping bag, haunted by a sense of foreboding.

Would he end up in intensive care? Would the Land Rover skid over a precipice? Would I ever see him again? And what did Cotopaxi have in store for me? Would I fall down a crevasse? Would there be an avalanche, or even an eruption?

The night before, a troop of hard-as-teak Special Forces from the Ecuadorian army had filled the hut with lewd guffaws, knowing winks and the persistent hiss of their pissing out the windows. Now that they had overrun Cotopaxi and marched away on their next Andean assignment with khaki sideboards lashed to their backs, our dormitory was nearly empty, a morgue in waiting. Outside, though, the mountain was having a fit.

Down in Quito, weather forecasts were unheard of because everyone knew what was coming: four seasons in one day, namely summer in the morning, spring at midday, autumn in the afternoon and winter at night. Here on the volcano, a hurricane straight out of the gates of Hell was shaking the hut, rattling its corrugated-iron roof, blasting through every nook and cranny into the dormitory and scouring my exposed face with a frozen flannel.

Incapable of even dozing in my bunk, I wrestled with apprehension about what lay up the mountain. That wind's a killer. We can't climb in this. Impossible. Wrong. At 1.00 in the morning, Alejandro gave me a tap on the shoulder; time to put on our gear and hit the road.

Norwegians say there's no such thing as bad weather, only wrong clothing, and I had the kit for the job. Back on Merseyside they might joke about it being cold enough for two pairs of shoelaces but here in the Andes I required the full Ellis Brigham – five layers, including treasured 1977 Liverpool shirt, on my upper body, three layers on lower, two pairs of gloves, three pairs of socks, double-skinned boots, alpaca balaclava, snow goggles, Petzl head lamp, climbing harness.

I joined my guide in the candlelit kitchen for a mug of maté de coca, declining some biscuits. My stomach was bubbling with fear and anticipation. On with our backpacks and, ice-axes in hand, the pair of us wrestled open the stout wooden door which the storm slammed shut behind us.

Welcome aboard! Cotopaxi had two more playmates. The wind sucked my breath away and shards of ice bombarded my balaclava. Thank goodness for the goggles. Without them, my corneas would have become a dart board.

Whoooh! Going to be some night.

Past a sign, "Peligro! Zona de avalanchas. Danger! Avalanche zone", Alejandro plodded up an incline of black ash that buried your boots with every step. My nose detected a distinct whiff of sulphur and, despite wind chill bringing the air temperature down to minus 30C or lower, the ash was emitting heat. This, along with the physical exertion, meant I was soon drenched in sweat, misting up my goggles.

On one of the Andes' loftiest peaks, I couldn't see a sausage. Picture this: a blind man eyeballing the Cyclops of Cotopaxi.

Not that I was making much headway. Relentlessly the gale would lift me on my toes before slumping me down.

Stop it! Stop it! Stop it!

While resting, I wiped the goggles'lenses with my mitts but the second I put them on again, they clouded over. I couldn't leave them off, though, because of those jet-propelled needles.

A figure loomed in front of us, a climber abandoning his ascent. Mumbling something in Spanish to Alejandro, he slithered past.

If only I could have gone down, too. But no, my guide ushered me onwards and upwards until we reached the start of the aerobic workout, the 50-foot-high base of the glacier enveloping the peak, where the temperature dropped noticeably, cooling me and restoring clarity to my goggles.

Gloves removed, we put on our crampons. My right one fitted without any difficulty but as my fingers grew numb, I was labouring to tighten straps on the other. Strain as I might, I could not pull one binding fully through its buckle.

After three or four minutes, my hands were as much use as frozen fish fingers. I gave up. The strap would have to remain loose.

Very, very stupid. A lost crampon on the glacier would be no barrel of laughs.

We roped together via our hip harnesses and clambered onto the ice cliff.

Alejandro leading, we climbed 25-foot pitches – swing your axe into the face, kick in with one crampon's lobster claw, kick the other in a bit higher, swing your axe, kick one crampon in, kick the other in a bit higher.

Once upon a wet autumn, I did a week's rock climbing course at the National Mountaineering Centre in Plas-y-Brenin, Snowdonia, where our instructor, Rowland Edwards, soloed up cliffs in a graceful vertical ballet.

Here in the Andes, as I mirrored Alejandro's movements, I was conscious of a symmetry between us, as artistic and fulfilling as Rowland's pas seul in Llanberis. The climbers' fellowship of the rope was holding me in its thrall.

With a couple more kicks, I stood alongside my guide on the lip of the glacier.

Before us stretched Cotopaxi – Neck of the Moon in Quechua, the Incas' language.

Stark against the sky, she was excruciatingly white, carpeted with shimmering crystals, a sparkling vision of pure beauty, like nothing I had ever beheld.

Above her lay a black-satin firmament strewn with starry diamonds, a million more than in England where we are flicked crumbs from the Andes' nightly banquet.

I was in another world. At that point, at that instant, I might have been scared, dead tired, worried about Russ, but I felt more alive than ever. Perhaps this is how a condemned man feels before the noose is slipped over his head.

Now, in starlight and storm, the hard slog began up a 45-degree incline.

Climbing manuals warn that some crevasses lurking on this glacier are more than 100 foot deep. Concentrate, dear Neil, concentrate.

With Alejandro using a pair of ski poles to probe the route, we picked our way through a jumble of seracs, glacial pinnacles, and enormous wind-sculpted mushrooms, diverting around glass-covered blotches and streams of murkiness in the ice that signified unseen depths below.

Until an intimidating crevasse blocked our path. A narrow bridge of snow, six feet long, crossed the void. I peered into the bluey-white abyss.

Flaming Alf Arrowsmith! Immediately below the arch, spears of ice pointed up, formed out of melting snow.

Land on those and it's goodnight, Vienna, goodnight, Liverpool, goodnight, Anfield, goodnight, world. You'd bleed to death on those spikes. Alejandro might have had biceps the size of Barcelona but even he could not haul you off them.

Prodding deftly with his sticks, he edged across the bridge, carefully, very carefully, until a gust of wind halted him. Like a high-wire artist in the circus, he leant forward, clasping the ski poles firmly to aid balance, and waited for the blast to pass.

Calm restored, he advanced gently to the far side where he lanced the snow, validating its solidity. Reassured, he turned towards me, leaving the poles loose on their wrist straps and securely gripping the rope that yoked us together.

My turn.

I restrained my instinct for self-preservation, the intuitive urge to gallop across – not recommended on a fragile snow bridge. Slower the better.

Gingerly I put one foot in the imprint of Alejandro's boot, then another in the next – and the wind rocked me. Cotopaxi was toying with another timid intruder.

I stood above the chasm, head spinning.

To steady myself, I shoved my ice-axe into the arch and shut my eyes. Those icy spikes were waiting.

"Ven! Come on!" Alejandro shouted.

I opened my eyes and steeled myself ...

Deep, deep breath. Go!

One hesitant, short step, another, a last quick stride – there!

The other side! Thank you, Lord!

Head pounding, heart pumping, I'd escaped Cotopaxi's man-trap.

I bent double, gasping for breath, unscrambling my brain.

The day before, when we practised ice techniques, I had quizzed Alejandro about how he could extricate a client from a crevasse. With a rope pulley, he answered.

Next question: What happens if you fall into a crevasse? "Auto-rescue," he replied. Not a reference to the Andean Automobile Association's all-terrain breakdown vehicle, I took this to mean self-rescue.

All well and good until, hours later in the hut's gloom, he'd been chatting about close shaves in the Andes and disclosed that after falling into one crevasse on Chimborazo, he'd been left unconscious and wedged in a cleft. Meanwhile his climbing partner was clinging on for dear life, tied onto his anchor of an ice-axe which he'd rammed into the snow above the sheer drop. By chance, Alejandro hadn't broken his neck and did regain his faculties, but the pair of them had a devil of a job getting him out of this hole.

Having negotiated our snow bridge, this tale began gnawing away at me. If Alejandro was knocked senseless or broke a leg in a fall, I wouldn't have the wherewithal to save him. I'd have to cut the rope with my axe, abandon him to the depths and look after No 1.

On the other hand, at dead of night, high up a bad-tempered mountain that could turn alarmingly nasty within seconds, I quite liked my guide's company. He was good for my humour and my health and I was growing increasingly fond of him.

After all, he had a significant role to play in my future – he could decide whether or not I saw Jamie Carragher score a 35-yard screamer at the Kop end. So I'd much rather Alejandro was around to watch over this vulnerable laddie. No Kopite ever walks alone and, high on choleric Cotopaxi, I preferred to have him alongside me ... but, perish the thought, what if he did get hurt? What if the pair of us were swept away by a snow slide? Walking tourist trails above Chamonix, I'd watched avalanches on Mont Blanc from afar and their shuddering energy concentrated your mind. Now if my partner and I got buried up here in the Andes, we'd suffocate in minutes, long before anyone could lift a spade to dig us out. Not an enticing prospect.

Alejandro led me on, meandering around and up Cotopaxi's minefield until, around 6am, I halted for yet another pant and detected a tinge, a hairline glint on the horizon to our left, beyond the Andes, in the Amazon's direction.

Nature had lit its daily fuse.

As I resumed my slog, this filament swelled and lengthened into a glow that spread across the earth's curvature. By visible degrees, night and its panoply of stars were being vanquished by the hidden sun's growing brilliance and intensity.

With a silver-grey tide flooding towards us, he made his entrance.

A dozen nuclear bombs detonated on the edge of space, sending a shock wave of retina-ravishing light across the white ocean below.

Rooted 5,000 foot above foaming clouds, in an orange, red, crimson, blue, yellow, black, white universe, I was an observer at the dawn of life, the birth of the solar system, the moment of creation, the Big Bang, as this fabulous sunrise heralded a new day.

A cosmic, biblical, humbling revelation. An illumination that would have cast any Jesuit down on his knees in prayer. A glimpse of Heaven.

From being a grain of sand, I'd become a god.

For a few seconds.

Boof! The gale buffeted me back to reality. I dragged myself from the threshold of paradise and slogged on. But as the golden chariot of the equatorial sun, now swathed in its cobalt-blue mantle, powered into the turquoise skies, I was losing it.

Bend into that hateful wind, drag leaden boots a few steps higher, lean on ice-axe, fight for breath, repeat again and again. A painful, unwinnable battle – and the crater was still hours away.

I might have completed 20-mile cross-country runs with the rabbits of rural Hertfordshire, pumped tons of iron in Westminster Lodge gym and muscled my way into the Sandon on numerous occasions but Cotopaxi was pulverising me with exhaustion. In medical phraseology, my biomechanics were buggered.

This wasn't Pillar or the Fairfield Horseshoe in a Lakeland February; this was the real deal in the Andes at 17,500 feet, three miles higher than Anfield's centre spot. Here the oxygen was half sea level's and my chest was croaking, legs wobbling, temples throbbing and fillings jangling.

I also had the salty taste of blood in my mouth...

I confess: My 50s had become the new 90s and Saga's Zimmer-assisted, extreme bungee-jumping course would have to go on hold for a while.

Reinhold Messner, the supreme Himalayan, has remarked that when you climb, you're not discovering how big you are but how small, how weak, how full of fear. In all honesty, my will to succeed had ebbed away since Russ's departure and now I was Shanks's caraway seed, as weak as a baby, petrified by the thought of crossing another crevasse.

Know how, after they've given you a general anaesthetic, the instant arrives when you're about to go under? Well this dead man climbing Cotopaxi had reached that point, only I'd never return if I did go under.

Danger can be addictive, until it becomes too dangerous, and my days were about to end with a single, downpage paragraph in the *Liverpool Echo*: "City man missing in Andes".

No longer could I ignore the mantra every mountaineer should chant: Getting to the top is optional, getting back down is not.

I felt a long, long way from Ullswater Street.

Mum was calling.

Like Roberto Duran in the eighth round of his ferocious world title bout with Sugar Ray Leonard, I gasped my words of surrender to Alejandro: "No más, no more."

To hell with a show-off photo on the summit, my high-altitude shamble was over. Alejandro and I began our descent.

To my relief, the downward route included a detour around Arrowsmith's crevasse – a snow bridge thawing in the sun was not my idea of an early-morning frolic – and at 8am I tottered into the hut, shunning my guide's offer of maté de coca. All I wanted was to lie down.

Festooned in my mountain gear, I collapsed onto the bunk, my body not so much a temple, more a tumbledown lean-to.

Three hours later, my deathlike slumber was cut short by Alejandro; we had to leave because our four-wheel-drive was waiting at the bottom of the mountain. I was going to see my son again.

As our Jeep crabbed down the gravel, Alejandro informed me that out of a dozen climbers who had set out for the summit, a couple of Germans had got there. I didn't feel quite so inadequate.

Ninety minutes later, I found myself back in Quito's Hostal Vicna where I was reunited with Russ who, as promised by Alejandro, had recovered from his soroche, mountain malady, and also a head-spinning midnight slalom down Cotopaxi in the clapped-out Land Rover. Its headlights were kaput: to navigate around lethal hairpins in the gloom, the driver's mate had to cling onto the bonnet while signalling directions with a torch.

As Russ tumbled around the cab, he felt too ill to care, experiencing delusions that rocks beside the track were turning into serpents. Now, safe within our hotel, his hallucinations had melted away and he appeared elated, possibly as a side effect of the supplemental oxygen at lower altitude.

Cotopaxi had not finished with me, though. I might have escaped impalement on her spears but she was about to exact a price for invading her privacy.

That night I crawled into my bed womb and was so knackered that, within an eye blink, I'd melted into the mattress. My deep sleep ended in panic.

I came to on the bottom of a swimming pool, flat on my back, throat and lungs full of water, drowning. I could see sunlight dancing on the surface but hadn't the strength to push myself up. I was paralysed. Like a goldfish in a bowl, I kept opening my mouth to ingest air, only for it to fill up with more liquid.

Unable to breathe, unable to move, unable to comprehend what was going on, a paroxysm of terror convulsed me.

Finally, finally, I burst out of this nightmare.

I awoke in bed, gurgling and gasping to disperse fluid in my lungs.

I sat up, gulping all the air I could, and with each mouthful, my distress eased.

I clambered out of bed, plonking myself down on a chair where my breathing settled into an uneasy, rasping rhythm, and for the rest of the night I dozed upright in that chair, draining congestion from my chest cavity. The drowning hysteria did not return.

So Cotopaxi's parting gift was a pernicious infection that only cleared up after a doctor prescribed horse-strength antibiotics.

A couple of days after our traipse up the mountain, we were wallowing in rest and recuperation in Quito when Pachamama, the Indians' Mother Earth, got hot under the collar: Tungurahua, a volcano three hours by road to the south, blew its top in spectacular fashion.

From the news film on TV, Ecuador's notorious Black Giant would be worth seeing, so Russ and I promptly caught a bus to the nearest town, Baños, an attractive spa resort, where we went straight to the taxi rank, asking a driver to clog it to the fireworks.

"Not worth going," he lamented. "Not a spark. It's asleep."

Then, ruminating on the tourists, and dollars, it might attract, he added: "Ojalá! Please Lord, it'll erupt again this weekend."

It didn't but we still had an agreeable couple of days in Baños, trawling around a market that sold everything from shrunken heads to Talking Heads, and catching up on our email in a crowded cybercafe.

No sooner had Russ lodged himself at a computer than a message dinged in: "Hi! I noticed your log-on. Where are you from? Are you on holiday?"

Russ glanced around to a smile from a girl of about 16 sitting directly behind. The romance of internet technology.

Regrettably, he had to shun her approach; bit too young.

As the name Baños indicates – Baths in English – the town's charm resides in its outdoor thermal spas and we quickly identified the best, a volcanically-heated waterfall tumbling down a cliff into its pool. There we soothed away all the aches and pains from capricious Cotopaxi.

Our Andean fling might not have gone strictly to plan, we might have both suffered illness, but at least Russ and I would be returning home safely, unlike Gary, the poor American lad.

22
Liverpool Will Not Leave Me

All the things that one has forgotten scream for help in dreams.

– Elias Canetti

THE summer of 2001 brought sad news for every Kopite: Joe Fagan and Billy Liddell had both passed away. Quiet, modest "Uncle Joe" was 80 while Billy, another gentle, unassuming man, was 79.

Having helped create the phenomenon of Liverpool Football Club, they had seen the side's incredible treble but would not be watching their latest endeavours in the reconditioned European Cup.

Back in 1982, Bob Paisley had forecast the advent of a Europe-wide league and, two decades on, Liverpool would be competing in just that, the Champions League, if they got through a preliminary round against Finnish team Haka. After a 5-0 win in Helsinki wrote another entry in the Owen book of football exploits – the first Anfield player to notch up a hat-trick in an away European game – the Reds cruised home 4-1 on their own soil to move into the competition proper.

Roy Evans had said: "Liverpool without European football is like a banquet without wine."

Once the team had devoured Haka, UEFA's sommelier was pulling on his white gloves and getting out his corkscrew.

Before the League campaign resumed, the minor issue of the Charity Shield needed settling with Manchester United in the Millennium Stadium, where we took a grip on the prize in the opening 15 minutes when Murphy was up-ended by Keane and McAllister lashed the spot kick past Barthez. Then Owen turned Gary Neville inside out before slotting the ball in to give a 2-1 victory.

Since Anfield South's roof was closed because of rain, Liverpool had become the first British team to bag a major trophy indoors. Their collection of silver had not been completed, though. In August they won the Super Cup in Monaco, shading European champions Bayern Munich 3-2, to take their trophy haul to five in six months, on the back of a run of 14 victories and one draw in 15 outings.

According to Babbel, his first season at Anfield had been "beautiful". For older fans, the German represented our new Emlyn Hughes, someone who would never wave a white flag, and Houllier agreed: "Markus would die for the shirt. He would play with a broken leg."

However, a couple of weeks into the League campaign, he was laid low with Guillain-Barre syndrome, a viral condition that drains all energy and has ended some sportsmen's careers. This was a blow to the squad and another came when McAllister had to drop out because his wife had cancer.

Meanwhile, Owen was the target of some sniping from Old Trafford's Jaap Stam, who went into print to say the Wonder Boy tag had been used too much for this "overrated" player. Top defenders could deny him space for his pace and "I find the hype that surrounds the Liverpool striker a bit over the top".

Only a bit? No need to be tactful. Say what you really think.

Michael gave his riposte on the pitch in Munich in September, scoring a hat-trick as Liverpool blitzed Germany 5-1 in England's World Cup qualifier, the other goals coming from Gerrard and Heskey. Acknowledged as the world's best keeper, Oliver Kahn described this defeat as "supergau", a nuclear explosion, adding: "The scars will last for life."

Across the continents, the result was greeted with disbelief, particularly in Santiago where Roger Lemerre, France's coach, thought an aide was pulling his leg when he told him the scoreline before a friendly with Chile. Still, West Ham's Steve Lomas managed to sum up the feat's magnitude: the Germans were "a very difficult team ... they had 11 internationals out there today".

To achieve his hat-trick, the first by anyone against Germany on their turf, Michael had done homework on Kahn's technique and noted he "stood tall", using his considerable height to intimidate opponents approaching goal.

England's coach, Sven-Goran Eriksson, put his finger on Owen's secret: "He has something very special. He has two things difficult to find in a player: he's very cold when he gets a chance and he's very quick. When you have that combination, it's a killer."

But that killer touch exacted a price on Michael's body, borne out by the presence of one concerned spectator in Munich, German orthopaedic surgeon Hans-Wilhelm Muller-Wohlfahrt, who treated the striker's hamstring strains.

By virtue of their disposal of Haka, Liverpool entered the Champions League group stages and Kopites purred with anticipation at the prospect of Anfield's next visitors, Boavista, on September 11. However, that day brought the horror of the 9/11 atrocities in the USA, a minute's silence before kick-off setting the tone for a sombre encounter.

Although the Kop did their bit to encourage our lads, the stadium was subdued, the action undistinguished, apart from Owen's pearler of a curler around the goalie to equalise after Silva tapped home for the Portuguese. By registering yet another OG, Owen goal, Michael became the first British player to score in every debut game in every senior competition: Premiership, FA Cup, League Cup, UEFA Cup, Champions League, Super Cup and Charity Shield.

Before the next tie, he signed a new contract, binding him to Liverpool until 2005 and reputedly worth £16 million, a good piece of business for the club, in the view of the guest of honour at our match with Dynamo Kiev. "Owen is the best striker in the world," Brazilian icon Jairzinho commented. "He has the ability of a South American player but also great strength."

Jari Litmanen, a recruit from Barcelona, got the winner against the Ukrainians, in the absence of Michael who was sidelined with a recurrence of his hamstring problems. His body was reacting once again to the pressures it had coped with since his teens, turning out for England Under-18s at the age of 16 and taking part in junior tournaments during the summer after gruelling seasons with his club.

Football had always come first for the teenager, as shown in a friendly before the World Cup in France when Morocco's keeper kneed his head, knocking him out. To ensure Owen couldn't swallow his tongue, Dion Dublin lifted him into the coma position until England's doctors ran up. "When he regained consciousness, Michael didn't know what he was doing," Glenn Hoddle recalled. "The first thing he did was plead not to be taken off. We gave him two minutes to regain his composure."

Three years later, in 2001, another medical emergency occurred, this time at Anfield and not involving Owen but potentially far graver.

In October, at half-time of the Liverpool-Leeds fixture, Houllier was racked by chest pain and had to be rushed to hospital. A cardiac artery had ruptured. Before being wheeled into Broadgreen's operating theatre, he asked the match result and, on hearing 1-1, inquired: "Who scored our goal?" Answer: Danny Murphy.

At 7pm, surgeons began repairing his torn aorta and they stayed on their feet until 6am when the open-heart procedure was concluded successfully.

Three factors were instrumental in saving the 54-year-old's life. First, the emergency arose in L4 where the club doctor, Mark Waller, diagnosed its seriousness. Second, a leading cardio-thoracic unit was situated in the city. Third, the rupture occurred at halftime. After the final whistle, the ambulance would have had to fight its way through gridlocked traffic.

More worryingly, less than 48 hours later the team were flying to their Champions League return with Kiev. If our manager had been struck down in midair, that would have delayed urgent treatment and also hospitals in Ukraine would not have been as sophisticated as in Liverpool.

Mercifully, Broadgreen's ultramodern facilities and world-class surgeons gave the most crucial result of the day, week, month or year to Gérard.

His place at the helm was filled by Phil Thompson, who assisted Le Boss's recuperation in intensive care by guiding the Reds into the Champions League second phase.

In Kiev, Murphy side-footed home after a 30-yard pass from Gerrard, who added a second to make it 2-1 against a side that had never lost on their patch to any British club, including Arsenal, Manchester United and Celtic

A home victory over Dortmund and clean sheets on their travels meant Liverpool led their group when Houllier was discharged from hospital for a period of convalescence, his 16-hour working days ended once and for all.

In the League, the lads also took top spot with a sequence of wins that included a 3-1 dispatch of Manchester United on our turf, John Arne Riise detonating one of his free-kick bombs and Owen, back to his predatory best, bagging a brace. Afterwards, Jacques Crevoisier, the Anfield coach, referred to Michael as "the Harry Potter of modern football", a young wizard on the pitch.

Another sorcerer, Robbie Fowler, was about to leave for fresh pastures. In August, he hadn't even been on the bench for the Charity Shield after Houllier dropped him because of a training ground bust-up and, come November, he agreed a transfer to Elland Road.

To many Kopites, his exit was unthinkable but for others it boiled down to the best deal for player and club. Unhappy as third striker behind Owen and Heskey, Robbie craved regular first-team football to strengthen his case for international call-ups.

"I've not been playing as well as I would have liked, so I think a change will do me good," he said. "Hopefully it will kick-start my career again."

If negotiations about a new contract had dragged on, he could have held out and quit like McManaman, on a Bosman free transfer, leaving the Reds without a penny for one of their most dynamic forwards. Instead, Leeds forked out £12 million, a tidy sum in anyone's transfer kitty, and Liverpool snapped up another goalscorer, Czech international Milan Baros, for £3.4m from Banik Ostrava.

As Robbie abandoned L4, Merseyside was saying goodbye to a music legend. George Harrison, the youngest Beatle who chatted to me in the Cavern, died at the age of 58 after a long battle with cancer. Paul McCartney said: "He was a lovely guy and a very brave man and had a wonderful sense of humour. He was really just my baby brother."

Yes, a lovely guy, George was graced with inner peace and beauty, as well as a generosity of spirit that shone throughout his life.

In the second round of Champions League group matches, Barcelona ran out 3-1 victors at Anfield, ending a winning streak masterminded by Phil Thompson. Michael netted to put us in the lead but missed what he deemed "a sitter", which would have made it 2-1 in our favour. In the second half, the Catalans played handsome football, earning a Kop ovation that gratified Patrick Kluivert. "I loved the fact the great Liverpool fans applauded us off," he said. Carlos Rexach, Barça's coach, agreed: "In world football, Anfield's fans have a great reputation. They are very knowledgeable and it was nice to be clapped off the pitch."

A fortnight later, the Reds defended stoutly to get a goalless draw with Roma in the Olympic Stadium, after which Francesco Totti, the Italians' hitman, spoke about contenders for European Footballer of the Year, to be announced in December.

"Owen is a rare talent and the important goals he has scored make him the No 1 man," he said. "I feel honoured to be on the same short list as him for the award.

"Liverpool would not have won five trophies this year without him, and the three goals he scored for England in Germany mark him down as a great player. I have been nominated for the award because I'm lucky enough to have a great team behind me. It's not the same with Owen. He scores goals out of nothing."

Totti's backing for Michael's cause was vindicated; leading football writers did vote him in as Europe's top footballer. The lad who from the age of seven had been the best player in every team he turned out for was the youngest recipient since Ronaldo of the Ballon d'Or, or Golden Ball.

That same month of December, the Reds were also voted Team of the Year in the BBC Sports Personality awards and became the first club to gain all three of World Soccer magazine's annual titles: World Team, Liverpool, in front of Bayern Munich and Argentina; World Manager, Gérard Houllier, ahead of Ottmar Hitzfeld and Sven-Goran Eriksson; and World Player, Michael Owen, beating Raul and Beckham.

These accolades climaxed our trophy-laden year of 2001. Now the objective was to make headway on the two major fronts, League and Europe. By December, the Reds had amassed a six-point lead in the Premiership but that had been frittered away by mid-January when they lay fifth, albeit only three points off the pace. They had also dropped out of the FA and League cups.

A spicy meeting at Old Trafford gave fresh impetus to their campaign. Bidding for a record 10th goal-scoring League match on the bounce, Ruud van Nistelrooy was backed every which way to hit the net and add to the Mancs' haul of 28 in nine matches. However, Liverpool's defence didn't give him a sniff, enabling Murphy to chip home for our fifth win over United in a row. Marvin Hagler, who held the world middleweight title from 1980 to 1987, had a motto, "Starve the doubt. Feed the faith", reckoning you were a loser in sport because you didn't believe you were good enough. Against United, Liverpool entertained no such reservations; they proved they were good enough.

After our Old Trafford belter, February brought more exhilaration as we routed Leeds 4-0 at Elland Road and Ipswich 6-0 at Portman Road. Having won seven of their previous eight games, the Tractor Boys were on a roll but Liverpool were different class, getting their goals through Owen (2), Heskey (2), Hyypia and new signing Abel Xavier.

George Burley, Ipswich's boss, conceded: "We were fortunate to get away with 6-0. It was men against boys in the second half. Liverpool were just phenomenal – Owen and Heskey were on top of the world."

Rodney Marsh, who was doing commentary for Sky Sports, declared: "In all my years, that has to be the closest thing to footballing perfection I have seen. Liverpool were brilliant in attack, superb in midfield, won every second ball, the defenders were brilliant and even the keeper made saves when he had to.

"It was just a brilliant, brilliant, brilliant display. It may have been six but it could've been 16."

With the Reds leading the Premiership again, they turned their sights on Europe, a 1-1 deadlock away to Galatasaray failing to bring the hellish reception promised to every team at the Ali Sami Yen stadium. In a reference to a Liverpool dance hall, visiting Scousers displayed a banner: "Welcome to Hell, my arse! If you think this is Hell, try the Grafton on a Friday night." That piece of advice now forms the backcloth of the Grafton's stage.

Next up were Barcelona, the sort of get-together worthy of an overseas trip and a chance to tick off the Camp Nou on my check list of stadia. A couple of mates, Stockport County nutter Steve Davenport and Red Cornishman Tim Ferrett, fancied coming along for the ride so we made all the arrangements and flew out.

Barcelona is a city and a club I have long admired and to understand what they both embody for the region of Catalonia, look back no farther than the Spanish Civil War. This began in 1936 when the military, led by General Francisco Franco and backed by the Catholic church and Establishment, sought to overthrow a democratically elected Left-wing government.

Pitting father against son, brother against brother, democrat against fascist, republican against royalist, regionalist against nationalist, Left against Right, the conflict went on to claim 500,000 lives, including Josep Sunyol, president of FC Barcelona, who was murdered by the general's soldiers in the Sierra Guadarrama mountains near Madrid.

Despite Hitler and Mussolini dispatching troops, bombers and munitions to aid their ally, Franco's army took three years to quell their republican foes in the peninsula, where Catalonia remained the principal stronghold of opposition until January 1939. Then fascist forces marched into Barcelona after a savage siege and instigated summary executions of so-called enemies of the state, the eventual death toll reaching 35,000 in the city alone.

Franco also exacted revenge on the region's culture. He banned books in Catalan and its use as an official language, prohibited the Sardana folk dance, made flying the Catalan flag a criminal offence and even changed the English name Football Club Barcelona to the Spanish Club de Fútbol Barcelona. Likewise, he punished the Basques, turning Athletic de Bilbao into Atlético de Bilbao.

Catalans and Basques have never forgiven Franco's tyranny. In 1964, the dictator marked the anniversary of his overthrow of democracy with billboards across Spain, stating "25 años de paz, 25 years of peace". In Madrid, Franco's capital, they were regarded with pride. In Catalonia, locals altered every one to read "25 años de paciencia, 25 years of patience". Their moment would come.

It did, in 1975: Franco was summoned by his maker to atone for his many sins and Catalonia secured regional autonomy. Its language, books, flag and folk dance were back – and the football club reverted to its original title.

My first inkling of Barcelona-Madrid hostility came after I hitch-hiked to the Spanish capital in 1966. Checking into a youth hostel, I asked the warden if he could recommend somewhere to eat, because people in Catalonia had told me meals could be pricey in Madrid. The Madrileño bridled. "Señor," he corrected, "you can eat a lot better and a lot cheaper here than in Barcelona." To prove the point, he forsook his desk and led me round the corner to a cheap and cheerful restaurant.

Against a background of civil war, the cities' football rivalry assumes a political, cultural and military dimension not found anywhere else in Western Europe. Catalan fans hate Franco's favoured club, Real Madrid, that symbol of fascist repression; supporters of the Merengues detest FC Barcelona, breeding ground of separatists and socialists.

Encapsulating Barça's emotional hold is their motto, "Som més que un club, We are more than just a football club". In shirts unblemished by any commercial sponsor, they represent a national team for seven million Catalans in the region, millions more who have emigrated to Latin America and the host of members of its 1,700 penyas, or supporters' branches.

For many of them, Spain are a "foreign" side and any Catalan playing for Madrid's selection is as disloyal as an Englishman turning out for Scotland.

Equally galling is the Champions Cup/Champions League table, since Real, "the best club in history", have won it nine times, compared with Barça's twice.

The manager who first broke the Catalans' jinx in the competition in 1992 was Johan Cruyff, El Salvador (The Saviour), who discovered politics were as important as tactics at the club, despite unprecedented honours at home and abroad. Eager to sign McManaman and Fowler in 1998, the Dutchman was informed by Josep Nuñez, the club president, that they would never meet Liverpool's asking price. Next, out of the blue, Cruyff read newspaper stories that Bobby Robson had been appointed to his job. Disregarding these, he drove to training at the Camp Nou where the vice-president, Joan Gaspart, banished him from the stadium with a contemptuous "You don't belong here any more".

Cruyff's contract had one week to run.

In spite of its chronicle of boardroom bloodletting, Barcelona is a rare entity, not owned by some faceless billionaire or distant multinational corporation but by 155,000 socis, or subscribing members, who run the club through elected nominees. They decide the budget, vote for or against the accounts, air their views on the team and bounce the president out if he's not delivering.

As a non-profit-making association whose excess income is ploughed back into the business, socis receive no dividends. As and when necessary, they dip into their own pockets, paying in 1957 for construction of the Camp Nou, or New Ground, which originally had a 150,000 capacity but was scaled back to 93,000.

Abiding by their socialist principles, socis have rejected proposals for a share flotation to raise capital, have spurned fortunes for shirt sponsorship and are planning to generate more revenue by building a leisure, entertainment and theme park on land next to the stadium.

Barça already possess one of Spain's biggest tourist attractions, the Camp Nou museum, which draws more than a million visitors every year, and on the afternoon of our European tie in 2001 my mates and I joined the queue of Catalan worshippers and Nordic tourists.

Inside, we lingered over a line-up of match posters dating back to the Twenties, one publicising a visit by Ilford of the English Isthmian League, but the trophy display was my must-see. Although Barça have been victorious in four Cup Winners and four UEFA cup competitions, seniority was given to the Champions League trophy, an inscription above it declaring, "La historia continua, The history continues".

And its chapters are not restricted to football. Facilities in the stadium complex extend to an indoor arena and ice rink, so the museum featured other sports: futsal, women's football, American football, baseball, basketball, wheelchair basketball, handball (Europe's crack team, with six European Cups), volleyball, rugby, swimming, roller hockey, field hockey, ice hockey, figure-skating, cycling and athletics (400 athletes in training). For older, retired supporters, Barça even has a thriving offshoot which organises social events, trips to away games and Catalan classes for non-speakers.

Som més que un club. That speaks for itself.

Having agreed the museum served as an excellent overture for that evening's main event, the three of us returned to our hotel off La Rambla to get ready for the game.

We were about to leave when I noticed Tim was going out in his LFC shirt. No jacket. My reaction: "If I were you, I'd cover up." Rather a coward than a punchbag for Catalan kick-boxers.

In point of fact, Tim had figured in a similar, but more menacing, precedent a few years earlier, while working on the outskirts of Los Angeles for a computer company. As he had no car, he used to travel by bus to the office and arrived one day in a Liverpool jersey.

A Mexican colleague was appalled. "Teem, Teem," he said. "No, no, no. They will keel you. Never wear red in the street. The Creeps will keel you."

The Creeps were the Crips, the blue-garbed street gang whose sworn enemies, the Bloods, could be distinguished by their red attire. For any Crip dawdling past the bus stop in his Dodge Ram, Tim's Carlsberg shirt would have been like a red rag to a bull, a brazen demand for a drive-by shooting.

In LA, Tim didn't wear his top again on the street. In Barcelona, he concealed his Liverpool jersey beneath a fleece.

Outside our hotel, we asked a taxi driver to drop us off at a hostelry not far from the Camp Nou and he conveyed us to a bodega, where we had a meal and a tincture or two. In Homage To Catalonia, George Orwell remarked: "How easy it is to make friends in Spain!" Well, Catalans are as warm as their Mediterranean sun and inside the bar we felt at home, chatting to matey locals, some of whom wanted us to win. Indeed, Tim thought the atmosphere was almost as convivial as in his local, The Cobweb in Boscastle, and that's saying something.

With kick-off creeping near, we set off.

As the three of us mooched in silence past the Miniestadi, or Mini Stadium, a modern 15,000-seat arena where reserves play, 50 or 60 teenage Catalans overtook us, flourishing scarves printed with "Barça O Muerte, Barça Or Death" and bawling a verse with puta, whore, in every line, doubtless a reference to Real Madrid.

Ahead, an interloper came around the bend, a Liverpool fan in red shirt and hat who sensibly took a wide berth into the road to avoid the gang.

Not far enough. One Barcelonista snotted him full in the face.

Hand holding jaw, the Scouser walked straight on.

What could he do against 50? And if Tim's top had been visible, he, and us, might have got the same treatment.

Through our turnstile, we found seats amid the Liverpool contingent at the top of a terrace overlooking the Gol Nord, lair of the Boixos Nois (Crazy Boys), Barça's hooligan firm. The rest of their supporters, those with some grey matter between their ears, are known as cules, or arses, after penniless youngsters who in past days would sit on a wall enclosing the ground, offering a row of backsides to passers-by.

From our specs, it was noticeable the stadium was not of uniform height all way round. It appeared like an enormous oval bowl tilted in a tectonic upheaval, its lowest side furnished with a narrow roof to shelter millionaires in their armchairs, rest of the arena open to the sun and rain.

Quite a venue. In 1981-82, average league attendances hit 100,000 when its capacity was increased to 115,000 for the World Cup, but now it has been reduced to a 98,800 all-seater, inciting a chant of "Shitty ground, shitty ground" from some Scouse comedians.

At the far end, surrounded by red and yellow flags, was a long banner bearing one word, "Almogavers", the 13th-Century Catalan knights who went into battle on foot against armies of cavalry and conquered large areas of the Mediterranean. A modern, political aspiration was publicised when, to chants of "Visca el Barça, Long live Barça" and "Visca Catalunya, Long live Catalonia", a poster was unfurled behind the goal, demanding in English, "Freedom for Catalonia". A message for Madrid and also King Juan Carlos, who was up in the presidential box.

Sun setting, floodlights on, both teams entered the white arena, with Barça in their traditional blue and scarlet jerseys which are believed to have been copied from Waterloo rugby club, since brothers Arthur and Ernest Witty, old boys of Crosby's Merchant Taylors' School, played prominent roles in founding the Catalan side in 1899.

Once the game kicked off, it developed into a cat-and-mouse affair, Barça probing and pressing, Liverpool absorbing and breaking. While their danger men, Rivaldo, Kluivert and tricky Saviola, got no change out of our defenders, we did create openings. From five yards out, goal gaping, Gerrard miskicked and then he outjumped their defence at a free kick, putting his header wide.

In the closing minutes, Baros came on as substitute and went on a mazy dribble across the edge of their box. With the Catalan defence spellbound, we bellowed for him to shoot but he took the ball too wide and, soon after, the referee blew for a goalless draw.

The local press had scorned Liverpool as 10 donkeys and Michael Owen. Now 11 donkeys had kept up with racehorses, 26 years after we'd prevailed over Barcelona on their patch.

While the Boixos Nois dispersed, sinister-looking riot police, faces masked by black scarves, kept us in our seats as Sammy Lee led the Reds' squad in their warm-down. Some 30 minutes later, we were allowed out to catch a bus to the Plaça Reial for a bevy.

Refreshed by this, Steve and Tim went back to our hotel but I elected for a nightcap in a bar next to the Boquería market where I picked over the bones of the match with a local called Joan (not someone awaiting a sex change operation, Catalan for John). I was sipping dark rum with Coke, so I bought him one and he reciprocated, toasting, "Salud y dinero y amor, Health and money and love". Then my new oppo inquired: "You like rum?"

I nodded.

"I can make rum," Joan continued. "Here, in this bar."

"Is that so? Prove it."

Joan, a David Bedford clone with ringlets of black hair tumbling down his head, was wearing a white T-shirt with Sitges in blue across the front. He flexed his right arm like a bodybuilder tensing biceps and, with the index finger of his left hand, made arcane signs on his elbow while whispering an unintelligible incantation.

He unbent his arm.

"Put your hand out," he instructed.

I did. Placing his fingers over my open palm, Joan rubbed the tips together. Drops of brown liquid fell into my hand.

I'll be jiggered!

"Try," he said.

I licked my palm and the liquid *was* rum.

"Again," Joan said. He repeated the procedure, bending his right arm and drawing symbols on the elbow with his finger.

Once more, drops of Nelson's blood fell from his fingertips into my palm. The impossible is not possible, yet I had seen and tasted it.

"How?" I had to know.

"I cannot tell you" was Joan's answer.

Several shorts later, from the bar's bottle, not Joan's digits, it was bedtime for me but, before leaving, I asked him: "Tell me the secret."

"Mira, look," he said, lifting the locks of black hair cascading over his right cheek. "You see ..."

Wedged out of sight behind his ear was ... a ball of cotton wool. "When you went to the caballeros, the gents, I wet it in my glass," he explained with a smile.

Crafty blighter. As he bent his arm and performed his incantations, my eyes focused on the finger describing cabalistic figures on his elbow. Meanwhile, the fingers of his right hand were squeezing rum out of the cotton ball, which then dripped into my palm.

A trickster bamboozling the gullible with sleight of hand.

Ignore the tatty old three-card trick – Joan is probably now making a fortune in Costa del Sol bars. You have been warned.

After the Barça stalemate, Liverpool were bottom of their group, on four points, while Galatasaray had five, Barcelona six and Roma seven. However, we could still qualify for the quarter-finals if we bettered the Italians by two goals at our place. A tough ask. Unbeaten for six months since losing to Real Madrid in the Champions League, Roma were Italian champions and top of Serie A.

The tie had a touching prelude as Gérard made his first appearance since the Leeds game and his lifesaving operation. Arriving unannounced at the ground at 5pm, he addressed the team: "I feel today will be something special, so I would like to be with you."

After both sides ran onto the pitch, he left the tunnel to a roar that resounded as far as Birkenhead and a chant of "Allez, allez, Gérard Houllier" split the night air as Roma manager Fabio Capello embraced him, leaving some Kopites with watery eyes.

From the instant of Le Boss's emergence on the touchline, the match was ours. Anyone would have judged the lads had been gorging on red meat for weeks as they went for the Italians' jugular. It took seven minutes to find it. Murphy was fouled in the box by Assunção; Litmanen coolly drilled the spot kick home.

On the bench, Gérard's face broke into a brief smile – until he remembered not to get too excited.

I Lupi, the Wolves, did not concede again until the 64th minute when, from a free kick, Heskey rose imperially to head in. An Anfield inferno illuminated the dark skies.

Before the tie, Roma ace Totti confessed how thrilled he was to be playing at Anfield, saying: "This is a temple of world football and I am dreaming of scoring a goal here."

He and his team-mates could not find the net, though, so the Reds went through to the quarter-finals. Afterwards, Capello admitted he had never seen Liverpool play with such aggression, while Thompson commented: "You could feel the passion rolling around the stadium. I know what it is like to play with an unbelievable force like that behind you. Anfield is still unique."

This night was up there with the best, and downcast Romans adopted the Spanish name for Liverpool, the Black Beast.

Now that Gérard was back, he revealed: "Some people said I should forget football. I replied I may as well stop breathing. Football is my oxygen, my life."

As he talked, he knew the medical facts: four out of 10 patients die within five years of open-heart surgery, six out of 10 within 10 years.

Given the uncertainties raised by Gérard's illness, Tommo had done well guiding our lads to the quarter-final and that proved their limit. After shading Bayer Leverkusen 1-0 in L4, Liverpool went down 4-2 in the BayArena where Xavier headed home and Litmanen scored through a superlative dribble and diagonal shot in the 79th minute to make the aggregate 3-3. Five minutes later, Lucio put the Germans through.

Some pundits had rubbished the Bundesliga side, who had lost only one home fixture all season and had already triumphed over Arsenal and Deportivo La Coruña. On the balance of possession and scoring opportunities, they were worthy victors and at full-time the travelling Kop chanted "Leverkusen".

A good League finish was now a must for Liverpool, who garnered 9 wins in their last 10 matches to gain second place, guaranteeing another tilt at the European crown and enabling Gérard to be positive in his end-of-term assessment. He stressed we had qualified with a month to go and lost just two out of 16 Champions League games.

Notwithstanding that, the euphoria of our trophy treble had been followed by the downer of a season without silver. We needed to win a premier trophy, the League or European title. We also had to have a better ground, one suited to the 21st Century. In May, Rick Parry announced plans for a 60,000-seat stadium in Stanley Park, which would retain the Anfield name while the old stadium would be converted into a public park.

This had to be our way forward. Much as we love Anfield, it is showing its age and you cannot stop progress. Take Bayern Munich. As I had seen, their Olympic Stadium was superior to most British grounds, yet they were transferring to the high-tech Allianz Arena. Meanwhile, over in the United States, American football clubs and college sides were demolishing impressive arenas built in the Seventies to replace them with even more modern facilities.

For years, Liverpool have trailed in the financial league and our only way of competing with Europe's best is to boost income, attracting more season ticket holders and increasing off-pitch revenues at a new Anfield.

Our heritage must be cherished but, as well as taking pride in the past, we have to build for the future. Rick Parry and the board were being far-sighted. However much it might hurt, we all had to share their vision.

* * * * * * * * * *

In successive seasons, we had finished fourth, third and second in the Premiership. Could we go one better in 2002-03?

Although our last League Championship had come in 1990, some people appeared to have forgotten our glorious record. Alex Ferguson, discussing the European Cup, said: "I think the history books tell you that Real Madrid, Bayern Munich, AC Milan and Ajax have all won it more than twice. We've only won it twice so that's an area we hope we can improve."

Kopologists remarked upon the omission of one multiple winner from his list. Bit odd.

An oversight? Judge for yourself from another comment. After Alan Hansen expressed the view that United's boss faced a challenge restoring Old Trafford's fortunes, Ferguson responded: "My greatest challenge was knocking Liverpool right off their f****** perch. And you can print that."

Gladly, Fergie, gladly. Don't you worry about that.

During the summer of 2002, Gérard tried to bolster his squad by recruiting El Hadji Diouf from Lens and Salif Diao from Sedan, both Senegalese internationals who arrived with substantial reputations. On his home debut against Southampton, Diouf netted twice. "Now you know more about him," Gérard told reporters. "He works his arse off. Actually, say, 'He covers the ground'. That sounds better."

In the European draw, the Reds had been grouped with Basle, Spartak Moscow and Valencia, the competition's surprise package. At their Mestalla stadium, coach Rafael Benítez said: "I have maximum respect for Liverpool but I have told my players they have to forget the Liverpool legend and concentrate on matters on the pitch."

Los Chés, the Lads, did just that, mauling us 2-0, while they won again, 1-0, on our patch. A formidable outfit, completely at ease with each other, they hogged the ball so intuitively that opponents were reduced to bemused onlookers. A team at its peak, one to watch.

The Reds bounced back, hammering Spartak Moscow 5-0 at Anfield through Heskey (2), Hyypia, Diao and another new boy, Bruno Cheyrou. In the return leg, Michael grabbed a hat-trick to make it 3-1, Spartak's first home loss to an English team.

Because they had only managed a 1-1 draw with Basle at home, Liverpool had to overcome them in Switzerland to reach the last 16 in the second phase. Trailing 3-0 after 45 minutes, the lads fought back gallantly to 3-3 but couldn't snatch a winner. One point behind the Swiss, they were out.

Now European manoeuvres were suspended, the Reds targeted a healthy spot in the Premiership. Ending a barren run of nine appearances without scoring in open play, Michael banged in a fine hat-trick against Manchester City, one day short of going a year undefeated at Maine Road. Then he pounced in the last minute against Chelsea to grab the points while Diao nicked the only goal at Elland Road to put us top of the League. However, during November and December, we hit an anaemic patch, taking three points from a possible 21 and slipping to fifth.

On Boxing Day, our opponents were Blackburn and, praying for a change of form, I motored north from St Albans for the festive fixture.

After a wee break at Hilton Park Services, I drove down the M6 slip road, by the side of which a bloke with a holdall was waiting for a lift. I stopped. Looking frazzled and dishevelled, he got in and informed me he was making for his mother's in Blackpool, for some Yuletide cheer to chase away a lonely Christmas.

A waiter by trade, he had gone down to Portsmouth because a mate held out the prospect of work. Once installed in his pal's digs, the Blackpudlian popped out to buy some food but, on return, found the landlord changing the door locks; his mate owed a packet in rent and had scarpered. Jobless, friendless and virtually penniless, the waiter was out on the street on Christmas Eve, leaving one escape route: hitch-hike back to Blackpool, a journey he managed as far as Birmingham city centre. There a copper directed him to a hostel with an empty bed.

He'd have been better off on a park bench.

That night in the dormitory, he hardly slept a wink because some very disturbed individuals were wrestling with diabolical spirits and, at dawn on Christmas Day, he fled to the tranquillity of the empty city.

With hardly any vehicles about, hitching to the M6 was impossible, so he trudged as far as the motorway where, cold and hungry, he spent Christmas Night under a bridge, sheltering from downpours. Next day, as more cars began moving around, he got a lift to Hilton service station where I picked him up.

On hearing I was going to watch the Reds, this sorry chap confessed he supported Leeds. A double-whammy: destitute and following a team diagnosed as an economic basket-case.

I dropped him off at Knutsford. While I cracked on to homely Anfield, he could try to reach the security of his mum's.

After parking in Pinehurst Avenue, my stroll to Anfield was the usual therapy on Boxing Day; a healthy treat after overdosing on food and drink, everyone in buoyant mood, children scampering along with mums and dads.

For some families, though, this was not an occasion for happiness and laughter. Around the Hillsborough memorial, as always at this time of year, a field of remembrance had blossomed and I contemplated "Kester Ball, 15" and the other names.

Never, ever, forgotten.

Our game with Blackburn finished 1-1, thanks to Riise whose goal was signalled by that perennial feature of Chrimbo on the Kop: amid the forest of arms hailing John's effort, a turkey drumstick was being brandished extravagantly like a cowboy's lasso. We still could not win but, back in the car, I reflected again on how Anfield is such a morale-booster. During November, December, January and February, the rain seems unrelenting, our cities are sombre and grey, daylight passes in a blink and Britons turn into duvet dwellers, pulling bed covers over their heads to keep out the cold.

For Reds, those months are always brightened by trips to L4, one of the most bracing elixirs on tap, a release valve we're so fortunate to possess.

In the media, Liverpool's rickety form was the topic of many column inches and much exhaustive analysis. While our rock-solid defence of the treble year had turned unreliable, the strikers were finding it difficult to score, main man Owen labouring and Heskey contributing little.

Tactically, we were one-dimensional and lacked creativity, since our charges of the Light Brigade down the middle failed to breech opposition resistance when width was required. The 3-3 Basle result that terminated our Champions League campaign had affected the squad more than anyone could have foreseen. Summer signings Diouf, Diao and Cheyrou had also not settled in and Djimi "The new Marcel Desailly" Traoré gave the ball away too often.

Worst of all, Houllier had lost his Midas touch, shuffling line-ups for no clear reason, apart from the creed of rotation, and allowing potential match-winner Litmanen to leave.

Giving his evaluation, Le Boss listed various negatives: our internationals from England, Senegal and Germany were still recovering from the previous summer's draining World Cup; Babbel and Hamann, two vital squad members, had been crocked; and we had lost an old pro who could alter the course of a game in a second, McAllister.

After this anatomical dissection of the team, papers saw in the New Year with stories about Gérard preparing to spend a £15 million war chest on fresh talent to stop the rot. Next day – Shock! Horror! – he informed the press he had no such plans.

To paraphrase Ecclesiastes, there's no new thing under the Sun.

Take my advice: Beware yarns that bellow "WORLD EXCLUSIVE!!!" and whose opening paragraph includes such words as shock, dramatic, stunning or, biggest giveaway, sensational. Hardly any story causes a sensation; in those exceedingly rare instances where it does, then the facts speak for themselves and sensational is redundant. So everyone should scorn this adjective as a ragged flag, waved in desperation to signal the last resort at the end of a wearisome day.

With the war chest story consigned to journalism's dustbin, Liverpool shaded Southampton 1-0 at the St Mary's Stadium in mid-January to clinch a first win in 12 Premiership games and end their worst League run for 50 years. The Saints were tricky opponents, not having lost on their own turf all season, but Heskey nicked it with his first League goal in four months. Another away success, 3-0 at West Ham, cemented the Reds' turnaround.

In the FA Cup, Crystal Palace had knocked us out, leaving the Worthington as our domestic target for silverware. Drawn against Ipswich, the tie appeared a shoo-in, although Dudek offered a chink of light. The previous Sunday, he had been at fault in two goals by Manchester United, raising expectations Chris Kirkland would replace him. Jerzy kept his spot and received a stirring reception at Anfield.

A Diao penalty resulted in a 1-1 deadlock with the Tractor Boys at 90 minutes, which extra time failed to settle, and the tie went to penalties. As the Sally Army was about to deliver lorryloads of sleeping bags, we won 5-4, prompting the team to whoop it up in the centre circle while Dudek slung his gloves into the Kop in gratitude for their support. Leaving the ground, I peered at my watch: 10.50pm, the latest I'd ever walked out of a match.

In the next round, Liverpool pipped Aston Villa 4-3 at Villa Park, moving into a semi with Sheffield United who took the first leg 2-1 at Bramall Lane. Back on home soil, the Reds resorted to another period of extra time to nab two goals without reply; they had reached the Millennium Stadium where Manchester United would be their opponents.

On paper, the Mancs were going to canter home, particularly as the Scousers faced a change of goalie. Kirkland, who had taken over from Dudek between the sticks, was robbed of his first appearance in a final by a cruciate ligament injury. Jerzy would turn out instead – to the glee of one Old Trafford fanzine which printed a front-page photo of Manchester players leaping around with a green and white Worthington Cup flag, beneath the headline, "News of Dudek's recall reaches the United dressing-room".

Well, oh, well. Liverpool soaked up early pressure, then turned the screw. Our first goal, a pile-driver from Gerrard, took a devilish deflection off Beckham's boot and arced over a despairing Barthez. Remember Greenhoff's jammy winner in '77? I do. What goes around comes around ...

The pain wasn't over for the Mancs. Be afraid, be very afraid, Michael is steeled to pounce.

Hamann, that meister of reading where the ball will be, positioned himself intelligently to nick it from Ferdinand and lay it off to Owen. With foot-to-the-floor F1 acceleration, he swept down on goal. A swing of his right boot and his arrow pierced United's net.

The Worthwhile Cup was ours and, to mark four exemplary saves, "dodgy keeper" Dudek was voted Man of the Match.

Once again, banners conveying Scouse wisdom were conspicuous in the Stadiwm y Milenium: "The distance between insanity and genius is measured only by success", "Our nation is Liverpool, our language is football" and, adorned with a painting of Michael, "A voice from above said to mankind – this shall be your gift".

What a gift. Victory over our pet adversaries on a perfect day, shared by TV audiences in 96 countries. Not only did we have the best team, best fans, best songs and best banners but we had also secured our seventh League Cup and 38th trophy, 10 more than the second-best club.

Amid the jubilation, hapless Kirkland was not forgotten. After the presentation ceremony, Gérard walked up to Chris and handed over his winner's medal.

"He said, 'This belongs to you'," the goalie revealed. "I was speechless. That gesture shows what kind of man he is and how much he thinks of his players. I'd played in all the games except one on the way to Cardiff and it was very hard to miss out. But for the boss to give me his winner's medal is something I'll never forget."

Naturally, United fans did not hang around, just like we wouldn't if we'd lost. As You'll Never Walk Alone boomed out, they left smartly, some to salve their bruised egos by singing In Your Liverpool Slum and that verse about building bonfires with Scousers on the top.

Long may they warble away. How reassuring to know our rivals need such ditties whereas we can't be fussed to make up any about them. For the greater their dislike, the more it tells you about our relative standings, the depth of their animosity dictated by the heights of our achievements. Heaven forbid that anyone should be apathetic to us; that would confirm the demise of the Mighty Reds. As George Bernard Shaw cautioned: "The worst sin towards our fellow creatures is not to hate them but to be indifferent to them."

Inferior clubs fulfil a primary function, too; just as Everest's scale and grandeur are accentuated by its subsidiary peaks of Nuptse and Lhotse, so Liverpool's prominence is underscored by lesser teams aspiring to its greatness. One Kop banner conveys this succinctly: "Above us only sky".

For Roy Keane, the defeat represented "a disaster". Wouldn't go that far, Roy. Scousers know the word disaster is reserved for far more serious issues.

No, I was just pleased our latest silver put more miles between us and them in the honours table. And as I've stressed to United mates ad nauseam, we need the other runners because otherwise there wouldn't be any race. Bear me out, Richard, Ken and Gordon. We all agree that without rivalries to fuel our passion, football would be very bland indeed. Barça and Real, Boca and River, Liverpool and the Republic of Mancunia ... what juicy pairings they are.

As consolation prize for third place in their European group, the Reds had been parachuted into the UEFA Cup where they disposed of Vitesse Arnhem and Auxerre through home and away victories. In the quarter-final, they met Celtic and a 1-1 result in Glasgow set us up nicely for the return. On our own patch, though, we just did not perform and the Bhoys got a brace to end our European travels, to the combined choirs' rendition of YNWA.

Now the lads had one aim: Champions League qualification, which relied on moving up from sixth in the Premiership.

On the M1 before the fixture with Leeds at Anfield, I passed a prehistoric Volkswagen Combi van, kiwi bird and NZ stickers on the rear.

Seeing its side painted with "Plan B" in large black letters made me smile. Perhaps Gérard's Plan B would put a smile on the Kop's face and our club in Europe's premier competition.

The Reds did resume winning ways with a 3-1 result that took them above Everton to fifth, a position they could not improve on despite four victories on the spin, including a 6-0 trouncing of West Brom at the Hawthorns. Owen nailed four of those to take his League total to 100.

In their last game, Liverpool had to beat Chelsea at Stamford Bridge to get into the Champions League. They went down 2-1, staying fifth and relegated to the UEFA campaign again.

The team's failings weren't difficult to diagnose. Even though they had the Premiership's best away form, home displays were substandard, bringing fewer victories than draws and losses and only 30 goals in 19 games at what used to be Fortress Anfield.

In attack, we relied too much on Owen. Someone had to supply more bullets and during the close season Houllier signed Leeds's Harry Kewell for that job.

Liverpool managed another stroke in the summer: the city was appointed European Capital of Culture for 2008, a fillip worth millions to Merseyside.

The West coast is the best coast because of its sunsets but when the panel of judges arrived at Lime Street, rain was pouring down, the sky was glowering and streets were empty, apart from people scurrying for shelter.

Our World Heritage city might have more public sculptures than anywhere except Westminster, the most listed buildings outside London and more Georgian houses than Bath but the dreary weather was not lending itself to positive first impressions for these strangers to Scouseology.

The judges were whisked off to Sacred Heart primary school in Toxteth where they asked the assembled children why their home town should be awarded this prestigious title. A forest of hands sprouted but, before he was singled out, a little boy couldn't contain himself.

"'Cos Liverpool's a brilliant city to live in," he yelled.

That comment registered with the judges. The voice of innocence was swaying the course of history.

****

When the Reds began pre-season games for 2003-04, a new banner trumpeted "18 League Championships, 4 European Cups, 1 Capital of Culture", yet once the League programme opened, our title aspirations were knocked as we lost to Chelsea, Arsenal and Portsmouth to slip into mid-table.

This poor form led to an alarming occurrence at Anfield. In December, we trailed from the 71st second against Southampton and never looked like grabbing an unwarranted win as it finished 2-1 to the visitors, our fourth home reverse.

What was abnormal was booing at half-time and full-time. How often has anyone heard that over the past 40 years? A rarity, but the crowd was aghast at the team's apathy.

Houllier had said his toughest challenges each week were post-match press conferences but during these he had been unfailingly patient and polite. Not for him the get-out clause used by one boss, ordering scribblers who posed awkward questions about multi-million-pound flops: "Go away and write your shite." So when Gérard addressed the media after our Saints upset, he was his habitually courteous self. However, his opening assertion that Liverpool should have won baffled listeners, although he did accept the team were going through "a difficult period", adding: "You just hold your head up."

After Le Boss had listed injured players such as Owen, Kewell, Finnan, Carragher, Baros and Henchoz, one reporter asked if he thought fans would be willing to swallow this explanation for mediocre performances. Gérard rose to the bait, referring to rumours the board had identified his replacement north of the border.

"OK, the supporters might not appreciate we have players missing but instead of just putting Martin O'Neill back in the picture, you in the media can portray properly what is happening," he said.

"My focus is my team. The chairman said something in his notes to shareholders last week that I've been saying all along, that our minimum aim has always been at least the Champions League, and you all said I'll get the sack if I finish fourth.

"So what? Listen, I've said enough. I've been fair to you and I've given you enough."

With that, he walked out. Very unlike Houllier.

For days afterwards, a media frenzy raged around the Reds, who were languishing ninth in the table, 16 points behind leaders Arsenal.

Everybody knew they had sustained injuries but the squad should be robust enough to cope. No, they were not delivering and our manager's stock response to setbacks, that he felt sorry for his players because they did not get what they were due, was wearing thin.

Form guide: Since Liverpool led the Premiership 13 months previously, they had won just 15 of 42 League fixtures. Yet Gérard had spent £113 million on players, several of whom had proved ill-fitted to the red jersey: for starters, Diao, Diouf, Cheyrou, Biscan, Traore.

Talking in general terms about football transfers, Alan Hansen said: "Whenever you're buying anybody, there's always an element of luck." Some of our recruits weren't just unlucky, they were bad, incapable of slotting in as cover for first-teamers. To make things worse, confidence and strength of will appeared wanting.

Liverpool had not sacked a boss for 50 years, but the buck had to stop with Houllier who let it be known he was irritated by criticism from former players such as Ian St John and Alan Kennedy, two of about 20 in the media. Among others plying their journalistic trade were Hansen, Tommy Smith, Barry Venison, John Barnes, Jan Molby, Jim Beglin, David Fairclough and Mark Lawrenson, who had consistently expressed admiration for Le Boss. Once Lawro went into print saying Gérard had gone as far as he could, judgement day was approaching. Now the Frenchman was walking through the wind and rain by himself, although a trophy would bring some sunshine. Bolton had already knocked Liverpool out of the Carling competition, Worthington's successor, when the Reds met Yeovil in the FA Cup in January. Even though the Glovers had been given substantial incentives, including hairstyles sponsored by local businesses, they could not manage an upset on their own turf.

A 2-0 victory allowed our lads to sidestep this banana skin and thwart the tabloids' craving for more fuel to throw on the "Houllier must go" conflagration.

Before the next round against Newcastle at Anfield, shown live on the BBC, disgruntled fans in the Centenary stand unfurled a poster: "Sort it out,

Houllier. Not good enough for Liverpool Football Club. No more expensive mistakes. We want the title."

A professionally made banner, I did wonder if a paper had helped pay for this message because, were the Reds to lose, its image would have filled back pages in every inquest story. Under-achiever Cheyrou spoilt this money shot, however, netting twice in a 2-1 win.

Now Soho Square's Cup lottery smiled on us again: Portsmouth on our patch in the next round. Despite Owen scoring in the second minute, Liverpool could not build on their advantage and Pompey nicked one in the second half to bring a tricky replay.

The outcome was what Kopites feared. After Michael missed a dubious spot kick, Portsmouth netted late on and we were out.

While pundits cranked up the heat on Houllier, one sicko's mental disorder took a nauseating turn. Overnight, someone in urgent need of psychiatric counselling sprayed, "Houllier, hope you die of Aids" on a wall at Melwood. Hope you, Mr Painter, got treated in time.

Liverpool's last possibility of silver rested with the UEFA Cup, in which they knocked out Olimpia Ljubljana and Steaua Bucharest through 4-1 and 2-1 aggregate victories.

The Thursday after the Portsmouth setback, they faced Levski Sofia in L4 where a 25yard Gerrard volley split asunder the Bulgarians' defensive wall. Immediately our captain legged it to the dugout to hug Le Boss. A bad week was ending and another deft goal, by Kewell, sealed victory.

In the away leg, a 4-2 victory put us into the next round against Marseille, who deserved a 1-1 draw at Anfield. Now the Reds had to win or achieve a 2-2 result in the Velodrome; they lost 2-1 and the trophy room's Brasso was back in its cupboard.

As in the previous year, Champions League qualification was now the sole priority for our lads, who had already captured one notable scalp, Chelsea, the side that scuppered our continental ambitions in 2002-03.

With Owen, Gerrard and Carragher out because of injuries, Heskey played like a man possessed at Stamford Bridge. When he whipped in a cross for Cheyrou to volley home, I kept schtum in the Shed End, although one Blues fan sitting behind did mutter in my ear: "You can clench your fists if you want."

Before the goal, residents of the Matthew Harding stand had been singing that tired taunt, "Champions League, you're having a laugh", so when full-time blew, the Scouse section had every right to go bonkers.

Liverpool's unexpected success, their first in 15 visits, ended seven defeats on the trot in SW6. Fifth in the League, it was time for the lads to grind out wins. Done! Just as McAllister had conjured up that last-gasp free kick winner at Goodison in 2001, so Hyypia directed a header into Wolves' net in the 92nd minute to grab the points at Anfield.

Another gratifying result came at Old Trafford. Gary Neville's scything tackle on Gerrard ticked all the penalty boxes and referee Mike Riley awarded a spot-kick that Murphy stroked home to earn victory.

Puzzlingly, this represented the first penalty scored against United on their own soil in 11 years. For background reading on this fact, which taxed the brains of statisticians, refer to Fergie's attack on intimidation of referees at Anfield, printed earlier.

Liverpool defeats of Middlesbrough and Birmingham guaranteed fourth place and a Champions League slot, without placating Houllier. The day before our last fixture, with Newcastle, he revealed the pressure he was under. "If people decide I'm not the right man in the right place, so what?" he asked the media at Melwood. "I am not important. I know it has been a rocky year – and I've heard and read that they want to go back to the 1960s and 1970s culture. Well, fair enough ... but not with me!"

Then he walked out ... again. Words can be swords and he was wounded but this untypical behaviour made speculation about his future even more feverish.

Against the Magpies, Liverpool played out a 1-1 stalemate, with Gerrard giving a wondrous display, capped by a 40-metre pass which Michael flicked home. Worth every penny for that alone.

At full-time, the players did a circuit of the pitch to the packed stadium's applause. It might have been a troubling season but the support from every corner of L4 was uplifting and you could tell the team appreciated it, although Gerrard, carrying his baby daughter, almost seemed an outsider. He waved, posed for photographs, but came across to me as preoccupied. Probably because the season had been a letdown.

Afterwards at the Windermere pub on Breck Road, the fans' consensus was they were glad the final final whistle had gone. If your team plays ugly and wins a trophy, that's acceptable. If it plays ugly and doesn't win anything, that's unacceptable.

For his part, Gérard lamented, "The draw with Newcastle was the minimum we deserved" – a verdict summing up his season – while he also termed qualification for Europe "a massive achievement". Sorry, mon vieux, that's the minimum to expect, as you have said.

By this time, supporters were facing facts. In his five-year plan, Houllier had spent £128 million on newcomers and recouped £45 million from sales, including £6.25 million for Heskey who had gone to Birmingham. Despite such expenditure, the Reds lagged 30 points behind champions Arsenal and 27 points above relegated Leeds. The team were stagnating.

In praise of Liverpool, Terry Venables once said: "There's a tremendous honesty about the club." Now that quality was required in spades by the board as it weighed up whether to say adieu to Le Boss.

Amidst all the conjecture, it was as plain as the birds on the Liver Building that our directors would be damned if they did and damned if they didn't but the uncertainty ended on May 24 when the guillotine fell on Gérard.

At a press conference, he admitted: "The reason we have agreed to part company is mainly because of the sudden excessive pressure on the board and myself. I thought it could be harmful for the players in next season's campaign and I also thought it could jeopardise their performance and achievement.

"The club comes first. I'm not here for myself, I'm here for the club. The club will always come first for me. I arrived here six years ago as a Liverpool supporter and I leave as an even bigger supporter. I may have left Liverpool but Liverpool will not leave me.

"The club is in my heart. It is one of the most fantastic clubs in the world. But the club needs to consider its roots and understand that it cannot always have a quick fix."

With these words, the French Kopite bowed out.

23
From Austria To Eternity

You can earn money or lose money but trophies are always in your history. That's what people remember.

– Rafael Benítez

ON June 16, 2004, Rick Parry welcomed Houllier's successor to Anfield – 45-year-old Rafael Benítez, former Real Madrid apprentice, health club manager and, most recently, architect of Valencia's rise.

After gaining a degree in physical education and a national diploma in football coaching, Benítez's curriculum vitae in the mid-Nineties had collected two noteworthy entries: youth team coach with Real and assistant to the manager, Vicente del Bosque. From the Bernabéu, he moved on to lead three Spanish clubs to success in each of his first years in charge: in 1997-98 he guided Extremadura to promotion from the Second Division; in 2000-01 he took Tenerife into the Primera Liga; the following season he piloted Valencia to their first Liga title in 31 years.

In 2003-04, his last term at the Mestalla, he landed the league once more and also the UEFA Cup, a double founded on an unyielding defence that conceded a miserly 26 goals, the Spanish champions' lowest for 30 years. With good cause, Los Chés were nicknamed "the crushing machine" because their bloody-minded intensity ground opponents down.

For Benítez to leave Real and Barcelona trailing in the honours race, exceptional flair was imperative, something that registered with Anfield's senior players who nominated Valencia when asked to pick the best side they'd encountered in the previous five years.

Addressing the media in L4, Benítez emphasised there was a lot right with the squad. "It's like a dream to join," he said. "Liverpool are the perfect club because we have very good players and very good staff. We need to work, we need to work well, we need to work hard and if we do that we will win."

Backing for the new hand on the tiller came from Phil Thompson who had left when Benítez arrived. "Things did need to be changed, without a doubt," he admitted.

The Reds had found a new manager, only their 11th since the war. Would they now lose their inspirational skipper? Driving down the M6 from the previous season's Newcastle game, I pondered on Stevie G's detachment during the parade at the end, reminiscent of Ray Clemence after the European Cup in Paris – on the periphery of the shindig. Next day, we read it had been Ray's last appearance for Liverpool. Could Stevie have had something like that in his thoughts?

Before England started their Euro 2004 campaign in Portugal, Benítez flew out to tell Gerrard, Owen and Carragher about his plans and to enlist their support. Despite this, as the tournament kicked off, tabloids published tales that Stevie had done a deal to join Chelsea for £120,000 a week.

Cynics say money doesn't talk, it bawls. Sometimes, though, it shouts so loud you can't hear it.

At the end of June, Liverpool summoned the press to a briefing from Stevie who announced he would not be quitting Anfield because he loved the club and its fans. London's *Evening Standard* had a different slant: He was staying because of threats to his family. Why didn't I think of that?

The media stirred things up again when Wayne Rooney, of Croxteth, Trafford and Effingham, penned a contract to tell his life story in *The Sun*, of all papers. How misguided. And he gets upset when some Kopites poke fun at "Fatboy Dim". Why give any excuse for yourself to be ridiculed?

Rooney's £250,000 deal led to widespread condemnation on Merseyside, which the tabloid sought to stem with an apology for its Hillsborough splash, saying it was "truly sorry", the false report was "the most terrible mistake in its history" and "we gladly say sorry again today, fully, openly, honestly and without reservation".

In response, Trevor Hicks told BBC Radio Merseyside he was not ready to forgive but he was prepared to accept an apology as the paper's first step towards making amends to the Hillsborough Families Support Group. If the HFSG approved *The Sun's* expression of regret, its managing editor had promised to campaign for victims. Now Liverpudlians waited to see whether editorial coverage would bear out his commitment.

In the Reds' pre-season friendlies, a 5-1 clobbering of Celtic in America sparked optimism that was bolstered by our first meaningful game, the Champions League qualifier against Austrian double-winners Grazer AK. Stevie G was on the mark with a brace of goals in their Arnold Schwarzenegger Stadium, putting us in a strong position for the return.

Friday the 13th of August brought news no Kopite could have predicted: Owen joined Real Madrid to "realise his ambitions". The question all hands asked: Did he jump or was he pushed?

Only a week before, he told the media negotiations about a new contract were going well and he expected to stay. Why had that changed?

The club's offer had been on the table eight months by the time Tony Stephens, the star's reclusive representative from the SFX agency, ended a six-month sabbatical. Nice work if you can get it. Then Stephens felt unable to enter into discussions straightaway because he was preparing his brief but Michael flew off to Portugal on Euro 2004 duty, after which came his annual holiday, delaying a settlement again.

All very confusing. Kopites wondered why everything had been allowed to drag on, like with McManaman. Could there be a hidden agenda?

Everybody in football knows Madrid are past masters in wily transfer dealing, ever alert to recruitment opportunities. One instance: at a UEFA banquet, club president Florentino Perez passed a serviette to Juventus's Zinedine Zidane on which he'd scribbled: "Do you want to play for Real?" Zidane wrote "Yes", passed it back and later signed for the Spaniards.

Papers carried well sourced stories that Owen had clashed with Benítez, who had pinpointed a clique of English players not complying with his squad ethic. Displeased with the way they stuck together in Melwood's canteen, he instructed them to mix more. Michael was one name mentioned, along with Murphy, who was soon transferred to Charlton.

The manager also let it be known he had no intention of building his team around Owen when other strikers such as Baros, Djibril Cissé and Sinama Pongolle were available. Put another way, no one had a right to play. Collective will took precedence over individual skill.

The boss's determination to impose himself was evident in a TV clip of a pre-season photo call, players lining up informally for the cameras at Melwood. With Benítez and Michael in the middle, the manager gave our striker a nudge, gesturing he should fold his arms like the others.

No question, the new man was imposing his authority, as he had done so forcefully at Valencia.

Take paella. For Valencians, this is sacrosanct, their daily sustenance, the dish they gave the world. That cut no ice with Benítez; for nutritional reasons, he limited it in players' diets. Sheer sacrilege for locals but, in the coach's eyes, an absolute necessity for his squad.

As Owen signed for Madrid, his fee was reportedly a snip at £8 million, meaning the Reds had lost another fortune on a star they had developed, again like McManaman. In 2001, when the Madrileños courted Michael, going public that they would love to sign him, Liverpool had put a £50 million price tag on his head. Now Stephens' sabbatical and all the other hurdles had cost us millions.

After his departure, Michael mentioned that as a plazzy, or plastic, Scouser, someone not born and bred in the city but adopted by it, he was not rated in quite the same way as Gerrard. Understandably so. Nonetheless, Anfield had seen the last of a prodigious goal-scorer, 158 in 297 appearances, and Kopites wondered who could fill his role.

In our first League fixture at White Hart Lane, Cissé offered a pointer, his crisp drive earning a draw that was applauded by Gérard Houllier, commentator at the game for French TV. Le Ex-Boss had forked out £14 million to sign the Auxerre forward.

Not that I saw much of Cissé's strike since my £42 seat came with a fully-fitted stanchion blocking the goal. On hearing this later in our office, a Chelsea wag commented that Spurs fans paid a premium for restricted views of their team.

For the Champions League return with GAK at Anfield, I wore my newest Liverpool shirt, "4 European Cups" on the back to remind the forgetful, although our listless display did not suggest that total would require updating by the campaign's close. After the Austrians nicked a goal, they grew in strength, keeping us on edge until the 90 minutes were up. We sneaked through 2-1.

This drab performance did not spoil the evening for one Kop virgin. I went to Anfield with an Austrian pal, Hans Schimmel, who supports Graz's other team, Sturm, and was backing the Reds. At the final whistle, no Kopite sang YNWA more lustily than he did.

Rightly, the 100-or-so Austrians gloried in their side's display but did not indulge in the shenanigans that blighted their derby with Sturm the previous March. Then, hormonal hooligans from both clubs, who share the Schwarzenegger ground, gained notoriety by using the stadium announcer to broadcast a ruck's time and venue.

During the match, Graz's George Sephton came on air, saying 10-year-old Brigitte should meet her mother outside a certain gate at full-time. Unknown to him, Brigitte was code for Brigata, or the Brigade, Sturm's ultras who wanted to commemorate the 10th anniversary of their inauguration by brawling with GAK's yobs, the mother.

As scheduled in this cryptic message, the rival packs locked horns in a brawl outside the appointed gate and forced the stadium to introduce a vetting system for future PA announcements.

Our struggle to hold GAK at Anfield did not bode well for the group stages. A 2-0 home victory over Monaco raised spirits that were rapidly deflated by a 1-0 defeat in Greece by Olympiacos and a goalless tie in L4 with Deportivo La Coruña, the previous year's beaten semi-finalists. Technically gifted, the Galicians were looking forward to three points at the

Riazor Stadium where only one English club had ever won. With – knock me over with a feather – Biscan playing a blinder, the Reds controlled the game and an own goal by Andrade put our campaign back on track.

Second in the group, we were on the brink of the knockout stages until defeat by Monaco meant we needed to blow Olympiacos away by two clear goals at Anfield to ensure qualification.

Plainly the Greeks hadn't read our synopsis. They got on the scoresheet first, through a Rivaldo free kick that prompted their 3,000 followers to belt out Jingle Bells, and by half-time they'd protected their lead, so our lads had to score three in 45 minutes to go through.

I couldn't see it happening.

Oh ye of little faith, see again.

Olympiacos boast one of the Continent's sternest defences, having conceded two goals in six outings, but within minutes of the restart substitute Sinama Pongolle cracks the ball in.

The Greeks, under the cosh, hold out until a quarter of an hour to go, when another sub, Neil Mellor, runs onto the park. His first act is to fire home, lashing in after the keeper pushes out a Núñez header.

As Kopites go ballistic, the lads turn the screw.

Four minutes remaining, Mellor heads on to Gerrard, arms aloft appealing for the ball.

From outside the box, our skipper unleashes a blistering half-volley that sends Anfield into orbit. A fabulous strike.

Bish, bash, bosh, one, two, three-one. We are through.

"I have not caught one as sweet as that for a long time," Stevie says. "That was one of the best goals I have scored." Amen.

Benítez praised our supporters, in his estimation the difference between the two sides, while next day the *Daily Telegraph*'s Henry Winter reported that Sven-Goran Eriksson viewed Stevie's thunderbolt over and over again on video. It was that good.

This breathtaking encounter provoked debate about the most memorable European nights in our Red bastion. Pour yourself a jug of jungle juice and brood over these contenders:

May 1965: Inter Milan, best side in the world, are destroyed 3-1 in the European Cup semi-final.

April 1966: In the Cup Winners' Cup, goals from Smith and Strong knock out Celtic, who had won 1-0 at Parkhead.

April 1976: After Bruges stun the Kop by taking a 2-0 lead in the first half, Kennedy, Case and Keegan turn the UEFA Cup tie on its head.

March 1977: In the second leg of the European Cup quarter-final, St Etienne are drubbed 3-1 and Liverpool are heading towards their first final.

November 1991: In the Cup Winners' Cup, Auxerre manage a 2-0 win over the Reds on their patch but Molby, Marsh and Walters bulge the net three times at Anfield.

March 2002: On Gérard Houllier's return to L4 after heart surgery, goals by Litmanen and Heskey against Roma put the lads into the Champions League quarter-finals.

December 2004: Requiring three in the second half against Olympiacos, the Reds do it with minutes to spare.

While Liverpool's European exploits were enthralling, their League form remained erratic. Against Bolton at the Reebok, they seemed ill at ease, possibly because new Spanish signings Xabi Alonso and Luís García were adapting to the formation. After a perfectly good goal by García was disallowed, the Reds went down 1-0, miring them in mid-table.

The fixture at Fulham showed how they could raise their game. Going two down before half-time, they bounced back to win 4-2, the first instance in 13 years that they'd come from behind to retrieve points away from home.

Before the Birmingham match in November, the fickle finger of fame was wagging away in the Centenary stand's car park, as a gleaming black saloon drew up and the sick-noted Smicer stepped out. People walked past with hardly a second glance – until Baros emerged through the other door. At once 10 autograph-hunters surrounded him.

I wondered why Milan wasn't already inside. He mustn't be fit. As Cissé was expected to be out for the rest of the season with a double leg break, the Czech remained our only top-class striker and we could toil to get goals.

Proceedings on the pitch bore that out, Liverpool wasting three or four good opportunities before the Brummies grabbed a goal in the closing minutes.

Rafa had no excuses. "We created many chances and did not score," he said. "Then we lose concentration for two seconds and that is enough. It was not bad luck."

A few days later, Emlyn Hughes died at the age of 57. During his Anfield career, he was the leader of a team that won two European Cups, two UEFA Cups, four League titles and one FA Cup. A flood of tributes testified to his stature but one in particular touched me. *The Echo* reported a fan as saying Emlyn would now be in Heaven signing 96 autographs – a wonderful image of a player whose commitment, desire and fervour have never been bettered by anyone with a Liver Bird on their chest.

Our departed skipper was respected throughout football and when a one-minute silence was announced before our next home fixture, Crystal Palace supporters broke into applause. A fine gesture by the South Londoners.

Liverpool won 3-2, following that up with an impressive victory over an Arsenal side who had only suffered one reverse in 54 games. During this purple patch, the Gooners had been in a league of their own and I suspected they would be a real test at our place. Once Alonso put us ahead, however, we called all the shots. Even though the visitors equalised with their sole attempt on target, our stand-in marksman Mellor unloosed a 25yard wonder goal to earn the points. Three seconds remained.

Next were Tottenham in the Carling Cup at White Hart Lane where Rafa put out a team of reserves, changing nine of the side that saw off Arsenal. The Academy lads did not let him down. Goalless after 90 minutes, Spurs scored in extra time, only for Kanouté to take leave of his senses, handling in the area. Sinama Pongolle equalised from the spot and also bagged the winner in a penalty shoot-out. Liverpool were in the semi.

Benítez understood where he was going and how to get there. "I know why I am here," he said. "It is not just to learn English but to win titles. That is my responsibility, that is my job and I am not fearful of the challenge. I know the history of this club. I know all the old glories in Europe and the passion of the fans. It is not a burden. It is why I left Spain to come to Liverpool. There are so many good things about this job. We will try to change matters that are not good enough for this club, pick up on the good things done by the last manager and strengthen others.

"I am very young as a manager but I have a lot of experience. The most important thing is that I am not afraid of what must be done. Each day I am learning."

Don Rafa's Anfield education had brought three exceptional victories in the fortnight straddling November and December: Arsenal in the League, Spurs in the Carling Cup, Olympiacos in the Champions League. Deliberating on this good run, Hyypia said the squad was now fitter and more disciplined, with a stronger team spirit, aided by roommates swopping around on away trips to get to know each other better.

This fitness and bonding continued to pay off over Christmas and New Year, a period of four wins and one defeat when Chelsea nicked a goal during final knockings. Liverpool outplayed the Londoners in L4 and should have had a penalty for Tiago taking the lace out of the ball but the referee was looking elsewhere. Another downer came after Frank Lampard clattered Alonso rather unfortunately, causing a fractured ankle. Our playmaker would be out for months.

Because of his casualty list, Benítez had to call upon the Academy again for the FA Cup tie at Burnley where the youngsters could not replicate their Spurs success. They went down 1-0, a reverse compounded by a 2-0 Premiership defeat at Southampton.

After that, the national press had a field day, knives flashing in the morning light, and one *Daily Mail* scribe filleted the Reds, "the worst Liverpool of the past 40 years". Now the second leg of our Carling semi with Watford took on added significance: having nosed ahead by a single goal in L4, Rafa would be shredded if we lost at Vicarage Road.

A Stevie Wonder effort blunted the backpage hacks' blades and sealed our third Cardiff appearance in five years. The downside: another player out, Sinama Pongolle.

Throughout the 90 minutes, hardcore Kopites who travel everywhere – Southampton on Saturday, Watford on Tuesday, Charlton the following Saturday – championed Rafa's cause, songs and chants telling the media how they rated him. Do any other fans stick up for their manager like we do?

On and off the terraces, the match took place in a good spirit, and Hornets supporters did not descend to that refrain synthesising poor personal hygiene, place of origin and state of illegitimacy. Normally so stale, this tedious perennial brought laughter to one game in which a member of the Hayes team from Middlesex was fouled by an opponent from Stevenage in Hertfordshire. "Dirty Northern bastard," screamed the Hayes crowd.

Praise be we English haven't plumbed the depths of fans in China who go way below the belt with their wounding chant of "You have no manners and are of low culture".

No, Watford's crowd were gracious in defeat.

Our opponents at the Millennium Stadium were Roman Abramovich's cash-rich Chelsea, informed by Red banners that "Your dreams are our reality" and "Money can't buy history, heart, soul". To encourage Rafa's compatriots, there was also "Nunca andan solos, You'll never walk alone".

Expecting the lads to repeat their ascendancy over the Blues at Anfield, my Carling scenario was given a perfect opening in the first minute: Riise volleyed home. After that, the lads sat back too much, conceding possession and inviting Chelsea to attack, although we did miss out on another penalty when Stevie G was flattened.

Inevitably, the Blues got a goal, the ball skidding off Gerrard's head to send the final into extra time. We ran out of puff, the Blues collared two more goals and the cup was lost, despite a late Núñez reply.

If this had been a contest between rival fans, it would have been a walkover for us. Cardiff council technicians measured the volume of our support as a world-record 131 decibels, the loudest crowd ever officially certified. On the pitch, however, the better side had won; fitter, more skilful, more tenacious.

Now Rafa had to settle for a twin-track approach, plotting Liverpool's progress in their European campaign while aiming for a top-four berth in the Premiership, to guarantee Champions League qualification.

On the domestic front, the team's form was consistently inconsistent, at turns exasperating and exhilarating. Take the game with Birmingham at St Andrews, what should have been a banker draw. The Reds lost 2-0 and well before full-time the Railway End emptied of Liverpudlians, deserting one of our worst displays, up there with that 2-0 failure at Southampton.

Yet, against Everton at Anfield, the dominant, potent Liverpool clocked on. The Blues, who had been fourth in the League all season, could not cope with the intensity and high tempo, going down 2-1. If the Reds reproduced that form more steadily, they'd be getting stuck into the top three of Chelsea, Arsenal and Manchester, instead of lying fifth.

At least in Europe, Rafa, the self-styled loner with a laptop, was getting his control commands right, despite a system overload of injuries and fixtures. The draw for the first knockout stage had pulled out Bayer Leverkusen and, before meeting them in L4 at the end of February, Liverpool had played 14 times since the Germans' winter break, compared with their six. In mid-December, Leverkusen drew 1-1 with Borussia Mönchengladbach, then took a Christmas and New Year holiday that dovetailed with eight days' recuperation in the Canaries. Bundesliga sides know how to protect squads from burnout.

By chance, Liverpool had no game the weekend before the home leg, so they managed a few days' rest, which must have helped them. On the night, they were irrepressible, rattling in three – a García strike and free kicks from Riise and Hamann – and leaving Leverkusen in disarray until a late Dudek fumble gave the Germans a lifeline for the return.

This result, best of all the European ties, was a slap in the face for analysts who maintained Liverpool were a one-man band, Gerrard FC. Our talismanic captain was suspended and the victory could be added to statistics proving we won more matches without him than with him. The same could be said when Michael Owen was at Anfield.

The night before the second leg in Germany, a familiar face entered Jameson's Irish bar in Cologne while hundreds of Scousers were taking the waters and watching AC Milan v Manchester United on TV.

Since his hotel telly was featuring a German game, Rafa Benítez was looking for somewhere to see Chelsea's clash with Barcelona. "It was like Jesus walking into a room," one Kopite said, as word of this visitation spread. What joy for the fans, particularly as, minutes after Rafa's entrance, Crespo dumped the Mancunians out of the Champions League. That set the seal on a hooley captured for posterity on cameras and mobile phones.

All those years ago during my *Echo* phase, I had a colleague, Martin Noot, who lived down Ullet Road. On my first visit to his flat, I was fascinated to see one living room wall was masked by a poster, some 20 foot across, printed with a Nietzsche quote in giant letters: "Life is a fountain of delight but where the rabble drinks, the wells are poisoned."

With all due deference, dear Friedrich Wilhelm, any Kopite worth his salt would have crawled buck-naked across 1,000 yards of the Cast-Iron Shore, shunning barrels of free booze served by bevies of buxom barmaids, to join the Red rabble in Jameson's. Do you honestly believe a single one of those present would have preferred to be in the plush Hotel Excelsior, sipping Singapore slings and schmoozing with UEFA's top brass?

Rafa's presence in the Irish bar turned on a fountain of proletarian delight that would lubricate yarns and irrigate Merseyside folklore for ages. I rest my case of Kölsch bier.

Since Dudek had gifted that late goal to the Germans on our patch, some disquiet had crept in about the return, especially as our walking wounded included a fresh casualty. Mellor had been ruled out for the rest of the season, the fifth squad member to sustain long-term injury, along with Cissé, Kirkland, Alonso and Sinama Pongolle. Add other players unavailable during the campaign – Gerrard, Baros, Smicer, García, Núñez, Finnan, Kewell and Josemi – and that made a grand total of 13, *of whom 10 required surgery*. We really couldn't afford any more casualties, on the pitch or in training.

Have no worries. In Leverkusen, in the season's most important fixture, the lads delivered a really professional performance, as García (two) and Baros (one) gave us a 6-2 aggregate victory over a side that had topped their group, putting three past each of Real Madrid, Roma and Dynamo Kiev. So the BayArena boys were no mugs but, despite losing to Liverpool, they were magnanimous enough to play YNWA on their Tannoy system and both sets of fans sang it together.

The Reds' display and Rafa's tactics brought fulsome praise. On the subject of our manager, Rick Parry commented: "We've all been very impressed. He has demonstrated all the qualities we thought he had. He's had rather more injuries than he might have expected, but the thing I like about Rafa is he's focused on the things he can influence and doesn't worry about those he can't.

"He's tough, he's resilient, he's ambitious, he's young and he is very, very hardworking." As one of Benítez's favourite Spanish proverbs puts it: Luck is in love with hard work.

The European quarter-final produced a pairing that could not have been laden with more emotion. Twenty years after that black night in Brussels,

Liverpool and Juventus were drawn against each other, an opportunity seized upon by our directors to salve past wounds and turn over a new leaf with the Italians.

Before kick-off at Anfield, supporters from both clubs carried a poster bearing the names of Heysel's 39 dead and "Memoria e amicizia, In memory and friendship" onto the pitch. A minority of Juve tifosi turned their backs, holding up an insulting finger and whistling You'll Never Walk Alone. One banner in Annie Road proclaimed the culprits: Drughi, the Droogs, now ruling the Stadio delle Alpi home end after a vicious head-to-head with their fiercest adversaries, the Fighters.

While a minute's silence was held for the Heysel victims and Pope John Paul II, who had just died, Kopites formed a mosaic, "Amicizia, Friendship", which most visiting fans clapped. They weren't all Drughi. However, the gesture that moved me came when someone held aloft "Martina Vive, Martina Lives", in tribute to someone who had passed away. Yes, she lives, like the memory of Heysel's dead must live on.

Despite the Drughi's snub at Anfield, I felt our club had done its best to extend the hand of reconciliation. Now we had to beat Juve over 90 minutes, a daunting task given that they had turfed out Real Madrid in the previous round and conceded only two goals in eight ties, earning the accolade of Europe's meanest defence.

Beforehand, their coach, Fabio Capello, said: "Anfield's atmosphere is so special." Never a truer word. The second the whistle shrills, Liverpool loose off a cyclone of attacks on the Zebras, who succumb twice.

What a start! Hyypia sends the crowd delirious when he slams a scorching volley in and then García loops an outrageous 30-yard shot over Buffon.

A Tornado jet breaks the sound barrier *inside* the Kop.

Liverpool two ahead, Juve wobbling.

Digging deep, the Italians pull themselves together but fail to capitalise on a couple of chances until after the break, nicking a goal when stand-in keeper Scott Carson does not snaffle up Cannavaro's soft header.

The Bianconeri cannot draw level, though, and Walton Breck's low-flying Tornado is back the instant full-time blows.

Little surprise that afterwards Del Piero tells Italy's media that the crowd's blood-andthunder passion has astonished him.

Spare a thought for one Liverpool fan. Martin Johnson, England's Rugby Union legend, possessed a ticket but found out he had another engagement that night. A charity do, he couldn't let them down so had to give Anfield a miss. Was he mortified when he heard about this humdinger of a collision.

The away goal put the Italians in good mettle for the second leg. Now a single goal would put them through and they'd won 11 of 42 matches during the season by that margin. All well and good, but if you don't have the ball or space to use it, you can't put it in the net.

In the Stadio delle Alpi, the Reds deployed a five-man midfield, retaining the ball, harrying and harassing, starving the Italians of goal openings, so Dudek was only called into action halfway through the second half.

Having stifled their opponents, Liverpool upped the pace and could have scored. They didn't but a clean sheet put them into the semi.

This immense result against Serie A's joint leaders astounded Europe and set off another debate about where it stood in the rankings of our away feats on the Continent.

We've already nearly come to blows over the best Anfield nights, so let's keep this one short and cordial: the 1-0 defeat of Barcelona in the UEFA Cup in 1976, the Catalans' first and only loss to an English club on their own patch; Benfica's 2-1 dismissal in the European Cup in 1978, ending their 46 games without defeat in the Stadium of Light; Benfica losing again on home soil, 4-1, in the European Cup in 1984; Owen's brace in 2001's UEFA Cup, halting Roma's season-long unbeaten spell. For me, though, the winner must be the 1984 European Cup final defeat of Roma in their own stadium.

Against Juve in Turin in 2005, Liverpool had refused to be intimidated and every Red was a colossus. Take Alonso. Since breaking his ankle in January, he hadn't turned out for the first team for three months but he still completed 90 minutes in the Stadio delle Alpi. Take Cissé. Six months after a double leg fracture at Blackburn that could have ended his career, he came on as substitute.

An injury-ravaged squad's sheer professionalism and lion-hearted defending had nullified one of the Continent's most formidable teams. From now on, we feared no one.

In the semi, the Reds were drawn against Chelsea, who'd already defeated us three times, twice in the League, once in the Carling Cup. All narrow losses, we were due a victory that would send us to the showpiece European final in Istanbul.

It all depended which Liverpool turned up on the night for the first leg at Stamford Bridge. Say no more. The tenacious, resolute Reds constructed an unbreachable defensive wall that secured a goalless draw and set them up nicely for the return.

Few matches have aroused such expectancy as the second leg, a monumental clash that has every Kopite licking his lips.

A spare is as rare as a diamond in a coal scuttle, and one fan stomps forlornly along Walton Breck Road, holding a placard adorned with a photo of a big-breasted blonde and the offer, "One night with my wife for a ticket".

Emission impossible, cock.

In Chelsea's dressing room, José Mourinho plays his trump card: he writes 33 in large red letters on the white tactics board, a reminder to his newly crowned Premiership champions of the points gap with Liverpool. That should gee them up.

Think again. Roman Abramovich might have spent £280 million on his squad but money is no substitute for human spirit. One dole-drawer on the Kop sees the social benefit of the Russian's billions, flourishing a banner, "Roman's taxes pay for my giro", and another pleads, "Make us dream."

You got it.

When both sides come out, the rafters are rocking to a noise that blows everyone away, including hardened hacks more used to dozing off at the Highbury library, Old Trafford theatre or Stamford Bridge bank. Every side of the stadium is jumping and it takes just four minutes for a new Krakatoa to erupt in L4.

As Baros pursues a subtle flick-on from Gerrard, our striker is flattened by Chelsea goalie Cech, leaving the ball to bounce free. García is nippiest, flicking it into the net where Gallas belts it back out.

Has it crossed the line?

Without hesitation, the linesman indicates: Yes.

Anfield establishes a ground-shaking high on the Richter scale.

That first goal is a vital breakthrough which the Londoners' protests cannot quash. Inane appeals. If it hadn't stood, there should have been a penalty and a sending-off for Cech.

The Fields of Anfield Road thunder out as Liverpool dig in to protect their lead, soaking up pressure, tackling with body-shattering bite, surging into attack.

Given an earful by Mourinho at the break, Chelsea try to raise the tempo, stroking the ball around smartly but failing to worry Dudek who only has one serious save to make. At the other end, Cissé can't take advantage of two chances as the clock winds down.

With seconds to go, our ordeal isn't over. An incomprehensible six minutes' extra time is announced.

No way!

As watch hands freeze, Eidur Gudjohnsen wastes a chance to snatch victory, firing wide from an angle.

Relief, head-holding relief.

After that miss, the lads cling on, the ref signals full-time and the ground exults like it hasn't since St Etienne. A tsunami of sound hurtles around the cosmos, segueing into You'll Never Walk Alone from every corner of the stadium.

The final whistle is too much for one commentator covering the tie for

Spanish TV. Michael Robinson, now the Castillian counterpart of Alan Hansen, screams with joy, then dissolves into tears.

As the crowd gives full throat to its spine-tingling YNWA, Mourinho shakes hands with most of our players and applauds the Main Stand before going down the tunnel. "I felt the power of Anfield and it was magnificent," he is chivalrous enough to say.

The atmosphere inside our Red citadel has stupefied Chelsea's captain, John Terry. "The Liverpool fans were amazing," he admits. "I have never heard anything like it before and I don't think I ever will again. I walked out into that cauldron and heard that singing and saw that passion. The hairs on my arms were standing up."

A conditioned reflex. People in the crowd felt as though they had been rapt in a force field, an electromagnetic charge that made them tingle. And if our lads fought like electrocharged lions, then Carragher reigned as king of the pride. A huge presence, he never shirked last-ditch tackles, ignoring the risk of a yellow card keeping him out of the final.

Mention must also be made of Didi Hamann, who returned after six weeks out through injury and sweated blood for the cause. Courage and character had won the day.

Having caught their breath again, veteran reporters from across Europe agreed the semi had been football's ultimate encounter while Carragher stressed the cardinal factor: "You can't buy fans like ours."

Twenty minutes after the game, a lonely figure walked across the pitch; Michael Owen making his way to the Main Stand from ITV's studio at the Annie Road corner where he'd been guest panellist. He had quit Liverpool to win the shiniest silver with Real Madrid but Juventus had turfed the Galácticos out of the Champions League. Meanwhile, his former club had reached the final with AC Milan, setting off alarm bells from the Atlantic to the Urals.

On an internet message board, someone in Sevilla warned: "Europa tiembla, vuelven los Reds, Europe's trembling, the Reds are back." Yes, whisper those dreaded words, Liverpool are back, and I wanted my brain back, too. For days afterwards, The Fields of Anfield Road was swirling around my head.

Even though they were finalists, the lads still had to secure their place in the following season's Champions League, some ambition given their schizophrenic behaviour on the domestic front. Routinely Jekyll and Hyde FC had been trailing the top four in the Pemiership and they couldn't improve on this, finishing fifth.

Blame it on our away form. During their travels, the Reds lost 11 matches, including defeats by Crystal Palace, Middlesbrough, Birmingham City,

Manchester City and Southampton, a sorry return that had to be compared and contrasted with a Continental campaign that had taken us to the final.

Now Kopites were organising their big trip to Istanbul where their unique qualities would be on show once again to the rest of Europe.

Why has the Kop become so celebrated? Why do fans across the planet associate this terrace with songs, wit and banter? Why has this stretch of concrete spawned such remarkable supporters? Why do they have a character all of their own?

Any analysis must focus on one trait, a finely honed sense of humour. Take a couple of mates when they bump into each other. Invariably their opening duologue goes along these lines:

First Scouser: "How're you diddling?"

Second Scouser: "Fine."

First Scouser: "Wife, kids, all right?"

Second Scouser: "Great."

First Scouser: "Heard this one? There's this magician, from Tuebrook, working on a cruise ship. Audience is different every week, so he does same old tricks, every show. Only problem is the captain and his parrot have to sit through the shows. After a couple of weeks, the parrot begins to understand how the magician's doing his tricks.

"Once it cottons on, it keeps shooting its mouth off during the show: 'Look, the rabbit's in his coat' or 'He's hiding flowers under the table' or 'Watch out, all the cards are ace of spades'.

"Magician can't say anything – has to bite his tongue because it's the captain's bird.

"Then, one night, middle of the Pacific, engine-room boiler overheats, explodes, blows a hole in the liner's side. In minutes, it sinks, drowning everybody on board.

"Obviously the magician's got a last trick up his sleeve. Ends up floating on a plank. Next thing, out of the sky, flutter, flutter, flutter, parrot lands on the plank.

"Magician looks at it, hate in his eyes, but doesn't say a thing. Parrot stares back, without opening its beak.

"This goes on, one day, two days, three days. Finally, fourth day, parrot's had enough. Squawks at the magician: 'All right, give up. Where've you hidden the ship?'"

Accept a joke like this for what it is: a present any Liverpudlian enjoys giving on a daily basis to whomever he may meet. In a city where everyone regards himself as a comedian, one of the most flattering references you can give any mate is "He's a good laugh" and this ability to amuse, this tonic of story-telling, has sustained Merseyside through its darkest moments, sparkling like a gem in the blackness of the Second World War and the postwar decades of decay and dereliction. One invaluable asset.

As evidence of that ability to provoke laughter, consider the rich lineage of comedic talent from Liverpool and its environs: Billy Matchett, Will Hay, Robb Wilton, Arthur Askey, Tommy Handley, Ted Ray, Ken Dodd, Jimmy Tarbuck, Faith Brown, Norman Vaughan, Tom O'Connor, Stan Boardman, Russ Abbot, Freddie Starr, Alexei Sayle, Kenny Everett, Johnny Kennedy, Les Dennis, Billy Mucho, Johnny Hackett, Jackie Hamilton, Stevie Faye, Pauline Daniels, Micky Finn, Mick Miller, Jon Culshaw, Paul O'Grady, Pete Price, John Bishop, John Martin.

A Comic Relief study unearthed the fact Liverpool has nurtured more comedians than any other city, confirmation that laughter is ambrosia for any Scouser. And boy can you miss it. When a journalist pal, Maurice Simms, emigrated from Merseyside to Toronto, as well as the harsh winters, he had to put up with the absence of humour in everyday life. "I miss the laughter," he told me. Whereas acquaintances here usually had fresh jokes to tell, Torontonians did not share this genetic compulsion to entertain.

Not just mates or neighbours want to put a smile on your face; my mother passed on funny stories she'd been told by the milkman or postman. The entrepreneur who parked his van, the mobile, outside her flats and sold groceries to residents was a case in point.

As well as serving her with sugar and milk, he'd supply a joke. Like the one she told me about a Liverpudlian who walks into a boozer, orders three pints, sips each glass until they are all empty and requests three more.

Intrigued, the barman asks why he's doing this.

"I've got one brother in Canada, another in Australia," the Scouser says. "We've agreed to have a drink together every Saturday. At this time they're both having three pints too."

The barman reckons this is a brill idea and over the next few months pulls three pints whenever the brother walks in.

One Saturday the brother asks for just two pints. "I'm sorry," the barman says. "One of your brother's died?"

The Scouser shakes his head: "No, they're both fine. I've just given up drinking."

Ignore the quality of the tale – recognise the wellbeing induced by making someone chuckle. Yet this fondness for jokes isn't a Liverpudlian's sole blessing. He has two other godsends – a passion for football and a love of music.

Chuck those into the Kop blender and, along with sportsmanship, you have components for the globe's most fabled terrace. Here are some examples of its anarchic humour and choral creativity, culled over the years:

● In April 1964, during Merseybeat's heyday, the BBC filmed a Panorama special about Liverpool, dispatching ace reporter John Morgan to Anfield for the Arsenal match. If the Reds won, they'd be champions again.

Everybody knew this documentary was being made and minutes before kick-off, as Morgan stood at the Kop end doing his introduction to camera, the crowd was ready. "ITV! ITV! ITV!" they chanted.

Once that died down, Morgan repeated his opening, until Kopites struck up with a refrain the Beeb did not wish to hear: "Ee-aye-addio, we haven't got a licence."

Morgan cracked off laughing.

As the Kop opened its catalogue of Beatles hits, the Beeb's man said "the music the crowd sings is the music Liverpool has sent echoing around the world" and quoted Wellington's reaction to his soldiers before the Battle of Waterloo: "I don't know what they do to the enemy but, by God, they frighten me."

The Reds went on to clinch the title with a 5-0 spanking of the Gooners.

● In the Fifties, an attempt was made to have organised singing with a brass band before kick-off but Kopites refused to join in, greeting every song with the comedy hit, Yes, We Have No Bananas. The band were given their marching orders.

● When Liverpool played Derby in 1963, a clash of heads left one County defender semiconscious on the grass, so the trainer dashed on and pulled him to his feet. The Rams man was groggy, collapsing into the trainer's arms and giving the Kop its cue for a Beatles hit appropriate to their clinch: "He loves you, yeah, yeah, yeah."

● During the Sixties, cashiers would carry match takings in wooden boxes along the cinder track to the Kemlyn stand. Every Saturday, conflicting chants of "Open the box!" and "Take the money!" rang out, references to Take Your Pick, a TV quiz show in which contestants could win a key to open one of several numbered boxes containing mystery prizes or alternatively to be sold for cash to the presenter, Michael Miles.

● In the European Cup semi with Inter Milan in 1965, a children's rhyme was adapted to remind Helenio Herrera, the Italians' manager, about our goals. Instead of "One, two, three, O'Leary", Kopites chirruped, "One, two, three, Herrera".

● During the 1966-67 European campaign, the visitors to L4 were Romanian champions Petrolul Ploesti, who, as their name signified, came from the oil-refining city of Ploesti. Coincidentally, an advertising campaign had begun on British telly with a distinctive jingle, "The Esso sign means happy motoring", and once the Reds had grabbed a brace of goals, the Kop tweaked this into "The Esso sign means happy footballing".

● In December 1967, Liverpool were leading Leeds 1-0 when Gary Sprake, United's keeper, swept up the ball during an attack. Since it was wet, he opted to throw out, rather than kick, but as he swung his arm, he changed his mind about the spot to aim for. Halfway through the fling, he sought to abort it.

Too late. The greasy ball shot out of his hand and into his own net! The Kop had its response ready: their cover version of Des O'Connor's hit, Careless Hands.

● The 1967-68 season brought a new marksman to Anfield, Tony Hateley, who signed from Chelsea for £96,000 and began with a bang – eight goals by mid-September. Then he entered a barren spell, incapable of even arousing an "Oooh!" from the crowd for a near-miss. In November, though, Liverpool faced Munich 1860 in the Fairs Cup and when Tony scored in the ninth minute, Kopites rejoiced with "Have we told you Hateley that we love you / Have we told you Hateley that we care". The Reds finished up 8-0 winners.

● That same season, Liverpool played Walsall in an FA Cup tie which could have been postponed because of fog so thick you couldn't see beyond the halfway line. Once the game did kick off, the Reds went ahead at the Annie Road end, although the Kop were unable to make out the marksman. "Annie Road, Annie Road, who scored the goal?" they asked.

From out of the pea-souper came a chant of "Tony Hateley, Tony Hateley", to which grateful Kopites responded with their adaptation of a Scaffold tune: "Thank you very much for the information."

● In the Sixties, Leeds's Jack Charlton was an old foe and Kopites knew how to celebrate his physical hallmark. To the tune of Al Jolson's Mammy, they belted out: "Charlton, Charlton, I'd walk a million miles to the end of your neck, Charlton."

● During another clash with Leeds, a tussle between Smith and Terry Yorath resulted in Tommy being heaved to the ground. Seeing red, he was on the point of getting stuck into Yorath when a pork chop struck his back, thrown by a Kopite who shouted: "Here's your dinner, Smithy. Leave him alone."

● In 1974, Dennis Law, who Shanks had nurtured as a lad way back when at Huddersfield, announced he would retire at the end of the season, so the Kop greeted him with "Dennis Law, Dennis Law, is it true what Shanks says, you're 64?"

● On one occasion, Smith took to the field in silver footwear, the kind you'd only ever see on the Empire's pantomime dame. Kopites, never averse to poking fun at their own, poured scorn on his fashion sense with "Where'd you get those boots?" He never wore them again.

● In 1978, after Sunday tabloids splashed news of marital turmoil for Peter Shilton because of his friendship with a woman called Tina, the England goalie ran out to, "Don't cry for me, Tina, Tina".

● Evertonians' lauding of their hero Bob with "Latchford walks on water" evoked the retort, "Latchford is a duck".

● After John Wark, playing for Ipswich, was decked by a ball to his bag of nuts, the trainer had to administer urgent first aid with a vigorous rubbing. While this was taking place, the Kop alerted John's other half with "Are you watching, Mrs Wark?" before switching to a false falsetto, eunuchoidal chant of "Johnny Wark, Johnny Wark".

● Kevin Francis, a 6ft 7in forward, was sized up with "There's only one Blackpool Tower" and "What's the weather like up there?"

● In 1979's FA Cup, Grimsby Town's raucous fans filled Annie Road, presenting an unmissable opportunity for Kop chants and songs based on trawling and chippies.

When the Mariners' contingent broke into a chorus, Kopites hit back with "You only sing when you're fishing" and encouraged Liverpool attacks with "In the net! (Clap, clap, clap) / In the net! (Clap, clap, clap)", which mutated into "Batter 'em! / Batter 'em!"

Their request was heeded. Five goals to the good, the Reds went sailing through, giving the Kop peace of mind to allocate piscatorial epithets to players. Neal was encouraged with chants of "Phil Seal!"; Dalglish was serenaded with "Kenny is a dogfish", a verse revamped to accommodate Thompson's nose in "Tommo is a swordfish"; Ray Kennedy was renamed "Stingray"; McDermott turned into "Terry McTurbot" (a contribution from patrons of that upmarket chippy in Allerton) and Case became "Oh Jimmy, Jimmy / Jimmy, Jimmy, Jimmy, Jimmy, Jimmy – PLAICE!"

● In the Eighties, a police sergeant with droopy, white moustache patrolled the touchline, stimulating a cry of "Ee-aye-addio, the walrus is a queer". A party of Americans in the Main Stand were at a loss to understand what sort of sports event they were attending.

● In 1983, filming took place at Anfield for Scully, a Channel 4 drama written by Alan Bleasdale about a tearaway who dreamt of playing for the Reds. Before a match, the first team agreed to run out with Drew Schofield in the lead role, wearing a No 7 shirt, and to the production crew's satisfaction, Kopites played their part by greeting the actor with "There's only one Franny Scully".

● In December 1987, Liverpool were leading Newcastle by a single goal when John Aldridge was tackled and tumbled over in the penalty box. The defender's challenge was perfectly fair but the referee blew for a penalty. Unable to comprehend this bizarre decision, Kopites could only deduce it was another Christmas present, acknowledged with "Nice one, Santa, nice one, son".

● After one match, Barnes joined customers queuing in a chippy near Anfield, where an incredulous Red gawped before asking: "You're John Barnes, aren't you?" "Yes," Barnes confirmed. "So you know Ian Rush, don't you?" the fan continued. "I know him well," said Barnes. "Why don't you bleedin' well pass the ball to him then?" the supporter demanded indignantly.

● During the period when Vinnie Jones was in his prime as a TV personality, he appeared in the Gladiators TV show and suffered a well-publicised disagreement with another contender, Wolfman. The Kop reminded Jones of this with "Who's afraid of the big, bad wolf? / Vinnie, Vinnie Jones".

● When Liverpool welcomed Manchester United to L4 in 1989, the Trafforders were irritated by the ref and sought solace in that hackneyed chant of "Who's the Scouser in the black?" Kopites enlightened them: "Johnny Barnes, Johnny Barnes, Johnny Barnes."

● During the Eighties, a biscuit bar was being widely advertised and the Kop used it to scoff at the visitors: "There's only one United – and that's a chocolate biscuit".

● In the early Nineties, the Kop was exhorting our lads to "Attack, attack / Attack, attack, attack" when a black cat scurried across the pitch. Within seconds, their chant was reworded into "A cat, a cat / A cat, a cat, a cat", followed by an update of a political message: "Moggie, moggie, moggie / Out, out, out."

● At his farewell appearance, crowd favourite Gary McAllister, who arrived at Anfield on a free transfer, was teased with "What a waste of money".

● While the Kop had no roof because of rebuilding, torrential rain drenched the crowd, who thumbed their noses up at the discomfort with "We only sing when we're soaking".

● And, finally, in 2004, Gérard Houllier's last year at Anfield, Djimi Traoré was doing his level best to be the French counterpart of Carlton Palmer, about whom Southampton manager David Jones once said: "He covers every blade of grass on the pitch. You have to when your first touch is as crap as that."

Taking a dim view of Djimi's clumsy technique, Kopites rearranged Dean Martin's Amore into "The prat (!!!) at the back who's going to get Houllier the sack / that's Traoré".

Now, in 2005, Gérard had gone, replaced by Rafa who had guided our lads to the Champions League Final.

On May 25 in Istanbul, the Kop would have a new audience for its lyrics and humour ... and the much maligned prat at the back might even make an appearance on club football's biggest stage.

24
Immortality In Istanbul

And gentlemen in England, now a-bed shall think themselves accursed they were not here.

– William Shakespeare

WHEN UEFA took out an injunction banning the sale of Istanbul tickets on websites, the words stable, door and horse sprang to mind. If football's rulers had planned allocations with greater consideration for the loyal fans of Liverpool and AC Milan who help keep their organisation so profitable, then touts would not be able to make a killing. Instead, two of the continent's best-supported clubs would each receive just 20,000 seats, the remaining 30,000 going to the Turkish FA and such worthy causes as the "football family", official sponsors, corporate guests and hospitality-mongers.

An affront to thousands of Scousers raring to attend the first European final in a Muslim city.

Unless you were willing to fork out £600 on eBay, that glorified, computerised car-boot sale, tickets weren't available in England, so Russ and I decided to make our own way to Turkey and to work the streets there for tickets. A Google doodle having turned up flights from London to Sofia to Istanbul, arriving Sunday before the game, we booked them and were all set … until I suffered a panic attack on the eve of departure, triggered by my resolve to help the environment.

It all began so calmly. Since we had a bundle of newspapers for recycling, I drove to Waitrose's car park where the council's steel container is situated. I carried my armful to the repository, only to discover the letterbox flap propped open with a plug of papers.

Some lazy so-and-so, too idle to put them in.

I pushed them through, followed by the first of my papers, until – surprise, surprise – a face popped into view. *Inside the flap. Staring out.*

"Hello," this bloke said.

"Hello," I replied. As you do, contemplating a face inside a great big shipping container next to a supermarket in St Albans.

"What's going on?" I inquired.

"Looking for my passport," Container Face retorted. "Wife threw it away with the papers, and we're off to Portugal next week."

I wished him well with his quest, offloaded my offering into the recycler's jaws and returned home, ruminating on life's adversities. But one person's misfortune can be another's wake-up call. I needed my passport. Where was it?

Since time immemorial, I'd always stored it in the Travel folder in my filing cabinet. Wasn't there. I extended my search to the rest of the cabinet, cupboards, drawers, bedrooms until, two-hour forensic examination of my home concluded, I found it: in a holdall, in the loft, where I'd abandoned it after a trip to Verona six months before.

My cardiac resuscitation effected, all systems go for Turkey. While one batch of fans were driving in a Hackney cab from Merseyside to the stadium 1,750 miles away, we took off for Istanbul on Sunday night, landing immediately after the earthquake.

The city was shuddering – all because Fenerbahçe had pipped arch enemies Galatasaray 1-0 to clinch the Super Ligi. I might have witnessed celebrations in Liverpool and elsewhere but our taxi crawl from airport to hotel confirmed no one is more lunatic about football than the Turks. Note that these are people who in extreme cases have committed suicide if their side have lost.

Fener's supporters have an idiosyncratic technique for geeing up players: at kick-off, they fall silent, and remain so for three minutes until, all together, governed by the second hands of watches, they explode into shouting and jumping that shakes their ground.

Now they were shaking Istanbul's city centre. Bedlam reigned as they blocked roads with cars and lorries, kept elbows jammed on horns, pounded drums, waved a forest of flags, brandished flares, set off bangers and launched rockets. They'd even fitted bouncy castles inside fleets of pogoing buses.

Eventually, by dint of playing chicken with other vehicles and scraping his wing mirrors across shop fronts, our driver manoeuvred through this chaos and delivered us to Taksim Square, to our hotel booked via the internet.

Supposedly a three-star establishment, our room left me musing if a minus sign had slipped from its classification, since you couldn't swing a gnat inside, never mind a cat. Flipping Nora, it was so cramped the only spot for our portable karaoke machine was on the lavatory cistern.

A previous guest had even vented his dissatisfaction by setting fire to my bed's foam-rubber mattress. At least that was the most plausible explanation for the fist-sized burn holes and extensive scorch marks visible through the flimsy sheet, although at check-in I should have twigged the grizzled desk jockey wasn't discussing tobacco, he was talking literally, when he inquired: "Smoking or non-smoking?"

A couple of years ago, driving through the food-coupon end of Las Vegas's strip, my eyes were caught by a neon billboard which damned a seedy motel with proprietorial praise: "Highly recommended – by the owner". Well, our Istanbul hotel should have had something of the sort, because no one else would have recommended it for 60 quid a night.

Despite that, finding accommodation on the web had been a chore, so the state of my mattress, loo's stench, stifling heat and carpet woven out of masticated chewing gum were unimportant.

We had reached Istanbul and we had beds.

Having verified that iron rungs fixed to the wall outside our fourth-floor window afforded escape in any conflagration, we went out on the lash, repairing to a British bar up the street where we savoured numerous Turkish sherberts in the company of a Scouse duo, a policeman and a lift technician who'd flown over from Toronto. Ignore Fiery Towers, Champions Cup week starts here.

Next morning at breakfast (wrinkled olives, couple of cucumber slices, fingernail of cheese), the waiter divulged that Fener celebrants firing guns in the air had wounded several people.

A word of warning: unless you want a hole drilled between your eyes, never lean over any balcony of any flat in Turkey to watch any jubilant supporters. Equally, you could get shot just walking down the road. Our waiter also informed us a man strolling past Taksim's Beatles Bar was hit by a stray bullet. OK, bit of an excuse, they *were* playing the Revolver album at the time. Given the availability of firearms and the fact two Leeds supporters had been stabbed to death outside nearby McDonald's in 2000, I did speculate how locals would react when we, outriders for the main Red invasion, hit the streets. After all, rumours had spread on the net that Islamic fundamentalists/Al Qaeda terrorists/Kurdish lager louts were plotting to murder a Liverpool fan, spread stories that Italians had done it and sit back as riots razed Istanbul.

Web of misinformation. As we traipsed through the city centre, the Turks could not have been friendlier. Spotting our LFC tops, drivers beeped and pedestrians even approached us to say "Get the cup" or "I hope you win on Wednesday". Genuine expressions of encouragement.

One FB FC supporter who had been at the title-clincher the night before told us Liverpool flags and scarves were on sale outside their stadium. I've no idea what Italians had done to antagonise Istanbullus but it was gin-clear they were siding with us. Russ and I felt at home.

As we sauntered along Istiklal Caddesi, the main shopping street, a TV crew pounced outside the North Shield pub.

"BBC North-West News," the woman reporter informed us. "Are you from Liverpool?"

On being told I was, she exclaimed: "Good! You're the first Liverpool fans from Liverpool we've come across."

She then interviewed me to camera about how we'd been received in Istanbul, my chance to give an upbeat account of our early impressions, larded with a description of the Turkish fad for chargrilled Dunlopillo at bedtime. A couple of minutes later, my Warholesque period of fame was over.

Not quite.

You wait ages for a No 26 bus and ... [Fill in the rest for your prize of two pints at the Sandon.]

At our first port of call on the tourist trail, the Blue Mosque, we were waylaid by another hack, from *The Times*, who scribbled down a carbon copy of my account of our first day, sensationalised with even more lurid details of the Istanbul penchant for scorching-hot mattresses and their side effects ... flames shooting through the hotel roof ... Scousers leaping out of upstairs windows ... our 10-storey-long escape rope of knotted sheets ... Hold the presses!

With that melodramatic narrative translated into shorthand, the reporter scurried away and my second spell of celebrity was terminated. What did Andy Warhol know ...?

After we'd circumambulated the Blue Mosque, Islam's cerebral architecture of the soul, we sat outside on a bench, attracting the attention of a party of schoolgirls who crowded around, keen to practise English. They told us they'd travelled 20 hours by coach to Istanbul from their home town of Trabzon, that distant UEFA outpost where Emlyn and the lads were awoken at daybreak by the muezzin's wailing call before their European Cup tie in 1976. It was also the venue which, according to Kop mythology, a solitary supporter managed to reach from Merseyside in those pre-charter flight years. If that *is* true, I'd love to buy him a pint of Cains bitter *and* a large rum chaser.

Russ – 6 foot 3, fair-haired, blue-eyed, skin the colour of Cat I'th Window farmhouse cream – was the centre of scrutiny as the girls quizzed us about Liverpool, our opinions on Turkey, the kinds of music he liked. At this, their teacher intervened. She had taught them the Beatles' Yesterday, to help improve their English accents. Would we like to hear it? Of course!

Yesterday may be the most recorded song ever and I might have heard hundreds of versions but the lasses' rendition will always remain with me.

While passers-by stopped and gawked, this choir of Turkish teenagers serenaded us at the Blue Mosque and by the time they hummed the final line, "I believe in yesterday", one soppy Scouser was struggling to swallow a rather large lump in his throat.

Having composed myself sufficiently to applaud their faultless performance, I couldn't hold back with my claim to fame: I told them the Beatles sang for me in the Cavern for 5p while I lunched on Mum's home-made lamb koftes. Well, they would never have heard of corned beef and piccalilli sarnies, would they?

The girls, and their teacher, swallowed the Cavern bit but not the lamb koftes.

All in all, a lovely interlude with charming youngsters. True, I'm a tad biased but could this have happened to supporters of any other team?

After goodbyes to our Trabzon friends, we gravitated to the next mosques, 1,400year-old Haghia Sophia and Istanbul's most voluptuous, Suleiman the Magnificent, inside which a chap was vacuuming the Stanley Park of a carpet. Drawing near, he jabbed a finger skyward, which I took to be a question: Do you want to go up the dome? I nodded.

He parked his Hoover and escorted us outside – to a mediaeval wooden door in the base of the tallest minaret. This was what his finger had been indicating.

Glancing around to confirm we weren't being clocked, he fished out a clunky jailer's key from his pocket and opened up this skyscraping stone pencil which has written Koranic messages in the heavens for centuries.

Nowadays, though, minarets have lost their purpose as a podium for summoning worshippers to prayer. The muezzin doesn't drag himself on high five times a day to muster the faithful; from ground level, he uses an array of loudspeakers, leaving the turret redundant.

Through its ancient entrance, all three of us crossed the threshold of a religious relic, dusty, musty, frequented by fluttering pigeons, a narrow staircase spiralling into blackness, a treadmill we panted up.

At the top of endless steps, our guide forced open a creaking door onto the muezzin's uppermost pulpit to behold a paradisiac panorama: one country, Turkey ... two continents, Europe and Asia ... three empires, Roman, Byzantine and Ottoman ... three capital cities, Byzantium, Constantinople and Istanbul ... three religions, Islam, Christianity and Judaism ... three rulers, Greeks, Romans and Ottomans ... the Golden Horn, Bosphorus, Sea of Marmara ... Sublime Porte, Bazaar Quarter, Galata Tower ... blocks of flats draped with gigantic blue and yellow Fenerbahçe flags ... Red ants tootling along cobbled streets to the strains of Scouser Tommy ... mosques and minarets, domes and spires, harems and hippodromes, caliphs and cabbies, belly dancers and beer bellies, sultans and shoppers, Whirling Dervishes and Wal-Mart, eunuchs and UEFA …

A transcendental spectacle that not even the crumbling balustrade above a vertiginous 200-foot drop could diminish.

Istanbul's high spot, bar none.

How many Muslims, not to mention Scousers, have drooled over Suleiman's magnificent vista? To think that if any infidel had violated this sacred spot a century ago, he might have paid with his head. But we had been there, seen all that, taken our photos and now wished to buy the T-shirt.

We began our treacherous descent, down the ladder-steep staircase, in the gloom, without any handrail. Inshallah, we'll get down in one piece. Stepping blindly into the abyss, I was sweating my hesitant feet wouldn't land squarely on each uneven step, aware any stumble could do some serious damage and compromise my attendance at the final.

Allah was willing. Neither of us fell headfirst and the Exalted One granted safe passage to the bottom.

There, the cost of our unsolicited trip was the subject of haggling with the Hoovercraft pilot, a practice in which we had already received intensive tuition while negotiating the Grand Bazaar's 4,000 shops.

Having been driven down to what probably constituted a day's wage, our guide dragged the creaky door ajar and peeped out. A dark suit strode past, obliging us to stand back, but once the coast was clear we scuttled away, the rarest perspective of Istanbul embedded in our memories.

That evening, history morphed into hostelry as we partook of refreshments around Taksim Square, the focal point for supporters appreciative of Turkey's healthy brand of Islam lite.

In one bar, a couple of fans told us about a rail journey from Sofia to Istanbul, 300 miles in a pedestrian 18 hours. At dead of night, at the back of Bulgaria's beyond, the train clanked to a halt to allow "a gang of gipsies" to clamber on board.

These were carrying screwdrivers which they used to remove panels in the carriage. Curious. Brick-shaped parcels were then inserted in the cavities and the panels reinstalled. Very curious.

As the Scousers contemplated this, the gang leader glowered at them, drew a finger across his throat and pulled back his jacket to reveal a pistol.

Not exactly the Southport line for the Liverpudlians, who judged it wise to avert their gaze and admire the gloom clinging to the window.

Once the gang had disembarked and the train resumed its course, the fans agreed moving to another carriage might be advisable. They upped and offed and reached Istanbul without being fingered by Turkish customs for smuggling whatever was inside the packages.

Now it was time for them and us to paint Taksim red. Discussing his mother city, Zinedine Zidane said: "There is a special culture in Marseilles. It is probably like Liverpool, very vibrant and very tough." Well, Turks and tourists around the square were being regaled with the Scousers' cultural speciality of pub singsongs. Inside and outside every watering hole, encores of old standards never faltered but one pertinent ditty was prominent: "Istanbul is wonderful / It's full of mosques, kebabs and Scousers". Never a truer word ...

Listening to our vocal repertoire, I reflected that every club is defined by several qualities but two carry more weight than most: its songs and its trophies. In both, Liverpool stand supreme.

We're dab hands at banners, too. Taksim's walls were plastered with them and an imaginative offering posed the question, "No small Toffees for feast tonight / Kopites party with Turkish delight / José ... Sir Alex ... London press / All choking on sweet success / Money, not love, is your drive / But tell us ... can you count to five?" and that theme was echoed by "Glazer's dollars or Roman's roubles? Rafa, just 5 euros, por favor!"

Alongside "Those who forget the past have no future / VE Day 25-05-05" and "Picasso was a painter, Alonso is an artist, Basque in his brilliance", another poster modernised Supercalifragilisticexpialidocious to commend an unlikely hero: "Super Croat Igor Biscan Used To Be Atrocious". While some comics sipping pints made me smile with "Battered husbands on tour", a serious note was struck by The Irregulars' "Do you think we would leave you dying? Justice for the 96".

"Never give up," the Dalai Lama keeps telling Tibet's oppressed people and Taksim's Scousers were repeating that message for the Hillsborough families. Your fight is our fight and we will never give up.

Next morning, Tuesday, we caught a leisurely ferry across the Bosphorus with three Thai telecom engineers who'd flown from Mosul in Northern Iraq. Pleasant lads, looking like teenagers rather than in their late-20s, with Liverpool badges neatly handsewn on their shirts, I did ask myself if briefcases bloated with Bush's dollars could compensate for the hazards of life in that wartorn country. At least here in Istanbul they were well away from the daily car bombs and AK47 ambushes.

After having had breakfast coffee in Europe and midday beers with the Bangkok boys in Asia, our thoughts began turning to tickets. Since we expected prices to fall as the final drew nearer, we'd already spurned some for £500 and £700 from Turkish touts and on Tuesday afternoon, we got down to business, combing bars around Taksim. The only sniff came from a Scouser selling one for £375, with a credit card slip to corroborate that was the price he'd paid. Carry on searching.

We planted ourselves in the middle of the square, asking passers-by about spares. Even though a bunch of Kopites couldn't supply tickets, they did present us with lager to rinse our dry throats and, as we opened the cans, Bingo! a lad from Robson Street offered a pair of seats for £500.

Since we'd heard forgeries were circulating, we studied the tickets' holograms carefully and they did appear genuine.

Judgement time! The deal was made, the cash exchanged and we'd be seeing the show. What's more, Russ and I would be sitting together.

That evening we could relax with some Runcorn lads we'd met – Mark and Joe Grimes and their mates – and shake a leg in Taksim's gargantuan knees-up.

The square was heaving with our fans. What a League of Nations: Irish, Norwegian, Japanese (Mum, Dad, red-shirted baby in a pram), Dutch, Welsh, Scottish, Thai ("We love the Red Swans", their nickname for our team), French, Czech, Polish, Singaporean ("We don't live in Liverpool but Liverpool lives in us"), Scousers from the USA and South Africa, Greek Australians ...

Yes, Greek *Australians*. Ignore Peter Kay's "*Garlic* (gulp!) *bread!*" These were Greek (gulp!) *Australians*! who'd flown around the globe, *with drums*, to bang out a backing beat for our lads. Mind-boggling.

The supporters' sheer diversity astounded me, underlining the aura and mystique Liverpool has for men and women of every race and colour.

No other club casts such a spell. No other city stirs imaginations like it does.

That's why, in Lima's fashionable Miraflores district, a Peruvian who has never set foot on English soil has called his bar after Liverpool and put our shirts on its walls.

That's why grounds on every continent have Kops who sing You'll Never Walk Alone.

That's why, in the Crimea in Ukraine, driving along the main road through the mountains to the Black Sea resort of Yalta, you can stop off at a pub called Liverpool.

That's why a branch of our supporters meets in Azerbaijan, in the Cavern Club at 12 Tgiyev Street, Baku.

That's why the Rush café in Clichy, Paris, is packed when our lads are on telly.

That's why the Mirage in Las Vegas spent £70 million on a state-of-the-art theatre for a Beatles spectacular sold out months ahead.

That's why CSKA Sofia feel honoured to be called Bulgaria's Liverpool, in acknowledgement of their domination of the country's game, with 30 league championships.

That's why, in far-off Western Australia in 2005, I noted a drinker in the Lucky Shag pub on Perth's waterfront reading a guide to the city's musical scene. Its title? Liverpool of the South Seas.

That's why, in the RSSSF, the world foundation of football statisticians, so many of its esteemed members single out the side from L4 0TH as their favourite.

And, finally, in this random paean of praise, that's why our fan club in Norway has 21,000 members. 21,000! More than any other team, an Oslo Viking told me proudly in Istanbul. Respect.

Yes, our city – through its people, football and music – has reached out and left an imprint on the psyches of millions. Our Camelot on the Mersey, our Avalon on Liverpool Bay, our Eden by the Irish Sea is the stuff of their fantasies.

I could go on and on about how it inspires, and I'd be glad to. Regrettably the publisher's just sent an urgent email, reading the Riot Act about how many more pages he can print. Let's call it a day, until my next stab at a book. Bear with me till then.

The morning of the final, Russ and I ogled Topkapi Palace's jewels, especially the blinding 86-carat Spoonmaker's Diamond which after being unearthed from a rubbish heap in 1669 was regarded as a fake and exchanged for three wooden spoons. Only *three*.

Golly! Why didn't they take it down to O'Hare's in Breck Road?

For dinner we tucked into a shish in Taksim and at 4 in the afternoon located the street from where buses would convey supporters to the stadium. Soon our coach was trundling towards the ground 20 miles away, escorted by car drivers who honked their horns while people along the route waved and clapped, one poster declaring, "Reds, club of the Labour class, welcome to Istanbul". No leg-pull, Kopites as liberating heroes. This must be how Bob Paisley felt when he rolled into Rome on a tank in '44. So where were all those Turkish extremists plotting to foment trouble between English and Italians?

At the end of our long and winding road, the coach dropped us a mile from the spanking-new Ataturk stadium, its twin roofs shaped like a giant pair of scimitars. Glinting in the sun, they were about to slash away at each other. How apt for a duel between England and Italy's foremost clubs.

Off we set down the freshly tarmacked road, beside a wire fence patrolled by soldiers ... farmers protecting their crops from famished Scousers, according to one joker. Across a wasteland, columns of Reds meandered towards our designated fans' zone where TV betting expert Angus Loughran was doing a report to camera for the ESPN channel, with a backcloth of rollicksome Scousers.

By this time we were getting peckish but the few food stalls were under siege and prices were extortionate – £2 for a packet of crisps. All the programmes had sold out, too. Since we needed some as mementos, we undertook a long trudge to the Rossoneri's end to investigate if they had any left in their kiosk but it was completely bare. The Italians' catering facilities were no improvement on ours, either.

After a natter with an AC tifoso, we trekked back to the Liverpool zone where dozens had hauled themselves onto the DJ's sound stage and were jumping about – so many that a Turk came on the PA system, asking them to clear off because the structure was in danger of collapse.

They ignored him.

As they leapt around, the announcer begged them to desist, to no avail.

"Just having a bit of fun, lah."

"No odds, mate. You think this geezer's overreacting but what if he's right and the stage does collapse and someone gets hurt? What message will that send out about reckless, irresponsible Scousers? What damage will that do to the club's search for investors?

"Remember, tabloid hacks are watching, waiting, hoping, even encouraging ... After all, news editors have been screaming down their mobiles all day, 'Give me a f****** incident!'

"Heysel ... Hillsborough ... Istanbul ... quite a hat-trick for some of the red-tops.

"No, lads. Behave. If you're told to get off the blinking stage, get off it."

I'd seen enough. I fancied hearing the Amsterdam band's set but, two hours before kick-off, wasn't going to hang around.

"Let's go inside," I told Russ.

We went directly to our gate, whose electronic box of tricks refused to read the barcode on my ticket when it was inserted.

Can't be a dud, surely. 250 quid for a dud!

A cold sweat gripped me ... until the steward opened the door manually and ushered me through, whole ticket intact in my hand. At least I'd have that as a memento.

We'd entered next to the VIP entrance where cries of "Diego, Diego" from Italians alerted us to Maradona's presence. He was chatting to admirers and looked considerably slimmer, fitter and smaller than I imagined, belying the photos of a 20-stone tub of lard that had filled front pages.

Shunning the offer of his trademark "El 10" autograph (know where you can stick your hand, Diego Armando), we toiled up steps higher than our old Kop's on Walton Breck Road to the refreshment area. We were starving but it took ages to get hot dogs and mineral waters from two lads striving manfully to serve hundreds of ravenous Liverpudlians.

Stomachs pacified, we sought out our seats at the top of the West stand, above the media section, halfway line below, affording a grand overview of the stadium, although not quite in the different time zone from the pitch that one Galatasaray supporter had warned us about.

Despite our early arrival, the waiting hours raced by until three sides of the stadium were saturated with Liverpudlians and both teams walked out for the 9.45pm kick-off. By now I was feeling queasy, not from the altitude but the excitement.

To everyone's surprise, Kewell was in the starting line-up – a bold stroke by Rafa who had noted how PSV's wingers ran Milan ragged in the semi-final.

The scene is set for a Reds triumph ... until 53 seconds of the match have elapsed. AC mount their first attack, Traoré commits a clumsy foul and Maldini volleys the free kick in.

The quickest goal ever in the Champions Cup, in Maldini's seventh final.

Bit of a choker.

José Mourinho has declared the Reds will have no chance if they concede first. Now we'll see – and worse is coming. Obviously not 100 per cent fit, Kewell has to go off, replaced by Smicer who can only stand and admire Milan's sumptuous football, orchestrated by Ricardo Izecson dos Santos Leite, alias Kaká. Ghosting through our defence in their all-white change strip, the Rossoneri set up Crespo twice to make it 3-0. A treble whammy.

We are being outclassed and when the ball strikes Nesta's elbow as he lies on the grass, Baros makes a nonsensical penalty appeal. That sums up our desperation.

Beforehand, squinting through my red-tinted glasses, I believed we were destined to win; by the half-time whistle, the Fates have deserted us. Conscious that in three finals, against Ajax, Barcelona and Steaua Bucharest, AC prevailed 4-0, I dread a worse humiliation in the second half ... 5-0, 6-0, a record thrashing. Michel Platini feels likewise, telling David Moores at the interval that it is now a question of damage limitation.

For my part, I'm praying. Come on, lads. Get a goal, just one. Make the scoreline respectable, give us some pride, then we can put it down to experience and go home.

My stream of introspection is halted by the singing of a hymn.

I've no inkling where it begins – North, West or East stands – but it radiates into the black ether, making time stand still as 40,000 lives are condensed into three metaphysical minutes.

From the core of their being, those sentimental, self-pitying, maudlin, hooked-on-grief Liverpudlians begin a You'll Never Walk Alone like I've only heard once before, at the FA Cup final with Everton after Hillsborough.

Not louder than ever, not more passionately, but with a visceral, ethereal, spiritual intensity that transcends the moment. Surely in far-off South Africa it even stirs the souls of Spion Kop's fallen.

Every line of its lyrics resonates with meaning, kindling hope in our hearts, reassuring us that a golden sky and the silver song of a lark will vanquish the dark and the storm.

With one voice, 40,000 believers are combining to articulate their dream and the world is bearing witness.

A tear-in-the-eye declaration, a defiant throw of the dice, further testimony to Liverpudlians' "strange brilliance", in Paul McCartney's perceptive words.

We might be down and out but our Scouse spirit refuses to be broken.

Please, please let our team hear us in their dressing room. This empowering anthem must – must – lift our bloodied troops who Rafa is contriving to rally. In a foreign language, not the Spanish he'd feel comfortable with, he is invoking a higher force to motivate his men, all "in shock", says Dudek.

"Don't let your heads drop," Rafa tells them quietly. "We are Liverpool, you are playing for Liverpool. Don't forget that. You have to hold your heads high for the supporters. You have to do it for them. They have come a long way. Don't let them down. You cannot call yourselves Liverpool players if you have your heads down.

"If we create a few chances, we have the possibility of getting back into this. Believe you can do it and you will. Give yourselves the chance to be heroes."

Out in the stadium, the final words of You'll Never Walk Alone have faded away, replaced by the North Stand jesting, "We're going to win 4-3".

Them Scousers again, laughing in the face of adversity. You can't help smiling. The rest of the break is a blur, a confusion of images and sensations that do not really register, a subliminal haze that only disperses when Liverpool come out for the restart.

Our midfield has been reinforced by Hamann in place of the injured Finnan. Now Gerrard will be able to push forward ...

The rest of the night is fact, fable, fairytale, fantasy, fiction.

From Liverpool River in Australia's Arnhem Land to Liverpool Bay in Arctic Canada, they will have heard about the Red storm, three dazzling goals during six minutes of madness.

Almost on the penalty spot, Gerrard sends a towering header into the corner of the net. 3-1. Game on!

Smicer's 25-yard drive zings past Dida. Vladi, in his last game for the Reds, has scored a second! 3-2.

Storming into the box, Stevie is tripped by Gattuso. Alonso places the penalty low to Dida's right. The keeper judges well, palming it onto the post, but Xabi follows up to blast into the roof.

Our placid playmaker, who says, "I prefer not to hate anyone, I prefer to just love Liverpool", has made it 3-3.

Yes, 3-3.

I repeat: 3-3.

Making Lazarus look like a legless gimp, the Reds have refused to die, clawing themselves out of the grave dug by Milan.

The most remarkable fightback in any European final. Ever.

On the precipitous West stand, I feel numb as the game moves into nailbiting extra time.

AC are dominant and in the 117th minute, Dudek pulls off a preposterous point-blank double save from Shevchenko, the most flabbergasting act of goalkeeping I have ever observed, a righteous hand of God rather than Maradona's thieving one. Truly the save that shakes the world.

Sheva, the goalscoring machine who treasures a pair of Rush's boots, just cannot get the ball in the net.

Crespo holds his head; now he knows the Milanesi will not win. "I knew that save was the moment we said bye-bye to the cup," he admits later.

The lads hang on – "running on empty", in Gerrard's phrase – until the referee gives the last blast on his whistle. All down to penalties.

In the centre circle, Carragher is waving his fist at Jerzy, getting him pumped up, but after going through an emotional wringer, I feel strangely unconcerned, detached from the shoot-out, as a chemical reaction occurs in my body and brain. Where once we'd been dead and buried, now a supernatural force has taken possession of me, the fans, the team, floating us inexorably towards that cup. An unstoppable momentum is carrying the resurgent Reds to victory.

The penalties begin. Serginho blasts over the bar: 0-0. Hamann slots in: 0-1. Dudek saves from Pirlo: 0-1. Cissé scores coolly: 0-2. Dudek dives but Tomasson's weak kick goes in the other corner: 1-2. Dida saves from Riise: 1-2. Kaká scores: 2-2. With me murmuring that Dida always dives to the right, Smicer fires home: 2-3.

The moment of truth. Shevchenko has a final chance to keep Milan in the shoot-out. If he doesn't score, they lose. As he trudges to the penalty spot, he looks like he's walking to the gallows.

With the clock showing 12.29am and 500 million watching, he runs up and strikes the ball sharply, straight down the middle.

Jerzy, diving away from the trajectory, stretches out his left arm and gets his fingertips to the ball. Saved!

2-3!

LIVERPOOL CHAMPIONS!

After 11 goals, all at the same end, the Italian end, we have won!

From their thrones on high, the 96 smile down. You've been with us every step of the way.

As every Red goes demented, Russ and I hug and dance, scream and howl.

Strangers you've never seen before in your life grab and squeeze and *kiss* you. Human warmth, the very essence of Anfield.

Scousers who've carried the ashes of fallen mates all the way from Merseyside to share this beatific moment cast them towards that great Anfield in the sky.

Tears are shed by grown men, even in the media section below where one broadcaster breaks down: Michael Robinson.

Jerzy, who only realises his save from Sheva has won the final when team-mates rampage towards him, is mobbed by, among others, Traoré, the prat at the back who was going to get Houllier the sack.

Like an Ashworth Hospital inmate who's just succeeded in scaling the wall after 30 years' plotting, Carragher gambols across the pitch, mouth agape in disbelief, socks around ankles, legs of elastic, and careers past Dudek in a maniacally wide arc to fans along the touchline to freak out with his people.

In the mêlée, I swear one Kopite bear-hugging Jamie is wearing a white cork motorcycle helmet. Or am I hallucinating?

Glorious, glorious delirium!

Beyond belief, beyond reason, beyond logic.

My last European Cup journey in 1985 had warped into Heysel's horror. This night of atonement has purged those frightful memories, the power and the glory have exorcised those demons. We are all in a state of grace.

When Huyton's finest, Stevie G, lifts la Coupe des Clubs Champions Européens amid a typhoon of red confetti, I pinch myself. Back in August the lads had been 33-1 outsiders, toiling against third-rate GAK; now they're champions, overcoming a 3-0 deficit, something no other team have done.

Before this, the 50th final, many pundits had discarded Liverpool as no-hopers who should prepare for the worst, like Julius Francis did before fighting Mike Tyson in 2000. Jittery Julius had so little confidence he sold advertising space on the soles of his boots. BUPA were said to have expressed an interest.

AC had been dismissive of the Reds, too. Silvio Berlusconi, the club's owner and Italy's prime minister, pontificated: "Liverpool are inferior to Milan. We are the leading players in world football, the standard-bearers of good play. We are winners, we want to win games in convincing fashion. This is a tradition that will continue on Wednesday."

Carlo Ancelotti, the Italians' coach, advised, "I'll tell you what we should not do, and that is to worry about Liverpool. They are such a defensive team", while Maldini boasted, "Liverpool don't know how to attack – caution is at the core of their game. We play properly; our defence is the best in Europe, and therefore the world."

Right, Paolo. Serie A *is* the most defensive and tactically astute league anywhere and Milan *are* the most unyielding exponents of its steely arts. But they did not have the courage, guts and self-belief of the Reds who, in the lyrics of the Mighty Wah!, played with a heart as big as the city of Liverpool.

An incredulous Maradona said: "Even the Brazil team that won the 1970 World Cup could not have staged a comeback with Milan leading 3-0. Liverpool showed miracles do happen. They proved football is the most beautiful sport of them all.

"After this game, my English team is going to be Liverpool. I came across some of their fans beforehand and they told me they were going to win but they would be made to suffer. It's just the way it happened. Liverpool are the best team in the world for what they have done in the Champions League. They deserved the cup."

On the terraces, every Red man and woman basked in celestial rapture, the deities sanctifying them and their heroes. Europe's finest side and finest supporters: an unbeatable partnership had brought victory.

Johan Cruyff, who's done and seen and heard everything in football, said: "There's not one club so united with its fans as Liverpool. I sat watching their fans and they sent shivers down my spine. A mass of 40,000 people became one force behind their team.

"For that, I admire Liverpool more than anything."

Cruyff and the rest of us had witnessed the match of a lifetime; for me, the most stupendous in 50 years. On this night, there was no better place to be on Planet Earth than Istanbul's Ataturk Stadium where I'd shared in the supreme sporting climax, a game that meant more to me than almost anything. All right, not quite up there with the birth of my children, but given a choice between winning the cup, in that fashion, and scooping the Lottery, there could be only one call: give me Ol' Big Ears every time.

Everybody has a chance of winning the Lottery; just buy a ticket and you might land the jackpot. But my good fortune goes off the radar, endowing me not with wealth but a wealth of priceless memories

The global population is estimated to be 6.5 billion, give or take 100 million, and actuaries have calculated we live an average 28,000 days. So what are the odds on any one of millions of football fans, British or foreign, experiencing a single night like Istanbul during their lifetimes? Being in that stadium, at that moment, 12.45am precisely on May 26, 2005, to see their captain lift the cup and their team crowned Kings of Europe? For the fifth time, in the most climactic final ever, 28 years since watching them secure their first trophy in Rome?

What are the odds on all that? I'd love to know. What I do know is I'm one lucky beggar.

In 2001, the lads regaled us with the finest UEFA Cup Final, against Alavés; now they'd given us the most sublime European moment ever, fulfilling Rafa's pledge to his wife Montse that he would be champion of the continent by the time he was 45. True to his word, on the banks of the Bosphorus, he had crafted a thing of beauty as the Reds conquered the Whites yet again.

And this fifth victory meant the game's most handsome cup was the Kop's to keep, for ever.

Let that roll off your tongue: Ours for ever. And again: Ours for ever. And again: Ours for ever.

[That's not enough. Carry on. – Editor]

Ours for ever. Ours for ever. Ours for ever. Ours for ever.

Ours for ever.

If only our time in the Ataturk could last for ever. Such greed. But once the players had completed their victory parade and disappeared down the tunnel, Russ and I dragged ourselves reluctantly out of the ground.

By this time, it was a cool 1.15 in the morning, authenticating the football quiz question to end all football quiz questions: Which team were losing the Champions League final on a Wednesday and won it on a Thursday?

Outside the stadium, we jumped on a coach back to the city centre. Beside me sat a Red from Falkirk, a British Asian who told me he managed a couple of restaurants in the town, which made it impossible for him to get down to Anfield, so this was the first time he'd seen the lads play.

Some baptism!

I warned him: "All matches aren't like this, you know."

While the pair of us were discussing events, one Scouser bemoaned the fact he was starving. "Champions League, we're having a laugh" as their template, his mates chorused: "Champions League, we fancy a kebab."

Then news percolated through from the front that our transport was bound for the airport, not the town.

"Taksim Square! Taksim Square!" the passengers chanted and our driver, appreciative of their faultless Turkish pronunciation, obliged.

By 3am, Russ and I were back in the Red bosom of Taksim, devouring valedictory kebabs.

We moseyed on to the street where our hotel was smouldering sullenly and settled into chairs outside the British bar with our latest pal, Efes Pilsen.

At another table with his mates, a fan in a wheelchair was humming the Istanbul signature tune, Johnny Cash's Ring of Fire. Then another disabled supporter trundled past in her chair, a white-haired lady wearing a red shirt and happily murmuring, "Campioni Liverpool". Two followers who'd undertaken arduous, 3,500-mile round trips for our lads.

Think of the discomfort, the hassle – nay, the distress and pain – they'd gone through for our team, and feel humble. They put the rest of us to shame.

At 5am, to a dawn duet of the muezzin's amplified call from the local mosque and one Scouse soloist's final croak of YNWA, we returned to our hotel room, flicking through international TV channels with their unending reports and replays of this great night. Wall-to-wall coverage during which I wondered: Did all this happen? Was I there? Did I enter a higher state of consciousness? Had I slipped into a parallel universe? Was it an out-of-body experience?

Inside the Ataturk, it had felt as though I had a twin brother and I was hovering overhead, watching him watch the final. Weird.

A couple of hours' fitful sleep in my red hotbed, more channel-hopping (the match was still featuring massively) and in the afternoon, with thanks for everything to Istanpool, as Turkish papers were headlining our side and their city, we grabbed a cab to Ataturk Airport. There we joined our brothers and sisters of the miraculous vision of Istanbul at the check-in desks. Boarding his private jet at the same time was a morose Berlusconi, accompanied by a personal guest beaming with joy: Sir Ivor Roberts, Britain's ambassador to Italy and, more relevantly, a Liverpool fanatic.

A short Airbus hop took us to Sofia where we needed to find overnight accommodation. Along the main drag of Vitosha Street, we tracked down a Soviet-era hotel (Who knows the Cyrillic letters for hotel? We had a job recognising them) and dipped into our mini bar while absorbing yet more replays of the final on Bulgarian, Polish, Russian, Romanian, Czech and Chinese TV.

A pizza, a deep sleep and at 5 next morning our Bulgarian Airways plane flew up and over a sunlit Southern Europe, its green earth enwreathed in a red halo. After soaring with angels in the Ataturk, I could have jetted home without an aircraft.

Back on terra firma in Blighty, my first act once I got through our front door was to gulp down some sparkling Hertfordshire tap water. After a week on the sauce, I was gagging for a glass of now-privatised corporation pop.

Then Russ and I flopped into armchairs, amid a welter of newspapers and video recordings, endeavouring to validate what appeared to have occurred on that barmy, unbalmy night in Turkey. Britain's bookies were hoping it hadn't happened, since I discovered punters had piled in at half-time with bets on our lads at up to 188-1, accruing winnings of £2 million.

Next I clicked on the internet to monitor what was being written, in-depth coverage that consumed me for hours. I just couldn't log off. Fact: No cup final can ever have generated so many megabytes across all the continents. An unbelievable succession of reports ... but were they all true?

Socrates, the Athenian philosopher, not the Brazilian footballer, reflected: "One must wait until the evening to see how splendid the day has been." I had to wait five days to awake from my state of suspended animation, with my voice back and a realisation that the otherworldly splendour of Istanbul was reality.

Five-star Liverpool *had* won! The Red phoenix *had* risen from the ashes.

I would have to buy a new shirt to replace my obsolescent "4 European Cups" design.

Now this "ordinary team", in George Graham's opinion, were revered as living legends, joining Real Madrid and Milan in the Big Three, the continent's trio of superpowers, and German market researchers also named them as Europe's best-supported club, with 18 million fans.

What a rollercoaster ride it had been to our silver *perch* atop Europe's lustrous summit. And as we lorded it over our lessers, what a sickener for those who envy our supremacy.

How did we do it?

When Real Madrid won in 1956, they played seven games; to triumph in the 2005 final, Liverpool turned out 15 times, coping during the season with a casualty list of 13 – seriously, 13! – members of the first-team squad. Don't ever forget that. And don't ever forget how Don Rafa refused to moan about injuries, setting an example to other managers who would wallow in such misery. So was it divine will that we should win the Champions Cup? Was our name on it?

Was our road to perdition and redemption mapped out from the very start?

If ever a case can be made for that in sport, here it is.

From the off, when another European Cup wasn't even a faint glimmer in any Kopite's glass eye, the dice rolled in sequence.

The grind to keep GAK at bay at Anfield; Stevie's late strike against Olympiacos; the cathartic, cleansing quarter-final with Juve; the controversial, all-hands-to-the-pumps victory over Chelsea in L4; the palpitating comeback against Milan; Jerzy's extraterrestrial double-stopper from Sheva; the penalties. Yes, all this was written in the stars.

Against Juve, Chelsea and AC, the experts were tipping us to fail, disregarding the possibility every underdog can have his day. And what a once-in-a-lifetime day and night we had in Istanbul. After first abandoning us, the Fates ruled our moment would come ... with goals again and again and again to haul us back onto football's pinnacle after we'd plummeted into its black hole.

How low we'd fallen in previous decades. Having coped with Heysel and the six-year European ban, our club was shattered by Hillsborough's hammer blow. For all the families, that disaster ended life as they knew it; for Liverpool Football Club, it terminated a golden age and brought decline.

In my simple opinion, Hillsborough wounded everyone far more deeply than we could ever have imagined. Any tragedy alters your attitude to life and the Anfield community, from players to coaches to cleaners to supporters, had a markedly subdued perspective after April 15, 1989, the day our world changed.

Once your kinsfolk have died in front of a TV audience of millions, then you must see success on the field in a different light. It can never be as important as it was.

To gain some understanding of the long-term effects of trauma on a club, look at Torino.

After a game with Benfica in Lisbon in May 1949, they were flying into Turin airport when their plane crashed into the basilica at Superga, killing 31 passengers, including the entire first team and their English coach, Leslie Lievesley.

League champions five times in six years, Il Grande Torino had just supplied 10 members of Italy's national side against Hungary and at the time of the disaster they were leading the First Division by four points. To complete their remaining fixtures, they had no option but select their youth team who were carried to the title on a tide of tears.

Since the Day Italian Football Died, Torino have won the League once, in 1976, and they have never recovered their former superiority. Yet Liverpool have endured more anguish than any other club. Why have they risen above adversity to recapture Europe's crown while another team has failed to cast off the shackles of misfortune? Why have our lads ultimately prospered, despite attempts by bottle-throwing, ticket-snatching, stadium-storming parasites to poison them with the twin cancers of disgrace and dishonour?

Could our true supporters offer a clue? At club after club, players sign up in a fanfare of publicity, kiss the badge, suck the ring and slope away; managers are chauffeured to the front door and sneak out the back; directors hog the limelight and slink into obscurity; chief executives swear allegiance, then swop sides for more loot; shareholders sit on their speculative investments and flog them off to the highest bidders.

The one constant, the only unchanging factor, the sole inalterable element is the fan, and there is none truer than the Kopite, the human thread running through Liverpool's vibrant tapestry.

Loyal, devoted, steadfast, unwavering, never prostituting his fervour, never substituting one team for another, never abandoning his birthright, never denying his love, the Kopite has a mystical bond with his team.

After Amberleigh House won the Grand National in 2004, giving Ginger McCain his fourth victory, 27 years after Red Rum's treble, the trainer said at Aintree: "You can keep Cheltenham with its caps and tweeds. This is a people's place and this is a people's race and the Liverpool people are stone-cold magic."

Stone-cold magic, that's what Kopites are, too, in their people's place.

You may drive a battered Metro or a gleaming Bentley, live in Sandhills or Heswall Hills, prop up the bar in the Labour club or golf club, but in the democracy of the Kop, you are neither better nor worse than the individual beside you.

Equals. One and the same. Kopites.

Money, status, religion, colour are left at the turnstile; through that gate we are all Liverpool fans and the team is our priority.

Elsewhere commercial lust might have bred a monster with a voracious appetite for lorry loads of pound notes but at least in L4 the affinity between supporter and club remains as strong as ever.

We should all be thankful Liverpool have retained their roots in the community. Even though over the years directors have of necessity adapted to the demands of sport as a business, they have not sold out to the ogre of Mammon and they have kept a caring face, as many individuals can testify.

Reflecting on the shared grief after Iraq hostage Ken Bigley was murdered in 2004, mayor Frank Roderick said: "Liverpool is a city where people belong to a great family." Well, like the rest of our fans, I belong to my club and my club belongs to me and together we form sport's closest family.

This symbiotic relationship is at its most intimate on the Kop, the soul of Liverpool Football Club, an expanse of mundane steps and seats which assumes a character and life of its own when filled with mankind. For the game's most devoted supporters, this unique terrace affords a meeting of minds and bodies, sense of identity, belief system and place of worship. Step inside and bask in Anfield's feel-good factor. The job, weather, mortgage, bank statement, school reports, car's faulty gearbox, even worries about your health, whatever's bothering can be discarded outside this brick-and-concrete antidepressant.

Through its doors lie freedom and escape from cold reality, an inner peace that does not just prolong lives but can save them, for you have found respite in a sanctuary emblazoned with countless treasures. Our city's motto could have been devised for Kopites: Deus nobis haec otia fecit, These gifts God has bestowed on us.

Take a snapshot of the inheritance of glittering prizes bequeathed by our club: we have won as many Champions Cups as all other English sides put together; we have amassed the same total of European prizes as Arsenal, Chelsea, Everton and Manchester United combined; we have gathered a record haul of League championships.

Regular pick-me-ups, doses of happiness hormone prescribed in silver cups, which fortify whether you've followed the Reds for five, 10, 20 or 50 years.

Shining affirmation, in Britain's biggest trophy room, that our dreams are others' delusions. A heritage that every one of us has a duty to cherish and protect for future generations.

And what a setting we, the custodians of this legacy, have for our triumphs. Listen to a German international and Champions League winner. "Anfield is the best stadium in the world," Karlheinz Riedle declared. "I've never played anywhere else that has an atmosphere to rival it." Lend an ear to Thierry Henry. "Liverpool's fans are just amazing," he confessed. "The best feeling I have at away games is at Anfield. It is just incredible. I love it. You get goose bumps when their supporters sing You'll Never Walk Alone."

"The best feeling" for a superstar, so how good does it get for a Kopite? For this 100-per-cent-partisan chronicler, Liverpool's half-century since the Fifties has been a unique saga that has encompassed the epic, tragic, heroic, dramatic, comic, poetic and lyric.

During those years, I have gone through every emotion life can throw at you.

Let's be blunt: Within Anfield's walls, I have experienced more agony and ecstasy, passion and apathy, bliss and frustration, euphoria and despair, elation and deflation than any other place on Earth, apart from the marital bedroom.

So you're panting for a climax? Come on the Kop.

Nowhere, and nothing, equals it, because Anfield is my drug, the match is my fix.

And all my exquisite highs in L4 have thoroughly eclipsed the discouraging lows. As an unashamed, unapologetic, unalloyed, unadulterated, unreconstructed lover of Anfield, my 50 years of adoration have comprised days, weeks, seasons and decades of joy that nobody could have foreseen down in the dumps of our distant, sunless Second Division Hades.

Carl Gustav Jung, the pioneering Swiss psychiatrist who visited Liverpool in 1927, slipped into a dream long afterwards, in 1961.

"I found myself in a dirty, sooty city," he recalled. "It was night, and winter, and dark, and raining. I was in Liverpool... In the centre [of a square] was a round pool, and in the middle of it a small island... On it stood a single tree; a magnolia, in a shower of reddish blossoms. It was as though the tree stood in the sunlight, and was at the same time the source of light...

"Everything was extremely unpleasant, black and opaque – just as I felt then. But I had had a vision of unearthly beauty, and that was why I was able to live at all.

"Liverpool is the pool of life."

Well, if Jung were a football fan, his magnolia in a shower of reddish blossoms would serve as a metaphor for Anfield, my vision of unearthly beauty, my source of light.

Since the Reds' Dark Age of relegation, it has been a privilege and an honour to follow the lads, trusty companions on my odyssey from the City of Champions to far foreign lands of promise.

And nothing can surpass the Ataturk for this Istanbul bore, the night that made me realise God sometimes is a Scouser.

Just as the cup remains ours for ever, that memory is mine for ever, because I was present when the Immortals won *our* Champions League trophy, the one that now takes pride of place in *our* stadium. No one can take that final away from me. While it has entered sporting annals, inspiring any team, in whatever shirt, that despairs of a lost cause, the spirit of Liverpool in Istanbul will also drip-feed me with contentment for the rest of my days.

Stuck in an interminable traffic jam, drenched on a roofless railway platform, delayed by an industrial dispute at an airport, wheeled on a trolley into A & E, dispirited by months of knockbacks from publishers, my therapy will entail neutralising the negative by calling to mind our salvation and resurrection as Turkish scimitars flashed overhead.

So if you're in the pub at closing time, with some poor sod expounding on how the big boss upstairs has dealt him a lousy hand, how his dreams have been tossed and blown away, cheer him up with the name engraved on every Kopite's heart: Istanbul.

When you go to a European Cup Final, see all hopes dashed, your side demolished by half-time, then you discover something precious.

You could throw in the towel, walk out, slit your wrists.

You don't. You discover new strengths in your team, and yourself. You learn that they, and you, can eventually prevail.

Because within that single word of Istanbul rests a universal lesson: keep the faith. Always.

And believe in your city, too.

Yoko Ono said, memorably: "This isn't just any city, this is Liverpool" and for playwright Alun Owen, it was a place that never let you go.

Precisely. Because, love it or loathe it, Liverpool is in your blood. It cannot leave you indifferent, as I know so well. Wherever I may have travelled, however far I may have wandered, my birthplace has retained its hold on me, as it has for umpteen others. And at its core lies my football club. To paraphrase Yoko, not just any club but Liverpool FC.

What a club.

Like all those sprinkled with her red stardust, Destiny's goddess embraced me that night in the Ataturk Stadium when our team and our supporters touched eternity.

Now, no matter what might lie ahead for this timid lad who once hid coppers down his socks in the Boys' Pen, I can luxuriate in a reservoir of pleasure that will last till the end of time.

I can sup for ever in my personal fountain of delight.

Pool of life. Pool of love. My beloved Liverpool.

****

Appeal for help

Tell me, dear reader, that it's true. All this did happen, didn't it? Or was I just dreaming again ...?

Thank you

W E ALL owe debts of gratitude to those who have helped us along life's shining path and I am indebted more than most. Since there'll never be a better chance to place my appreciation on the record, I must take advantage of this once-in-a-lifetime opportunity. Kindly bear with me and read on.

Special thanks for their assistance with this book go to Steve Davenport, Dr Angus Bell, Mark Grimes, Dr Glyn Phillips, Commodore Ronald Warwick, Liverpool FC's Press Office, the staffs of St Albans Central Library and the British Library, and Simon Lowe of Know The Score Books.

For their friendship, kindness, inspiration and company in the pub, I am also grateful to:

Tom Abbott, Chris Abbott, Bill Abrams, Bou Acha, Ruth Ackers, Bob Adams, Richard Adamson, Uli Aeb, John Aldridge, Barry Allen, Mark Allen, Tim Allen, Bill Amos, Jim Anderson, David Andrews, Anton Antonowicz, Dennis Archdeacon, Bob Armstrong, Hugh Ash, Joe Ashton, Tina Asu, Davie Atherton, Thomas Atherton, Lewis Atkinson, Pete Atkinson, Keith Austin, Tim Austin, Lisa Aylett.

Steve Bailey, Austin Baillon, Julia Baillon, Mike Baker, Pam Baker, Phil Baker, Robert Baker, Ron Baker, Sue Balding, Dave Balmforth, Antoine Balzan, Joe Bangay, Paddy Barclay, Eddie Barford, Sue Barker, Peter Barnes, Becky Barrow, Chris Barrow, Brian Bass, Lyn Bateson, Geoff Baylis, Brian Bell, Diane Bell, Ken Bennett, Trevor Berry.

Charlotte Beugge, Kate Bevan, Tony Bevins, Geoff Bigg, Evelina Bigg, Bob Bird, Bob Blair, John Blake, Ian Blunt, Graham Bolton, Pete Bolton, Graham Booth, Tony Boram, Bill Bothwell, Peter Bowes, Tommy Boycott, Barry Bradburn, Marcia Brackett, Sue Brattle, Jim Brennan, Steve Brennan, Brian Brett, Dai Bridgman, Nicholas Broadbridge, Simon Brodbeck, Sue Bromley.

Peter Brooks, Tony Brooks, Harold Brough, Edna Brown, Ian Brown, Mike Brown, Roy Brown, Malcolm Bruce, Ken Bruff, Roger Bryan, Jackie Buckingham, Joe Buckingham, Tony Buckingham, Mick Burke (Journalist),

Mick Burke (Everest climber), Steve Burley, Mike Burnham, Gordon Burnett, Alan Burns, Julio Burriel.

Barbara Calderbank, Bill Caldwell, Tony Callaghan, Ian Callister, Alistair Campbell, Ewan Campbell, Ian Campbell, Al Capper, John Carey, Alan Carins, Patrick Carnwath, Andy Carson, Kit Carson, Mike Carter, Frank Cartwright, Pauline Cartwright, Jim Cassidy, Steve Castelli, Adam Cathro, Brian Caven, Chi Chan, Mike Charters, Frank Chester, Trevor Chester, Barbara Chevalier, Eric Chinn, Andrew Clark, John Clarke, Mike Clayton, John Clemison, Pat Codd.

Don Cole, Eric Cole, Roger Collier (*Mirror* man), Roger Collier (*Star* man), Patrick Collins, Alex Collinson, Jeff Connor, Syd Connor, Clare Conteh, Joan Conway, Bob Cook, Norman Cook, Blanche Cooke, Ronnie Cooke, Joe Cool, Bob Coole, Martin Cornell, John Corse, David Coss, Bob Cowans, Vernon Cowen, Ian Cowie, Jonathan Cox, David Coxon, Ian Craig, Luiz Craveiro, Marcos Craveiro, Bill Crawford, George Cregeen, Lester Critchley, Pat Critchley, Peter Crompton, Ann Cummings, Eddie Cummins, Jonathan Cundy.

Nick Dallman, Christine Dando, Jim Dandy, Jacqueline Darwin, Ray Darwin, Rob Davenport, Bryn Davies, Nicholas Davies, Rick Davies, Roger Davies, Rosemary Davies, Trevor Davies, John Dawes, Mike Deary, Bill Deedes, Jenny Delaney, Gerry Dempsey, Bernard Depledge, Dick Derwent, Jill Derwent, Julian Desser, John Dewsnap, Terry Dickie, Mark Dickinson, Richard Dillon, Tom Dobney, Alan Doddridge.

Alan Donaldson, Howard Donaldson, Peter Donlan, Phyllis Donlan, Diane Donne, Jim Donohue, Charles Douglas-Home, Henry Russell Douglas, John Dowling, Irene Dowling, Fred Dring, Regina Duarte, Richard Duckenfield, Linda Duff, Mary Duffy, Paddy Duffy, Olly Duke, Brian Dunlea, Helen Dunne, Phil Durrant, Yvonne Dutilh, Syd Dye, Bob Dyson.

Alison Eadie, Andrew Eames, Paul Eaton, Dennis Edensor, Alan Edwards, Rowland Edwards, Bill Elliott, Keith Elliott, Steve Ellis, Charlie Ellwood, Ben Elton, Doris Emery, Russell Emery, Duggie Enefer, Alan Evans, Glyn Evans, Roy Evans, Roy Eves, Jack Fafargue, Adam Faith, Linda Faram, Freddie Fargher, Neil Farley, Tim Ferrett, Dan Field, Robbie Firth, Paul Fitzpatrick, Bill Fletcher, Jack Fletcher, Joe Fletcher, Lilly Fletcher.

John Falding, Terry Foley, Paul Findlay, Paul Foot, Russ Forgham, Brian Forster, John Foster, Paul Fourdrinier, George Fowler, Simon Fowler, Tony Fowler, Howard Foy, Dave Francis, Ian Francis, Kevin Francis, Keith Franzke, Alistair Fraser, Alan Freeman, Bill Freeman, Roger French, Anne Fussell.

Danny Gallagher, Mike Gallemore, Ronnie Gallemore, Christine Garbutt, John Garton, Dave Gaskill, Jim Gaskin, Donna Gee, Garth Gibbs, Sally Gilbert, Tom Gilchrist, Bill Giles, Shirley Giles, Mike Gillender, Mike Glover,

Simon Godley, Andrew Golden, Bill Golden, Eric Goodman, Ian Gore, Scott Gormley, Joelle Goût.

John Grabham, Vicky Graham, John Grant, Bobby Gray, Ian Gray, Sandra Gray, Steve Greaves, Alf Green, Gerry Greenberg, Roy Greenslade, Alf Gregory, John Grewcock, Roly Gribben, Charlie Griffin, Nick Griffiths, Rachel Griffiths, Joe Grimes, Peter Grimsditch, Fatima Guetlef, Graham Gurrin, George Guy, David Gwynne.

Bill Hagerty, Denis Hamilton, Terry Hamilton, Ian Hamilton Fazey, Michael Hamlyn, Phil Hammond, Peter Hanlon, Alan Hansen, Dave Harbord, Trisha Harbord, David Hardy, George Hardy, Irene Hardy, Joan Hardy, Norman Hardy, Pat Hardy, Ian Hargraves, Ted Harriott, Dale Harrison, George Harrison (Over The Mersey Wall), Ted Hart, Maurice Hart, Stan Hayton, George Heap, Colin Henderson, Liz Henderson, Clarrie Henley, Steve Henry.

Dave Hepworth, Adrian Herbert, Louis Heren, Sylvie Hernalsteen, John Hetherington, Dave Highet, Barry Hill, Brian Hill, Dennis Hill, Peter Hill, Denise Hillman, Ken Hillman, Barry Hilton, Linda Hilton, Harry Hitchen, Marie Hitchen, Andy Hoban, Rodney Hobson, David Hockney, Neville Hodgkinson, Peter Hodgson, Ted Hodgson, Keith Hoggins, Roy Holden, Martin Holderness, Dick Holland, Jimmy Holland, Pete Hollinson, Bronwen Holly, Ken Holman, Joe Holmes, John Honeywell, Ian Hosie, Eddie Houghton, Keith Houghton, Margaret Houghton, Peter Houghton, Rob Houghton, Gérard Houllier.

Gordon Howard, Geoff Howlett, Val Huggins, Glenys Hughes, Harry Hughes, Margaret Hughes, Mike Hughes, Trevor Hughes, Bob Hugill, Irvine Hunter, Walter Huntley, Nick Hurst, Ted Hurst, John Husband, Peter Hussey, Chris Hutchins.

Peter Igglesden, Oguzhan Imrak, Sammie Ireland, Brian Jackson, Eddie Jacobs, Pat Jacobs, Suzy Jagger, Chris James, Derek Jameson, Sue Jansen, Bill Jarvis, Shane Jarvis,

Rob Jeacock, Alick Jeans, Andy Jennings, Dave Johnson, Frank Johnson, Jimmy Johnson, Brian Jones, Ceri Jones, Dave Jones (Chester Races), Dave Jones (Chester Romans), Glyn Jones, Harold Jones, Hilda Jones, Hugh Jones, John Jones, Steve Jones.

Martin Kaye, Margaret Kaye, Peter Keame, Martin Keates, Bill Keenan, Tony Keenan, John Keith, Brian Kelly, Joe Kelly, Olive Kelly, Vin Kelly, Ian Kelso, Johnny Kelso, Alan Kennedy, Nick Kent, Richard Kettlewell, Philip Key, Tom King, Simon Khalil, Peter Kilner, Jack Kirwan, Mike Klempner, Geoff Kuhillow.

José Lalaguna, Richard Lambert, Jon Lambeth, Duncan Lamont, Tony Lanagan, Vic Lanser, Derek Larmon, Rodney Lascelles-Smith, Kevin Lavelle,

Helen Lawrence, Ken Lawrence, Julie Leadbetter, Chris Leake, Eric Leatherbarrow, Kay Lee, Simon Lee, Claud Lescure, Bernard Levin, Peter Levy, Ray Liderth, Marjorie Liderth, Paul Liderth, Gillian Linscott, Jamie Littlejohn, Stan Liversedge, Terry Lloyd, Christine Long, Ken Loran, Steve Lord, Bill Lowe, Edna Lowe, Brian Luckett, Ted Lupton, Linda Lusardi, David Luxton, Charles Lyte.

Jean McAnally, Anne MacDonald, Allan McKenzie, Marilyn McKenzie, Frances MacNamara, Tommy MacNamara, Crawford McAfee, Reg McConville, Florrie McCouig, Doug McCouig, Irene McDermott, Susan McDermott, Tommy McDermott, Bob McGrae, Peter McGregor, Gerry McIver, Jimmy McIver, Iain McKie, Louise McKie, Pauline McLeod, Eddie McMahon, Eileen McMahon, David McMaster, Bill McMath, Sheila McMath, Alastair McQueen, Rob McSweeney, Ross McWhirter.

Alfredo Machado, Gloria Machado, Victor Mallet, Frank Malley, Dave Manktelow, Bernie Manning, Colin Margerison, Pam Marsden, Consuelo Martinez, Fiona Mason, Walter Mason, Geoff Mather, David Maude, Keith Meadows, Jennifer Melling, Wallie Melling, Kevin Memery, Willie Mercer, Jacques Mercier, Charlie Methven, Penny Meyrick, Ramón Michan, Brian Millhouse, Doreen Millhouse, Gary Millhouse, Harry Millhouse, Lee Millhouse, May Millhouse, Ray Mills.

David Millward, Jimmy Milne, Roy Milner, Joe Minogue, Tim Minogue, Andy Moncur, Nina Montagu-Smith, Eric Montauriol, Steve Mooney, Charles Moore, Peter Moorhead, Chris Moorhouse, José Maria Morales, Kevin Moran, Ronnie Moran, Bert Morgan, Johnny Morgan, Sheridan Morley, Mansell Morris, Andy Morton, Peter Muller, Barry Munden, Leo Muray, Iain Murray, Jim Murray, Neil Murray, Rob Murray, Ian Myerscough.

David Nathanson, Terry Newell, Mike Niblock, Brian Noble, Jean Noble, Graham Noble, Steve Nolan, Martin Noot, Brian Nugent, Robin Oakley, Paul O'Brien, Carrie O'Grady, Steve O'Hare, Paddy O'Neill, Alistair Osborne, Bill Owen, Jim Owen, Liz Owen.

Mick Page, Bob Paisley, Rick Papineau, Ian Park, Freda Parker, Ian Parker, Stan Parker, Richard Parrack, Campbell Paterson, Terry Pattinson, Derek Payne, Dave Peacock, Jean Peacock, Herbert Pearson, Simon Pearson, John Penrose, Inéz Peraza de Ayala, Nick Petkovic, Robert Philip, Stephen Phillips, Norman Pickles, Leon Pilpel, Allan Pinch, Ian Pollock, Robin Popham, Dick Porter, Robin Porter, Sonia Porter, Phil Posting, Roy Povey, Peter Preston, John Price, Sammy Prince, Gill Pringle, John Proctor, Marje Proops, John Pugh, Ray Purcell, Steve Purcell.

Dave Radford, Keith Raffaelli, Eamonn Rafferty, Raj Ramyead, Shashi Ramyead, Kate Rankine, Sonny Rao, William Rees-Mogg, Martin Reeve,

Margaret Renn, Dave Reynolds, Ken Reynolds, Trevor Reynolds, Rodney Rice, Keith Richmond, Ron Ricketts, Jimmy Riddell, Mary Riddell, Norman Rigby, Joe Riley, Flavia Rima, Roly Rimmer, Cyril Ritson, Dan Roberts, Glyn Roberts, Ronnie Roberts, Cath Robinson, Di Robinson, Ernie Robinson, Joe Robinson, Lucy Robinson, Peter Robinson, Phil Robinson, Jeff Robson, Mark Roe, Rob Rohrer, Paul Rollinson, Robin Ronalds, Johnnie Rosh, Brian Rostron, Jack Rowe, Vernon Rowe, Bill Rowntree, Chris Roycroft-Davis, Dave Rushby, Vince Ryan, Terry Ryle.

Gloria Salgado de Reyes, Delphine Sauzay, Mark Savage, Dave Saxby, Bet Scally, Ted Scally, Diane Schimmel, Hans Schimmel, Jim Seddon, Anne Segal, John Sellers, John Sergeant, Ray Setterfield, Minesh Shah, Stephen Shakeshaft, Jimmy Shakespeare, Bill Shankly, Shiv Sharma, Rochelle Shavinsky, Roy Shaw, Fred Shawcross, Enid Shelmerdine, Bernard Shrimsley, Maurice Simms, Alison Simms.

Dave Simpson, Jocelyn Sizer, Dave Skeggs, Malcolm Skeggs, Margery Skeggs, Maureen Skilling, Peter Sloane, Jo Smalley, Tim Smart, Dennis Smith, Eric Smith, Ken Smith, Mike Smith, Tim Smith, Tommy Smith, Tony Smith, Mary Smithies, Pat Smyllie, Jim Soar, Philippa Soden, Neil Sowerby, John Stacey, Ken Stamp, Bob Staton, Brian Statter, John Stead, Alison Steed, Ian Stephenson, Peter Steward, Alastair Stewart, Bill Stock, Pete Storah, Richard Stott.

Mike Strutt, Martin Strydom, Alec Stuttard, Mike Sumner, Brian Sutherland, Don Sutton, Peter Swift, Phil Swift, Alan Sykes, Mal Tattersall, Bridget Taylor, Mike Taylor, Noreen Taylor, Phil Taylor, Tim Taylor, George Thaw, Aubrey Thomas, Cassandra Thomas, George Thomas, Mick Thomas, Nigel Thomas, Ron Thomas, David Thompson, Richard Thompstone, Ra Tickell, Ken Tossell, George Trefgarne, Donald Trelford, Alan Trewennick, Andy Trimbee, Sonny Tucker, Bruce Turner, Lloyd Turner, Steve Turner, Tony Tweedie.

Sam Uba, Bill Varty, Linda Varty, Andy Veitch, Eugenie Verney, Tim Verney, Brenda Vigus, Carol Wakefield, Dave Wakefield, Don Walker, Johnnie Walker, Mike Walker, Guy Waller, Pauline Wallin, Trevor Walls, Connor Walsh, Jan Walsh, Douglas Walters, Sam Wanamaker, Bob Ward, Doreen Wareing, Bob Waterhouse, Roger Watkins, Bill Watts, Tina Weaver.

Jean Webster, Les Webster, Pat Welland, Roy West, Annie Westhead, Ethel Westhead, Bill Wheeler, Brian Whitaker, Bob Whiting, Keith Whittaker, Paul Whyles, Paul Wilcox, Charlie Wilkinson, Anne Williams, Barbara Williams, Alvin Williams, Harry Williams, Flossie Williams, Ray Williams.

Peter Willis, John Willman, Dennis Wills, Chris Wilson, David Wilson, Dick Wilson, Edna Wilson, Kevin Wilson, Mollie Wilson, Simon Winchester, Henry Winter, George Withy, Chris Wood, Gerry Wood, Bill Woodcock,

Leslie Woodhead, Giles Wordsworth, Christine Worthing, Martin Worthing, Colin Wright, Gordon Wright, Ian Wright, Jez Wright, Melanie Wright, Ivor Wynne Jones, Lou Yaffa, Horace Yates, Peter Zimmerman, Maggie Zimmerman and Jan Zygadlo. And – finally – bar staff everywhere, especially the Standard's psychopathic alsatian.

Bibliography

John Aldridge: My Story (Hodder & Stoughton); Bill Shankly, Stephen F Kelly (Virgin); Billy Liddell, John Keith (Robson Books); Bob Paisley: Manager of the Millennium, John Keith (Robson Books); The Boot Room Boys, Stephen Kelly (Collins); The Cassell Soccer Companion, David Pickering (Cassell); A Cellarful of Noise, Brian Epstein (Souvenir Press); The Complete Beatles Chronicle, Mark Lewisohn (Chancellor Press); The Daily Telegraph Football Chronicle, Norman Barrett (Hutchinson); Dalglish, My Autobiography, Kenny Dalglish with Henry Winter (Hodder and Stoughton); The Day of The Hillsborough Disaster, Rogan Taylor, Andrew Ward and Tim Newburn (Liverpool University Press).

The Essential Shankly, John Keith (Robson Books); Everton v Liverpool, The Great Derbies, Brian Barwick and Gerald Sinstadt (BBC); Faith of Our Fathers: Football As A Religion, Alan Edge (Mainstream); Football Memories, Brian Glanville (Virgin); Fowler: My Autobiography, Robbie Fowler (Pan); Gérard Houllier: The Liverpool Revolution, Stephen F Kelly (Virgin); Gerrard: My Autobiography, Steven Gerrard (Bantam Press); Golden Past, Red Future, Paul Tomkins and Jonathan Swain (Anchor Print); Hamlyn Illustrated History Of Liverpool, Stephen F Kelly (Hamlyn); Hell Razor, Neil Ruddock (HarperCollinsWillow); Hillsborough: The Truth, Phil Scraton (Mainstream Publishing); The Ian Callaghan Story, Ian Callaghan and John Keith (Quartet Books); I Did It The Hard Way, Tommy Smith and David Stuckey (Arthur Barker).

Into The Red, John Williams (Mainstream); John Barnes: The Autobiography (Headline); Kennedy's Way, Alan Kennedy and John Williams (Mainstream); The Kop, Stephen Kelly (Virgin); Liverpool: A Complete Record 1892-1990, Brian Pead (Breedon Books); Liverpool Club of the Century, Ian Hargraves, Ken Rogers and Ric George (Liverpool Echo); Liverpool FC: The Ultimate Book of Stats and Facts, Dave Ball and Ged Rea (Bluecoat Press); Liverpool In Europe, Steve Hale and Ivan Ponting (Guinness); Liverpool From The Inside, Stan Liversedge (Mainstream); Liverpool My Team, Steve Heighway (Souvenir Press); Liverpool's Greatest Players: The Official Guide, David Walmsley (Headline).

The Liverpool Story, Derek Hodgson (Arthur Barker); Liverpool Versus Everton. Michael Heatley and Ian Welch (Dial House); Liverpool: Wondrous Place, Paul Du Noyer (Virgin); Match of the Day, The Complete Record Since 1964, Compiled by John Motson (BBC); Memories, Dreams, Reflections, Carl Gustav Jung (HarperCollins); Michael Owen: In Person, by Michael Owen (Harper Collins); Michael Owen: Off The Record, Michael Owen and Paul Hayward (CollinsWillow); The Official History of The Football Association, Bryon Butler (Queen Anne Press); The Official Liverpool FC Illustrated History, Jeff Anderson and Stephen Done (Carlton).

Passing Rhythms: Liverpool FC and the Transformation of Football. Edited by John Williams, Stephen Hopkins and Cathy Long (Berg Publishers); Pelé: My Life and the Beautiful Game, Pelé with Robert L Fish (New English Library); Peter Beardsley, My Life Story (CollinsWillow); The Real Bill Shankly, Karen Gill (Trinity Mirror Sport Media); The Red Revolution, Conrad Mewton (Mainstream); The Rough Guide to Liverpool FC, Dave Cottrell and Mark Williams (Rough Guides); The Saint: My Autobiography, Ian St John (Hodder & Stoughton, 2005); Sami Hyypia: From Voikaa to the Premiership, Sami Hyypia (Mainstream).

A Season on the Brink, Guillem Balague (Orion); Shankly, Bill Shankly (Arthur Barker, 1976); The Shankly Years: A Revolution In Football, Steve Hale and Phil Thompson (Ebury Press); Shanks for the Memory, John Keith (Robson); Shout! The True Story of The Beatles, Philip Norman (Corgi); Souness: The Management Years, Graeme Souness and Mike Ellis (Andre Deutsch); Stand Up Pinocchio, Phil Thompson (Trinity Mirror Sport Media); Stick It Up Your Punter, Peter Chippindale and Chris Horrie (William Heinemann); Story Of Football, Martin Tyler (Marshall Cavendish Books); Tall, Dark and Hansen, Alan Hansen (Mainstream); Toshack, Chris Hughes (Virgin Books); When You Walk Through The Storm, Sean Smith and Anne Williams (Mainstream).

Journalography

Daily Express, Daily Mail, Daily Mirror, Daily Telegraph, Financial Times, France Football, L'Equipe, Liverpool Daily Post, Liverpool Echo, London Evening Standard, Mail on Sunday, Marca, Sunday Express, Sunday Telegraph, Sunday Times, The Guardian, The Observer, The Times.

Webography

http://talklfc.com; www.bbc.co.uk; anfield-online.co.uk; bootroom.org; contrast.org/hillsborough; eurosport.com; fifa.com; football365.co.uk; 4thegame.com; historia.org; icons.com; iffhs.de; itv-football.co.uk; koptalk.co.uk; lfchistory.net; lfconline.com; liv.ac.uk/footballindustry; liverpoolfc.tv; liverpool.rivals.net; liverpoolway.co.uk; liverweb.org.uk; raotl.co.uk; redandwhitekop.com; rsssf.com; shankly.com; shanklygates.co.uk; skysports.com/football; soccerbase.com; soccerbooks.co.uk; soccernet.espn.go.com; soccer-sites.com; sportinglife.com/football/news; teamtalk.com; thefa.com; theglobalgame.com; thisisanfield.com; uefa.com; worldstadiums.com; ynwa.tv

Unbelievably abridged beerography

Adnams' Broadside, Alhambra Negra (Spain), Antarctica and Brahma (Brazil), Bent's Red Label Stout, Brain's Premium Bitter, Cain's Bitter and Premium Lager, Carlton Gold, Victoria Bitter, Swan Lager and Vintage Amber Ale (Australia), Charles Wells Bombardier, Cusqueña, Cristal and Arequipeña (Peru), Dos Equis, Modelo Especial and Sol (Mexico), Duvel, Kwak and Mort Subite (Belgium), Efes Pilsen (Turkey), Fischer Bitter, Jenlain Biere de Garde and Pelforth Brune (France), Fuller's London Pride and ESB, Greene King Abbot Ale and IPA, Higson's Pale Ale, Holt's Bitter and Mild, Hook Norton Old Hooky, Hyde's Mild, Ind Coope Mild, Jennings' Cumberland Ale and Sneck Lifter, Marston's Pedigree, McMullen's Original AK, Pilsner Club (Ecuador), Samuel Smith's Bitter, Sharp's Doom Bar, Shepherd Neame Bishop's Finger, St Austell HSD, Tetley Bitter, Threlfall's Bitter, Thwaites' Lancaster Bomber, Waitrose Vintage Cider, Walker's Bitter, Wychwood Circle Master and Fiddler's Elbow, Young's Bitter and Special.